PERFORMING COPYRIGHT

Based on empirical research, this innovative book explores issues of performativity and authorship in the theatre world in light of copyright law and addresses several inter-connected questions: who is the author and first owner of a dramatic work? Who gets the credit and the licensing rights? In what circumstances can a director or actor obtain joint authorship rights with the writer? Given the nature of theatre as a medium reliant on the re-use of prior existing works, tropes, themes and plots, what happens if an allegation of copyright infringement is made against a playwright? Furthermore, who possesses moral rights over the work?

To evaluate these questions in the field of theatre, the opening two chapters of the book outline its core themes and examine the history of the dramatic work both as text and as performative work. The third chapter explores the concepts of authorship and joint authorship under copyright law as they apply to the actual process of creating plays, referring to legal and theatrical literature, as well as empirical research. The fourth chapter looks at the notion of copyright infringement in the context of theatre, noting that cases of alleged theatrical infringement reach the courts rarely in comparison with music cases, and assessing the reasons for this with respect to empirical research. The fifth chapter examines how moral rights of attribution and integrity work in the realm of theatre. The book concludes with a prescriptive comment on how law should respond to the challenges provided by the theatrical field, and how theatre should respond to law.

Original and innovative, this book proposes a ground-breaking approach to study the implications of copyright law in society and makes a strong case for the need to consider the reciprocal interaction between law and practice.

Performing Copyright

Law, Theatre and Authorship

Luke McDonagh

•HART•
OXFORD • LONDON • NEW YORK • NEW DELHI • SYDNEY

HART PUBLISHING
Bloomsbury Publishing Plc
Kemp House, Chawley Park, Cumnor Hill, Oxford, OX2 9PH, UK
1385 Broadway, New York, NY 10018, USA
29 Earlsfort Terrace, Dublin 2, Ireland

First published in Great Britain 2021

A catalogue record for this book is available from the British Library.

Library of Congress Cataloging-in-Publication data

Names: McDonagh, Luke, author.

Title: Performing copyright : law, theatre, and authorship / Luke McDonagh.

Description: Oxford, UK ; New York, NY : Hart Publishing, an imprint of Bloomsbury Publishing, 2021. | Includes bibliographical references and index.

Identifiers: LCCN 2021004274 (print) | LCCN 2021004275 (ebook) | ISBN 9781509927036 (hardback) | ISBN 9781509949168 (paperback) | ISBN 9781509927043 (pdf) | ISBN 9781509927050 (Epub)

Subjects: LCSH: Copyright—Performing rights. | Copyright.

Classification: LCC K1447.2 .M33 2021 (print) | LCC K1447.2 (ebook) | DDC 346.04/82—dc23

LC record available at https://lccn.loc.gov/2021004274

LC ebook record available at https://lccn.loc.gov/2021004275

ISBN: HB: 978-1-50992-703-6
ePDF: 978-1-50992-704-3
ePub: 978-1-50992-705-0

Typeset by Compuscript Ltd, Shannon

For Rothna

ACKNOWLEDGEMENTS

I am grateful to the London School of Economics for awarding me the LSE Fellowship from 2011–13 which enabled me to conduct the empirical case study that underpins this book. I would also like to thank the Queen Mary Intellectual Property Research Institute for providing me with access to the Herchel Smith Intellectual Property Collection at the Institute of Advanced Legal Studies. The librarian Malcolm Langley has been of great assistance to me during the past several years. I would also like to thank all my colleagues at the London School of Economics for their support, as well as former colleagues at Queen Mary, University of London, Cardiff University and City, University of London.

I am particularly indebted to – and humbled by – the generosity of the following people for reading draft chapters and giving me invaluable feedback – Thomas Poole, Hugh Collins, Martin Husovec, Daniela Simone, Carys Craig, Jonathan Griffiths, Elena Cooper, Chen Wei Zhu, Michael Lobban and Brent Salter. In addition, I would like to thank Ronan Deazley and Tomás Gómez-Arostegui for giving me advice and assistance on copyright history.

I am grateful to several other people who have offered encouragement and advice during this project: Marc Mimler, Gaetano Dimita, Guido Westkamp, Maria Frabboni, Uma Suthersanen, Noam Shemtov, Brian Murray, Kenneth Madden, Alain Pottage, Tatiana Flessas, Siva Thambisetty, Dev Gangjee, Mara Malagodi, Enrico Bonadio, Patrick Goold, Elaine Fahey, Andrew Murray, Conor Gearty, Abenaa Owusu-Bempah, Paula Westenberger, Henrique Carvalho, Giuseppina D'Agostino, Stavroula Karapapa, Shane Burke, Danilo Mandic, Ana Alba Betancourt, Kazuhiro Ando, Tatsuhiro Ueno, Alan Read, Peter Searles, Claire Banyard, Mathilde Pavis, Hyo Yoon Kang, Marta Iljadica, Jose Bellido, Roberta Bassi, Linda Staniford, and Rosemarie Mearns.

I give particular thanks to the 20 anonymous interviewees who gave their time generously.

I would like to thank the McDonagh family in Galway – Thomas, Bridget, Sarah, Nicholas and Paul – for their constant support.

This book is dedicated to Rothna Begum. Rothna's support, proof-reading and literary advice during the long Covid-19 lockdown, when the bulk of this book was written, was essential. I could not have done it without her.

TABLE OF CONTENTS

Acknowledgements vii
Table of Cases xiii
Table of Legislation xxiii
Abbreviations xxvii

1. **Introduction – Copyright and Authorship on Stage** **1**
   The Rationale for this Book 1
   Overview of Jurisdictional Limitations and Thematic Scope 3
   A Theoretical Approach to Law and Authorship 4
   Copyright's Cultural Turn 7
   Empirical Methodology 9
   Using Bourdieu to Frame the Empirical Case Study 12
   Overview of Chapters 13

2. **'The Play's The Thing …' But What's the Play? And Who Owns It?** **19**
   Introduction 19
   Assessing the Relevance of Literary Theory and Theatre Studies on Legal Issues of Authorship 22
   Tracing the Influence of Law on Theatre and Theatre on Law: The Role of the Inns of Court and the Impact of the Stationers' Company in the Elizabethan and Jacobean Eras (1558–1625) 23
   Law and Theatre: Assessing the Theatrical Text and Authorship During the Elizabethan and Jacobean Eras (1558–1625) 26
   Ownership of Plays in the Elizabethan and Jacobean Eras (1558–1625) 26
   Theatrical Collaboration as Polyvocal Authorship in the Elizabethan and Jacobean Eras (1558–1625) 29
   An Unstable Text in the Elizabethan and Jacobean Eras (1558–1625) 31
   A Case Study on Authorial and Textual Instability – Thomas Kyd and *The Spanish Tragedy* 1594–1613 33
   The Publication of Shakespeare's *First Folio* (1623) and the Beginning of his Acclamation as the English Author-Figure Par Excellence 35
   Was Ben Jonson the First Self-conscious 'Author' in English Theatre? 37
   How Reconceptualising Anonymity Influenced Authorship During the Seventeenth Century 38
   Censorship of Theatre Texts in the Sixteenth and Seventeenth Centuries 39

Material Matters – Printing, 'Piracy' and 'Blocking' in the Pre-Statutory Copyright Era 1557–1709 40
The Changing Nature of Theatre and the Playwright's Status, Post-Restoration (1660–1709) 42
The Statute of Anne 1710 and the Recognition of Authors as Owners 44
Changes to Theatrical Culture Post-Statute of Anne 1710 47
Defining the Boundaries of Copyright Protection under the Statute of Anne 1710 49
The Changing Appreciation of What Copyright Protected 1710–1832 – From the Print-commodity to the Performance-commodity 50
The Reforms Brought About by the 1833 Act and 1842 Act – The Right to Perform a 'Dramatic Piece' 53
The Problem of Dramatisations Post-1833 55
Authorship and Joint Authorship Under the 1833 Act and 1842 Acts 56
What Were the Boundaries of the 'Dramatic Piece' 1833–1911? 58
US Comparison under the 1856 US Copyright Act 60
International Copyright: The Berne Convention 1886 61
The Imperial Copyright Act 1911 62
Conclusion 63

3. Copyright Law and Performing Authorship in Theatre – Exploring the Contrasting Roles of the Playwright, Director and Performers 67
Introduction 67
Understanding the Work in Modern Copyright Law 69
Original Dramatic Works under the Copyright, Designs and Patents Act (CDPA) 1988 69
Original Musical Works 72
Original Literary Works 73
Original Works in EU Copyright Law – Assessing the 'Dematerialised' Work of Originality 75
Original Works – Comparative Insights 77
Summary of the UK Position on Originality of Dramatic Works 81
Authorship and Ownership of the Economic Rights 82
Overview of Joint Authorship 83
Joint Authorship of Dramatic Works in the UK 83
Joint Authorship of Musical Works in the UK 87
Joint Authorship – Comparative Insights 88
Beyond the Individual – Exploring Theatrical Authorship as a Social Practice 91
Evaluating the Original Dramatic Work as Theatrical Text – 'Fully Formed' or 'Devised/Revised'? 94
Joint Authorship: How Do Dramatic Works Get Created Via the Workshop Process? 97

The Role of the Writer 100
The Role of the Director 102
The Role of the Actors (Performers) 103
The Final 'Transcendent' Work 104
Is the 'Workshopped' Play a Work of Joint Authorship? 105
The Importance of Contracts 108
Assessing the Legal Problems that can Arise from Sharing Ownership.......113
Conclusion 114

4. When Does Copyright Infringement Occur on 'The Haunted Stage'? 117
Introduction..117
Claims of Plagiarism and Infringement in Theatre in Historical Perspective 1709–1911 118
Infringement of Copyright under the 1911 Act and the 1956 Act 121
Infringement of Copyright under the CDPA 1988 123
How Much (or How Little) Needs to be Copied? The Meaning of 'Substantial Part' 123
Assessing the Copying of Plots and Characters in Light of the Idea/Expression Dichotomy 125
New Adaptations of Public Domain Works 127
Comparative Insights...128
How Prevalent are Disputes in the UK Theatre Field? 133
Empirical Insights 133
The Defence of Fair Dealing under the CDPA 136
The Purposes of Criticism or Review, Quotation and Parody in the CDPA 137
Assessing the Fairness of the Dealing under the CDPA 139
Comparative Insights...141
Exploring the Possibility of Incorporating an Open 'Fair Use' Standard in the UK 143
Conclusion 146

5. Copyright's Role in Enforcing Credit and Control in Theatre 149
Introduction..149
Moral Rights and Dramatic Works...151
The Attribution Right 153
The Integrity Right...154
Investigating the 'Integrity-based Objection' in the Context of Theatre 155
Godot (France)..157
Heretic (Australia) 158
Clybourne Park (Germany)..158
The Playboy of the Western World (Ireland)..159
Summary of Comparative Insights 160

Analysing the 'Aura' of the Work of Drama....161
Evaluating the 'Trajectory' of the Work of Drama....162
The Link between the Play's Trajectory and the Public Domain....166
How Prevalent are Integrity-based Objections in Theatre Practice?....168
What to do about Beckett? Views from the Field....175
Examining the Play's Trajectory – What Makes *King Lear* Different from *Waiting for Godot*?....176
Conclusion....178

6. How Should Law Respond to the Challenges of the Theatrical Context? How Should Theatre Respond to Law?....180
Introduction....180
The History of Authorship of Plays and the Shifting Property Boundaries of Ownership – The Text as Commodity....181
Copyright Law, Authorship and Joint Authorship of Plays in the Contemporary Theatre Field....183
Copyright Infringement – A Rare Occurrence in the Contemporary Theatre Field?....185
Copyright and Moral Rights in the Theatre Field – The Issue of Integrity Looms Large....186
Conclusion....187

Annex I – Interview Questions....190
Index....193

TABLE OF CASES

UK

Paul Allen (trustee of Adrian Jacob, deceased) v Bloomsbury Publishing and JK Rowling [2010] EWHC 2560 (Ch) 124
Ashdown v Telegraph Group Ltd [2002] Ch 149 .... 136, 140
Austin v Columbia [1917–1923] MacG CC 398 .... 125, 127
Autospin (Oil Seals) v Beehive Spinning [1995] RPC 683 123
Bach v Longman 98 ER [1777] 1274 50
Baigent and Leigh v The Random House Group [2006] EWHC 719 (Ch) 74
Baigent and Leigh v The Random House Group [2007] EWCA Civ 247 .... 74, 126, 129, 133
Bamgboye v Reed [2004] EMLR (5) 61 .... 82, 152
Banner Universal Motion Pictures Ltd v Endemol Shine Group Ltd and Others [2017] EWHC 2600 (Ch) 70
Barfield v Nicholson (1824) 2 Sim. and Stu. 1; 57 ER 245 57
Beckingham v Hodgens [2003] FSR 238 .... 86, 87
Beloff v Pressdram [1973] 1 All ER 241 .... 137, 140
Bolton v British International Pictures [1936–45] MacG CC 20 122
Burnett v Chetwood [1816] EngR 26; (1720) 2 Mer 441, 441; [1816] EngR 26; 35 ER 1008 50
Brighton & Dubbeljoint v Jones [2004] EWHC 1157 (Ch); [2004] EMLR 507 .... 58, 70–73, 84–85, 95–97, 104–05, 107–09, 115–16, 154, 183–84, 188
Cala Homes (South) Ltd v Alfred McAlpine Homes East Ltd [1995] FSR 818 87
Cary v Longman [1801] EngR 198; (1801) 1 East358, 361; [1801] EngR 198; 102 ER 138 50
CBS Records Australia Ltd v Gross (1989) 15 IPR 385 127–28
Coffey v Warner/Chappell Music [2005] FSR (34) 747 124
Coleman v Wathen (1793) 5 D. & E. 245 52
Confetti Records v Warner Music UK Limited [2003] EMLR 35 155–56
Corelli v Gray [1913] TLR 570 .... 72, 121, 125
Cumberland v Planché (1834) 1 Ad & E 580; SC 3 N & M 537; LJ 3 KB 194 54
Designers Guild Limited v Russell Williams (Textiles) Ltd [2001] FSR 113 123–24

Donaldson v Becket (1774) 4 Burr 2408; 98 ER 257 50
Donoghue v Allied Newspapers Ltd [1937] 3 All ER 503 89
Express Newspapers v News (UK) Ltd [1990] FSR 359....56
Exxon Corporation v Exxon Insurance Consultants [1982] RPC 69....76
Francis Day & Hunter v Bron [1963] Ch 587 122
Francis Day & Hunter Ltd v Twentieth Century Fox Corporation Ltd [1940] AC 112.... 74, 76
Fisher v Brooker [2006] EWHC 3239 (Ch); [2007] EMLR 9....73, 83, 87, 106
Fisher v Brooker [2008] EWCA Civ 287 ....73, 83, 87, 106
Fisher v Brooker [2009] UKHL 41; [2009] 1 WLR 1764....73, 83, 87, 106
Fylde Microsystems v Key Radio Systems Ltd [1998] FSR 449....87
Glyn v Weston Feature Film Co [1916] 1 Ch 261 122
Gyles v Wilcox [1740] EngR 77; (1740) Barn Ch 368; 26 ER 489....50
Godfrey v Lees [1995] EMLR 307 87
Hadley v Kemp [1999] EMLR 589 87
Hanfstaengl v Empire Palace [1894] 3 Ch 109....139
Hatton v Kean (1860) 29 L.J.C.P. 20 57
Harman Pictures v Osborne [1967] 1 WLR 723 ChD 122
Hawkes and Sons (London) Ltd v Paramount Film Service Ltd [1934] Ch 593 122
HRH the Prince of Wales v Associated Newspapers [2007] 3 WLR 222.... 138, 140
Hubbard v Vosper [1972] 2 QB 84 139–40
Hyperion Records Ltd v Warner Music (UK) Ltd 19 May 1991, Ch D, unreported 77
Hyde Park Residence v Yelland [2000] EMLR 363 140
Joy Music Ltd v Sunday Pictorial Newspapers (1920) Ltd [1960] 2 QB 60....139
Kelly v Cinema Houses [1928–35] MacG CC 362....122
Kennard v Lewis [1983] FSR 346 (Ch D)....139
Kenrick v Lawrence (1890) LR QBD 99 56
Kogan v Martin [2019] EWCA 1645. ....7, 71, 85–86, 94, 106, 184
Ladbroke (Football) Ltd v William Hill (Football) Ltd [1964] 1 WLR 273 ....74–76, 122, 126
Levy v Cave (Ct. C.P.), The Times, 14 December 1870....57
Levy v Rutley (1870–71) L.R. 6 C.P. 523 .... 57, 89
Longman v Winchester (1809) 16 Ves Jr 269 120
Ludlow Music v Robbie Williams [2001] FSR 271 122
Macklin v Richardson (1770) Amb. 694....51
Maclean v Moody (1858) 20 Sc. Sess. Cas. 2nd Ser. 1154 56
Martin v Kogan [2017] EWHC 2927 (IPEC) 73
Martin v Kogan [2021] EWHC 24 (IPEC) 71, 85
Marzial v Gibbons (1873–1874) L.R. 8 Ch. App. 518....57
Merchandising Corporation of America Inc v Harpbond Inc [1983] FSR 32....73

Millar v Taylor (1769) 4 Burr 2303; 98 ER 201 .... 49, 53, 119
Milligan v Broadway Cinema Production [1923]
Scots Law Times 35 122
Morris v Kelly (1820) 1 J&W 481 52
Morrison Leahy Music Ltd v Lightbond Ltd [1993] EMLR 144 154–55
Murray v Elliston (1822) 5 B and A 657 53
Newbery's Case (1773) Loft 775; 98 ER 913 50
Newspaper Licensing Agency v Marks & Spencer [1999] EMLR 369 140
Newspaper Licensing Agency v Marks & Spencer [2000]
4 All ER 239 .... 136–37, 140
Newspaper Licensing Agency v Marks & Spencer [2001]
UKHL 38; [2003] 1 AC 551 124
Newspaper Licensing Agency v Meltwater [2010]
EWHC 3099 (Ch) 70, 74–75, 117
Newspaper Licensing Agency v Meltwater [2011] EWCA Civ 890;
[2012] Bus LR 53 70
Norowzian v Arks Ltd (No 2) [2000] FSR 363 .... 4, 69–70
Nova Games Ltd v Mazooma Productions Ltd [2007] RPC 589 69–70
Pasterfield v Denham [1999] FSR 168 155
Planché v Hooper (1844) The Times, 19 January 1844, 7c 54
Pope v Curl [1741] EngR 500; (1741) 2 Atk 342; 26 ER 49, 119
*Public Relations Consultants Association Limited v The Newspaper
Licensing Agency Limited and Others* [2013] UKSC 18 .... 70, 76
Pro Sieben Media v Carlton Television [1999] FSR 610 136–39
*R (On the Application Of) v Secretary of State for Business,
Innovation and Skills* [2015] EWHC 2041 and [2015]
EWHC 1723 135
Ravenscroft v Herbert [1980] RPC 193 122
Ray v Classic FM plc [1998] FSR 622 87
Reade v Conquest (1861) 142 Eng. Rep. 297 (CPD) 55, 120
Reade v Lacey (1861) 70 Eng. Rep. 853 (KB) 55
Redwood Music v Chappell [1982] RPC 109 72
Rees v Melville [1911–16] MacG CC 168 .... 121, 125
Robertson v Lewis [1976] RPC 169 128
Russell v Smith (1848) 12 QB 217 55
SAS Institute Inc v World Programming Ltd [2010] EWHC 1829 (Ch) 76
SAS Institute Inc v World Programming Ltd [2013]
EWHC 69 (Ch) 75–77, 124
Sawkins v Hyperion Records Ltd [2005] EWCA Civ 565; [2005]
1 WLR 3281 .... 56, 72, 75, 94, 123,
126, 151, 153
Sayre v Moore (Unreported, Lord Mansfield CJ, 1785) 50
Scholtz v Amasis & Fenn [1905–10] MacG CC 216 59

Schweppes Ltd and Others v Wellingtons Ltd [1984] FSR 210 (Ch D)....................139
Shepherd v Conquest (1856) 17 CB 427; 139 ER 1140 57
Shelley v Ross (1870–71) L.R. 6 C.P. 531; Bail Court 7 June, The Times, 8 June 1871..58
Shetland Times Limited v Wills [1997] EMLR 277 76
Sony/ATV v WPMC Ltd [2015] EWHC 1853 (Ch)..144
Stationers' Company v Seymour (1677) 1 Mod. 256..42
Stationers' Company v Bradford (12 June 1700) C37/692..45
Stationers' Company v Partridge (1709) HLS MS 110..45
Sweeney v Macmillan Publishers Ltd [2002] RPC 35 133
Tate v Fullbrook [1908] 1 KB 821..58
Temple Island Collections Ltd v New English Teas Ltd & another [2012] EWPCC 1..124
Tidy v Trustee of the Natural History Museum [1996] 39 IPR 501 155–56
Tinsley v Lacy (1863) 1 Hem. & M. 747.. 56, 120
The Controller of Her Majesty's Stationery Office, Ordnance Survey v Green Amps Ltd [2007] EWHC 2755 (Ch) 140
Toole v Young (1874) 9 LR 523.. 55, 120
Tonson v Collins (1761) 1 Black W. 301 49
Twentieth Century Fox Film Corp v Anglo-Amalgamated Film Distributors [1960] 2 QB 60..139
University of London Press Ltd v University Tutorial Press Ltd [1916] 2 Ch D 601 49
Wall v Taylor (1882) 9 QBD 727 at 730 54
Walter v Lane [1900] AC 539... 56, 89
Warne & Co v Seebohm (1888) 39 Ch D. 73 .... 56, 120
West v Francis (1822) B & Ald 738...120
Williamson Music Ltd v Pearson Partnership Ltd [1987] FSR 97..139
Wiseman v George Weidenfeld and Nicholson Ltd [1985] FSR 525 .... 83, 113
Wood v Boosey (1868) LR 3 QB 223..72

Ireland

Adigun v McEvoy & Ors [2013] IEHC 342...159
Arambe Productions Limited v. Abbey Theatre and Roddy Doyle (IEHC filing, settled 2013) 159
Gormley v EMI Records (Ire) Ltd [2000] 1 IR 74 .... 79, 88
Phonographic Performance (Ireland) Ltd v Foyle [2015] IEHC 778 79
Sony Music Entertainment Ireland Ltd v UPC Communications Ireland Ltd [2016] IECA 231..79

EU

Bezpecˇnostnı' Softwarova' Asociace-Svaz Softwarove' Ochrany v Ministerstvo Kultury (Case C–393/09) [2010] ECR I-1397 70
Deckmyn v Vandersteen (Case C-201/13) EU:C:2014:2132 (3 September 2014) 139
Eva Marie Painer v. Standard VerlagsGmbH et. al. (Case C-145/10) 1 December 2011, EU:C:2018:798 70
Football Association Premier League Ltd & Others v QC Leisure & Others; Karen Murphy v Media Protection Services Ltd (Joined Cases C-403/08 and C-429/08) ECLI:EU:C:2011:631, [2012] Bus LR 1321 75
Football Dataco Ltd v Yahoo! UK Ltd (Case C-604/10) [2012] ECR I-0000, [2012] Bus LR 1753 .... 70, 75
Funke Medien NRW GmbH v Bundesrepublik Deutschland (Case C-469/17) EU:C:2019:623 .... 75, 138, 142, 148, 186
Infopaq International A/S v Danske Dagblades Forening (Case C-5/08) [2009] ECR I-6569 (ECJ (4th Chamber)); [2009] ECDR 16 259 ....69–70, 74–81, 117, 124
Levola Hengelo BV v Smilde Foods BV (Case C-310/17) [2018] EU:C:2018:899 ....69, 76–77
Pelham GmbH and Others v Ralf Hütter and Florian Schneider-Esleben (Case C-476/17) 29 July 2019, EU:C:2019:624 ('Pelham') 138, 186
Spiegel Online GmbH v Volker Beck (Case C-516/17) 29 July 2019, EU:C:2019:625 ....138, 148, 186

France

Godot (TGI Paris 3rd Chamber) 15 October 1992, (1993) 155 RIDA 225 .... 155, 157
Hugo v Plon SA (Cour Cass 1 ch civ) 30 January 2007, (2007) 212 RIDA 248 152
Turner Entertainment Company v Huston (Cour Cass 1 ch civ) 28 May 1991; (CA Versailles ch civ reunites) 19 December 1994, (1995) 164 RIDA 389 155

Germany

Kraftwerk v Moses Pelham Decision of the German Federal Supreme Court no. I ZR 112/06 (November, 2008)..141

USA

A & M Records, Inc v Napster, Inc., 239 F. 3d. 1004 (9th Cir. 2001)......129
Aalmuhammed v Lee, 202 F.3d. 1227 (9th Cir. 2000)......90
Alexander v Irving Trust Co., 132 F. Supp. 364 (S.D.N.Y. 1955)......131
American Geophysical Union v Texaco Inc., 60 F. 3d. 913 (2d. Cir. 1994)......142
Apple Computer, Inc v Microsoft Corp., 35 F.3d. 1435 (9th Cir. 1994)......133
Arnstein v Porter, 154 F. 2d. 464 (2d. Cir. 1946)......129–30
Baker v Selden, 101 U.S. 99 (1880), 25 L. Ed. 841......78
Bill Graham Archives v Dorling Kindersly Ltd., 488 F. 3d. 605 (2d. Cir. 2006)......129, 142
Blanch v Koons, 467 F. 3d. 244 (2d. Cir. 2006)......129, 144
Bright Tunes Music Corp. v Harrisongs Music, Ltd et al., 420 F. Supp. 177 (1976); *ABKCO Music, Inc. v Harrisongs Music, et al*, 508 F. Supp. 798 (1981); on appeal, 722 F. 2d. 988 (1983); again after remand, 841 F. 2d. 494, and again 944 F. 2d. 971 (1991)......129
Burroughs v Metro-Goldwyn-Mayer, Inc., 519 F. Supp. 388 (S.D.N.Y. 1981)......133
Cain v Universal Pictures Co., 47 F. Supp. 1013 (S.D. Cal. 1942)......132
Campbell v Acuff-Rose, 114 S. Ct. 1164 (1994)......129, 142, 144
Chappell v Fields, 210 F. 864 (2d. Cir. 1914)......61
Childress v Taylor, 798 F. Supp. 981 (S.D.N.Y. 1992)......89–90, 106
Daly v Palmer, 6 F. Cas. 1132 (S.D.N.Y. 1868)......59, 120
D C Comics v Towle, 802 F.3d. 1012 (9th Cir. 2015)......133
Einhorn v Mergatroyd Productions, 426 F.Supp. 2d. 189 (S.D.N.Y. 2006)......90, 131
Eldred v Ashcroft, 1123 S. Ct. 769 (2003)......129
Feist Publications Inc v Rural Telephone Service Co Inc., 499 US 340 (1991)......78, 129–30
Fogerty v Fantasy, Inc., 510 US 517 (1994)......130
Foxworthy v Custom Tees, Inc., 879 F. Supp. 1200 (N.D. Ga 1995)......133
Frye v YMCA Camp Kitaki, 617 F.3d. 1005 (8th Cir. 2010)......132
Garcia v Google, Inc., 786 F.3d. 733 (9th Cir. 2015)......90
Google LLC v. Oracle America, Inc., 593 US (2021)......142
Gutierrez v DeSantis, No. 95-1949 (S.D.N.Y. filed Mar. 22, 1995)......90, 131
Grand Upright Music, Ltd v Warner Bros. Records Inc., 780 F. Supp. 182 (1991)......130
Harper & Row, Publishers, Inc v Nation Enterprises, 105 S. Ct. 2218 (1985)......130, 144
Holmes v Hurst, 174 US 82 (1899)......120
Idema v Dreamwork, Inc., 162 F. Supp. 2d. 1129 (C.D. Cal. 2001)......132

International Film Service v Affiliated Distributors, 283 F. 229 (S.D.N.Y. 1922) 61
Kalem v Harper Brothers, 222 U.S. 55 (1911) 61
Kaseberg v Conaco LLC, 260 F.Supp. 3d. 1229 (S.D. Cal. 2017) 133
Kelly v Arriba Soft, 280 F. 3d. 934 (9th Cir. 2002) 142
Peter Letterese and Associates, Inc. v World Institute of Scientology, 533 F.3d. 1287 (11th Cir. 2008) 130
Litchfield v Spielberg, 736 F. 2d. 1352 (9th Cir. 1984)
Los Angeles News Service v Reuters Television International Ltd., 149 F. 3d. 987 (9th Cir. 1998) 144
Mantello v Hall, No. 97cv8196 (S.D. Fla. filed Mar. 21, 1997) 90
NBA v Motorola, 105 F. 3d. 841 (2nd Cir. 1997) 78
Novak v National Broadcasting Co., 716 F. Supp. 745 (S.D.N.Y. 1989) 131
Newton v Diamond, 388 F. 3d. 1189 (9th Cir. 2003) 130
Nichols v Universal Pictures Corporation, 45 F.2d. 119 (2d. Cir. 1930) 78, 131
Perfect 10, Inc v Amazon.com, Inc., 487 F. 3d. 701 (9th Cir. 2007) 130, 142
Salinger v Random House, Inc., 811 F.2d. 90 (2d. Cir. 1987) 131
Seltzer v Sunbrock, 22 F. Supp. 621 (S.D. Cal. 1938) 78
Sheldon v Metro-Goldwyn Pictures, 81 F. 2d. 49 (2d. Cir. 1936) 61
Shipman v RKO Radio Pictures, 100 F. 2d. 533 (2d. Cir. 1938) 61
Skidmore v Led Zeppelin, 905 F.3d. 1116 (9th Cir. 2018) 130
Sony Corp of America v Universal City Studios, Inc., 104 S. Ct. 774 (1984) 130, 144
Southco Inc v Kanebridge Corp., 324 F. 3d. 190 (3d. Cir. 2003) 130
Suntrust Bank v Houghton Mifflin Co., 268 F. 3d. Cir. 1257 (11th Cir. 2001) 130, 142, 145
Taylor Corp v Four Seasons Greetings, LLC 315 F.3d. 1039 (8th Cir. 2003) 132
Thomson v Larson, 147 F.3d. 195 (2d. Cir. 1998) 203-20 .... 78, 90
The Andy Warhol Foundation for the Visual Arts, Inc. v Goldsmith, decision of March 26 2021 (2d. Cir. 2021) 142
Warner Bros. Entertainment Inc. v RDR Books, 575 F. Supp. 2d. 513 (S.D.N.Y. 2008) 133
Warner Bros Pictures, Inc v Columbia Broad Sys, Inc., 216 F.2d. 945 (9th Cir. 1954) 133
Williams v Crichton, 860 F. Supp. 158 (S.D.N.Y. 1994) 130
Williams v Gaye, 895 F.3d. 1106 (9th Cir. 2018) 130

Canada

CCH Canadian v Law Society of Upper Canada [2004] SCC 13 ....78, 129, 140–41
Cinar Corp v Robinson [2013] 3 SCR 1168 79

Cummings v Global Television Network Quebec, Limited Partnership [2005] Q.J. No. 6707 (Que. S.C) 79
Denis Desjardins Inc v Jeanson [2010] QCCA 1287 128
Hutton v Canadian Broadcasting Corp. [1989] A.J. No. 1193 (Alta. Q.B.) 79
Neudorf v Nettwerk Productions Ltd., et al. [1999] B.C.J. No. 2831 (B.C.S.C.); [2000] RPC 935 ....89–90, 106
Neugebauer v Labieniec [2009] FC 666 89
Productions Avanti Ciné-Vidéo Inc. c Favreau [1999] 177 DLR (4th) 568 141
Robertson v Thomson Corp (2006) SCC 43 78

India

RG Anand v Delux Films, (1978) 4 SCC 118 129
Bradford v Sahara, 2004 (28) PTC 474 (Cal) 129
Eastern Book Company v DB Modak, (2008) 1 SCC 112 79
Mansoob Haider v Yashraj Films, 2014 (59) PTC 292 (Bom) 129
Najma Hcptulla v Orient Longman Ltd, AIR 1989 Del 63 88
Nav Sahitya Prakash and Ors v Anand Kumar and Ors, AIR 1981 All 200 88
Twentieth Century Fox Film Corp v Sohail Maklai Entertainment Pvt. Ltd., 2010 (112) BomLR 4216 129
Zee Telefilms Ltd. v Sundial Communications Private Ltd., 2003 (27) PTC 457 (Bom) (DB) 129

Israel

Elisha Kimron v Herschel Shanks [1993] 7 EIPR D-157 56
The Football Association Premier League v Ploni (2009) Case 1636/08 Motion 11646/08 (District Court of Tel Aviv) 146

Australia

Acohs Pty Ltd v UCorp Pty Ltd [2010] FCA 577 88
Autodesk Inc v Dyason (No 2) [1993] HCA 6; (1993) 1976 CLR 300 128
Career Step, LLC v TalentMed Pty Ltd (No 2) [2018] FCA 132 88
CBS Records Australia Ltd v Gross [1989] FCA 601; (1989) 15 IPR 385 127
Data Access Corporation v Powerflex Services Pty Ltd [1999] HCA 49; (1999) 166 ALR 228 128

Fairfax Media Publications Pty Limited v Reed International Books Australia Pty Limited [2010] FCA 984 .... 77, 80
IceTV Pty Ltd v Nine Network Australia Pty Ltd [2009] HCA 14; (2009) 239 CLR 458 .... 77, 80, 88
Larrikin Music Publishing v EMI Songs Australia [2010] FCA 29 128
Network Ten Pty Ltd v TCN Channel Nine Pty Ltd (2004) 218 CLR 273 141
Primary Health Care Limited v Commissioner of Taxation [2010] FCA 419 88
Sydney Ltd v Shortland County Council (1989) 17 IPR 99 141
TCN Channel Nine Pty Ltd v Network Ten Ltd [2001] FCA 108 141
Telstra Corporation Limited v Phone Directories Company Pty Ltd [2010] FCA 44 88
Telstra Corporation Ltd v Royal & Sun Alliance Insurance Australia Limited [2003] FCA 786 128
Zeccola (First Instance) [1982] AIPC 90-019 (Supreme Court of Victoria) 128
Zeccola v Universal City Studios [1982] FCA 241; (1982) 67 FLR 225 128

New Zealand

Green v Broadcasting Corp of New Zealand [1989] 2 All ER 1056 .... 70, 80

TABLE OF LEGISLATION

UK

An Act for the Encouragement of Learning by Vesting the Copies of Printed Books in the Authors or Purchasers of Such Copies during the Times Therein Mentioned 1709 (Statute of Anne)................ 37, 119
Copyright Act 1775 120
Copyright Act 1836 120
Copyright Act 1842 ....55–56, 120
Copyright Act 1911 ....20, 62–63, 69, 121
Copyright Act 1956 122
Copyright, Designs and Patents Act 1988 ....3, 69–72, 74–75, 83, 123, 140, 151, 153
Dramatic Copyright Act 1833...120
Dramatic and Musical Performers Protection Act 1925 69
Dramatic and Musical Performers Protection Act 1958 69
Engraving Copyright Act 1734...120
Engraving Copyright Act 1767 120
Fine Art Copyright Act 1862. 56
Human Rights Act 1998 140
Lectures Copyright Act 1835 120
Prints Copyright Act 1777...120
Prints and Engraving Copyright (Ireland) Act 1836 120
Sculpture Copyright Act 1814 120
Theatres Act 1843 .... 43, 55
Theatres Act 1968 92
Theatrical Licensing Act 1737...46

EU

Directive 93/98/EEC of 29 October 1993 harmonizing the term of protection of copyright and certain related rights OJ L 290, 24.11.1993 .... 83, 152
Directive 2001/29/EC of the European Parliament and of the Council of 22 May 2001 on the harmonisation of certain aspects of copyright and related rights in the information society 82, 137

Directive 2006/116/EC of the European Parliament and of the Council of 12 December 2006 on the term of protection of copyright and certain related rights OJ L 372/12, 27.12.2006 152
Directive (EU) 2019/790 of the European Parliament and of the Council of 17 April 2019 on copyright and related rights in the Digital Single Market and amending Directives 96/9/EC and 2001/29/EC (Text with EEA relevance.), OJ L 130, 17.5.2019....137

USA

United States Copyright Act 1831 59
United States Copyright Act 1856 60
United States Copyright Act 1976 ....61, 77, 89, 137–38, 142

Australia

Copyright Act 1968 ....80, 88, 128, 141
Copyright Amendment Act 2006 141

Canada

Copyright Act, R.S.C. 1985, c. C-42 ....79, 88, 128, 141
Copyright Modernization Act 2012 141

India

Copyright Act 1957 78

Ireland

Copyright and Related Rights Act 2000 ....3, 78, 88, 123, 137–38

Germany

German Act on Copyright and Neighbouring Rights 1965 (Urheberrechtgestz) 141

Israel

Israeli Copyright Act 2007 146

International

Agreement on Trade-Related Aspects of Intellectual Property Rights, Annex 1C of the Marrakesh Agreement Establishing the World Trade Organization (15 April 1994) 61, 70, 138, 140–41
Berne Convention for the Protection of Literary and Artistic Works (September 9, 1886; revised 1896 (Paris), 1908 (Berlin), 1914 (Additional Protocol), 1928 (Rome), 1948 (Brussels), 1967 (Stockholm), 1971 (Paris) – as amended 1979)..........................61–62, 70, 76, 138, 140, 145, 152, 154
International Convention for the Protection of Performers, Producers of Phonograms and Broadcasting Organizations of 1961 (Rome Convention).. 61, 70
Universal Copyright Convention of 1952 61
WIPO Copyright Treaty of 1996 .... 61, 140
WIPO Performances and Phonograms Treaty of 1996 61

ABBREVIATIONS

AC	Law Reports, Appeal Cases
All ER	All England Law Reports
Burr	Burrow's King's Bench Reports
Bus LR	Business Law Reports
CA	Court of Appeal
CA 1911	Copyright Act 1911
CA 1956	Copyright Act 1956
CA 1963	Copyright Act 1963
CBNS	Common Bench Reports, New Series
CC	Creative Commons
CDPA	Copyright, Designs and Patents Act
CJEU	Court of Justice of the European Union
Ch/Ch D	Law Reports, Chancery Division
Civ	Civil Division
CRRA	Copyright and Related Rights Act
ECDR	European Copyright and Designs Reports
ECHR	European Convention on Human Rights
ECJ	European Court of Justice
EIPR	European Intellectual Property Review
EMLR	Entertainment and Media Law Reports
ER	English Reports
EU	European Union
EWCA	England and Wales Court of Appeal
EWHC	England and Wales High Court

FCA	Federal Court of Australia
FSR	Fleet Street Reports
HMSO	Her Majesty's Stationer's Office
ICPPA	Industrial and Commercial Property (Protection) Act
InfoSoc	Information Society Directive
IP	Intellectual Property
IPO	Intellectual Property Office
IPR	Intellectual Property Reports
IR	Irish Reports
JP	Justice of the Peace Reports
LJ PC	Law Journal Reports, Privy Council
LR	Law Reports
MacG CC	MacGillivray's Copyright Cases
MCPS	Mechanical Copyright Protection Society
NGO	Non-governmental Organisation
NZ	New Zealand
PPL	Public Performance Limited
PRS	Performing Rights Society
QB/QBD	Law Reports, Queen's Bench Division
RIDA	Revue Internationale de Droit d'Auteur
RPC	Reports of Patent, Design and Trademark Cases
SACEM	Société de Auteurs, Compositeurs et Éditeurs de Musique
SCC	Supreme Court of Canada
SCOTUS	Supreme Court of the United States of America
TCE	Traditional Cultural Expressions
TK	Traditional Knowledge
TLR	Times Law Reports
TRIPS	Agreement on Trade-Related Aspects of Intellectual Property Rights

UK	United Kingdom
UKHL	United Kingdom House of Lords
UKSC	United Kingdom Supreme Court
US/USA	United States/United States of America
WCT	WIPO Copyright Treaty
WIPO	World Intellectual Property Organisation
WLR	Weekly Law Reports
WPPT	WIPO Performers and Phonograms Treaty

1

Introduction – Copyright and Authorship on Stage

The Rationale for this Book

It goes without saying that theatre involves performance, but what is perhaps less appreciated is that law too is 'a performative mode of practice'.[1] The tasks that copyright lawyers and judges perform – often during the theatre of the trial – shape the boundaries of copyright law, which in turn affects the way works of theatre are perceived as objects of property. With this in mind, the theatre world itself presents a fascinating setting for exploring the legal concepts of the copyright work, authorship, joint authorship, infringement and moral rights from an interdisciplinary perspective.[2] These notions do not have a stable, inherent meaning – they are infused with normative content only through the practice, or the performance, of law. As theatre practitioners and copyright owners have made claims, and sought enforcement of rights, legal jurists have, through processes of legal

[1] A Read, *Theatre & Law* (Basingstoke: Palgrave Macmillan, 2016) 3. See also M Leiboff, 'Law, Muteness and the Theatrical' (2010) 14 *Law Text Culture* 384; P Goodrich, 'Rhetoric and Somatics: Training the Body to do the Work of Law' (2001) 5 *Law Text Culture* 241; M Del Mar, 'The Education of Attention and Encounter in the Legal Academy' in Z Bańkowski and M Del Mar (eds), *The Moral Imagination and the Legal Life: Beyond Text in Legal Education* (Farnham, UK: Ashgate, 2013) 33; G Calder, 'Embodied Law: Theatre of the Oppressed in the Law School Classroom' (2009) 1 *Masks: An Online Journal for Law and Theatre* 11; S Ramshaw, *Justice as Improvisation: The Law of the Extempore* (Abingdon, UK: Routledge, 2013); S Ramshaw, 'Jamming the Law: Improvisational Theatre and the "Spontaneity" of Judgment' (2010) 14 *Law Text Culture* 133.

[2] S Katyal, 'Performance, Property, and the Slashing of Gender in Fan Fiction' (2006) 14 *American University Journal of Gender, Social Policy, and Law* 461; CJ Craig, 'Reconstructing the Author-Self: Some Feminist Lessons for Copyright Law' (2006) 15 *American University Journal of Gender, Social Policy, and Law* 207; JE Cohen, *Configuring the Networked Self: Law, Code, and the Play of Everyday Practice* (New Haven, CT: Yale University Press, 2012); MA Lemley, 'Faith-Based Intellectual Property' (2015) 62 *UCLA Law Review* 1328; P Jaszi, 'Is There Such a Thing as Postmodern Copyright' (2009) 12 *Tulane Journal of Technology & Intellectual Property* 105; J Butler, *Gender Trouble* (New York: Routledge, 1990); S Stern, 'Copyright, Originality, and the Public Domain in Eighteenth-Century England' in R McGinnis (ed), *Originality and Intellectual Property in the French and English Enlightenment* (New York: Routledge, 2008) 85; P Jaszi, 'On the Author Effect: Contemporary Copyright and Collective Creativity' in M Woodmansee and P Jaszi (eds), *The Construction Of Authorship: Textual Appropriation In Law and Literature* (Durham, NC: Duke University Press, 1994) 29; D Oliar and C Sprigman, 'There's No Free Laugh (Anymore): The Emergence of Intellectual Property Norms and the Transformation of Stand-Up Comedy' (2008) 94 *Virginia Law Review* 1787.

reasoning and improvisation, defined the content of what the law protects. This book explores how the essential copyright law concepts have been developed in the context of theatrical practice and performance, drawing on insights from literary studies, theatre and performance studies, anthropology and sociology, as well as the core study of law.[3] As the first academic monograph that focuses solely on the relationship between UK copyright law and historical and contemporary theatre this book fills an important gap in the scholarship. Until the last few years monograph studies of copyright law were focused overwhelmingly on literature (and to a lesser extent, music); whereas this book fits within an emerging field concerned with the copyright claims over visual art, dance and performance.[4]

My focus on theatre illuminates the fact that what is protected by the law – embodied by the script of the play, known under UK copyright as the dramatic work – is an allographic, rather than an autographic, work of art.[5] Specifically, it is a performative work, a text which is typically intended to be performed by people other than the playwright. Moreover, the dramatic work is often authored via a collaborative workshop process, with several participants – the playwright, the director, the actors – making creative contributions. This raises several questions: who, after this process, is the author and first owner of the work? Given the nature of theatre as a medium reliant on the re-use of prior existing works, tropes, themes and plots, what happens if an allegation of copyright infringement is made against a playwright? Furthermore, who possesses moral rights over the work – namely, the right to be named as author and the right to control the integrity of the work?[6] Although major

[3] M Rose, *Authors in Court: Scenes From the Theater of Copyright* (Cambridge, MA: Harvard University Press, 2016); S Shepherd and M Wallis, *Drama/Theatre/Performance* (London: Routledge, 2004) 1; P Sidney, *The Defence of Poetry* (JA Van Druten ed, Oxford: Oxford University Press, 1975) 45 (originally published 1579–80); J Dryden, *Of Dramatic Poesy and Other Critical Essays* (G Watson ed, London: Dent, 1968) 87 (originally written 1665–66); ST Coleridge, *Coelridge's Shakespearean Criticism* (TM Raysor ed, London: Constable & Co., 1930) 209; S Johnson, *Dr Johnson on Shakespeare* (WK Wimsatt ed, Harmondsworth: Penguin, 1969) 70–71 (originally published 1765); W Hazlitt, *Selected Writings* (J Cooke ed, Oxford: Oxford University Press, 1991) 330.

[4] E Cooper, 'Book Review: Becoming Property: Art, Theory and Law in Early Modern France and Copyright and the Value of Performance, 1770–1911' (2020) 16 *Law, Culture and the Humanities* 504. See also D Miller, *Copyright and the Value of Performance, 1770–1911* (Cambridge: Cambridge University Press, 2018); E Cooper, *Art and Modern Copyright: The Contested Image* (Cambridge: Cambridge University Press, 2018); W Slauter, *Who Owns the News? A History of Copyright* (Stanford: Stanford University Press, 2019) and A Kraut, *Choreographing Copyright: Race, Gender, and Intellectual Property Rights in American Dance* (Oxford: Oxford University Press, 2015).

[5] N Goodman, *Languages of Art* (Indianapolis: Hackett Publishing Co, Inc, 1976) 99–123. Goodman uses autographic to define works bound by material form such as paintings and sculptures (which he argues can be 'forged'). He uses allographic to define works legitimately realisable in innumerable ways (via copying and performance) such as literature, drama and music. As I note in chapter three, in copyright law there is some conceptual vagueness about the distinction between literary and dramatic works, with the performative quality said to distinguish drama from literature.

[6] A Gilden 'Intellectual Property's Queer Turn' in S Stern, M Del Mar and B Meyler (eds), *The Oxford Handbook of Law and Humanities* (Oxford: Oxford University Press, 2020) 549. See also S Burke, 'Copyright and Conceptual Art' in E Bonadio and N Lucchi (eds), *Non-Conventional Copyright – Do New and Atypical Works Deserve Protection?* (Cheltenham: Edward Elgar, 2018) 44; HY Kang, 'Is There (Should There Be) a Law & Humanities Canon?' (2019) 16 *Law, Culture and the Humanities* 1; M Mimler, 'On How to Deal with Pandora's Box – Copyright in Works of Nazi Leaders' in E Bonadio and N Lucchi (eds), *Non-Conventional Copyright – Do New and Atypical Works Deserve Protection?*

theatres use standard contracts to try to clarify some of the above issues, in general theatre – which thrives in part due to public subsidy – tends to be less integrated into the web of business contracts found in the TV and film industries.[7] This leaves much room for regulation of theatrical ownership practices via social norms.[8] Yet, as I show over the course of this book, although the practices of theatre are profoundly social and normative, they are also bounded by legal constructs.

Overview of Jurisdictional Limitations and Thematic Scope

This book, including its empirical case study, is focused on stage plays as dramatic works rather than on works of musical theatre (musicals, operas, etc) or works of choreography (dance). Performance studies is an extraordinarily rich and varied field and there is simply no way to encompass every aspect of theatre within a single monograph, especially where significant studies have already been produced on, for example, choreography.[9] Over the course of this book, my focus is limited to copyright in the underlying dramatic work itself, not related rights such as performers' rights or the rights in set design. Since my aim in this book is to explore authorship of plays as dramatic works – texts that can be performed from a script – certain aspects of contemporary theatre are thus excluded, such as 'immersive' theatre. Yet, as I describe in chapters two and three, by zeroing in on the dramatic work I can study its relationship with law during different time periods and with respect to a wide spectrum of theatrical forms from devised to text-based theatre.

This study focuses primarily on the UK jurisdiction. The empirical study was similarly undertaken with UK-based participants. However, my intention is that this book will be relevant to legal scholarship more broadly.[10]

(Cheltenham: Edward Elgar, 2018) 432; T Flessas and L Mulcahy, 'Limiting Law: Art in the Street and Street in the Art' (2018) 14 *Law, Culture and the Humanities* 219.

[7] CL Fisk, 'Will Work for Screen Credit: Labour and the Law in Hollywood' in P McDonald, E Carman, E Hoyt and P Drake (eds), *Hollywood and the Law* (London: Palgrave, 2015) 235, 240.

[8] See generally J Silbey, *The Eureka Myth: Creators, Innovators, and Everyday Intellectual Property* (Redwood City, CA: Stanford University Press, 2014) and M Iljadica, *Copyright Beyond Law: Regulating Creativity in the Graffiti Subculture* (Oxford: Hart, 2016). See also RC Ellickson, *Order Without Law: How Neighbors Settle Disputes* (Cambridge, MA: Harvard University Press, 1991).

[9] Kraut (n 4).

[10] Copyright, Designs and Patents Act (CDPA) 1988, available at www.legislation.gov.uk/ukpga/1988/48/contents. Ireland is a close comparator – since independence in 1922 it has maintained standards very close to those of UK copyright law. The Copyright and Related Rights Act (CRRA) 2000 follows the terms of the CDPA. There is however a lack of relevant Irish case law on dramatic works. As a result, UK court precedents can be said to have persuasive authority in Irish law (albeit Ireland has a written constitutional document). See, eg R Kennedy, 'Was it Author's Rights All The Time?: Copyright as a Constitutional Right in Ireland' (2011) 33 *Dublin University Law Journal* 253. Ireland, as a continuing EU member, may end up diverging from UK case law in years to come, should the UK pursue a course away from the terms of EU law (which remain binding in Ireland).

On authorship, joint authorship, infringement and moral rights I draw on comparative insights from case law in common law jurisdictions such as the US, Canada, Australia, Ireland and India. I refer to EU law on several points of relevance, including on originality; and I make comparative reference where civil law jurisdictions provide fascinating counter examples to the UK common law system of protection – for example, France in the case of moral rights and Germany in the case of 'free use'.

A Theoretical Approach to Law and Authorship

In assessing the relationship between the categories of 'authorship' and 'work' in theatre, legal scholarship is not the 'be all and end all'.[11] Taking an interdisciplinary perspective, I am guided not only by legal scholars but also by thinkers from the fields of theatre studies, literary studies, anthropology and sociology.[12]

Philosophers have long mused upon the concept of ownership as applied to different forms of writing, including literature and drama. Almost 2,000 years ago, when considering the sale of books in *De Benficiis*, Seneca – a playwright as well as a philosopher – made a distinction between the thing itself and its use, and between the original piece of writing and its copy.[13] When Immanuel Kant considered the question of whether it ought to be prohibited to publish an unauthorised version of an author's text, he referred to Roman law's separation between *opus* (work of art) and *opera* (speech in action).[14]

What is fascinating about a work of theatre is that it problematizes such distinctions – between original and copy and between work of art and speech in action. As noted earlier, dramatic works are allographic, attaining their ideal expression in performance; the printed form, by contrast, is often seen as secondary (or at least not as authoritative as the performed text in action).

[11] W Shakespeare, *The Oxford Shakespeare: Macbeth* (N Brooke ed, Oxford: Oxford University Press, 2008) Act I, Scene vii.

[12] R Barthes, 'The Death of the Author' 5/6 *Aspen: The Magazine in a Box* (R Howard tr, 1967), available at www.ubu.com/aspen/aspen5and6/index.html; M Foucault, 'What Is an Author?' in JM Marsh, JD Caputo and M Westphal (eds), *Modernity and its Discontents* (New York: Fordham University Press, 1992) 299, 305 (original essay dating from 1969 and seen by many as a response to Barthes); and P Bourdieu, *The Logic of Practice* (Stanford CA: Stanford University Press, 1990). See also Shepherd and Wallis (n 3) and Goodman (n 5).

[13] LA Seneca, *De Beneficiis* (67 AD); *On Benefits*, addressed to Aebutius Liberalis (A Stewart tr, London: George Bell and Sons, 1887), available at www.gutenberg.org/files/3794/3794-h/3794-h.htm. See also NT Pratt, *Seneca's Drama* (Chapel Hill: University of North Carolina Press, 1983).

[14] I Kant, 'On the Wrongfulness of Unauthorized Publication of Books (1785)' in P Guyer and AW Wood, *The Cambridge Edition of the Works of Immanuel Kant* (Mary J Gregor ed, tr, Cambridge: Cambridge University Press, 1996) 27. In the UK it is possible for a work to fall into more than one category of work eg in *Norowzian v Arks Ltd (No 2)* [2000] FSR 363 it was held that a film can also be a dramatic work. Thus, a literary work such as a novel that is later read out (performed) on stage could be considered as a dramatic work in that context as well as being a literary one in its original form/context.

In this book when considering theories of authorship and the work I take as my primary inspiration insights from the path-breaking 1960s–1970s work of Roland Barthes and Michel Foucault. Barthes and Foucault are often *authorised* as the key philosophers of post-modern authorship.[15] Their work enables a re-categorisation of the 'the singular, autonomous author as a discursive formation embedded in particular historical conditions and disciplinary needs'.[16] By setting out how concepts of theatrical authorship have changed over time, this book embraces these theoretical ideas, outlining the multi-faceted – and even poly-vocal – nature of theatrical authorship.

In particular, I make use of Barthes' distinction between the work and the text, which he utilises to separate – or liberate – the author from the text.[17] What Barthes calls the 'work' is what may be viewed casually by the reader, with its meaning almost taken for granted; by contrast he argues that 'a text's unity lies not in its origin but in its destination'.[18] The post-modern reader approaches the 'text' to make it revelatory, creating a network of meanings and interpretations between reader and text, with the author far removed. For this reason Barthes' states 'the birth of the reader must be at the cost of the death of the Author'.[19] In this chapter – and in those that follow – I refer back to this distinction as a way of deepening the understanding of the dramatic text as allographic work (of art) and copyright work (in law). As I explore, the work of drama is often authored via a collaborative process, which de-centres the author figure from the resultant text. Furthermore, the text that is produced is performative, typically brought to life on stage in front of an audience by parties – director, actor, producer – other than the author.[20] What emerged in theatrical history were two historical commodities of value – print and performance – arising from the the same text. Print was the first to gain legal protection; by contrast it took much longer for the law to protect performances via property rights.[21]

[15] This is not to say they are the only thinkers who problematise the nature of authorship. While insights from their work are appropriate for my study, which is focused on Western concepts of theatre and authorship, several prominent scholars have analysed indigenous modes of authorship and ownership, providing a rich critique of intellectual property law – see, eg K Bowrey, 'Alternative Intellectual Property?: Indigenous Protocols, Copyleft and New Juridifications of Customary Practices' (2006) 6 *Macquarie Law Journal* 65 and D Wassel, 'From Mbube to Wimoweh: African Folk Music in Dual Systems of Law' (2010) 20 *Fordham Intellectual Property, Media and Entertainment Law Journal* 289.

[16] H Hirschfeld, 'Early Modern Collaboration and Theories of Authorship' (2001) 116 *Theories and Methodologies* 609, 619–20. See also E Ostrom, *Governing the Commons* (New York: New York University Press, 1990).

[17] For a critical view of the use of literary theory in copyright analysis, see HB Holland, 'Social Semiotics in the Fair Use Analysis' (2011) 24 *Harvard Journal of Law & Technology* 335, 358.

[18] Barthes (n 12) 148.

[19] ibid.

[20] E Ioannidou, 'From Translation to Performance Reception: The Death of the Author and the Performance Text' in E Hall and S Harrop (eds), *Theorising Performance: Greek Tragedy, Cultural History and Critical Practice* (London: Bloomsbury, 2010) 208.

[21] See generally L Febvre and H-J Martin, *The Coming of the Book – The Impact of Printing, 1450–1800* (London: Verso, 1997). See also JS Peters, *Theatre of the Book, 1480–1880: Print, Text, and Performance in Europe* (Oxford: Oxford University Press, 2000).

Along with Barthes, Michel Foucault's work on authorship is essential to my analysis. Foucault focuses on how authors are often heralded as the epitome of the 'writer as genius'. On this it is notable that playwrights are typically acclaimed as among the finest author-geniuses: Shakespeare is the quintessential English author, his works both read as literature and performed as drama. The influence of playwrights even stretches to the critique itself: when Foucault wrote his famous essay 'Who is an author?' during the 1970s he quoted Samuel Beckett:

> 'What does it matter who is speaking,' someone said, 'what does it matter who is speaking.'[22]

It is perhaps revealing, however, that there is a minor difference in the English translation of Foucault when compared with Beckett's own English version of the line (originally written in French):[23]

> 'What matter who's speaking, someone said what matter who's speaking.'[24]

In both translations there are no question marks. Yet the first appears to be related in the third person perspective by the author (or 'God' voice) and the second translation appears to be a line spoken in the first person, as if a person were relating what someone else has said. Even here, we are left with the question – *who* is speaking?

In theatre the person speaking is typically an actor, not the writer. So to ask about who is speaking is to necessarily contemplate the relationship between author and performer. There may be talent – even genius – in both. Yet traditionally copyright law recognises solely the writers as authors of texts (recognised in law as works), and actors as merely the authors of their performances when these are recorded (eg on film), that is, performers' rights, which tend to be much less valuable than authors' rights.[25]

Ultimately, Foucault claims that what we think of as the author is 'a certain functional principle by which, in our culture … one impedes the free circulation, the free manipulation, the free composition, decomposition, and recomposition of fiction'.[26] Why is this important? For Foucault the answer is that the performance of the author function is inevitably more complex than the simple ascription of 'genius' to a single figure could ever encompass. This book aims to demonstrate that this is profoundly true in the theatrical context: to 'perform' the role of the author is to become, in law, the copyright owner. It is this notion that gives this book its title. Yet, there are other 'performers', and consequently other claims to the work, and these too require analysis.

[22] Foucault (n 12) 101.

[23] A Hird, '"What Does it Matter Who is Speaking," Someone Said, "What Does it Matter Who is Speaking?": Beckett, Foucault, Barthes' (2010) 22 *Samuel Beckett Today/Aujourd'hui* 289.

[24] S Beckett, 'Text 3, Texts for Nothing' in *The Grove Centenary Edition, Vol. 4: Poems, Short Fiction Criticism*, P Auster (ed) (New York: Grove, 2006) 302.

[25] R Arnold, *Performers' Rights*, 5th edn (London: Sweet & Maxwell, 2015). As noted earlier, my focus in this book is on authorship of the copyright work rather than the 'related rights' of performers.

[26] Foucault (n 12) 118–19.

Copyright's Cultural Turn

It took time for the deconstruction of the 'cult of the author' by scholars such as Foucault, Barthes and Masten to influence copyright law and scholarship.[27] As recently as the mid-1990s Bently could state with confidence that the 'death of the author' critique 'appears so far to have had no significant influence on copyright law which has continued to employ romantic images of authorship'.[28] That has now changed; copyright has since the mid-1990s undergone a 'cultural turn' via the work of legal scholars such as Woodmansee, Cohen, Coombe, Pottage, Craig, Macmillan and Sherman.[29] In addition to enriching legal scholarship this body of research is even beginning to have an impact on copyright case law.[30]

One crucial aspect of creative practice that has become more perceptible in legal debates as a result of this scholarship is collaboration, which is evident in theatre in the 16th century, through the Romantic period, and up to our present day.[31] Although some specific practices may have changed during the past five centuries, the process of developing plays remains inherently dynamic and collaborative in nature. As Keller relates:

> The theatrical process consists of everything that takes place between the first writing down of dialogue or the first day of rehearsal and the final curtain on opening night. This process is a dynamic, evolving one, and all of its elements are organic: plays are created out of people, either from the improvisational acting efforts of a group or from the individual contributions of a writer, a director, the dramaturge, set, costume and lighting designers, perhaps a choreographer, and, of course, actors. All of these people work together to bring a play to fruition.[32]

[27] ibid. See also J Masten, *Textual Intercourse: Collaboration, Authorship, and Sexualities in Renaissance Drama* (Cambridge: Cambridge University Press, 1997) and Barthes (n 12). For assessment of the 'cultural turn' more generally see F Jameson, *The Cultural Turn: Selected Writings on the Postmodern, 1983–1998* (London: Verso, 1998).

[28] L Bently, 'Copyright and the Death of the Author in Literature and Law' (1994) 57 *The Modern Law Review* 973.

[29] A Chander and M Sunder, 'Copyright's Cultural Turn' (2013) 91 *Texas Law Review* 1397. See also M Woodmansee, 'The Genius and the Copyright: Economic and Legal Conditions of the Emergence of the "Author"' (1984) 17 *Eighteenth-Century Studies* 425; CJ Craig, *Copyright, Communication and Culture: Towards a Relational Theory of Copyright Law* (Cheltenham: Edward Elgar, 2011); JE Cohen, 'Creativity and Culture in Copyright Theory' (2007) 40 *UC Davis Law Review* 1151; RJ Coombe, *The Cultural Life of Intellectual Properties: Authorship, Appropriation and the Law* (Durham NC: Duke University Press, 1998); B Sherman and L Bently, *The Making of Modern Intellectual Property Law* (Cambridge: University Press, 1999); A Pottage, *Figures of Invention* (Oxford: Oxford University Press, 2011); F Macmillan, *Intellectual and Cultural Property: Between Market and Community* (London: Routledge, 2020).

[30] *Kogan v Martin* [2019] EWCA 1645, citing the work of D Simone, *Copyright and Collective Authorship: Locating the Authors of Collaborative Work* (Cambridge: Cambridge University Press, 2019) in reassessing the joint authorship test.

[31] See generally J Cox and D Kastan (eds), *A New History of Early English Drama* (New York: Columbia University Press, 1997).

[32] S Keller, 'Collaboration in Theater: Problems and Copyright Solutions' (1986) 33 *UCLA Law Review* 891, 908–09.

It is on collaboration that legal-feminist thought becomes vitally relevant. Krause argues that the 'institution of authorship' can distract from the collective realities of cultural production, where the role of collaborators, especially women, is minimised due to the 'elective affinity of the concept of the author with modern, western individualism'.[33] To critique our universal authorship presumptions, we must first acknowledge that promoting individual – and typically, male – authorship is in many cases a deliberate strategy. The institutions of, for example, literary scholarship, literary publishing and historical biography all have an interest in producing (and reproducing) the idea of a sole 'genius' author to an audience.[34] Put simply, it is easier to sell an individual mythology than to explain the complexities involved in collaboration, especially when apportioning the roles of others may reduce the image of the 'great man' in history.[35] Moreover, as a society, we often seem to find the idea of the individual genius alluring, even comforting.

Yet, historicising the single author image as part of our own view of modernity is exactly what many post-modern scholars have sought to do in the wake of Foucault and Barthes. The 'great man theory' originally ascribed to Thomas Carlyle, and occasionally applied by scholars such as Harold Bloom to a select group of women such as Mary Ann Evans (George Eliot) and Jane Austen may be alluring, but it is sometimes – perhaps often – not reflective of collaborative realities. In fact, understanding collaboration is the key factor in making authorship of theatrical works truly 'visible'.[36] As we shall see, the Elizabethan period provides rich accounts of collaborative theatricality; but so too do the later periods including our contemporary one.[37] Indeed, it is possible that Elizabethan theatrical practitioners understood better than we do that what is created in theatre is a collaborative product that ought not be attributed to a single individual.[38] Yet, as copyright law came into focus during the eighteenth and nineteenth centuries by recognizing the property claims of writers *as authors*, this vital insight about collaborative creativity in theatre appears to have been lost. Modern copyright law struggles to recognise the collaborative product of theatre for what it is. In evaluating theatrical creativity in the past and present I aim in this book to link the historical and the contemporary, showing how understanding history may aid our current task – the construction of authorship and ownership.[39]

[33] M Krause, 'Practicing Authorship: The Case of Brecht's Plays' in C Calhoun and R Sennett (eds), *Practicing Culture* (Oxford: Routledge, 2007) 217. See also T Moi, *Sexual/Textual Politics* (London: Methuen, 1985).

[34] ibid, 216. See also P Bourdieu, *The Rules of Art: Genesis and Structure of the Literary Field* (Cambridge: Polity Press, 1996) and L Ede and A Lunsford, *Singular Texts/Plural Authors: Perspectives on Collaborative Writing* (Carbondale: Southern Illinois U, 1990).

[35] BA Spector, 'Carlyle, Freud, and the Great Man Theory More Fully Considered' (2016) 12 *Leadership* 250.

[36] B London, *Writing Double: Women's Literary Partnerships* (Ithaca, NY and London: Cornell University Press, 1999).

[37] Hirschfield (n 16). See also WJ Ong, *Orality and Literacy* (London: Routledge, 1982) 72.

[38] J Stillinger, *Multiple Authorship and the Myth of Solitary Genius* (New York: Oxford University Press, 1991) 182.

[39] M Heidegger, *Being and Time* (New York: Harper and Row, 1962) 424–55, noting that the present does not necessarily yield the future we anticipate.

Looking forward, Foucault evokes 'a future in which fiction seems to circulate unlimited by authorial or other constraints' – yet Masten argues that even Foucauldians should admit that it is 'pure romanticism' to imagine a culture devoid of all such mechanisms.[40] So what can we achieve in terms of legal and cultural reforms? Over this book this question will remain central – and, as I explain below, there is no way to answer it without speaking directly to those who work in the theatre field and evaluating their responses.

Empirical Methodology

In recent years qualitative empirical studies have shed light on the collaborative nature of artistic creativity in a range of areas, providing insights that have forced scholars to grapple with the practical consequences of copyright's individualistic approach to authorship, ownership and the control of cultural works.[41] This book fits within that analytical framework.

Here I describe the methodology of the qualitative empirical research underpinning the book's case study – the detailed set of 20 interviews I conducted during 2011–13. The empirical study was a necessity due to the lack of UK case law on dramatic works and the scarcity of existing data.[42] In order to probe the key issues in detail I needed to speak with those in the field.[43] I undertook the empirical interviews between November 2011 and March 2013, featuring a representative sample of participants in the UK theatre community – actors, playwrights, directors and other participants, as detailed below.[44]

Having received ethics approval from my institution, the initial stages of the study design primarily concerned identifying a broad 'universe' of potential participants.[45] This universe was obviously wide-ranging – the UK has a very large theatre sector featuring innumerable theatre companies, ranging from small, regional theatres to London's thriving commercial scene, as well as the major public-funded theatres around the country. When collating the list of possible respondents I was careful to create a representative sample, accommodating this

[40] J Masten, 'Beaumont and/or Fletcher: Collaboration and the Interpretation of Renaissance Drama' (1992) 52 *English Literary History* 337, 351.

[41] See, eg L McDonagh, 'Plays, Performances and Power Struggles – Examining Copyright's Integrity in the Field of Theatre' (2014) 77 *The Modern Law Review* 533; Silbey (n 8); and Iljadica (n 8).

[42] A rare example of a study focusing on authorship of plays in the UK is D Wu, *Making Plays: Interviews with Contemporary British Dramatists* (London: Palgrave MacMillan, 2000), though there is no reflection on legal issues in this book. On the Australian context see B Salter, 'Taming the trojan horse: an Australian perspective of dramatic authorship' (2009) 56 *Journal of The Copyright Society of The USA* 789.

[43] The annex explains the question design and interview process and provides the full questionnaire.

[44] For anthropological insight into the researcher's experience of entering the cultural field see R Wagner, *The Invention of Culture*, 2nd edn (Chicago: University of Chicago Press, 1981) 1–16.

[45] For discussion of the way the 'field' is constructed in relation to empirical research, see S Dalsgaard, 'The field as a temporal entity and the challenges of the contemporary' (2013) 20 *Social Anthropology* 213. This must be contrasted with Bourdieu's notion of 'field' as discussed later on in this chapter.

diversity – I made efforts to ensure that I had an equal spread of participants, from the experienced to the newcomers, and from the established names to the fringe players.[46] As a result, the participants who were interviewed during the period between November 2011 and February 2013 were varied in terms of careers and their perspectives – some had worked exclusively in London and the South-East, while others had worked all around the UK as well as abroad.[47]

I made contact with the participants using two main methods. First, 14 interviewees agreed to participate after I initially made direct contact with each of them, inviting them to participate. I chose these interviewees based on their characteristics in light of the need to form a representative sample, examining factors such as the level of establishment a participant had within the field, their level of experience, and where relevant, the size of the theatre company the participant typically worked at/with. I contacted them one by one via email accessed from their personal or professional websites, or via their agents. The second method I used was the 'snowball' method. I used this method where participants were willing to provide me with contact details for other potential participants. In this respect, two participants informed me of others who might be interested in participating. Six participants were contacted in this way and agreed to participate. Overall, I conducted interviews with 20 participants. These anonymous participants, whom I have categorised as anon 1–20, fell into an array of diverse categories:

- Four playwrights (anon 1-4).
- Two producers (anon 5-6).
- Two actors (anon 7-8).
- One director-artistic director (anon 9).
- One director-artistic director-playwright (anon 10).
- One director-associate director (anon 11).
- One associate literary director (anon 12).
- One actor-deviser (anon 13).
- One actor-dramaturge (anon 14).
- One actor-director-playwright (anon 15).
- One actor-producer-deviser (anon 16).
- One playwright-artistic director (anon 17).
- One playwright-performance artist (anon 18).
- One deviser-choreographer (anon 19).
- One academic working in the field of drama (anon 20).

[46] Regarding analysis of what the appropriate length of research projects is, see G Marcus, 'How short can fieldwork be?' (2007) 15 *Social Anthropology* 353.

[47] The interviewees agreed to participate voluntarily under the condition of anonymity. They gave up their time generously, for which I am most grateful. All data is held and used anonymously in accordance with the Data Protection Acts and the EU General Data Protection Regulation (GDPR).

It is clear from the different descriptions given above that it is not uncommon in the theatre world for the same person to hold a number of different roles. For example, the actor-director-playwright that I interviewed was, at the time of interview, engaged in a purely acting role, but he was due to move on to a purely directing role shortly afterwards. Similarly, the actor-dramaturge was at the time of interview engaged in an acting role, but she had previously worked as a dramaturge. The director-artistic director-playwright was currently performing the artistic director role at his fringe theatre company, though over the course of his career he had gained experience at directing, and occasionally at devising and playwriting. This diversity of roles ultimately proved useful to the study as many participants had experience of performing different roles within the theatre world and could reflect on the different perspectives gained from each role.

It is crucial to note the limitations of the empirical research methodology and data.[48] The guiding research hypothesis at the heart of this book is 'What effect, if any, does copyright law have on creative practices in the realm of theatre?' As noted earlier, this book does not attempt to address all issues relating to copyright and theatre – my focus is on authorship/joint authorship of the dramatic work (chapters two and three), the right to exclude others (chapter four on infringement) and the right to be credited and to control artistic interpretations (chapter five on the moral rights of attribution and integrity). Other intellectual property (IP) issues such as performers' rights, trade marks, rights over set design etc do not form part of the study. Given both the relatively small size of the sample, and the diversity of views on the issue of copyright and theatre uncovered by this book, it is clear that no qualitative study can claim to produce a definitive statement on the subject. Nonetheless, this study represents the first monograph from a legal scholar that engages empirically with the question of how copyright actually relates to the creative practices of artists in the realm of theatre in the UK. In this regard, it works alongside other recent empirical studies which have attempted to illuminate the realities of how copyright works in atypical or 'negative' spaces – spaces where the normal assumptions and practices of copyright law must be called into question.[49]

[48] For commentary on the limitations of empirical research more generally, see J Faubion and G Marcus (eds), *Fieldwork Is Not What It Used to Be: Learning Anthropology's Method in a Time of Transition* (Ithaca NY: Cornell University Press, 2008).

[49] See recent research in the fields of musicians, magicians, stand-up comedians, theatre directors and other types of artist, eg J Leach, 'Constituting aesthetics and utility: Copyright, patent and the purification of knowledge objects in an art and science collaboration' (2012) 2 *Journal of Ethnographic Theory* 247; J Yoshin, 'Secrets Revealed: Protecting Magicians Intellectual Property without Law' in CA Corcos (ed), *Law and Magic: A Collection of Essays* (Durham NC: Carolina Academic Press, 2010) 123; Oliar and Sprigman (n 2) and E Bonadio and N Lucchi, *Non-Conventional Copyright – Do New and Atypical Works Deserve Protection?* (Cheltenham: Edward Elgar, 2018).

Using Bourdieu to Frame the Empirical Case Study

In the theatrical context creativity is very much a social practice.[50] As I explore in chapters three to five, the interviews demonstrate that 'power struggles' concerning the integrity of dramatic works commonly take place between the various 'agents' active in the field of theatre, such as playwrights, directors and actors. The plays that are created are constitutive of this complex, iterative process.[51]

Due to the fact that creativity in theatre is primarily social, the sociologist Pierre Bourdieu's work provides a useful intellectual framework for examining the interview data. For Bourdieu, society exists as 'as an array of fields with specific forms of capital that are objects of struggle'.[52] These capitals include economic (money and property), cultural (information, knowledge, education etc.), social (acquaintances and networks) and symbolic (legitimacy and prestige).[53] Capitals can also transfigure from one form into another; for example cultural capital can be transformed into symbolic capital, something which can give an agent a great deal of leverage when power struggles take place.[54] Meanwhile, the concept of 'habitus' refers to an agent's social knowledge – framed by internalised past experiences – something that allows the agent to know which behaviours to select in order to achieve a desired result.[55]

Within this prism, it can be said that in the field of theatre there are various agents occupying an assortment of roles such as playwright, director, actor, producer, dramaturge, performance artist etc, with each agent possessing different capitals within the field. Sometimes agents perform multiple roles simultaneously, meaning they possess a multiplicity of capitals. Regarding the various capitals and habitus each particular agent possesses within the field of theatre, 'experience' and 'peer-esteem' are key factors. A track record of success as a director, actor, playwright, producer etc gives that person a high level of cultural capital in the form of acquired knowledge, as well as social capital, in the form of acquired networks. These forms of cultural and social capital often transform into symbolic capital, in the form of prestige, which can be used advantageously within the power struggles which occur. This might be used to negotiate a higher level of compensation – economic capital – in the form of a payment fee or royalties. Symbolic capital can also be used to gain leverage during a power struggle over the creative direction of the project. As I explore in chapter three, the interview data demonstrate that

[50] P Bourdieu, *The State Nobility: Elite Schools in the Fields of Power* (Stanford CA: Stanford University Press, 1996) 264–74.

[51] J Lennard and M Luckhurst, *The Drama Handbook* (Oxford: Oxford University Press, 2002) 155.

[52] DL Swartz, *Symbolic Power, Politics and Intellectuals – The Political Sociology of Pierre Bourdieu* (Chicago IL: University of Chicago Press, 2013) 47.

[53] P Bourdieu, 'The Forms of Capital' in JG Richardson (ed), *Handbook of Theory and Research for the Sociology of Education* (New York: Greenwood Press, 1986) 243.

[54] Swartz (n 52) 50.

[55] P Bourdieu, *Distinction – A Social Critique of the Judgment of Taste* (Cambridge MA: Harvard University Press, 1984) 471.

an inexperienced agent – such as a young writer or actor – will find it much more difficult to exert leverage within a power struggle since that person will likely lack the necessary economic, cultural, and social capitals, as well as the necessary habitus, to obtain the desired result.[56]

The specific role the agent plays will also affect the types of capitals that agent possesses. For instance, a director may possess a relatively stable level of economic capital if they are a salaried member of staff within a theatre company. However, a director may not be in a salaried position as they may be brought in by a theatre company just to stage a single production – a much more precarious situation. Yet, directors are typically the primary ones 'in charge' of the production. Moreover, as the interview data outlined in chapters three to five demonstrate, once the production process begins, directors need to make use of their habitus in order to maintain creative control over the project while also keeping other agents, such as writers and actors, on board.

Artistic directors typically oversee and approve a theatre company's entire set of productions. This is a relatively powerful position to be in, and one which involves the use of economic, cultural and social capitals. Producers, by contrast, often deal primarily at the level of economic capital, but they may also avail of social capital with respect to the networks they have access to. Like directors, producers often work in-house within theatre companies; though at the high-end of the market in London's 'West End' producers may work relatively independently in order to provide the finance and business arrangements for the staging of particular productions. Actors are typically freelance and they will generally be paid a union fee, per day of work, unless they are able to make use of their symbolic capital – reputation, prestige, popularity – to negotiate an increased fee. This brings us finally to playwrights, who tend to be freelance, and they are often paid just a one-off fee for their work – effectively a copyright licence fee – to cover the entire initial run of the production.[57] Depending on how the negotiation process goes, they may also receive a royalty based on ticket-sales. Moreover, playwrights also tend to retain copyright in the resulting play, something which gives them a potentially powerful economic capital when disputes arise.

Overview of Chapters

Following this first chapter, chapter two examines the history of the dramatic work both as print-text and as performative commodity, referring to legal, literary

[56] S Henley and T Allen-Martin, 'Tree. A Story of Gender and Power in Theatre' *Medium* (2 June 2019), available at https://medium.com/@toriandsarahburnbright/tree-a-story-of-gender-and-power-in-theatre-23b8a2468224.

[57] The 2015 Writers Agreement and *The Working Playwright* (Writers' Guild of Great Britain, 2019) aim to deal with such negotiations in advance: see https://writersguild.org.uk/wp-content/uploads/2015/02/WGGB_booklet_jun12_contracts_i.pdf.

and theatrical studies relevant to the period 1558–1911.[58] In chapter two I am interested in two related but distinct issues: authorship and the work.[59] How did authorship of theatre occur in the late sixteenth and early seventeenth centuries? It was profoundly *polyvocal*, with the individual playwright one creative contributor among several others (theatre managers, actors, other writers, Stationers, and even censors) to the malleable text.[60] Furthermore, I ask: what exactly was the work of theatre in the time of Elizabeth I? It was not a copyright work in the modern sense of a property-object encompassing a bundle of rights (to copy, publish, perform, adapt, etc). Rather, theatre houses in the sixteenth century took ownership of scripts as valuable *performance* texts, attempting to prevent them from being performed elsewhere using informal norms; while the Stationers exercised their legal monopolies to control the play-texts as *print* commodities. To a great extent, the Elizabethan dramatist *neither owned nor controlled either commodity*.[61] I examine how during the late Elizabethan and Jacobean eras burgeoning printing technology enabled the rise of a market for play-texts by popular writers such as Shakespeare and Ben Jonson to be published in book form, which in turn began to alter conceptions of the dramatic text as property during the 17th century. I outline how, post Statute of Anne 1710, claims of performance rights and adaptation rights challenged copyright law's view of what the law protected as text, leading to the reforms of 1833 and 1842, which provided legal recognition to the *performance-commodity* for the first time, and contributed to the emerging 'work' concept.[62] Overall, chapter two seeks to map out the historical relationship between the collaborative artistic practices of theatre and the legal institutional philosophy of copyright. The key mechanism of copyright law is traced from the era of the Stationers' Company to the Statute of Anne 1710, and up to the 1911 Copyright Act, via the ownership of plays as 'books' (1710), to 'dramatic pieces' (1833), and finally to 'dramatic works' (1911).

Chapter three explores the legal concepts of authorship and joint authorship of the dramatic work under copyright law in our contemporary period, referring

[58] See, eg, J Feather, 'The Book Trade in Politics: The Making of the Copyright Act of 1710' (1980) 8 *Publishing History* 19; T Ross, 'Copyright and the Invention of Tradition' (1992) 26 *Eighteenth-Century Studies* 1; J Hughes, 'The Philosophy of Intellectual Property' (1988) 77 *Georgetown Law Journal* 287; J Waldron, 'From Authors to Copiers' (1993) 68 *Chicago-Kent Law Review* 841 and Masten (n 27).

[59] For perspectives of authorship which take account of non-individualist practice see Craig (n 29), Coombe (n 29) and K Aoki, '(Intellectual) Property and Sovereignty: Notes Toward a Cultural Geography of Authorship' (1996) 48 *Stanford Law Review* 1293.

[60] Masten (n 27). See also Barthes (n 12) and Foucault (n 12).

[61] DA Brooks, 'Dramatic Authorship and Publication in Early Modern England' (2003) 15 *Medieval & Renaissance Drama in England* 77. See also P Blayney, 'The Publication of Playbooks' in J Cox and DS Kastan, *A New History of Early English Drama* (New York: Columbia University Press, 1997) 383; HT Gómez-Arostegui, 'What History Teaches Us About Copyright Injunctions and the Inadequate-Remedy-at-Law Requirement' (2008) 81 *S. Cal. L. Rev.* 1197; JJ Marino, *Owning William Shakespeare: The King's Men and Their Intellectual Property* (Philadelphia: University of Pennsylvania Press, 2011); B Lauriat, 'Literary and Dramatic Disputes in Shakespeare's Time' (2018) 9 *Journal of International Dispute Settlement* 45; and J Loewenstein, *Ben Jonson and Possessive Authorship* (Cambridge: Cambridge University Press, 2002) 10–18.

[62] Miller (n 4).

to case law from the twentieth and twenty-first centuries. I explore the actual processes of creating contemporary plays, referring to legal and theatrical literature, as well as empirical research, considering social norms in the context of the law of copyright.[63] I note that copyright law typically prizes individual authorship, which is also often valorised by the publishing industry. While copyright scholars merely *critique* this focus on individual authors, theatre practitioners actually put their challenges to the myths of singular authorship into *practice*, via collective processes of devising and revising plays. In the first part of chapter three I assess the current law on: (i) the copyright work, (ii) originality and (iii) authorship and joint authorship of plays. I explore legislation and case law in the UK jurisdiction on the question of how to define works of drama in light of the concept of originality, making comparative reference to relevant rules and case law approaches in common law jurisdictions such as the US, Canada, Australia and India.[64] In the second part of chapter three I explore theatre studies literature concerning the way works of drama are created via processes of *devising* and *revising* of texts, referring to insights from the 20 empirical interviews I undertook between 2011–13 with UK theatre participants. On the question of how dramatic works are authored I keep in mind Masten's point that in the modern world collaboration is often viewed 'as a mere subset or aberrant kind of individual authorship'.[65] I aim to show that in contemporary theatre, collaboration is far from aberrant – it is, in fact, the norm. Individual authors – Samuel Beckett, Harold Pinter, Martin McDonagh, etc – sometimes do provide dramatic works to theatre companies that are 'fully-formed'. Yet, most works involve an amount of collaborative devising or revising via the workshop and rehearsal process. These processes can alter the play substantially before it becomes a final text. In the case of devised theatre – Complicité, Frantic Assembly, Forced Entertainment, etc – or where a play is revised through workshops – common with the plays of David Hare, David Edgar, Caryl Churchill, etc – the final play as performed is constitutive of a highly collaborative process. In light of this, I consider questions of credit and ownership.[66] I reflect on how authorship relates to ownership, as well as the way plays are licensed and how revenues are distributed.[67] The chapter concludes by considering whether copyright law, as currently legislated, can take account of the above processes, and what reforms, if any, might better facilitate the creative processes of theatre.

Chapter four examines the notion of copyright infringement in the context of theatre. I show that in many ways, theatre takes place on a 'haunted stage' – throughout theatrical history, virtually every aspect of plot, character

[63] See, eg Craig (n 2); Simone (n 30); Coombe (n 29).
[64] McDonagh (n 41).
[65] Masten (n 40) 341.
[66] E Cooper, 'Joint authorship and copyright in comparative perspective: the emergence of divergence in the UK and USA' (2015) 62 *Journal of the Copyright Society of the USA* 245.
[67] *The Working Playwright* (n 57) aims to deal with such disputes in advance. For data on theatre sales see uktheatre.org/theatre-industry/news/2018-sales-data-released-uk-theatre-and-society-of-london-theatre/. For the Society for Theatre Research see www.str.org.uk/publications/annual-publications/. For Theatre collecting societies see www.concordtheatricals.co.uk/resources/intro-to-licensing.

and stage production has been recycled, even 'plagiarised'.[68] How does the idea of copyright infringement operate in this theatrical context? It goes without question that the verbatim copying of dialogue, or the taking of a very short amount of text from one work and using it in another, is likely to amount to copyright infringement under UK law. Dialogue and text aside, the more difficult question is where to draw the line between copyright infringement and the creative re-use of theatrical tropes, characters and scenarios. How can copyright law draw a line between the acceptable 'evoking' of another writer's work and infringement? I assess the doctrine of copyright infringement and the various fair dealing exceptions/limitations under UK law, with comparative insights drawn from jurisdictions such as the US, Canada, Australia and India. Relying on literature from theatrical studies, as well as the empirical case study, this chapter reveals insights about the way theatrical participants (directors, playwrights, actors, producers) regulate – or choose *not* to regulate – disputes about copying, allegations of plagiarism and cases of infringement. I note that cases of alleged theatrical infringement reach the courts comparatively infrequently in comparison with eg music cases. I assess the reasons for this with reference to the empirical research. The interview data show that re-interpretation, and even copying, is a commonplace 'natural' part of the theatrical creative process. Litigation is rare. Moreover, participants possess divergent views on the rights and wrongs of copying. At times, the UK theatre participants appear to regulate themselves – this regulation is *normative* but not legal, with a resolution found outside of the mechanisms of copyright law. Even in relatively clear cases of copying, artists are wary of entering the arena of law, fearing both the costs of litigation and that the ultimate result could be a 'bad precedent' that restricts the overall freedom to create.[69] Chapter four concludes by reflecting on the legal ramifications of the theatrical creative process and assessing the social norms at play.[70]

Chapter five examines the way moral rights of attribution and integrity apply in the context of theatre. The narrative of moral rights tends to emphasise the inherent link between the artist and the work of art, a point I examine in disputes over theatrical integrity which have occurred in Australia, France, Germany and

[68] M Carlson, *The Haunted Stage: The Theatre as Memory Machine* (Ann Arbor, MI: Michigan University Press, 2001).

[69] See generally R Tushnet, 'Free to Be You and Me? Copyright and Constraint' (2015) 128 *Harvard Law Review Forum* 125; R Tushnet, 'My Fair Ladies: Sex, Gender, and Fair Use in Copyright' (2006) 15 *American University Journal of Gender, Social Policy, and Law* 273 and A Chander and M Sunder, 'Everyone's a Superhero: A Cultural Theory of Mary Sue Fan Fiction as Fair Use' (2007) 95 *California Law Review* 597.

[70] E Fauchart and E Von Hippel, 'Norms-Based Intellectual Property Systems: The Case of French Chefs' (2008) 19 *Organization Science* 187; Oliar and Sprigman (n 2); D Fagundes, 'Talk Derby to Me: Intellectual Property Norms Governing Roller Derby Pseudonyms' (2011) 90 *Texas Law Review* 1093; E Sarid, 'Don't Be a Drag, Just Be a Queen-How Drag Queens Protect their Intellectual Property without Law' (2014) 10 *FIU Law Review* 133.

Ireland.[71] In this vein, I note that it is commonly argued that moral rights protect 'the superior interests of human genius' by ensuring that the work is kept 'as it emerged from the imagination of its author'.[72] The notion of a singular, Romantic author is clearly the archetype here, rather than any idea of authorship which reflects the collaborative nature of theatre.[73] It is also sometimes argued that along with the need to protect 'the personality interests of the individual artist' moral rights also protect the public interest by 'preserving' the work for the public.[74] Nonetheless, there is a counter-argument, one which is framed around the need to allow creative reinterpretation of the work by others.[75] In this view, Adler argues that the right of integrity 'threatens art because it fails to recognize the profound artistic importance of modifying, even destroying, works of art, and of freeing art from the control of the artist'.[76]

On attribution I explore how credit is awarded for theatrical plays and productions, a topic also relevant to chapter three. I demonstrate that it is typically the case that the agreements between writers and theatres specify that only the writer should get credit as author for the script (dramatic work).[77] Be that as it may, in theatre everybody tends to get some form of credit in the programme, from the writer to the director, and from the actors to the production staff; and when plays are published the original cast and director are usually provided in the text, providing an additional layer of attribution.

It is the second moral right – integrity – that is particularly fraught in this context and the bulk of this chapter concentrates on this right. Working together – sometimes radically – is central to the practice of drama and the creation of plays. How does this dramatic collaboration affect perceptions of the integrity of the work – and crucially the question of who gets to control the work? Cox and Kastan remark:

> Of all literary forms, drama is least respectful of its author's intentions. Plays inevitably register multiple intentions, often conflicting intentions, as actors, annotators, revisers,

[71] JH Merryman, AE Elsen and SK Urice, *Law, Ethics and the Visual Arts*, 5th edn (Alphen aan den Rijn, The Netherlands: Kluwer Law International, 2006) 423, arguing that to mistreat the work is to mistreat the artist.

[72] JH Merryman, *Thinking about the Elgin Marbles: Critical Essays on Cultural Property, Art and Law*, 2nd edn (Alphen aan den Rijn, The Netherlands: Kluwer Law International, 2009) 412, quoting from *Millet*, Tribunal de la Seine, 20 May 1911 (1911) Amm. I. 27, a case where the son of the great French artist Jean-François Millet took a case to prevent the publication of reproductions of his father's paintings, allegedly because they were so poorly produced the reproductions 'distorted' his father's works.

[73] See Craig, (n 2); Simone (n 30); Coombe (n 29).

[74] AM Adler, 'Against Moral Rights' (2009) 97 *California Law Review* 263, 270.

[75] LA Mills, 'Moral Rights: Well-Intentioned Protection and its Unintended Consequences' (2011) 90 *Texas Law Review* 443. See also MA Hamilton, 'Appropriation Art and the Imminent Decline in Authorial Control over Copyright Works' (1994) 42 *Journal of the Copyright Society of the U.S.A.* 93 and M Rimmer, 'The Grey Album: Copyright Law and Digital Sampling' (2005) 114 *Media International Australia* 40.

[76] Adler (n 74) 265.

[77] This is envisaged by the Writers' Guild in *The Working Playwright* (n 57).

collaborators, scribes, printers, and proofreaders, in addition to the playwright, all have a hand in shaping the text.[78]

I refer to cases where playwrights, such as Samuel Beckett, David Williamson and Clive Norris, have made *integrity-based objections*. The theoretical concepts of 'aura' and 'trajectory' are useful to this exploration.[79] Analysis of Benjamin's aura concept helps to explain why playwrights often show *anxiety* regarding maintaining the integrity of the dramatic work – put simply, they fear the audience will *fail to perceive the intended meaning of the play*. This relates to what Latour and Lowe describe as the trajectory of the dramatic work from its first performance onward.[80] I show that different jurisdictions (eg UK, Ireland, France, Italy, Australia) take varying approaches to resolving disputes over 'integrity'. I conclude by suggesting that in integrity disputes, the right to freedom of expression under the European Convention on Human Rights (ECHR) ought to be taken into account alongside the author's rights.[81]

Chapter six concludes the book with a succinct comment on how law should respond to the challenges provided by the theatrical context, and reflects on how theatre could respond to law.[82] On this, I note that theatre is often a centre of resistance to prevailing political and cultural currents – whereas law (especially in cases of intellectual property) can sometimes, perhaps often, be the tool of the powerful. One of Shakespeare's most famous jokes – about the sort of utopia a popular rebellion could envisage – still has a potent sting: 'The first thing we do, let's kill all the lawyers!'[83]

[78] Cox and Kastan (n 31). See also Sherman and Bently (n 29) and R Deazley, *Rethinking Copyright: History, Theory, Language* (Cheltenham: Edward Elgar, 2006).

[79] W Benjamin, 'The Work of Art in the Age of Mechanical Reproduction' in *Illuminations* (H Arendt ed, H Zohn tr, New York: Schocken Books, 1968) 217.

[80] B Latour and A Lowe, 'The migration of the aura, or how to explore the original through its fac similes' 1, 5–6, available at www.bruno-latour.fr/sites/default/files/108-ADAM-FACSIMILES-GB.pdf – originally published in T Bartscherer (ed), *Switching Codes: Thinking Through Digital Technology in the Humanities and the Arts* (Chicago: University of Chicago Press, 2010) 275. With regard to the life and 'trajectory' of instruments see also B Latour, *We Have Never Been Modern* (Cambridge MA: Harvard University Press, 1993) 17 and I Hacking, 'Artificial Phenomena' (1991) 24 *The British Journal for the History of Science* 235.

[81] The EU has not sought to harmonise moral rights so there are divergences between eg the UK and France on integrity. The philosophical link of 'personality' between artists and their works has its roots in Kantian and Hegelian thought. See, eg W Fisher, 'Theories of intellectual property' in S Munzer (ed), *New Essays in the Legal and Political Theory of Property* (Cambridge: Cambridge University Press, 2001) 171; H Breakey, 'Natural intellectual property rights and the public domain' (2010) 73 *The Modern Law Review* 208, 210; A Drassinower, *What's Wrong with Copying?* (Cambridge, MA: Harvard University Press, 2015) 147; A Chander and M Sunder, 'The Romance of the Public Domain' (2004) 92 *California Law Review*.

[82] Shepherd and Wallis (n 3) 21.

[83] W Shakespeare, *The Oxford Shakespeare: Henry VI: Part Two* (R Warren ed, Oxford: Oxford University Press, 2003) Act IV, Scene ii.

2

'The Play's The Thing ...' But What's the Play? And Who Owns It?

Introduction

One of the many things we learn from *Hamlet* is 'the play's the thing' – an object.[1] As with many other 'things', the law protects plays as objects of *property*.[2] But what exactly is the play as protected by copyright law? And who owns it? In this chapter I explore the history of authorship and ownership of plays from the Elizabethan period up to the early twentieth century (1558–1911) by analysing both theatrical and legal developments.

A note of caution is necessary. The narrative sweep of this chapter covers a large amount of material, spanning more than four centuries. Legal scholars have devoted entire books to micro-historical studies within this period.[3] Within the limitations of the length of this chapter my aim is to build upon these valuable historical studies to contribute a novel account of the emergence of the author-figure as owner of the dramatic work under UK copyright law. In addition to being

[1] W Shakespeare, *The Oxford Shakespeare: Hamlet* (S Wells ed, Oxford: Oxford University Press, 2008) Act II, Scene ii.

[2] B Sherman, 'What is a work?' (2011) 12 *Theoretical Inquiries in Law* 99, 120. See also A Pottage, *Figures of Invention* (Oxford: Oxford University Press, 2011); ZK Said, 'Copyright's Illogical Exclusion of Conceptual Art That Changes over Time' (2016) 39 *Colum. J. L. & Arts* 335; HY Kang, 'Is There (Should There Be) a Law & Humanities Canon?' (2019) 16 *Law, Culture and the Humanities* 1; A Rahmatian, *Copyright and Creativity: The Making of Property Rights in Creative Works* (Cheltenham: Edward Elgar, 2011); J Sanders, *Adaptation and Appropriation* (New York: Routledge, 2006); PK Saint-Amour (ed), *Modernism and Copyright* (Oxford: Oxford University Press, 2011); T Flessas and L Mulcahy, 'Limiting Law: Art in the Street and Street in the Art' (2018) 14 *Law, Culture and the Humanities* 219; A Drassinower, *What's Wrong With Copying?* (Cambridge, MA: Harvard University Press, 2015); G Frosio, *Reconciling Copyright with Cumulative Creativity – The Third Paradigm* (Cheltenham: Edward Elgar, 2018); K Bowrey, *Copyright, Creativity, Big Media and Cultural Value: Incorporating the Author* (Abingdon: Routledge, 2020).

[3] D Miller, *Copyright and the Value of Performance, 1770–1911* (Cambridge: Cambridge University Press, 2018); E Cooper, *Art and Modern Copyright: The Contested Image* (Cambridge: Cambridge University Press, 2018); and W Slauter, *Who Owns the News? A History of Copyright* (Stanford: Stanford University Press, 2019). See also M Rose, *Authors and Owner – The Invention of Copyright* (Cambridge, MA: Harvard University Press, 1993); L Goehr, *The Imaginary Museum of Musical Works: An Essay in the Philosophy of Music* (Oxford: Clarendon Press, 1992) and A Barron, 'Copyright Law's Musical Work' (2006) 15 *Social & Legal Studies* 101.

a useful contribution to the literature, this chapter lays the groundwork for my exploration of the modern law of copyright in the chapters that follow.

The significance of theatre to daily life during the often-tumultuous period from 1558–1911 is unquestionable: it is not an exaggeration to say that theatre was the primary public forum of art.[4] During the passing of these centuries England was transformed by momentous events including civil war (1642–51), restoration of the monarchy (1660) and the 'glorious revolution' (1688–89). The modern state of the United Kingdom of Great Britain and Ireland emerged via unions with Scotland (1707) and Ireland (1801), with the Imperial Parliament at Westminster forming the centre of the British Empire by the time of the Copyright Act 1911. Theatre reflected these events and was shaped by them, via constant state censorship and even by the shutting down of all theatres (as happened most dramatically in 1642–60).

At various points during this long period theatrical innovations influenced the law's perception of dramatic texts. The property boundaries of the play shifted, with the text being first protected via law solely as a print-commodity, and later additionally as a performance-commodity.[5] The law's impact on theatre was no less profound, with the literary activities of lawyers at the Inns of Court influencing the development of English tragedies.[6]

In the Elizabethan period the majority of plays were not published at all, and if so only in 'Quarto' form.[7] Playwrights were sometimes named as authors in printed play-texts registered at the Stationers' Company but not always, and they did not receive royalties. After the Statute of Anne 1710 legal claims made by playwrights, publishers and theatre owners (some of whom had received legal training at the Inns of Court) helped establish key case law principles concerning the 'right to copy' – the dramatic print-commodity under copyright. Later on, seminal cases such as *Macklin v Richardson* (1770) and *Murray v Ellison* (1822) stirred public debate over the commodification of performances and the ultimate question of 'how and what we value in art' – issues we still grapple with today.[8]

[4] S Shepherd and M Wallis, *Drama/Theatre/Performance* (London: Routledge, 2004) 1; J Dryden, *Of Dramatic Poesy and Other Critical Essays* (G Watson ed, London: Dent, 1968) 87 (originally written 1665–66); ST Coleridge, *Coleridge's Shakespearean Criticism* (TM Raysor ed, London: Constable & Co., 1930) 200; S Johnson, *Dr Johnson on Shakespeare* (WK Wimsatt ed, Harmondsworth: Penguin, 1969) 70–71 (originally published 1765), W Hazlitt, *Selected Writings* (J Cooke ed, Oxford: Oxford University Press, 1991) 330.

[5] Miller (n 3) 27–31 and 128–30.

[6] P Raffield, *Shakespeare's Imaginary Constitution* (Oxford: Hart Publishing, 2010); A Moore, *Shakespeare Between Machiavelli and Hobbes: Dead Body Politics* (Lanham: Lexington Books, 2016); E Heinze, '"Were it not against our laws": Oppression and Resistance in Shakespeare's Comedy of Errors' (2009) 29 *Legal Studies*; BJ Sokol and M Sokol, *Shakespeare's Legal Language* (London: Continuum, 2004) 316.

[7] Several Shakespeare plays were published during his lifetime in Quarto form, but Shakespeare's posthumous *First Folio* (1623) featured a large number of previously unpublished plays – see E Smith, *Shakespeare's First Folio: Four Centuries of an Iconic Book* (Oxford: Oxford University Press, 2016).

[8] Miller (n 3) 31.

My concern in this book is UK law, so it is appropriate to begin in the first part of this chapter by analysing drama as it emerged in England.[9] I explore the nature of dramatic authorship from an interdisciplinary perspective, considering law, theatre studies, literary studies, anthropology and sociology. As acknowledged earlier, several important studies on copyright history in non-literary forms (visual art, news, theatre & music performance) have been published in recent years.[10] This chapter contributes to this flourishing field of research by mapping out how plays came to be protected as works – property objects encompassing a bundle of rights to eg copy, publish, perform, adapt, etc.

My focus in this chapter is on two related issues: authorship and the work. How did *authorship* of theatre occur in the sixteenth century and seventeenth century? On this I explore whether individual playwrights were viewed as authors of plays; and I trace how conceptions of authorship (and ownership) changed over time, especially in the eighteenth century and nineteenth century.

Furthermore, what exactly was *the work* of theatre in the time of Elizabeth I? I consider how theatre houses in the sixteenth century took ownership of scripts and examine how the burgeoning printing technology and market for books began to alter conceptions of dramatic texts as property during the seventeenth century and early eighteenth century. I outline how from the mid-eighteenth century until the early 1900s claims for performance rights and adaptation rights challenged the way copyright law gave protection to plays.

Overall, this chapter seeks to map out the relationship between the artistic practices of theatre and the legal institutional philosophy of copyright, explaining how the modern law of copyright came to protect plays as works. I begin this process with a commentary on my theoretical approach before I assess theatrical authorship in the Elizabethan period. The key mechanism of copyright law is considered in order to trace the dramatic text's emergence as property object, from its early legal form in the era of the Stationers' Company to the Statute of Anne 1710 and up to the 1911 Copyright Act, when the print and performance commodities were subsumed within a bundle of rights encompassed by the copyright 'work'.

[9] Theatre is such an extraordinarily multi-faceted subject, rooted in many different linguistic and performative cultures, that to explore theatrical cultures beyond the English-language world is beyond the capacity of this chapter. Where useful I refer to theatrical works as they developed in other major European countries including Italy and Russia; at times I refer back to examples from Greek and Roman theatre, especially where they influenced English-language theatrical works during the past 500 years. For a reasonably comprehensive overview of theatre in the global context see JR Brown, *The Oxford Illustrated History of the Theatre* (Oxford: Oxford University Press, 1995). For an account of the fascinating process by which copyright emerged in France see K Scott, *Becoming Property: Art, Theory and Law in Early Modern France* (New Haven: Yale University Press, 2018).

[10] See, eg Miller (n 3); J Feather, 'The Book Trade in Politics: The Making of the Copyright Act of 1710' (1980) 8 *Publishing History* 19; T Ross, 'Copyright and the Invention of Tradition' (1992) 26 *Eighteenth-Century Studies* 1; J Hughes, 'The Philosophy of Intellectual Property' (1988) 77 *Georgetown Law Journal* 287 and J Waldron, 'From Authors to Copiers' (1993) 68 *Chicago-Kent Law Review* 841.

Assessing the Relevance of Literary Theory and Theatre Studies on Legal Issues of Authorship

In line with copyright scholarship's 'cultural turn', I argue in this chapter that insights from theatrical and literary studies facilitate a more holistic apperception of theatrical creativity relevant to questions of law. In particular, Jeffrey Masten's path-breaking approach to theatrical authorship is invaluable.[11] Masten builds upon the work of Barthes and Foucault to argue that the figure of the individual author in theatre is a constructed (or 'produced') one that often does not reflect the social reality. As I outline in detail below, our individualist assumptions about authorship in theatre, and ownership of plays, are very different from what occurred in practice in the Elizabethan period (and indeed, in later eras to varying degrees).[12] The presumption of the individual author in theatre must, therefore, be questioned. The author-figure is not 'produced once and for all'.[13] The concept can be unpacked, enabling a richer study of the authorship process:

> We might note that the presumed universality of individuated style depends on a network of legal and social technologies specific to a post-Renaissance capitalist culture (for example, intellectual property, copyright, individuated handwriting).[14]

In critiquing our universal authorship presumptions, it is important to acknowledge that promoting individual – and typically, male – authorship is in many cases a deliberate strategy.[15] Krause claims that the institutions of, for example, literary scholarship, publishing and historical biography all have an interest in producing (and reproducing) the idea of a sole 'genius' author to an audience.[16] Although some level of simplification may be inevitable, it is hard not to conclude that it is easier to sell an individual mythology than to explain the complexities involved in collaboration, especially when apportioning the roles of others may reduce the

[11] J Masten, *Textual Intercourse: Collaboration, Authorship, and Sexualities in Renaissance Drama* (Cambridge: Cambridge University Press, 1997). See also R Barthes, 'The Death of the Author' 5/6 *Aspen: The Magazine in a Box* (R Howard tr, 1967), available at www.ubu.com/aspen/aspen5and6/index.html and M Foucault, 'What Is an Author?' in JM Marsh, JD Caputo and M Westphal (eds), *Modernity and its Discontents* (New York: Fordham University Press, 1992) 299, 305 (original essay dating from 1969 and seen by many as a response to Barthes).

[12] J Masten, 'Beaumont and/or Fletcher: Collaboration and the Interpretation of Renaissance Drama' (1992) 52 *English Literary History* 337, 352. See also WC Booth, 'The Rhetoric of Fiction and Nehamas, "The Postulated Author and Critical Monism as a Regulative Ideal"' (1981) 8 *Critical Inquiry* 133–49.

[13] M Krause, 'Practicing Authorship: The Case of Brecht's Plays' in C Calhoun and R Sennett (eds), *Practicing Culture* (Oxford: Routledge, 2007) 217.

[14] Masten (n 12) 342. See also K Pistor, *The Code of Capital: How the Law Creates Wealth and Inequality* (Princeton, NJ: Princeton University Press, 2019); JE Cohen, *Between Truth and Power: Legal Constructions of Informational Capitalism* (Oxford: Oxford University Press, 2019) and S Thambisetty, 'Liza's Bucket: Intellectual Property and the Metamodern Impulse' (2020) 19 *LSE Law, Society and Economy Working Papers* 1.

[15] Krause (n 13) 217. See also T Moi, *Sexual/Textual Politics* (London, UK: Methuen, 1985).

[16] ibid, 216. See also P Bourdieu, *The Rules of Art: Genesis and Structure of the Literary Field* (Cambridge: Polity Press, 1996) and L Ede and A Lunsford, *Singular Texts/Plural Authors: Perspectives on Collaborative Writing* (Carbondale: Southern Illinois U, 1990).

image of the 'great man' in history.[17] The 'great man theory' originally ascribed to Thomas Carlyle, and occasionally applied by scholars such as Harold Bloom to a select group of women authors such as Mary Ann Evans (George Eliot) and Jane Austen may be alluring, even comforting; but it is sometimes – perhaps often – not reflective of collaborative realities.[18] At the same time, my intention here is not to remove the author-figure completely, merely to widen and deepen the understanding of authorship in the collective medium of theatre.[19]

Collaboration is a constant. It is evident in theatre in the sixteenth century, through the early modern and Romantic periods and up to our present day.[20] Acknowledging the collaborative realities of theatre is perhaps the key factor in understanding how to make authorship of theatrical works truly visible.[21] Nonetheless, as we shall see, collaboration has worked differently from era to era, with legal concepts and case law influencing theatre practices. As I explore below, the Elizabethan period provides rich accounts of collaborative theatricality.[22] Tracing the arc of recognition of authors' rights in the sixteenth and seventeenth centuries reveals enthralling insights not only about authorship but also, as the title of this chapter suggests, what the play is today as an object of property: the dramatic work. But before discussing the theatres themselves, it is necessary to ground my analysis by outlining the place of law viz the theatre world of the mid-1500s.

Tracing the Influence of Law on Theatre and Theatre on Law: The Role of the Inns of Court and the Impact of the Stationers' Company in the Elizabethan and Jacobean Eras (1558–1625)

At the dawn of the Elizabethan age in the 1550s there was a boom in litigation, causing an increased demand for lawyers, judges and administrators.[23] The legal

[17] BA Spector, 'Carlyle, Freud, and the Great Man Theory More Fully Considered' (2016) 12 *Leadership* 250.

[18] L Bently and L Biron, 'Discontinuities between legal conceptions of authorship and social practices: What, if anything, is to be done?' in M van Eechoud (ed), *The Work of Authorship* (Amsterdam: Amsterdam University Press, 2018) 237.

[19] B Boyd, 'Review of Brian Vickers, *Shakespeare Co-Author: A Historical Study of Five Collaborative Plays*' (2003) 54 *Shakespeare Quarterly* 458, 460–61 noting that a kind of individuated authorial ambition can be traced in Western theatre to classical antiquity, as evidenced by the plays of the Greek and Roman playwrights that survived, though it is likely collective creative practices occurred during this period that cannot be evidenced in the records that remain.

[20] S Keller, 'Collaboration in Theater: Problems and Copyright Solutions' (1986) 33 *UCLA Law Review* 891, 908–09.

[21] B London, *Writing Double: Women's Literary Partnerships* (Ithaca, NY: Cornell University Press, 1999). See also M Woodmansee, 'The Genius and the Copyright: Economic and Legal Conditions of the Emergence of the "Author"' (1984) 17 *Eighteenth Century Studies* 425, 440.

[22] H Hirschfeld, 'Early Modern Collaboration and Theories of Authorship' (2001) 116 *Theories and Methodologies* 609, 619–20. See also E Ostrom, *Governing the Commons* (New York: New York University Press, 1990).

[23] J Winston, *Lawyers at Play: Literature, Law and Politics at the Early Modern Inns of Court, 1558–1581* (Oxford: Oxford University Press, 2016) 50–73.

field flourished and became more professionalised. A significant Elizabethan innovation was the use of printed law reports alongside manuscript reports.[24] Meanwhile, the Inns of Court thrived, becoming relatively secular and liberal spaces, not just for legal training but for philosophical thought, debate and the performance of plays.[25] The works of Ovid and Cicero were translated and became an influence on the development of English legal rhetoric.[26] Perhaps the great legal thinker of the period – Sir Edward Coke – while 'neither a dramatist nor a friend to actors' nonetheless 'recognised and embraced the dramatic medium through which English law manifested itself to its audience'.[27]

Buoyed by the liberal atmosphere, lawyers at the Inns of Court such as Barnaby Googe, George Turberville and Sir Thomas North translated plays by Roman philosophers such as Seneca and Plutarch that shaped English renaissance theatre in innumerable ways.[28] Key elements of Senecan drama that were co-opted into English theatre include the use of violence (and even gore) onstage as well as the presence of supernatural figures on stage (ghosts, demons, etc).[29] Senecan tragedy's sense of inferiority, often expressed in monologue, influenced Shakespeare's classic plays *Titus Andronicus* and *Hamlet*.[30] In addition, Shakespeare relied heavily on the works of Plutarch – as translated by Sir Thomas North – for the plot of *Antony and Cleopatra*.[31]

Printing technology enabled the diffusion of these translations – though it is worth noting that printing was severely regulated by law. From its formal incorporation via Royal Charter in May 1557 the Stationers' Company possessed a near-exclusive jurisdiction to register and copy books for printing.[32] Only members of the company could print books (unless the Crown had granted a direct privilege).[33] Within the system controlled by the Stationers Company, the market for printed books and play-texts expanded steadily. The plays of Seneca were among the most commonly printed and widely read, becoming so popular that in England among the literary class it was possible to speak of a 'Senecan vogue'.[34]

[24] P Raffield, *The Art of Law in Shakespeare* (Oxford: Hart, 2017) 8.

[25] Winston (n 23) 123.

[26] Raffield (n 24) 12.

[27] ibid, 3. See also WR Prest, *The Inns of Court under Elizabeth I and the Early Stuarts 1590–1640* (Harlow: Longman, 1972) and I Williams, 'He Creditted More the Printed Booke": Common Lawyers' Receptivity to Print, c.1550–1640' 28 (2010) *Law and History Review* 39.

[28] Winston (n 23). See also C Perry, *Shakespeare and Senecan Tragedy* (Cambridge: Cambridge University Press, 2020) and S Elsky, *Custom, Common Law, and the Constitution of English Renaissance Literature* (Oxford: Oxford University Press, 2020).

[29] ibid.

[30] Perry (n 28).

[31] R Miola, *Shakespeare's Reading* (Oxford: Oxford University Press, 2012) 106–09.

[32] I Gadd, 'The Stationers' Company in England before 1710' in I Alexander and HT Gómez-Arostegui (eds), *Research Handbook on the History of Copyright Law* (Cheltenham: Edward Elgar, 2016) 81–95. For the early history of the Stationers' Company see PWM Blayney, *The Stationers' Company and the Printers of London, 1501–1557* (Cambridge: Cambridge University Press, 2013).

[33] For example, the universities at Oxford and Cambridge had their own right to print.

[34] DA Brooks, 'Dramatic Authorship and Publication in Early Modern England' (2003) 15 *Medieval & Renaissance Drama in England* 77. See also P Blayney, 'The Publication of Playbooks' in J Cox and DS Kastan, *A New History of Early English Drama* (New York: Columbia University Press, 1997) 383 and L Febvre and H-J Martin, *The Coming of the Book – The Impact of Printing, 1450–1800* (London: Verso, 1997).

While the translations are acknowledged as influential, that Elizabethan lawyers were enthusiastic writers and performers of plays is perhaps less widely known.[35] It is notable that the first 'English tragedy' – *Gorbudoc* – was authored jointly by two lawyers, Thomas Norton and Thomas Sackville, and was performed first at Inner Temple by actors from the Inns.[36] Later, the Inns would be referenced (and satirised) by Ben Jonson in 1599 in *Every Man out of His Humour*; and celebrated plays such as Shakespeare's *Comedy of Errors* and *Twelfth Night* were performed at the Inns in 1594 and 1602 respectively.[37] Indeed, a deep fascination for law and legality is visible in Elizabethan play-texts, particularly those of Shakespeare. Raffield notes that 'the *agon* of the trial is represented to great dramatic effect in, for example, *The Merchant of Venice, Measure for Measure, King Lear* and *The Winter's Tale*';[38] while Heinze argues that Shakespeare's history plays explore the conditions for how a functional and just legal order can be established.[39]

Thus, the Elizabethan age saw the flourishing of the legal profession (via the Inns) and the expansion of printing (via the Stationers' Company). Rather than the common law courts or the Court of Chancery, if disputes arose involving infringement of the right to copy under the Stationers' privileges resolution was sought at The Court of Assistants, the Court of Star Chamber and the Court of High Commission.[40]

The activities of lawyers and printers cannot be separated from the great blossoming of English theatre in the latter half of the sixteenth century. Over the remainder of this chapter, as my focus turns to questions of theatrical authorship and legal ownership, it is worth bearing in mind the connection between the institution of law and the business of printing – this helped shape the ways in which the play has come to be seen not just as a work of art, but as an object of property under copyright.[41]

[35] Winston (n 23) 1–15.

[36] N Jones and PW White, 'Gorboduc and Royal Marriage Politics: An Elizabethan Playgoer's Report of the Premiere Performance' (1996) 26 *English Literary Renaissance* 3.

[37] M Knapp and M Kabialka, 'Shakespeare and the Prince of Purpoole: The 1594 production of "The Comedy of Errors" at Gray's Inn Hall' (1984) 4 *Theatre History Studies* 71. Twelfth Night was performed at Inner Temple in 1602, an event still celebrated by the Inns today, available at www.innertemple.org.uk/who-we-are/history/historical-articles/gorboduc-or-the-tragedy-of-ferrex-and-porrox/.

[38] Raffield (n 24) 9.

[39] E Heinze, 'Power Politics and the Rule of Law: Shakespeare's First Historical Tetralogy and Law's "Foundations"' (2009) 29 *Oxford Journal of Legal Studies* 139. See also Q Skinner, *Forensic Shakespeare* (Oxford: Oxford University Press, 2014).

[40] HT Gómez-Arostegui, 'What History Teaches Us About Copyright Injunctions and the Inadequate-Remedy-at-Law Requirement' (2008) 81 S. Cal. L. Rev. 1197, noting at 1221–22 that only after 1660 did copyright claims come to the Court of Chancery, apart from one exception – *Wolfe v Payne*, C33/29, f. 143v, C33/30, f. 143v (Ch. 1563/4), which Gómez-Arostegui cites at fn 116 as the 'first copyright injunction ever granted by the Court of Chancery'. See also WA Jackson, *Records of the Court of the Stationers' Company, 1602–1640* (London: Bibliographical Society, 1957).

[41] Miller (n 3). For philosophical underpinnings see I Kant, 'On the Wrongfulness of Unauthorized Publication of Books (1785)' in P Guyer and AW Wood, *The Cambridge Edition of the Works of Immanuel Kant* (Mary J Gregor tr, Cambridge: Cambridge University Press, 1996) 27–35; LA Seneca, *De Beneficiis* (67 AD); *On Benefits*, addressed to Aebutius Liberalis (Translated by A Stewart, London: George Bell and Sons, 1887), available at www.gutenberg.org/files/3794/3794-h/3794-h.htm; NT Pratt, *Seneca's Drama* (Chapel Hill: University of North Carolina Press, 1983) and Aristotle, *Poetics* (A Kenny ed, Oxford: Oxford University Press, 2013).

Law and Theatre: Assessing the Theatrical Text and Authorship During the Elizabethan and Jacobean Eras (1558–1625)

In the Elizabethan period (1558–1603) and into the Jacobean era (1603–25) we can observe the practices of theatre working in tandem with early capitalist market forces. As today, the production of culture was one in which questions of ownership and value were not merely relevant – they were vital.[42] I explore theatrical production in the Elizabethan period here by focusing on five crucial characteristics: first, a type of 'ownership' of plays in performance, by theatre companies, and in print, by the Stationers; second, 'polyvocal' collaborative authorship; third, textual instability, as evidenced by, for example, *The Spanish Tragedy* which was printed in at least ten different versions; fourth, the changing nature of 'anonymity' in literary practice; and fifth, censorship.

As the Elizabethan age gave way to the Jacobean period, and eventually the 'interregnum' and restoration, I mark how during the seventeenth century there was a gradual shift towards greater recognition of the individual writer, presaged by the actions of Ben Jonson in the early 1600s and the posthumous publication of Shakespeare's *First Folio* in 1623. At the same time, the growing market and tensions between publishers and the Stationers' Company led eventually to the first copyright statute – the Statute of Anne in 1710.

Ownership of Plays in the Elizabethan and Jacobean Eras (1558–1625)

Although today we have no compunction about individual authorship and attribution – of 'Shakespeare's tragedies', 'Marlowe's plays' or 'the works of Ben Jonson' – it is important not to forget that in the Elizabethan period playwrights were not treated as authors in the sense of owning their writings. Statutory copyright had yet to emerge and printing was controlled by the Stationers' Company.[43] During the sixteenth and seventeenth centuries, although some play-texts could be said to exist as print-commodities, as they were registered at the Stationers' Company and printed for sale, usually in 'Quarto' form, a great many significant plays went unpublished – and even where a play was published, authorship was not always ascribed to the text.[44] The idea that the playwright could own property

[42] Winston (n 23). See also R Knutson, *Playing Companies and Commerce in Shakespeare's Time* (Cambridge: Cambridge University Press, 2001).

[43] R Deazley, *On the Origin of the Right to Copy* (Oxford: Hart, 2004). See also Blayney (n 34).

[44] Shakespeare's First Folio contained several previously unpublished plays – G Egan, 'The Provenance of the Folio Texts' in E Smith (ed), *The Cambridge Companion to Shakespeare's First Folio* (Cambridge: Cambridge University Press, 2016) 68–85.

in the dramatic text being performed by the company 'would have been difficult to comprehend for the majority of writers in the Elizabethan period'.[45] Playwrights could not enter their texts onto the the Stationers' register, nor could they own copyright privileges.[46] Playwrights lacked the essence of ownership: control. Once a dramatist had developed a text whatever 'ownership' a writer could claim was inevitably short-lived:

> Strictly speaking, a playwright owned a copy of a play, a manuscript distinguishable from a scribal copy only by the fact that it was a unique copy …[47]

Acting companies purchased such texts from writers for a flat fee of between £6–10; and in a practical sense, that transaction brought to an end any claim the writer might have had to 'own' the play.[48] Litman remarks:

> Theatre managers valued playwrights as they valued actors, and paid them in the same fashion. Scripts once acquired entered a theatre company's repertory, where they could be revived, adapted, rewritten, performed, and printed without any further license from the writer.[49]

After a play's performances had run their course, actors sometimes sold their copies of the play-text for print.[50] Thus, play-texts could be sold as print-commodities without the permission of the playwright and then published without attribution. It was the publisher who would register the play-text at the Stationers' Company in order to obtain the right to print the 'book' in perpetuity. To the extent the play operated as a print-commodity, it was the publisher who benefited from its exploitation; and it was the publisher who controlled the legal privilege, which could be asserted in a case of alleged 'piracy' at a number of legal venues, such as the Court of Assistants.[51] Concepts of authorship and ownership in the individualist sense were not absent entirely, but they were only dimly perceived.[52]

Apart from printed playbooks, during the Elizabethan period in England the most profound way that plays could be said to be 'owned' was not by individual

[45] B Salter, 'Taming the trojan horse: an Australian perspective of dramatic authorship' (2009) 56 *Journal of The Copyright Society of The USA* 789, 815. See also R Knutson, *The Repertory of Shakespeare's Company, 1594–1613* (Fayetteville: University of Arkansas Press, 1991).

[46] Blayney (n 34) 394–99.

[47] J Loewenstein, 'The Script in the Marketplace' (1985) 12 *Representations* 101, 102.

[48] ibid. Loewenstein notes that printers sometimes gave 'limited privileges' of revision to authors. See also Z Lesser, *Renaissance Drama and the Politics of Publication: Readings in the English Book Trade* (Cambridge: Cambridge University Press, 2004).

[49] JD Litman, 'The Invention of Common Law Play Right' (2010) 25 *Berkeley Tech. L. J.* 1381, 1390. See also T Stern, *Rehearsal from Shakespeare to Sheridan* (Oxford: Oxford University Press, 2000) 129–31 and 241–45 and J Milhous, 'The First Production of Rowe's "Jane Shore"' (1986) 38 *Theatre J.* 309, 312.

[50] Loewenstein (n 47) 105–06.

[51] Gómez Arostegui (n 40). See also E Arber (ed), *A Transcript of the Registers of the Company of Stationers of London 1554–1640* (London: Privately Printed, 1875), available at https://catalog.hathitrust.org/Record/001168984.

[52] L Bently, 'Copyright and the Death of the Author in Law and Literature' (1994) 57 *The Modern Law Review* 973, 978. See also M Woodmansee and P Jaszi (eds), *The Construction of Authorship: Textual Appropriation in Law and Literature* (Durham, NC: Duke University Press, 1994).

authors but by acting companies.[53] Such companies emerged as a result of the growth of an early capitalist marketplace for theatrical works and performances, which benefited the shareholders of various medium- and large-scale theatre companies – entities which in effect can be described as early versions of the 'joint venture of limited liability'.[54] Theatres operated under severe economic pressures, knowing they could be forced to close by outbreaks of plague.[55] Nonetheless, when times were good the shareholders of companies like the Lord Chamberlain's Men (later the King's Men) or the Admiral's Men would receive a stable income.[56]

It is notable that, in general, early modern prologues and epilogues spoken on stage did not name authors, whether individuals or collaborators.[57] During the Elizabethan period actors on stage would instead refer to a playwright merely as 'our poet', increasing the sense that the theatre company not only owned the play, but that the role of the poet/writer was subsumed within collective management:

> On the margins of dramatic representation – in inductions and epilogues – the Elizabethan play is regularly represented by the speaking actor as 'ours,' the possession and, indeed, the product of the actors. Where the playwright is mentioned, he is almost never 'the Author' or 'the Playwright'; he is 'our poet,' an adjunct to the proprietary group of performers. Of course, playwrights almost always wrote the prologues to their scripts. Still, the marketplace was such that authorial assertions of preeminent domain were all but unthinkable.[58]

The acting company took ownership – and thus, control – of the play in the performance context, and would thereafter rework the text, adding edits and improvisations as it was performed.[59] In a way, what the company took control of was an early version of what Miller calls the performance commodity.[60] Unlike play-texts as print-commodities, this performance-commodity did not have the force of legal protection. Instead, mindful of competition and market saturation, theatre companies operated a system of informal, reciprocal social norms to regulate their activities, ensuring they did not perform each other's plays without permission.[61]

[53] R Dutton, *Licensing, Censorship and Authorship in Early Modern England* (London: Palgrave MacMillan, 2000) 91.

[54] Masten (n 12) 339.

[55] B Freedman, 'Elizabethan Protest, Plague, and Plays: Rereading the "Documents of Control"' (1996) 26 *English Literary Renaissance* 17, 19–25.

[56] See generally JJ Marino, *Owning William Shakespeare: The King's Men and Their Intellectual Property* (Philadelphia: University of Pennsylvania Press, 2011).

[57] T Stern, 'Review of Authorship and Appropriation: Writing for the Stage in England, 1660–1710' (2002) *The Scriblerian* 73. See also P Kewes, *Authorship and Appropriation: Writing for the Stage in England, 1660–1710* (Oxford: Clarendon Press, 1998).

[58] Loewenstein (n 47) 102. M Straznicky (ed), *The Book of the Play: Playwrights, Stationers, and Readers in Early Modern England* (Amherst, Boston: University of Massachusetts Press, 2006).

[59] JS Peters, *Theatre of the Book, 1480–1880: Print, Text, and Performance in Europe* (Oxford: Oxford University Press, 2000), 1, 4–5. See also Marino (n 56).

[60] Miller (n 3).

[61] B Lauriat, 'Literary and Dramatic Disputes in Shakespeare's Time' (2018) 9 *Journal of International Dispute Settlement* 45.

Thus, we can observe that even as early as the Elizabethan period plays provided two potential sources of value: print and performance. However, in practice dramatists neither owned nor controlled either one of these sources of value.

Theatrical Collaboration as Polyvocal Authorship in the Elizabethan and Jacobean Eras (1558–1625)

As contemporary readers of plays, or as theatre-goers, it is hard to escape a presumption of 'writing as composition' by a defined author. Yet, this assumption does not actually reflect the practices of Elizabethan dramatic authorship. To comprehend the nature of theatrical creativity during this period we are advised by theatre studies scholars like Cox and Kasten to 'dislodge authors and scripts' from the centre of our minds and open our perspective to the 'collaborative sense of early English dramatic activity by focusing on the conditions and constraints of playmaking, the networks of dependency, both discursive and institutional, that motivated and sustained it'.[62] A form of authorship certainly existed – but it must be contextualised 'within the social and material circumstances in which early English drama was enabled and inhibited'.[63]

The most obvious way that this collaboration manifested itself is in the work undertaken by playwrights labouring together. Masten notes that during the period 1590–1642 there is evidence that almost two-thirds of the plays referenced in the papers of the contemporary theatre manager Philip Henslowe 'reflect the participation of more than one writer'.[64] Working together – sometimes radically – was therefore central to the creation of plays during the Elizabethan and Jacobean periods. Virtually all major playwrights of the time – including Christopher Marlowe, Ben Jonson, Thomas Middleton, and of course, William Shakespeare – wrote plays collaboratively.[65] Attribution was not always given. As noted earlier, play-texts were sometimes printed without naming any author; and even where there were printed title-page statements of singular authorship these tended to obscure and simplify the practical circumstances of composition.[66]

[62] J Cox and D Kastan, 'Introduction: Demanding History' in J Cox and DS Kastan (eds), *A New History of Early English Drama* (New York: Columbia University Press, 1997) 1–6. See also J Clare, 'Shakespeare and Paradigms of Early Modern Authorship' (2012) 1 *Journal of Early Modern Studies* 137.

[63] G Egan, 'What is Not Collaborative about Early Modern Drama in Performance and Print?' (2010) 67 *Shakespeare Survey* 18, 20–28. See also P Pender and A Day (ed), *Gender, Authorship, and Early Modern Women's Collaboration* (London: Palgrave Macmillan, 2017) and Hirschfeld (n 22) 614–15.

[64] Masten (n 12) 347, referring to Philip Henslowe.

[65] B Vickers, *Shakespeare, Co-Author: A Historical Study of Five Collaborative Plays* (Oxford: Oxford University Press, 2002). See also Boyd (n 19) 460–61 and W Shakespeare, *The New Oxford Shakespeare: Modern Critical Edition – The Complete Works* (G Taylor, J Jowett, T Bourus and G Egan eds, Oxford: Oxford University Press, 2016) and G Edelstein, 'Collaborating on Credit: Ben Jonson's Authorship in Eastward Ho!' (2020) 50 *English Literary Renaissance* 233.

[66] Masten (n 12), 339.

The most famous example of a consistent writing partnership during the Jacobean era is that of Francis Beaumont and John Fletcher. Yet the Beaumont and Fletcher example is utilised by Masten to demonstrate that even attributing plays to a limited number of joint authors does a disservice to the creativity involved in theatrical authorship at this time. Masten argues that although authorship in their plays is 'intermittently present' it does not appear in 'anything approaching a definitive or monolithically singular form'.[67] As mentioned earlier, once a dramatist sold a script to a theatre company, the company took control of it and made significant edits, allowing for improvisation, thus 'unsettling' the text. Taylor views collaboration during this period as a type of artisan production.[68] Certainly, collaboration within theatre companies was the normal playmaking practice.[69] For Masten the 'ample evidence of the frequent revision of play-texts' indicates the existence of a 'a diachronic form of collaboration' involved in creating an iterative play-text.[70] Theatrical authorship ought, therefore, to be viewed as *polyvocal*: the 'joint accomplishment of dramatists, actors, musicians, costumers, prompters (who made alterations in the original manuscript) and … managers'.[71]

For Masten the type of collaboration at stake involved 'a dispersal of author/ity, rather than a simple doubling of it; to revise the aphorism, two heads are different than one'.[72] It is therefore appropriate to view the practices of polyvocal authorship as radical – not as merely 'a more multiple version' of singular authorship. This analysis does not erase or minimise the role of the writer – it contextualises it and enriches our understanding.[73] Only by taking this contextual approach can we observe 'the different configuration of authorities controlling texts' and 'constraining their interpretation'.[74] The writer played an important role, but the writer was only one active party within a greater collaborative enterprise.[75]

Masten opines that only by 'ignoring the theatrical as a mode of (re)production' can these texts be 'read from the post-Enlightenment perspective of individual authorship, the now-victorious mode of textual production and the site of Foucault's critique'.[76] Even the way play-texts are archived in the post-Elizabethan era can reveal a bias towards the existence of a mythological single

[67] ibid, 347.

[68] G Taylor, 'Artiginality: Authorship after Postmodernism' in G Taylor and G Egan (eds), *The New Oxford Shakespeare: Authorship Companion* (Oxford: Oxford University Press, 2016).

[69] See, eg H Hirschfeld, *Joint Enterprises: Collaborative Drama and the Institutionalization of the English Renaissance Theatre* (Amherst: University of Massachusetts Press, 2004) and D Nicol, *Middleton and Rowley: Forms of Collaboration in the Jacobean Playhouse* (Toronto: University of Toronto Press, 2012).

[70] Masten (n 12) 339.

[71] GE Bentley, *The Profession of Dramatist in Shakespeare's Time 1590–1642* (Princeton: Princeton Univ. Press, 1971) 198.

[72] Masten (n 11) 19. See also Hirschfeld (n 22) 619–20.

[73] Vickers (n 65).

[74] Masten (n 12) 338.

[75] J Loewenstein, *Ben Jonson and Possessive Authorship* (Cambridge: Cambridge University Press, 2002) 10–18.

[76] Masten (n 12) 341.

author. The will to nominate a play's 'date of composition' by its nature 'assumes a relatively limited amount of time during which a text was fully composed and after which it was merely transmitted and corrupted'.[77] This is obviously problematic in this broader understanding of collaboration.[78]

Instead of assuming retrospectively the existence of a singular author, Masten contends that we must accept that 'collaborative texts produced before the emergence of authorship are of a kind different (informed by differing mechanisms of textual property and control, different conceptions of imitation, originality, and the "individual") from collaborations produced within the regime of the author'.[79]

Even if we do not accept all Masten's contentions, it is clear that during the Elizabethan and Jacobean era the modern ideas of individual authorship and ownership did not yet hold sway – and, of course, copyright law as we know it did not yet exist.[80] As I now explain, the polyvocal nature of authorship left the text itself in an unstable state.[81]

An Unstable Text in the Elizabethan and Jacobean Eras (1558–1625)

Elizabethan and Jacobean theatrical texts defy easy categorisation because they 'strikingly de-naturalize the author-text-reader continuum assumed in later methodologies of interpretation'.[82] To understand what has survived as text it is necessary to accept the norms of company ownership and polyvocal authorship.[83] The writer may have originated a text, or adapted a text from an earlier work (for example, the plot and basic characters of Shakespeare's *The Comedy of Errors* are taken wholesale from an earlier work – *Menaechmi* by Plautus).[84] However, as outlined earlier, once the company took ownership, the text was shaped by several other parties (actors, musicians, costumers, prompters, managers). It is important, therefore, to acknowledge the 'inseparability of the textual and theatrical production of

[77] ibid, 340.

[78] R Knutson, 'Working playwrights, 1580–1642' in J Milling and P Thomson (eds), *The Cambridge History of British Theatre* (Cambridge: Cambridge University Press, 2004) 339–63.

[79] Masten (n 12) 346.

[80] T Stern, '"Whether one did Contrive, the Other Write,/Or one Fram'd the Plot, the Other did Indite": Fletcher and Theobald as Collaborative Writers' in D Carnegie and G Taylor (eds), *The Quest for Cardenio: Shakespeare, Fletcher, Cervantes, and the Lost Play* (Oxford: Oxford University Press, 2012) 115–30.

[81] A kind of polyvocal authorship can be observed in works of traditional folklore and cultural heritage, as well as some classics from the world of the ancient Greeks – L McDonagh, 'Protecting traditional music under copyright (and choosing not to do enforce it)' in Bonadio and Lucchi (eds) (n 2).

[82] Masten (n 12) 338.

[83] See S Orgel, 'What Is a Text?' in DS Kastan and P Stallybrass (eds), *Staging the Renaissance: Reinterpretations of Elizabethan and Jacobean Drama* (New York: Routledge, 1991) 84; J Knapp, *Shakespeare Only* (Chicago: University of Chicago Press, 2009).

[84] R Lyne, 'Shakespeare, Plautus, and the discovery of New Comic space' in C Martindale and AB Taylor (eds), *Shakespeare and the Classics* (Cambridge: Cambridge University Press, 2011) 122–38.

meaning in a context that did not carefully insulate the writing of scripts from the acting of plays'.[85] The result was that, in comparison with our modern understanding, the Elizabethan text was typically in a semi-permanent unsettled state – it would often change from performance to performance.[86] Writers, often different from those who originated the play-text, would add materials (new scenes, additional prologues/epilogues, new songs, etc) to existing texts. Virtually any play 'first printed more than ten years after composition and … kept in active repertory by the company that owned it is most likely to contain later revisions by the author or, in many cases, by another playwright.'[87] An example is *Dr Faustus* – a play attributed to Christopher Marlowe, but which also passed through several other hands, thus existing as a text 'patched' together.[88] As Masten relates, *The Knight of the Burning Pestle* (attributed to Francis Beaumont|) is a manifestation of Barthes' phrase in 'The Death of the Author' that a text is often 'a tissue of quotations drawn from the innumerable centres of culture'.[89] In a similar vein, the play registered with the Stationers and printed in 1594 as *The Taming of a Shrew* has little in common – other than a basic plot – with the text printed as *The Taming of the Shrew* in the posthumous 1623 *First Folio*.[90]

Writers were not the only creative parties making edits to the text during the Elizabethan period.[91] Actors too 'performed' authorship. The company would work collaboratively with a manuscript, revising it and allowing improvisation by actors during performances.[92] Improvisation was so commonplace the term 'tarltonising' (after the comedic actor Tarlton) arose to describe actors' improvisation in verse (though the term began to fall out of favour in the 1590s).[93] There is no doubt that improvisation was vital to the process until at least the late Elizabethan era.[94] The Lord Chamberlain's Men revised the plays in their repertoire continuously in

[85] Masten (n 12) 340.

[86] C Hoy, 'Critical and Aesthetic Problems of Collaboration in Renaissance Drama' (1976) 19 *Research Opportunities in Renaissance Drama* 4.

[87] GE Bentley, *The Profession of Dramatist in Shakespeare's Time 1590–1642* (Princeton, NJ: Princeton Univ. Press, 1971) 263.

[88] T Stern, *Documents of Performance in Early Modern England* (Cambridge: Cambridge University Press, 2009).

[89] Masten (n 12) 349.

[90] Marino (n 56) 48–74.

[91] Censors were also involved in 'editing' texts as discussed later on in this chapter.

[92] Masten (n 12) 339.

[93] C Lehmann, *Shakespeare Remains: Theater to Film, Early Modern to Postmodern* (Ithaca, NY: Cornell University Press, 2002) 80.

[94] Indeed, as I shall consider later on in the book, modern theatrical improvisation and devised theatre has deep roots in theatrical practice, whether in Greek, Roman or English theatre. See, eg Keller (n 20) 908–09, 'Much new dramatic work is created in these contexts. Sometimes a play without a prior history does open at a big commercial house, but the usual pattern involves a workshop production or a resident/regional theater production, and then possibly an off-Broadway engagement before an opening at a major New York or, occasionally, Los Angeles theater. Even those plays or musicals which are initially scheduled for a Broadway run usually have an extensive out-of-town "try-out" period. These earlier productions pro-vide opportunities to work through the play's problems, allowing major changes and revisions to be made in relative safety and obscurity.'

many ways, including updating topical references and adding/removing satirical comments on their rival companies' plays.[95]

Ultimately, Cox and Kastan remark that we should view this theatre world as one in which 'actors, annotators, revisers, collaborators, scribes, printers, and proofreaders, in addition to the playwright, all have a hand in shaping the text'.[96] The combination of authorial and textual instability confirms that theatrical playwriting was indeed 'polyvocal'.[97] Everyone – from those involved in the first performance to later archivists – could be said to perform a role in the authorship of the play.[98] It is this idea that inspired the title of this book: *Performing Copyright.*

Despite the evidence of polyvocal collaboration and unstable play-texts, later considerations of Renaissance drama have nevertheless tried to 'produce' an authorial 'univocality' which naturally privileges the writer.[99] To try to address this privilege, I consider here one of the most famous play-texts of the period – *The Spanish Tragedy*. As we shall see, this play provides a fascinating case study for the way authorship and texts were perceived at the time.

A Case Study on Authorial and Textual Instability – Thomas Kyd and *The Spanish Tragedy* 1594–1613

Along with *Gorbudoc*, *The Spanish Tragedy* was perhaps the crucial play of early modern English theatre. It cast an impression on almost every theatrical tragedy that came in its wake, including those of Shakespeare and Marlowe. It was performed very often at the Rose Theatre, and was among the most highly performed plays of the Elizabethan period and immediate post-Elizabethan era. As such it represents a useful case study of textual instability and authorial attribution.

The origins of *The Spanish Tragedy* can be traced to the mid-sixteenth century. It was published in at least 10 different versions during the period 1594–1613, demonstrating that the text was in an unsettled state during this period.[100] As noted earlier, multiple 'collaborators' – including actors and writers – were adding to the text as it was being performed. Most famously, Ben Jonson was commissioned

[95] Marino (n 56) 107–42.
[96] Cox and Kastan (n 67).
[97] Masten (n 12) 339.
[98] LB Petersen, *Shakespeare's Errant Texts: Textual Form and Linguistic Style in Shakespearean 'Bad' Quartos and Co-authored Plays* (Cambridge, Cambridge University Press, 2010).
[99] Masten (n 12) 340.
[100] E Smith, 'Author v. Character in Early Modern Dramatic Authorship: The Example of Thomas Kyd and The Spanish Tragedy' (1999) 11 *Medieval and Renaissance Drama in England* 129, 131–32. Smith shows that *The Spanish Tragedy* avoids the author function in favour of a 'character-function' which positions Hieronimo as the author of the play, that is until 1612 when Kyd began to be attributed. Indeed, more than one character in *The Spanish Tragedy* takes on the title of 'author' including Hieronimo, Lorenzo, and Andrea's Ghost. See T Kyd, *The Spanish Tragedie* (1587), available at www.gutenberg.org/files/6043/6043-h/6043-h.htm.

to write additional passages for an extant version of *The Spanish Tragedy* in the 1590s.[101]

Yet, despite the play's value as commodity in print and performance, and its undoubted influence, questions of attribution seem to have been an afterthought. As Smith argues:

> Given the evidence for the play's popularity, it might be expected that Kyd – or some other playwright – would want to claim authorship, or that an author would be subsequently added to playtexts published after his death … And yet none of the early editions or references to performances of *The Spanish Tragedy* associates the play with Kyd's name. There is no mention of Kyd on the title pages of the numerous editions of the play.[102]

By contrast, around the same period, Marlowe was attributed as the writer of a similarly popular play, *Dr Faustus*, with the printed text bearing Marlowe's name in the (posthumous) quarto of 1604; furthermore, Shakespeare and Jonson 'used, or allowed the usage of, their names to authorise their work in early publication'.[103] Kyd's authorship was not asserted clearly until around 1612, when Thomas Heywood's *An Apology for Actors* was published.[104] It is generally accepted today that Kyd was the originator of the script.[105] Yet, Smith argues that whether or not Kyd wrote *The Spanish Tragedy* is actually 'of lesser interest (as well as being ultimately unverifiable, in the absence of additional external evidence) than the effects of the absence of a named author-figure in the play's reception'.[106] What this reveals is that in the Elizabethan era it was even possible for the text of the most influential tragedy of the period to circulate in print and be performed widely in the absence of a definitive named author-figure.

In light of the way *The Spanish Tragedy* was perceived, Smith cautions against reifying the Elizabethan theatrical author 'in hindsight', emphasising that such early modern theatrical texts 'defy a post-Romantic scripting of the author-figure' because they are works 'frequently attributable to more than one hand, or with later revisions by the author or another writer, with cuts and alterations made by the actors'.[107] Such texts can be defined by their 'authorlessness' (in the modern sense) because the way they were created was 'plural and collaborative', that is, polyvocal.[108]

We can nonetheless observe the significance of the gradual change in the fact that even though *The Spanish Tragedy* was originally printed without attribution,

[101] ibid. See also D Kezar, 'Shakespeare's Guilt Trip in Henry V' (2000) 61 *Modern Language Quarterly* 431.

[102] ibid. See also B Vickers, 'Shakespeare and the 1602 Additions to The Spanish Tragedy: A Method Vindicated' (2017) 13 *Shakespeare* 101.

[103] ibid. See also Petersen (n 98) and Marino (n 56).

[104] ibid.

[105] D Freebury-Jones, 'The Diminution of Thomas Kyd' (2019) 8 *Journal of Early Modern Studies* 251.

[106] Smith (n 100).

[107] ibid.

[108] Masten (n 12) 337, quoting Jean-Christophe Agnew's comparison with the joint venture company.

eventually the name of an author-figure – Thomas Kyd – began to be ascribed to it (in the Jacobean era). This gives weight to the argument that 'the playwright as author-figure' grew in esteem and began to emerge in the public imagination during the seventeenth century.[109] There is little doubt that the luminaries Shakespeare and Jonson were central to this paradigm shift.

The Publication of Shakespeare's *First Folio* (1623) and the Beginning of his Acclamation as the English Author-Figure Par Excellence

Today Shakespeare's fame as an author is incalculable. I do not intend to probe his life or analyse the plays he wrote in detail – the academic literature on Shakespeare is voluminous and in many respects the plays speak for themselves as evidence of his poetic brilliance and insightful philosophical outlook. However, there are two aspects of his career that are worth highlighting here, as they are important for understanding authorship and ownership of plays during the period. First, it is notable that Shakespeare was active in theatre in capacities other than playwriting (acting, management); and second, the surviving Shakespearean texts are testaments not only to his brilliance, but also to his successful collaborations with other writers, and more generally to the vibrancy of polyvocal theatrical authorship.[110]

On the first, recalling the earlier discussion of whether writers 'owned' plays in the Elizabethan era, it is revealing that even William Shakespeare did not – and, in all likelihood, could not – rely on playwriting as a way to make a living. To obtain a steady income he needed to play multiple roles, becoming, in addition to a writer, an actor, a producer and, effectively, a business manager.[111] Thus Shakespeare fulfilled several different roles in in theatre companies over his career, most notably in the Lord Chamberlain's Men (and the successor company – the King's Men).[112]

[109] Kewes (n 57). See also Knutson (n 45).

[110] Vickers (n 65). See also J Clare, 'Shakespeare and Paradigms of Early Modern Authorship' (2012) 1 *Journal of Early Modern Studies* 137–53.

[111] Shakespeare was a founder of an acting company (The Lord Chamberlain's Men) and a shareholder in the Globe Theatre – D Price, 'Evidence for A Literary Biography' (2004) 72 *Tenn. L. Rev.* 111, 133–34. See also Knutson (n 45). Certain well-known actors, such as Richard Burbage, also benefited as shareholders.

[112] Vickers (n 65). The question of whether Shakespeare's works should be viewed primarily as performative texts or as literature to be read in print is one of the most vexed questions in all of English scholarship. I do not profess to provide a definitive answer here – nor could anyone. Yet it is certainly the case performance was the priority as it was the major way that Shakespeare would receive an income; print by contrast largely provided an income to the Stationers. Shakespeare may have received some benefit arising from increased fame due to publication, but this would have been secondary to his primary purpose of putting on plays successfully – see eg D Bruster, 'Shakespeare the Stationer' in M Straznicky (ed), *Shakespeare's Stationers* (Philadelphia: University of Pennsylvania Press, 2013) 112–31, 112–14.

For the second, given that neither the theatrical copyright 'work' nor modern authorship had yet been conceived in the terms we understand them today, we should not allow 'the singular figure of Shakespeare' in our modern imagination to obscure the fact that collaboration, in various forms, was a major – and perhaps the dominant – contemporary form of textual and theatrical production.[113] As noted earlier, Shakespeare was a serial collaborator.[114] Shakespeare crafted several plays with other writers, including *Titus Andronicus* (with George Peele), *Timon of Athens* (with Thomas Middleton), *Pericles* (with George Wilkins) and *Henry VIII* and *The Two Noble Kinsmen* (with John Fletcher).[115] This list was expanded as recently as 2016 when *The New Oxford Shakespeare* credited Christopher Marlowe as a co-author of the *Henry VI* cycle of plays (Parts One, Two and Three).[116] To view Shakespeare as a collaborator does not in any way lessen the stature of his works – rather it enriches our understanding of them.[117] Moreover, it would surely be unjust to allow Shakespeare's poetic brilliance to overshadow the substantial and essential input of other parties.[118] The texts that have survived have done so in varying forms – in the first published 'quarto' version of *Hamlet*, which is much shorter than the later versions, the famous 'To be or not to be' soliloquy does not assert 'that is the question' – it declares 'that is the point'.[119] Such variances should not necessarily be viewed as 'corruption' – they instead reflect the polyvocal nature of authorship that Masten describes.[120]

Indeed, although Shakespeare is the greatest and most iconic of all Elizabethan/Jacobean playwrights, it is arguable that at the time Ben Jonson had a greater sense of himself as an author. This is evidenced by Jonson's attitude to his published works, which, as I explore below, marks him out from his contemporaries (and, to some extent, from the prevailing norms of polyvocal authorship). By contrast, our modern understanding of William Shakespeare as English author par excellence begins with the posthumous publication of the *First Folio* in 1623 – organised by the actors John Heminges and Henry Condell – which called attention to his unique genius.[121] It included numerous previously unpublished plays, proving that several major Shakespeare works were not registered at all at the Stationers' Company during his lifetime, demonstrating how distant the world of print and publication often was from performance. While Shakespeare is undoubtedly the greatest playwright in English theatrical history, we turn now to Ben Jonson, perhaps the key *author-figure* of the time.

[113] Masten (n 12) 339.
[114] Vickers (n 65) and Boyd (n 19) 460–61.
[115] Vickers (n 65).
[116] W Shakespeare, *The New Oxford Shakespeare: Modern Critical Edition – The Complete Works* (G Taylor, J Jowett, T Bourus and G Egan eds, Oxford: Oxford University Press, 2016).
[117] Vickers (n 65).
[118] Marino (n 56) 5.
[119] Shakespeare (n 1).
[120] Masten (n 12).
[121] Egan (n 63).

Was Ben Jonson the First Self-conscious 'Author' in English Theatre?

Ben Jonson can be viewed as the pivotal self-conscious author working in the English theatrical tradition. Loewenstein argues that Jonson's attitude towards publication marks him out from his contemporaries and anticipates the later emergence of authors as possessive owners of copyright in their works:

> Not until 1709 did the Statute of Anne formally locate the origins of literary property rights in authors, as opposed to stationers, but the publication of Jonson's *Folio Workes* nearly a century earlier marks a crucial moment in that history of the cultural marketplace, and in the history of the bibliographic ego, from which later developments in legal history derive.[122]

Jonson's view towards publication was ahead of his time. Jonson arranged for printing of his preferred manuscript versions of plays and emphasised his authorial status by adding paratextual material (prologues, epilogues, dedications, etc) to manuscripts before printing.[123] McMillan opines that Jonson cared deeply about his literary status and 'made a campaign out of turning plays into respectable literature'.[124] By contrast, Gurr questions whether Shakespeare truly took an interest in the printing of his plays – for instance, in the case of *Henry V* Shakespeare allowed the theatre company to arrange for printing of the company's shortened performance text rather than his superior manuscript version, which only received posthumous publication.[125]

Jonson pursued multiple avenues of revenue to earn an income primarily from his writings. First, he 'sold plays to acting companies'; second, he made appeals for patronage based on his manuscripts; third, he sold 'masques' to the Royal court for performances at, for example, the Banqueting House at Whitehall; and finally, he sold 'verse' for registration at the Stationers' Company and thereafter print dissemination.[126]

During the 1590s Jonson formed a business relationship with Philip Henslowe, the prominent theatrical manager of the Rose Theatre and 'The Admiral's Men' – though Loewenstein cautions 'it would not be far from the truth to say that he was indentured to Henslowe'.[127] This relationship blossomed at the end of the Elizabethan era as the market for plays in printed form grew in significance. Henslowe arranged for Jonson's texts, including Jonson's paratextual additions, to

[122] Loewenstein (n 47) 110.

[123] Peters (n 59) 136. Although Jonson also worked as an actor (as Shakespeare did) his efforts to derive an income from his writings mark him out.

[124] S McMillin, 'Professional Playwriting' in DS Kastan (ed), *A Companion to Shakespeare* (Oxford: Blackwell, 1999) 226–38, 238.

[125] A Gurr, 'Shakespeare's Lack of Care for His Plays' (2015) 2 *Memoria di Shakespeare: A Journal of Shakespearean Studies* 161, 161–62. Gurr's view can be contrasted with that of Erne who makes the claim that Shakespeare did intend his plays to be read – L Erne, *Shakespeare as Literary Dramatist*, 2nd edn (Cambridge: Cambridge University Press, 2013).

[126] Loewenstein (n 47) 102.

[127] ibid, 103. Peters (n 59).

be registered at the Stationers' Company, which provided the acting company with a potential additional source of income once audiences for formerly popular plays had begun to dwindle.[128]

Jonson's self-conscious approach to authorship only increased during the Jacobean era. As noted earlier, acting companies typically purchased plays from writers for a flat fee and such transactions effectively brought to an end the writer's 'ownership' of the work;[129] and when the playwright was referred to on stage, it was typically as 'our poet' and almost never as the 'author' or the 'playwright'.[130] Jonson began to challenge these presumptions, engaging with acting companies with a higher level of agency than most writers. This is evident in the prologue he wrote for *Bartholomew Fayre* in 1614 which, unusually, referred to a contract between 'the Hearers' (the audience) and 'the Author' (Jonson, as playwright).[131] This was a radical moment in the history of authorship in theatre because it presented the playwright, rather than the actors, as the originator (not merely 'our poet') of the play in the mind of the audience.[132] It is not difficult to see how this individualist turn presaged the move, over the decades that followed, towards appreciating the unique 'voice' of the author. Indeed, the efforts of Jonson, and the posthumous appreciation of Shakespeare, meant that as the Jacobean era gave way to the Caroline period (1625–49), the perception of theatrical authorship was already beginning to stabilise around an author-figure. The idea that such an author should also own property in the play was not far off. On this too, Ben Jonson was ahead of his time, advocating publicly for increased legal rights for writers.[133] There is no doubt that the author's rights tradition in English theatre found an early paragon in Ben Jonson.[134]

How Reconceptualising Anonymity Influenced Authorship During the Seventeenth Century

Masten posits that although it does not identify anyone the term 'anonymous' signifies a definable 'space for identity, a need to know "who is speaking"'; as such, this supports Foucault's contention that 'the author has a particular point of emergence as a cultural fiction'.[135] Today we are intrigued by anonymity – at times it frustrates us because when reading a text or listening to a speech we want to know 'who is speaking'.

[128] ibid, 104. See also AW Pollard, *Shakespeare's Fight with the Pirates and the Problems of the Transmission of His Text*, 2nd edn (Cambridge: Cambridge University Press, 1920) 35–52.

[129] ibid, 102, noting that 'printers conventionally gave limited privileges of revision to authors'.

[130] ibid, 102.

[131] B Jonson, *Bartholomew Fair* (1614), induction, lines 58, 64–66, 73–82, available at www.gutenberg.org/files/49461/49461-h/49461-h.htm.

[132] Loewenstein (n 75) 103.

[133] J McKeough, K Bowrey and P Griffith, *Intellectual Property: Commentary and Materials*, 4th edn (London: Butterworths, 2007) 21.

[134] Peters (n 59) and McMillin (n 124).

[135] Masten (n 12).

Yet, in the Elizabethan age anonymity was not applied to texts.[136] As Masten relates, only in the late seventeenth century was the term ascribed to literature and dramatic playbooks.[137] As described earlier, the polyvocal nature of theatrical authorship of the time meant that dramatic texts passed through several sets of hands. Even where plays were published, they were often printed without written ascription of authorship – thus Masten quips that such texts were not even attributed as 'anonymous'.[138] In fact, Masten refers to Elizabethan play-texts as 'pre-anonymous' because anonymity as we know it had not yet 'emerged' – it would only do so as the author concept itself began to change:

> Anonymous, in other words, only assumes its textual associations as a marking of difference from a new concept of authorship.[139]

When, towards the latter half of the seventeenth century, the idea of an individual author began to gain currency, there was a concurrent turn towards recognising that same individual's 'authority' over the text. To stamp 'anonymous' on a text became a way to recognise the insistence of the authorship question. In other words, the use of anonymous as a placeholder brings up the Beckett/Foucault concern once more, our need to know *who* is performing the author function? Masten argues:

> The historicity of that need is registered in the word anonymous, which supports Foucault's contention that the author has a particular point of emergence as a cultural fiction.[140]

From the late seventeenth century onward the term anonymous began to 'signal the authorization of a text, the importance of someone, anyone, speaking' – indicating that the emergence of an author-figure was marked concurrently 'by the notice of its absence'.[141] As the understanding of 'anonymous' changed this coincided with a general shift towards focusing on authors over texts in literary circles and theatrical scholarship.[142] Tracing the 'authorial lineage' of the play became more important.[143] Therefore, questions of attribution and anonymity became more vital just as the individual theatrical author mythos began to materialise.

Censorship of Theatre Texts in the Sixteenth and Seventeenth Centuries

The final factor that is worth considering (briefly) in the context of theatrical authorship in the Elizabethan and Jacobean eras is the way that censorship, and

[136] Smith (n 100).
[137] Masten (n 12). See also Smith (n 100), noting that the first *Oxford English Dictionary* citation of this usage ('anonymous', 2) is dated to 1676.
[138] ibid, 363.
[139] ibid, 337.
[140] ibid, 337. See also Bently (n 52) 978.
[141] ibid, 337.
[142] Masten (n 12) 337. See also Bently (n 52) 978.
[143] ibid, 347.

the attendant threats of state sanction (actions for sedition) influenced the creation of play-texts. Although censorship is less useful to assisting this book's analysis of questions about copyright and authorship, and thus I do not go into it in great detail here, it undoubtedly played a part in the polyvocal theatrical authorship of plays. The power of the state to make edits to play-texts was significant. As Litman states, theatre was 'closely supervised by the crown'.[144] The key authority in the Elizabethan and Jacobean eras was the Master of the Revels, who was in charge of stage censorship.[145] Only once approved by the Master did a play-text become exploitable, and thus valuable, with respect to performance and print. For this reason, Loewenstein argues that once a text was approved by the Master of the Revels 'the mark of ideological control' was 'converted into something like an intellectual property right'.[146]

A classic example of the influence of the censor on a text is provided by the play *Sir Thomas More* concerning the Tudor lawyer who was eventually sentenced to death for his refusal to recognise Henry VIII as Supreme Head of the Church in England. As recorded by the British Library:

> The work was initially written by Anthony Munday between 1596 and 1601. The Master of the Revels, Edmund Tilney, whose role included stage censorship, refused to allow *Sir Thomas More* to be performed, perhaps because he was worried that the play's depiction of riots would provoke civil unrest on the streets of London. After the Queen's death in 1603, Shakespeare was brought in to revise the script, along with three other playwrights.[147]

We can thus observe that in this case the censor was 'making changes and demanding others' – effectively becoming a co-author of the manuscript along with the collaborating writers.[148]

Material Matters – Printing, 'Piracy' and 'Blocking' in the Pre-Statutory Copyright Era 1557–1709

As noted earlier, with very few exceptions, from 1557 the Stationers' Company held the exclusive right to print works.[149]

With printed plays becoming more popular in the book-selling marketplace, during the Elizabethan and Jacobean eras 'piracy' of printed texts – including plays – emerged as a major problem for publishers. In the posthumous Shakespeare *First Folio* published in 1623 Heminges and Condell refer to the

[144] Litman (n 49).
[145] R Dutton, *Mastering the Revels: The Regulation and Censorship of English Renaissance Drama* (Iowa: University of Iowa Press, 1991).
[146] Loewenstein (n 75) 31.
[147] See www.bl.uk/collection-items/shakespeares-handwriting-in-the-book-of-sir-thomas-more.
[148] Masten (n 12) 340.
[149] M Rose, 'The Public Sphere and the Emergence of Copyright: Areopagitica, the Stationers' Company, and the Statute of Anne' (2009–10) 12 *Tulane Journal of Technology and Intellectual Property* 123.

existence of 'stolne, and surreptitious copies' of the plays.[150] Resolution of disputes arising over 'pirate' editions of books, including play-books, could occur through formal and informal mechanisms of quasi-arbitration that could be used to deal with the Stationers' disputes.[151] Claims could be taken to The Court of Assistants or The Court of Star Chamber. Yet, it is worth recalling that disputes over the right to print a given text could be resolved via law without any consideration of an author-figure.[152]

In the context of theatre, the existence of 'blocking' registrations posed a challenge. Theatrical impresarios, including Henslowe, sometimes deigned to register plays at the Stationers' Company to secure the exclusive right to print a particular text, a right which in some cases they had no intention of ever exercising.[153] Here we can observe, perhaps for the first time in England, that the publishers and the theatre were to some extent in competition for the public's attention. Registering a play but not actually printing it was an attempt by Henslowe (founder of The Rose Theatre and The Fortune Theatre) to prevent any other theatres from being able to access copies of the text in order to stage it.[154] The use of the play-book as print-commodity and the staging of the play-text as performance commodity could lead to an increase in each one's value – but the use of one could also affect the other negatively.

Piracy disputes and the 'blocking' registrations of plays indicate how unsettled the state of literary property was at the time of pre-statutory copyright. For licensing and registration, flexible, though complex, conventions had developed concerning the right to copy in such a way that avoided elaboration of ideas of literary property as belonging to authors.[155] Indeed, the modern conception of authorial copyright ownership was 'effectively preempted, if not mooted, by the original structures of copyright'.[156]

Nonetheless, as the seventeenth century went on, the Stationers' system proved inflexible – and even corrupt in some respects.[157] With the increase in competition and the tussle for control, authors began to come into focus.[158] The commodification of the play raised questions about ownership of its value:

> … within the theater, more than within the book trade, imperfectly rationalized economic relations and a marketplace made harrowingly unstable by plague and censor generated a new kind of theft and a new kind of ownership. Authors had been compensated, by stationers or, in the case of playwrights, by acting companies, for little more than the scribal labor of generating a unique but reproducible text – a scribal and not a creative act. But now that plays were being sold by acting companies and pirated by individual actors or individual stationers, an economic value relatively autonomous

[150] Erne (n 125) 280–83, referring to 'Heminges and Condell's "Stolne, and surreptitious copies" and the Pavier quartos'.
[151] Lauriat (n 61).
[152] Loewenstein (n 47) 105.
[153] ibid, 105.
[154] ibid, 105.
[155] ibid, 105. Litman (n 49).
[156] ibid, 105.
[157] ibid, 105–6.
[158] Barron (n 3).

> from either the author's scribal labor or the stationer's reproductive and disseminative labor began to inhere in script.[159]

The value of play-books, even in 'pirate' versions, had increased. Yet, the rights of playwrights as authors remained barely perceptible in a fog of legal relationships that benefited publishers and booksellers. A Star Chamber degree in 1631 had emphasised the Stationers' monopoly, and it was given statutory imprimatur via The Licensing Act 1662. Even so, the courts were beginning to perceive, and acknowledge, the possibility of authorial ownership. Although not a case about a theatrical text, the ruling of the Court of Common Pleas in *Stationers' Company v Seymour* (1677) is relevant as it raised questions about whether authors possessed a kind of common law literary property in their writings.[160] Gómez-Arostegui demonstrates that during the mid-to-late seventeenth century there was some implicit Parliamentary and judicial acceptance that authors owned a form of literary property in their writings, but it was never given definitive approval by the courts.[161]

The Licensing Act 1662 continued in force, via amendments, with some lapses, until 1695. The Stationers agitated for the renewal of their monopoly rights. The eventual outcome of this struggle was the push for statutory copyright. In time, this would bring the role of the author as *owner* to the fore. Simultaneously, from the Restoration (1660) onwards, a turn toward individual author-figures is visible in theatrical practice.

The Changing Nature of Theatre and the Playwright's Status, Post-Restoration (1660–1709)

The theatres were closed from 1642–60 during the English civil war and the rule of Oliver Cromwell. After the restoration of Charles II in 1660 the theatre market was revived – but in an altered state. Post-1660 the theatre market became more heavily regulated and restricted than it had been under Elizabeth I, James I or Charles I. Charles II issued a monopoly (patent) to two theatres – one run by William Davenant and the other by Thomas Killigrew.[162] Only these two could

[159] Loewenstein (n 47), 105–6.

[160] *Stationers' Company v Seymour* (1677) 1 Mod. 256. See also HT Gómez-Arostegui, 'Stationers v Seymour (1677)' in J Bellido (ed), *Landmark Cases in Intellectual Property Law* (Oxford: Hart, 2017) 21–58.

[161] R Deazley and E Cooper (eds), 'What is the Point of Copyright History? Reflections on Copyright at Common law in 1774 by H. Tomás Gómez-Arostegui' (2016) 4 *CREATe Working Paper* 1.

[162] D Ganzel, 'Patent Wrongs and Patent Theatres: Drama and the Law in the Early Nineteenth Century' (1961) 76 *PMLA* 384–96. In 1661 Davenant's 'Duke's Company' was based at Lincoln's Inn Fields but in 1671 moved to Dorset Garden. In 1663 Killigrew's company was based at Theatre Royal, Drury Lane. In Dublin, the Theatre Royal opened its doors in 1662. In 1682 the King's Company was taken over by Duke's to form United Company with Thomas Betterton. Betterton later received a licence from William III to found a new theatre, first at Lincoln's Inn in 1695 and in 1720 the Theatre Royal Covent Garden. Samuel Foote founded the Theatre Royal, Haymarket, in 1766, which became

stage performances of serious dramas, (though other theatres could perform comedy and pantomime).[163] Notably, women were allowed to perform on stage for the first time and the first female playwrights – such as Susan Centlivre – began to receive attention.[164]

Yet, the great blossoming of English 'Renaissance' theatre – typified by the polyvocal productions of the late sixteenth and early seventeenth centuries – was over. Collaborative writing between playwrights had its 'heyday at the turn of the sixteenth century' and thereafter gradually declined.[165] The theatre environment transformed from a context where 'creative originality and independence of voice had been little prized' to one where individual authors were increasingly appreciated and rewarded.[166] Thus, towards the end of the seventeenth century a more author-centric model emerged.[167] As Kewes states this can be evidenced by the fact that the post-1660 period saw 'a growing concern with the integrity of an author's œuvre'.[168] This manifested itself most obviously in changes to the way plays were catalogued – during the 1650s they were 'lists of titles of plays' – the plays rather than authors were the 'commodity for sale' in print; but by the time of Gerard Langbaine's catalogues of the 1680s–1690s 'the organizing principle shifts from play to author'.[169]

As the 1700s began there was a rise in public consumption of works of literature and drama.[170] As Stern remarks, the need to have 'a single identifiable author with a known body of work became an increasingly important sales pitch'.[171]

The theatrical marketplace had changed to the benefit of the dramatist. Even if their work is not as critically lauded today, post-1660 writers such as Dryden, Otway, Lee, Behn, and later, Congreve, Vanbrugh, and Farquhar, gained 'a contemporary esteem equal, even superior, to their illustrious predecessors Shakespeare, Jonson, and Fletcher'.[172] This increased further from 1699 when it became more common for playwrights to be identified in playbills.[173]

the third patent theatre, operating in summer. As the eighteenth century went on further letters patent were granted to theatres: Theatre Royal, Cork (1760), Theatre Royal, Bath (1768), Theatre Royal, Liverpool (1772), Theatre Royal, Bristol (1778) and Theatre Royal, Birmingham (1807).

[163] The patent monopolies on the performance of serious plays lasted until their revocation via the Theatres Act 1843 (6 & 7 Vict., c. 68).

[164] DP Fisk, 'The Restoration Actress' in SJ Owen (ed), *A Companion to Restoration Drama* (Oxford: Blackwell, 2001) 69–91. See also W Van Lennep, EL Avery, AH Scouten, GW Stone and CB Hogan, *The London stage, 1660–1800: a calendar of plays, entertainments & afterpieces, together with casts, box-receipts and contemporary comment: Compiled from the playbills, newspapers and theatrical diaries of the period* (Carbondale, Illinois: Southern Illinois University Press, 1960–1968), accessible at https://catalog.hathitrust.org/Record/000200105.

[165] Stern (n 57) 73.

[166] ibid.

[167] Kewes (n 57).

[168] ibid.

[169] ibid.

[170] Krause (n 13) 217.

[171] Stern (n 57) 73.

[172] Kewes (n 57).

[173] Stern (n 57) 73. See also T Stern, '"On each Wall and Corner Post": Playbills, Title-pages, and Advertising in Early Modern London' (2006) 36 *English Literary Renaissance* 57.

On the key issue of ownership, authors gradually began to be viewed as the 'sole begetters of their works'.[174] Kewes argues the existence of the Restoration 'benefit' – a custom of giving a portion of revenues from the playhouse's third night to the author as payment for a play – encouraged authors to write; though Stern notes that a similar benefit existed pre-Restoration in the 1620s.[175] Nonetheless, there is no doubt that the idea that the playwright ought to be viewed as 'owner' of the text became 'a matter of heated dispute from the 1660s onwards'.[176] In the aftermath of the 'glorious revolution' of 1688–89 and the Act of Union 1707, regulation of the right to copy by Parliament, in the form of legislation, would soon come to pass.

The Statute of Anne 1710 and the Recognition of Authors as Owners

In 1710 the first copyright statute – the 'Statute of Anne' – came into force.[177] The Act can be viewed as the foundation of legislative copyright in the modern UK and the common law world.[178] Historians of copyright – such as Rose and Deazley – have undertaken significant studies of the Statute of Anne in historical context.[179] I do not intend to explore this period in detail, but it is important to highlight some key issues that relate to authorship and ownership of plays.

The first question to consider is – why was the Act passed? The need for a copyright statute arose due to substantive conditions central to the print industry,[180] such as the existence of printing technology, the demise of the previous system of state licensing, a governmental acceptance of the concept of 'intellectual property', and a rapidly expanding market for books and play texts – and later, sheet music.[181] Consequently, the rationale behind the Statute of Anne was concerned primarily 'with "books" and their "proprietors" (ie, the Stationers), not authors and

[174] Kewes (n 57).
[175] ibid.
[176] ibid.
[177] An Act for the Encouragement of Learning by Vesting the Copies of Printed Books in the Authors or Purchasors of Such Copies during the Times Therein Mentioned 1710 (Imp) 8 Anne, c 19. (the Statute of Anne), available at http://avalon.law.yale.edu/18th_century/anne_1710.asp.
[178] Kewes (n 57).
[179] See, eg Rose (n 3) and Deazley (n 43). See also D Ross, 'Copyright and the Invention of Tradition' (1992) 26 *Eighteenth-Century Studies* 1. See also Feather (n 10). For further detail on these issues see generally J Locke, *Two Treatises of Government* (Cambridge: Cambridge University Press, 1988) (originally published 1689). See also W Gordon, 'A Property Right in Self-Expression: Equality and Individualism in the Natural Law of Intellectual Property' (1993) 102 *Yale Law Journal* 1533; B Sherman and L Bently, *The Making of Modern Intellectual Property Law* (Cambridge: Cambridge University Press, 1999) and Waldron (n 10).
[180] D Hunter, 'Musical Copyright in Britain to 1800' (1986) 67 *Music and Letters* 269, 274. See also Deazley (n 43) xix.
[181] Deazley (n 43) xix. See also J Raven, 'The Book Trades' in I Rivers (ed), *Books and Their Readers in Eighteenth-Century England: New Essays* (London: Continuum, 2001) 1–34.

their works'.[182] The assumption was that the Stationers would continue to assert control of cultural production.[183] The Statute of Anne provided that the owner of the book's 'Copy' possessed 'the sole liberty of printing and reprinting' it. An infringer would be liable to 'forfeit such Book or Books, and all and every Sheet or Sheets' giving the owner the right to 'forthwith Damask and make Waste Paper of them'.[184]

The second question is: how did this law affect the status of authors? As noted earlier, dramatists had largely lacked control over print and performance in the Elizabethan/Jacobean eras; and although the concept of an author's literary property under common law had been present in judicial reasoning in the mid-to-late seventeenth century it remained of ambiguous legality.[185] Although the 1710 Act was intended to protect publishers' interests rather than those of writers, the Act nonetheless anticipated the emerging importance of the author's role. As Bently notes:

> The 1710 Act refers to 'authors' and makes the continuation of the copyright term from 14 to 28 years dependent upon the author's survival … Additionally, the Stationers' use of the claims of authors in inducing Parliament to pass the Statute indicates that authorship also had some rhetorical power.[186]

In making the author's role explicit, the Act followed the logic of the rhetorical discussion of the author as *owner* of common law literary property in pre-1710 court rulings involving the Stationers, while also limiting the duration of copyright.[187] In the theatrical context, references to the role of the author in legislation can be seen in the light of the playwright's improved economic status at the dawn of the 1700s, which in turn inspired new conceptions of what constituted authorship.[188]

By the end of the eighteenth century the author-figure as *owner* had truly emerged in philosophy and law. Bently remarks that 'the link established in law between an author and a work, and the romantic conceptualisation of the work as the organic emanation from an individual author, emerged simultaneously at the end of the eighteenth century'.[189] The material and the philosophical worked in tandem as technology and trade allowed post-Enlightenment ideas about

[182] Bently (n 52) 975.

[183] Salter (n 45) 811. It is less relevant to authorship questions, but it is notable that statutory copyright, enforced in the courts, also brought with it even greater potential power to censor works of literature.

[184] Section 1 of the Statute of Anne 1710.

[185] HT Gómez-Arostegui, 'Copyright at Common Law in 1774' (2014) 47 *Conn. L. Rev.* 1. For a Scottish perspective on the debate see H MacQueen, 'Literary property in Scotland in the eighteenth and nineteenth centuries' in I Alexander and HT Gómez-Arostegui (eds), *Research Handbook on the History of Copyright Law* (Cheltenham: Edward Elgar, 2018) 119–38. See also Deazley and Cooper (n 161).

[186] Bently (n 52) 975. See also Feather (n 10).

[187] Gómez-Arostegui (n 160) at 51, referring to *Stationers' Company v Seymour* (1677) (n 160), *Stationers' Company v Bradford* (12 June 1700) C37/692 and *Stationers' Company v Partridge* (1709) HLS MS 1109.

[188] Stern (n 57).

[189] Bently (n 52) 974.

the individual to circulate in print, helping to create a new respect for authorial 'geniuses'.[190] Copyright law's framing of authorship in the late eighteenth century was thus influenced by a critical ferment – the confluence of the material and the philosophical.[191]

John Locke's *Two Treatises of Government* (1689), which advocated a theory of individual labour-property rights as natural rights, was an influential contemporary text.[192] Rose ties Locke's labour theory of property individualism to the the later romanticism of Coleridge.[193] Thus, at the end of the eighteenth century Lockean property discourse 'which speaks of a natural right of property in the products of labour' was blended with a growing acceptance that 'heroic' individual authors create literary, musical and dramatic works of art.[194] As Woodmansee remarks, the legacy is that 'a piece of writing or other creative product may claim legal protection only insofar as it is determined to be a unique original product of an intellection of a unique individual (or identifiable individuals)'.[195]

Our modern understanding of the author – in terms of the literary imagination and legal personhood under copyright – was certainly consolidated during the Romantic period.[196] In theatre there was a continuing shift towards recognising individual authorship, which created a presumption of originality on the part of the increasingly 'professionalised' writer in line with the ethos of the evolving copyright law.[197] Over time, writers began to benefit from the new legal form of authorship.[198] A more authorial view of composition took hold.[199] Thus, at the end

[190] Although many scholars accept that 'Romantic author' idealism influenced copyright law, not all scholars agree. Saunders claims the discourse of Romantic aesthetics is overstated and should not be allowed to overwhelm legal scholarship, viewing the fields of art/aesthetics and copyright as fundamentally separate – D Saunders, 'Dropping the subject: An argument for a positive history of authorship and the law of copyright' in B Sherman and A Strowel (eds), *Of Authors and Origins* (Oxford: Clarendon Press, 1994) 95–96. Barron is also sceptical of how influential Romanticism has been on the development of case law principles – A Barron, 'Copyright law and the claims of art' (2002) 4 *Intellectual Property Quarterly* 368, 374–80. For a comparative outline of early copyright theory in Germany see Kant (n 41).

[191] Salter (n 45) 792.

[192] Locke (n 179). See also S Stern, 'From Author's Right to Property Right' (2012) 62 *University of Toronto Law Journal* 29.

[193] Rose (n 3).

[194] Bently (n 52) 975. See also M Chatterjee, 'Lockean Copyright versus Lockean Property' (2020) 12 *Journal of Legal Analysis* 136.

[195] M Woodmansee, 'On the Author Effect: Recover Collectivity in The Construction of Authorship' (1992) 10 *Cardozo Arts & Ent. L.J.* 279.

[196] Censorship of plays by the Lord Chamberlain via the Theatrical Licensing Act of 1737 lasted until 1968.

[197] Kewes (n 57). See however Litman (n 49) 1395 noting that the Act 'made no immediate observable difference in the lot of dramatists'. The question of plagiarism in theatre grew in importance at this time – I reflect on this in ch 4 of this book.

[198] Krause (n 13) 217.

[199] E Cooper, 'Copyright and Mass Social Authorship: A Case Study of the Making of the Oxford English Dictionary' (2015) 24 *Social & Legal Studies* 509, noting that there were examples of collective authorship of literary works under the 1842 Act that do not fit within the idea of Romantic, individualist authorship.

of the eighteenth century the acceptance of Romantic 'genius' authors *as owners* was well under way.[200]

Nevertheless, the link between copyright and romanticism should not be overstated. As explored above, the idea of the theatrical author as a possessive public agent, as well as the rhetoric of literary property, can be observed in the post-Restoration (1660) period (and even earlier in the atypical figure of Ben Jonson). Moreover, as I outline below, the law at the end of the eighteenth century did not yet protect a 'copyright work' in the modern sense of a broad property-object encompassing a bundle of rights – only print was given statutory protection, with performance falling outside the scope of the Act.

Changes to Theatrical Culture Post-Statute of Anne 1710

When Queen Anne – whom the 1710 statute is named after – passed away in 1714, George I became the new King. Theatre was not valued as highly by the new monarch and as a result the status of actors in Crown circles lessened.[201] Nonetheless, the public remained in thrall. During the eighteenth century several small theatre companies 'sprang up' to compete with the two patent theatres by performing comedies, although 'extensive government regulation and uncertain finances kept them from gaining a foothold'.[202] When Parliament passed the Licensing Act in 1737 the performance of 'legitimate' or serious drama remained limited to the two theatre companies that possessed the royal patent. The Act affirmed that all scripts had to pass through the approval of the censor – the Lord Chamberlain – prior to initial performance.[203] The overall effect was to limit opportunity for 'serious' dramatists – it became harder to find venues for new scripts and some would-be dramatists 'shifted their efforts to poetry or novels'.[204] The market for printed novels was such that several great writers began to establish themselves, including Samuel Richardson, an author who was certainly aware of, and willing to assert, his copyright under the Statute of Anne.[205]

The restrictive theatrical scene may be one reason why the legacy of eighteenth century theatre is not as rich as that of the Elizabethan/Jacobean period. During the eighteenth century the works of Shakespeare were revived and adapted – albeit

[200] FM Scherer, 'The Emergence of Musical Copyright in Europe from 1709 to 1850' (2008) 5 *Review of Economic Research on Copyright Issues* 3, 11.

[201] Litman (n 49). See also RD Hume, 'Theatres and Repertory' in J Donohue (ed), *The Cambridge History of British Theatre: Volume 2 1660 to 1895* (Cambridge: Cambridge University Press, 2004) 53–70.

[202] ibid.

[203] Theatrical Licensing Act of 21 June 1737, 10 Geo. II c. 28.

[204] Litman (n 49).

[205] JR Alexander, 'Richardson and Copyright' (2012) 59 *Notes and Queries* 219.

often as 'tragedies with happy endings' as in the case of the Nahum Tate version of *King Lear* – with famous performances by leading actors such as David Garrick;[206] meanwhile Restoration comedies such as Congreve's *The Way of the World* (1700) remained popular.[207] Today the most respected of the eighteenth century playwrights who wrote for the London stage are two Irish writers of satire: Oliver Goldsmith (1722–74), whose most famous work – *She Stoops to Conquer* (1773) – continues to be revived frequently in the twenty-first century; and Richard Brinsley Sheridan (1751–1816) who wrote *The School for Scandal* (1777) and several other popular plays.[208] Authorship of theatrical works was more individualist than in the Elizabethan/Jacobean eras, but it still thrived on collaborative input, with several parties – writers, actors and theatre managers – 'playing at authorship'.[209] For example, Goldsmith engaged the actor and manager David Garrick to write the prologue to *She Stoops to Conquer*, which introduced the play's comedic style and themes to the audience.[210]

Post-1710 the legal print rights the individual playwright could claim continued to increase in practice. During the mid-to-late eighteenth century theatre companies began to agree contracts with writers that allowed the playwrights to keep ownership of the play in its printed form – this allowed writers to make agreements directly with the Stationers.[211] By the end of the eighteenth century the two 'patent' theatres began to pay authors flat fees rather than the prior system of partial performance 'benefit'.[212] The theatres intended to limit their cost outlay, but the impact on writers was that on average, by contracting with the publishers themselves they received a greater amount of money than in the earlier periods – as well as acknowledgment of authorial ownership.[213] As a result, Litman states, by the end of the 1700s 'it was becoming possible for at least some playwrights to earn a living writing for the theatre'.[214]

To understand the nature of the legal rights the dramatists possessed in this respect, the key cases decided during the eighteenth century and early nineteenth century on the question of what copyright protected in the context of drama must be examined. What these cases reveal is that legal claims over plays could no longer be limited to

[206] CB Hardman, '"Our Drooping Country Now Erects Her Head": Nahum Tate's "History of King Lear"' (2000) 95 *The Modern Language Review* 913.

[207] See www.bl.uk/collection-items/congreves-the-way-of-the-world.

[208] Sheridan, along with his compatriot playwright Charles Macklin, would come to influence the law on performance rights, as outlined later on in this chapter. See D Worrall, 'Charles Macklin and Arthur Murphy: theatre, law and an eighteenth-century London Irish diaspora' (2020) 14 *Law and Humanities* 113. See also www.bl.uk/restoration-18th-century-literature/articles/18th-century-british-theatre.

[209] EH Anderson, *Eighteenth-Century Authorship and the Play of Fiction: Novels and the Theater, Haywood to Austen* (London: Routledge, 2009) 1–20.

[210] See www.bl.uk/collection-items/first-edition-of-she-stoops-to-conquer-1773#.

[211] Litman (n 49).

[212] House of Commons Report from the Select Committee on Dramatic Literature with Minutes of Evidence (1832), available at www.copyrighthistory.org/cgibin/kleioc/0010/exec/ausgabe/%22uk_1832%22.

[213] Litman (n 49).

[214] ibid, 1397.

printed play-texts – the commodification of performance as a source of value in the theatre market led to numerous claims for exclusive rights to perform plays.[215]

Defining the Boundaries of Copyright Protection under the Statute of Anne 1710

The terms of the Statute of Anne stated that the owner of the book's 'Copy' possessed 'the sole liberty of printing and reprinting' it.[216] Kaplan argues that 'the draftsman was thinking as a printer would – of a book as a physical entity'.[217] It did not take long for this to became untenable. As we shall see, by the end of the eighteenth century it became clear that the courts viewed copyright as applying to an immaterial text, though one limited to the words on the page.

Deazley notes that one of the earliest cases taken under the 1710 Act by a living author, *Gay v Read* (1729), concerned the text of a dramatic opera (*Polly, an Opera* – also known as *The Beggar's Opera*); whereby, the author John Gay sought, and was granted, a preliminary injunction to prevent unauthorised printing of the playbook, which, after his death in 1737, was extended to a permanent injunction in *Baller v Watson* (1737).[218]

Early case law also saw significant copyright precedents developed in seminal rulings such as *Pope v Curl* (1741).[219] The case involved the writer Alexander Pope, who as one of the most 'professionalised' contemporary authors was assertive over his interests in court.[220] The court ruled that although the letters in question belonged to the recipient, the literary copyright remained with the author, and therefore the recipient did not have a licence to publish them.[221] The case was important for an early consideration of whether copyright protected not just books, but also something intangible: the literary content.

Two subsequent cases are central to this question and are known as the 'literary property debate' cases. As noted earlier, prior to the Statute of Anne there had been some rhetorical acceptance of the idea that at common law there existed a form of author's 'literary property'.[222] In *Millar v Taylor* (1769)[223] it was ruled that

[215] Miller (n 3).

[216] Section 1 of the Statute of Anne 1710.

[217] B Kaplan, *An Unhurried View of Copyright* (New York: Columbia University Press, 1967) 9. For a continental philosophical perspective of the distinction see F Kawohl and M Kretschmer, 'Johann Gottlieb Fichte, and the Trap of Inhalt (Content) and Form: An Information Perspective on Music Copyright' (2009) 12 *Information, Communication & Society* 205 and M Biagioli, 'Genius against Copyright: Revisiting Fichte's Proof of the Illegality of Reprinting' (2011) 86 *Notre Dame Law Review* 1847.

[218] Deazley (n 43) 60–64 referring to unreported case records in the National Archives, London – *Gay v Read* (1729) c.33 351/305 and *Baller v Watson* (1737) c.33 369/315.

[219] *Pope v Curl* (1741) 2 Atk. 342. The defendant was Edmund Curll but the transcript of the judgment refers to 'Curl'. See also *Tonson v Collins* (1761) 1 Black W. 301.

[220] M Rose, 'The Author in Court: Pope v Curll (1741)' in M Woodmansee and P Jaszi, *The Construction of Authorship* (Durham, NC: Duke University Press, 1994) 211, 228.

[221] Bently (n 52) 975.

[222] Gómez-Arostegui (n 160).

[223] *Millar v Taylor* (1769) 4 Burr 2303.

such a right did exist in the form of a perpetual exclusive right belonging to the author which was not removed by the time-limited right provided for in the 1710 Act. Yet, the outcome of *Donaldson v Becket* (1774)[224] was that any common law literary property right was extinguished as soon as the work was published (when it became in effect the statutory right under the 1710 Act).[225]

A substantive consequence of the debate was the application of the common law notion of property (object-ownership) to intangible, literary texts, which enabled the further conceptual development of statutory copyright law, including the emergence of the idea/expression distinction and the broader copyright work concept.[226] Discussion of the distinction between the material (the text printed in book form) and intangible property (the text as intangible content) would continue to raise important questions through the centuries that followed.[227] For present purposes, the key contemporary question was as follows: what happened if the printing of the text was not in dispute but rather its public performance?[228]

The Changing Appreciation of What Copyright Protected 1710–1832 – From the Print-commodity to the Performance-commodity

As stated earlier, by the Elizabethan era plays had become print-commodities with a measure of legal protection via the Stationers' monopoly rights. The Statute of Anne marked the first time that writers were, at least nominally, recognised as possessing explicit legal ownership rights over this print commodity. Notably, the Statute of Anne referred only to the protection of books/printed texts.[229] While the marketplace for printed playbooks continued to expand during the early-to-mid

[224] *Donaldson v Becket* (1774) 4 Burr 2408.

[225] Gómez-Arostegui (n 185). See also P Masiyakurima, *Copyright Protection of Unpublished Works in the Common Law World* (Oxford: Hart, 2020).

[226] R Kennedy, 'Was it Author's Rights All The Time?: Copyright as a Constitutional Right in Ireland' (2011) 33 *Dublin University Law Journal* 253. See also Stern (n 192).

[227] I Alexander, *Copyright Law and the Public Interest in the Nineteenth Century* (Oxford: Hart 2010) 81–90 and 273–74. These questions include: was the intangible protected content limited to the words expressed or did it include other key elements that might fall into the category of ideas, like detailed plots, scenarios and characters? These are questions that continue to recur in copyright scholarship today.

[228] Translations were also the subject of much judicial debate at this time: *Burnett v Chetwood* [1816] EngR 26; (1720) 2 Mer 441, 441; [1816] EngR 26; 35 ER 1008, 1009 (Parker C). *Gyles v Wilcox* [1740] EngR 77; (1740) Barn Ch 368; 26 ER 489. *Newbery's Case* (1773) Loft 775; 98 ER 913. *Sayre v Moore* (Unreported, Lord Mansfield CJ, 1785), discussed in *Cary v Longman* [1801] EngR 198; (1801) 1 East 358, 361; [1801] EngR 198; 102 ER 138, 139–40 (Lord Kenyon CJ).

[229] The analogy with musical performance has been explored by several scholars – D Hunter, 'Musical Copyright in Britain to 1800' (1986) 67 *Music and Letters* 269, 274; M Carroll, 'Whose Music is it Anyway? How We Came to View Musical Expression as a Form of Property' (2004) 72 *University of Cincinnati Law Review* 1405, 1463; A Barron, (n 3) 106; and J Small, 'J.C. Bach Goes to Law' (1985) 126 *The Musical Times* 526. See also *Bach v Longman* 98 ER [1777] 1274.

eighteenth century, in the context of theatre tensions arose over performing – rather than merely printing – dramatic texts.[230] Miller argues that the courts at this time were grappling with understanding performance as a source of value worthy of protection, that is, as the performance-commodity.[231]

Theatre managers and playwrights often took copyright cases to the Court of Chancery, overseen by the Lord Chancellor, seeking injunctions.[232]

The first of the key Chancery rulings relevant to performance was in the 1770 case of *Macklin v Richardson*, which concerned the play *Love a la mode* by Charles Macklin.[233] Macklin had performed *Love a la mode* on many occasions but it had not yet been printed. This was deliberate – Macklin kept control over copies of the text to try to prevent others from performing it. To get around this, the defendants had employed a scribe to attend a performance and transcribe the play; the defendants then published the first act of the play in their magazine and intended to publish the second act. The defendants argued that since the play had been performed publicly, this ought to entitle anyone in the audience to make use of the play in any way they saw fit, including printing it. As a result of the literary property debate, there was ambiguity about whether, when a work had been performed, but not printed, an author retained a right at common law to authorise first publication. The court found for the plaintiff, granting an injunction to prevent unauthorised printing of the second act, holding that performance did not equate to publication. The ruling therefore confirmed that the right to authorise first printing of the play belonged to the author; but its consequences for performance were ambiguous. If a play was published in print, then it could be performed without permission or payment, since performances were not protected. However, the possibility of common law literary property in *unpublished* texts remained alive; moreover, if a playwright/company could maintain control over their copies of an unpublished play-text as Macklin had done, no other theatre would be able to perform it for the simple reason that they could not obtain the text.

This is an instance where the law affected theatre practices directly and considerably. Its impact among theatre practitioners was to encourage playwrights and theatres to hold back from publishing plays in print, so to keep an exclusive right to perform the work.[234] Gerland notes that in the 1750s and 1760s the publication of new plays provided lucrative revenues to printers, with several plays, such as Isaac Bickerstaffe's *Maid of the Mill*, selling out multiple print runs; but by the 1770s the supply of new plays in print dried up, exemplified by the fact that Richard Brinsley

[230] Kewes (n 57).
[231] Miller (n 3).
[232] O Gerland, 'The Haymarket Theatre and Literary Property: Constructing the Common Law Playright, 1770–1833' (2015) 69 *Theatre Notebook* 74, 79–80. More generally, Gómez-Arostegui (n 185) notes that Chancery was favoured over the King's Bench by most claimants in copyright infringement cases post-Statute of Anne because they preferred the injunctive remedies available at Chancery, rather than penalties and forfeitures available under the Act.
[233] *Macklin v Richardson* (1770) Amb. 694
[234] JR Stevens, *The Profession of the Playwright* (Cambridge: Cambridge University Press, 1992) 86.

Sheridan's popular play *The School for Scandal*, first staged in 1777, was deliberately kept unpublished (in authorised form) until the 1800s.[235] Miller relates that the effect was to create a norm that plays should not be performed without permission of the author; a norm that appears to have been in effect in spite of – or perhaps more accurately, because of – the absence of a performance right under the law.[236] Indeed, Gerland notes that between 1777–1800, the London patent theatres – Drury Lane, Covent Garden Theatre and Haymarket (which since 1766 had been the third patent theatre, issued to Samuel Foote) – generally cooperated so that only Drury Lane showed performances of *The School for Scandal*.[237]

In addition to court actions and the norms of co-operation, Boorman notes that arbitration was also used by theatre companies to resolve legal disputes.[238] In 1795 theatre proprietors Samuel Ireland and Richard Brinsley Sheridan signalled their willingness to go to arbitration, allowing the solicitor Albany Wallis to decide the terms for the staging of the play *Vortigern* (a play initially falsely attributed to Shakespeare).[239]

That the performance of a published play was not protected by copyright was emphasised in *Coleman v Wathen*, a case taken to the King's Bench in 1793.[240] The dispute concerned *The Agreeable Surprise* – a comic musical, the libretto of which had been written by the Irish dramatist John O'Keefe. O'Keefe assigned copyright to the Haymarket Theatre, where performances became extremely popular.[241] When the defendant staged an unauthorised public performance of *The Agreeable Surprise* the manager of the Haymarket Theatre – George Colman, a trained lawyer – took action, claiming the public performance undertaken without permission was equivalent to an unauthorised print publication under the Statute of Anne. The court rejected this analogy, with Kenyon CJ noting that the Statute of Anne 'only extends to the publication of the book itself'.[242] Therefore, a performance of the text from memory (by the actors) could not be described as akin to an unauthorised reprinting under the Statute of Anne (the implication being that a performance was not publication, and publication solely meant printing).[243]

235 Gerland (n 232) 77.
236 Miller (n 3).
237 Gerland (n 232) at 81.
238 F Boorman, 'Theatrical arbitration in late-Georgian England' (draft article on file with author).
239 J Kahan, *Reforging Shakespeare: The Story of a Theatrical Scandal* (Bethlehem, PA: Lehigh University Press, 1998) 127–29. See also RB Sheridan 'Richard Brinsley Sheridan to Samuel Ireland, 9 Jun. 1795' in C Price (ed), *The Letters of Richard Brinsley Sheridan, vol. II* (Oxford: Clarendon Press, 1966) 17.
240 *Coleman v Wathen* (1793) 5 D. & E. 245.
241 WJ Burling, *Summer Theatre in London, 1661–1820, and the Rise of Haymarket Theatre* (London: Associated University Presses, 2000) 150–51.
242 *Coleman v Wathen* (n 207) 245. See R Deazley, *Rethinking Copyright* (Cheltenham: Edward Elgar, 2006) 30.
243 ibid. See also *Morris v Kelly* (1820) 1 J&W 481 and I Alexander, '"Neither Bolt nor Chain, Iron Safe nor Private Watchman, Can Prevent the Theft of Words": The Birth of the Performing Right in Britain' in R Deazley, M Kretschmer and L Bently (eds), *Privilege and Property: Essays on the History of Copyright* (Cambridge: Open Book Publishers, 2010) 321, available at https://books.openedition.org/obp/1083?lang=en#text.

In the 1822 case of *Murray v Elliston*[244] the influence of the earlier *Millar* and *Donaldson* 'literary property' sagas became clear. The case concerned Lord Byron's *Marino Faliero*. Lord Byron had assigned the copyright to the plaintiff who published it in print. The defendant sought to put on a public performance of the play at the Drury Lane Theatre without the permission of the plaintiff copyright owner. The plaintiff based his claim on the common law right to literary property rather than on the Statute of Anne.[245] The court nonetheless ruled for the defendant, arguing that 'an action cannot be maintained by the plaintiff against the defendant for publicly acting and represented the said tragedy, abridged in the manner aforesaid'.[246] The case confirmed that an unauthorised performance of a published play was considered legally acceptable under the Statute of Anne, with the courts maintaining a print-centric approach to copyright.[247] As the theatre market suffered a decline in the 1820s, the prior system of monopoly patents and co-operative norms began to break down; that performances went unprotected became a particular point of controversy, leading to calls for reforms to assist in the revitalisation of the theatre industry.[248]

The Reforms Brought About by the 1833 Act and 1842 Act – The Right to Perform a 'Dramatic Piece'

In the early 1830s the writer and MP Edward Bulwer-Lytton began to consider reforms of copyright in the theatrical context. In 1832, Bulwer-Lytton established the Select Committee on Dramatic Literature to consider the full picture of theatre in what was (after 1801) the United Kingdom of Great Britain and Ireland.[249]

The committee took note of the fact that copyright protection was limited to printing plays. A play 'could be performed by any theatre that could get its hands on a script' due to the fact that performances of plays were generally believed to be in the public domain.[250] On this, Miller notes that the hearings revealed tensions between the beneficiaries of the print and performance commodities.[251]

[244] *Murray v Elliston* (1822) 5 B and A 657.
[245] R Deazley, 'Commentary on Dramatic Literary Property Act 1833' in L Bently and M Kretschmer, *Primary Sources on Copyright (1450–1900)*, available at www.copyrighthistory.org/cam/tools/request/showRecord?id=commentary_uk_1833.
[246] *Murray v Elliston* (1822) 5 B. & Ald. 657 at 661. CB Collins. 'Playright and the Common Law' (1927) 15 *California Law Review* 381, 382–83.
[247] YH Lee, 'The persistence of the text: the concept of the work in copyright law – Part I' (2018) *Intellectual Property Quarterly* 22, 33.
[248] Alexander (n 243) 325–31. See also Miller (n 3) 56–57.
[249] See Report from the Select Committee on Dramatic Literature: with the Minutes of Evidence (1831–32) Paper No. 679, VII: 1. K Newey, 'The 1832 Select Committee' in J Swindells and DF Taylor, *The Oxford Handbook of the Georgian Theatre* (Oxford: Oxford University Press, 2014) 140–55.The Statute of Anne had not applied to Ireland and so it was perceived as a market where piracy of playbooks thrived – Gerland (n 232). For a thorough assessment of Irish theatre history through a legal lens see WN Osborough, *The Irish Stage: A Legal History* (Dublin: Four Courts Press, 2015).
[250] Litman (n 49) 1398.
[251] Miller (n 3) 57–63.

The committee also found that since the late eighteenth century new, smaller theatres had been formed to challenge the dominance of the two 'patent' theatres.[252] These non-patent theatres were – despite it being against the law – increasingly performing serious dramas.

Shifts in the market contributed to the need for reform. Litman states:

> When there had been only two theatre companies, the risk from competition was small, since the companies appear to have followed an informal practice of declining to poach each other's scripts or actors. In those circumstances, publication of a new play netted the company or playwright some extra money from the publisher without threatening performance revenues.[253]

This had now changed. As noted earlier, publishers had begun to send stenographers to attend the performances of unpublished plays to write down the dialogue as 'new' play-text. They would then publish the unlicensed printed verses, sometimes – though not in the case of *Macklin* – facing few legal consequences.[254] The law needed reform to protect performances and to take account of the new theatres.[255]

The Dramatic Literary Property Act was passed in 1833.[256] It created a new right of representation that for the first time gave authors (or their assignees) the legal right to control public performances.[257] The 1833 Act provided the author of 'any tragedy, comedy, play, opera, farce, or any other dramatic piece or entertainment' the exclusive right of performing or representing it at 'any place or places of dramatic entertainment'. The Dramatic Authors' Society was founded and acted as the first licensing agency for plays.[258] An example of the performance right being asserted by a dramatic author is *Planché v Hooper* (1844), a case where the Theatre Royal at Bath staged Planché's play *White Cat* without his authorisation.[259]

Nevertheless, several writers struggled to assert the right. Theatres and publishers often claimed to be the assignees of this authorial right based on prior assignments and thus claimed control of the performance right. This was a claim bolstered in *Cumberland v Planché*,[260] where it was held that the publisher of a play had in 1828 acquired the performance right as part of its contract to purchase the entirety of the copyright from the author. This was, of course, highly controversial because when the contract was agreed in 1828 the new right did not yet exist; yet it was held in *Cumberland* that the publisher could still exercise it, post-1833.[261]

[252] Litman (n 49) 1398.
[253] ibid.
[254] ibid, 1398–99.
[255] Alexander (n 227) 327–28. For an account of the debate over property in print and performance in contemporary France, see JC Ginsburg, 'A Tale of Two Copyrights: Literary Property in Revolutionary France and America' (1990) 64 *Tulane Law Review* 991.
[256] Dramatic Literary Property Act, 1833, 3 & 4 Will.IV, c.15.
[257] Litman (n 49) 1399–1401.
[258] M Banham, *The Cambridge Guide to the Theatre* (Cambridge: Cambridge University Press, 1995) 302.
[259] *Planché v Hooper* (1844) *The Times*, 19 January 1844, 7c.
[260] *Cumberland v Planché* (1834) 1 Ad & E 580; SC 3 N & M 537; LJ 3 KB 194.
[261] Deazley (n 245). See also *Wall v Taylor* (1882) 9 QBD 727 at 730.

Eventually this prompted an additional reform – an early proponent of which was the lawyer, MP and playwright Thomas Noon Talfourd – that was enacted in the form of the Copyright Act 1842,[262] which stated that the public performance right in the context of drama could be the subject of a separate assignment from the traditional 'print' copyright.[263] Furthermore, a dramatic piece's first public performance was stated to be akin to publication for the purpose of copyright law.[264] Shortly thereafter, the Theatres Act 1843 abolished the exclusive right of the patent theatres to produce serious drama on stage.[265] The combined effect of these reforms was that the performance commodity was now, finally, protected by the law.[266]

The Problem of Dramatisations Post-1833

Despite the reforms of 1833 and 1842, the definition of protected dramatic pieces as 'any tragedy, comedy, play, opera, farce, or any other dramatic piece' did not prevent unauthorised adaptations of *literary* texts such as novels. As novels were not 'dramatic pieces' within the meaning of the 1833 Act, authors could not control public performances of plays adapted from their novels.[267] In other words, although the *performance right* protected plays, under statute there was no *adaptation right* that would allow an author to prevent an unauthorised dramatisation and performance of a play based on, for example, a published story or novel.[268]

Cases such as *Reade v Conquest*[269] and *Toole v Young*[270] confirmed that copyright in the novel as literary text did not go so far as to prevent unauthorised parties from performing publicly plays based on such novels. The lack of such a right angered some of the prominent novelists of the period, including Charles Dickens.[271] It became a practice for novelists to create and 'stage' their own dramatisation of a novel in order to claim the performance right – for example Bram Stoker did this in 1897 by engaging the well-known Victorian actor Henry Irving to perform *Dracula* on stage for just two paying customers.[272]

[262] Copyright Act 1842, 5 & 6 Vict., c.45.

[263] C Seville, *Literary Copyright Reform in Early Victorian England: The Framing of the 1842 Copyright Act* (Cambridge: Cambridge University Press, 1999).

[264] Litman (n 49), 1400, suggests the 1842 Act mean that playwrights lost 'any common law public performance rights in their scripts upon the initial public performance'.

[265] Theatres Act 1843 (6 & 7 Vict., c. 68).

[266] Miller (n 3) 66.

[267] Lee (n 247) 34.

[268] B Lauriat, 'Charles Reade's Roles in the Drama of Victorian Dramatic Copyright' (2009) 33 *Colum J L & Arts* 1.

[269] *Reade v Conquest* (1861) 142 Eng. Rep. 297 (CPD). See also *Reade v Lacey* (1861) 70 Eng. Rep. 853, 854 (1861) (KB) and *Russell v Smith* (1848) 12 QB 217.

[270] *Toole v Young* (1874) 9 LR 523.

[271] JR Planché, *The Recollections and Reflections of J.R. Planché* (London: Tinsley Brothers, 1872) 50–51.

[272] Seewww.bl.uk/romantics-and-victorians/articles/bram-stokers-stage-adaptation-of-dracula–Lauriat (n 268). For more on theatricality in the Victorian era see B Murray, 'H.M. Stanley, David Livingstone, and the Staging of "Anglo-Saxon" Manliness' (2013) 129 *Scottish Geographical Journal* 150.

This was further emphasised in the cases of *Tinsley v Lacy*[273] and *Warne & Co v Seebohm*[274] where it was held that although it was not against the law to perform publicly an unauthorised dramatisation of a novel, to publish that dramatisation in a printed form would amount to copyright infringement.[275] Thus only if the theatrical adaptation were published would a copyright claim be available; a mere public performance did not violate the law.[276]

Authorship and Joint Authorship Under the 1833 Act and 1842 Acts

Singular authorship in the Victorian era was assumed to be linked with the physical act of, for example, putting pen to paper. This can be observed from *Kenrick v Lawrence*[277] – a case which involved a basic drawing protected by the Fine Art Copyright Act 1862.[278] Similarly, under the Copyright Act 1842, putting pen to paper appears to have been key. There was not yet a specific legal requirement that a copyright text (or dramatic piece) be 'original'. In 1900 it was held in *Walter v Lane*[279] that even a verbatim copy of a speech by Lord Rosebery as transcribed by a reporter could be protected by copyright.[280] Yet, as Gravells opines, *Walter v Lane* ended up having an unexpected afterlife as a precedent for the low threshold of originality:

> Most notably, and somewhat paradoxically, the case has come to be regarded as a legitimate starting point for judicial consideration of the notion of 'originality', which was, according to the majority of the House of Lords, neither an express nor an implied precondition of copyright protection under the then current 1842 Act.[281]

If singular authorship was viewed in relatively technical, functionalist terms, what about joint authorship? The possibility that there may be more than one author was not expressly covered by the terms of the Copyright Act 1842. Nonetheless, the cases of *Maclean v Moody* (1858)[282] and *Marzial v Gibbons* (1873–74) suggest

It is unclear how effective such 'copyright performances' were, legally speaking as noted in B Weller, *Stage Copyright at Home and Abroad* (London: The Stage, 1912) 5.

[273] (1863) 1 Hem. & M. 747.

[274] (1888) 39 Ch D. 73.

[275] E Cutler, *The Law of Musical and Dramatic Copyright* (London: Cassell & Co., 1892) 14–17.

[276] *Warne & Co v Seebohm* (1888) 39 Ch D. 73. Miller (n 3), Lauriat (n 268) and Lee (n 247) 36.

[277] (1890) 25 QBD 99.

[278] Fine Arts Copyright Act, 1862, 25 & 26 Vict., c.68.

[279] *Walter v Lane* [1900] AC 539. See also *Sawkins v Hyperion Records Ltd* [2005] EWCA Civ 565.

[280] Copyright Act 1842, s 2 and s 3 (5 amp 6 Vict. c. 45).

[281] N Gravells, 'Authorship and Originality: The Persistent Influence of Walter v. Lane' (2007) *Intellectual Property Quarterly* 267, 278; J Pila, 'An Intentional View of the Copyright Work' (2008) 71 *The Modern Law Review* 535, 548. The case is cited in twentieth and twenty-first century cases such as *Express Newspapers v News (UK) Ltd* [1990] FSR 359 and *Sawkins v Hyperion Records Ltd* [2005] EWCA Civ 565. See also the Israeli case *Elisha Kimron v Herschel Shanks* [1993] 7 EIPR D-157.

[282] *Maclean v Moody* (1858) 20 Sc. Sess. Cas. 2nd Ser. 1154.

it was acceptable.[283] However, joint authorship was explicitly envisaged in the context of dramatic pieces under sections I and IV of the Dramatic Literary Property Act, 1833.[284] This is the primary reason why the Victorian cases on claims of co-authorship centred on plays. There is, perhaps, another factor. In the Victorian era theatre went through periodic spells of decline and lull, but it nonetheless remained the primary public forum of art, with famous actors such as Henry Irving, Edward Gordon Craig and Ellen Terry being hailed for their performances;[285] meanwhile, the most popular playwrights included the Irish dramatists Dion Boucicault, Oscar Wilde and George Bernard Shaw.[286] Drama was in the public eye and the newly protected performance commodity was capable of generating substantial revenues – this made a successful copyright claim for joint authorship potentially lucrative.

Studying the facts of the disputes on drama and authorship reveals the power relations that existed between theatre managers and playwrights in the nineteenth century.[287] At the time it was common for theatre managers to try to prevent rival theatres from staging the plays that dramatists had previously written for them.[288] One tactic to this end was for the theatre manager to attempt to claim a share of ownership in the copyright in the dramatic piece, and thus the ability to stop that play from being performed elsewhere.

A relevant dispute came to court in 1856 – *Shepherd v Conquest* – where the courts ruled that the dramatist, not the theatre proprietor, was the author of the dramatic piece.[289] However, in the 1860 case of *Hatton v Kean*, the courts came to the opposite conclusion, holding that a theatre manager was the author of the dramatic piece in question – a dramatico-musical Shakespeare adaptation – in circumstances where it had been the manager who had 'employed' the dramatist-composer to create the work, even in the absence of written assignment.[290]

Levy v Rutley (1870–71) is the essential case of this period because it established the principle that joint authors of a dramatic work must pursue a common design.[291] The facts of *Levy* concerned the dramatic piece *The King's Wager; or*

[283] *Marzial v Gibbons* (1873–1874) L.R. 8 Ch App. 518.

[284] Deazley (n 245).

[285] ibid.

[286] See generally A Jenkins, *The Making of Victorian Drama* (Cambridge: Cambridge University Press, 1991). Since the principal jurisdiction of this study is the UK my focus is on the major Victorian dramatists who worked in London. But there is no doubt that at this time non-English language European theatre was more innovative than British theatre, with the works of eg Chekhov and Ibsen breaking down barriers of what 'modern' theatre could be. See, eg R Gilman, *The Making of Modern Drama* (New York: Farrar, 1972) and R Leach, *The Makers of Modern Theatre – An Introduction* (Oxford: Routledge, 2004).

[287] E Cooper, 'Joint authorship and copyright in comparative perspective: the emergence of divergence in the UK and USA' (2015) 62 *Journal of the Copyright Society of the USA* 245, 250.

[288] ibid. Cooper notes that such disputes were between theatre managers claiming to be 'employers' while claiming playwrights were mere 'employees'.

[289] *Shepherd v Conquest* (1856) 17 CB 427; 139 ER 1140, 1147.

[290] *Hatton v Kean* (1860) 29 L.J.C.P. 20, 25. See also *Barfield v Nicholson* (1824) 2 Sim. and Stu. 1; 57 ER 245.

[291] *Levy v Rutley* (1870–71) L.R. 6 C.P. 523. See also *Levy v Cave* (Ct. C.P.), *The Times*, 14 December 1870 at 11.

The Camp, the Cottage and the Court written by the playwright – Thomas Egerton Wilks. The plaintiff was a theatre manager who had added a scene and made some edits to the text before it was staged, later claiming that this made him a joint author of the play. This claim was rejected on the basis that there needed to be a *common design* between the two parties and this was sorely lacking in this case.[292] As Cooper states, *Levy* 'had merely made subsequent additions and alterations, there being no common design with Wilks'.[293] A similar ruling was made *Shelly v Ross*[294] where it was held that making minor alterations and edits to a piece of drama could not suffice as the basis of a joint authorship claim.

One aspect that is particularly notable about these decisions is acceptance by the courts of the *norms* of theatre practice. The courts took account of the fact that theatre managers – who often performed a role somewhat akin to the modern theatre director of today – often made alterations to play-scripts before putting them on stage. The courts rejected the idea that this ought to make such contributions sufficient to create a joint authorship interest. Cooper notes: 'The approach in *Levy* therefore ensured that the usual activities of theatre managers, in making subsequent alterations to play scripts, would not be sufficient to find a claim to joint authorship.'[295]

The immediate effect of these decisions was to support the position of the dramatists in their negotiations with theatre managers during the Victorian era. Even more importantly, these rulings also form the backbone of judicial analysis of joint authorship in modern copyright law, with *Levy* in particular continuing to be cited in contemporary case law.[296] As I explore in the next chapter, this case anticipates debates over theatrical authorship that continue today.[297]

What Were the Boundaries of the 'Dramatic Piece' 1833–1911?

As the twentieth century began, several theatrical copyright cases arose that gave some clarity to defining the boundaries of the dramatic piece under the 1833 Act. In *Tate v Fullbrook*[298] the case concerned a performative musical-hall sketch – 'Motoring or the Motorist'. The plaintiff had originated the general idea of the sketch and had enlisted a co-author to compose the dialogue. The defendant was a performer who had initially acted in the sketch, and who had later developed his

[292] I reflect further on this common design requirement in ch 3 when considering joint authorship of contemporary works of theatre.
[293] Cooper (n 287) 256.
[294] *Shelley v Ross* (1870–71) L.R. 6 C.P. 531; Bail Court 7 June, *The Times*, 8 June 1871 at 10.
[295] Cooper (n 287) 257.
[296] ibid, 258, noting divergence between UK and US positions can be traced to these cases.
[297] *Brighton and Dubbeljoint v Jones* [2004] EWHC 1157 (Ch); [2004] EMLR 507.
[298] *Tate v Fullbrook* [1908] 1 K.B. 821.

own sketch based on very similar characters and the same central comedic motif. Importantly, however, the dialogue was not the same in the defendant's work as in the plaintiff's sketch. In the first instance the court stated that infringement had occurred due to copying of 'the verbal composition of the author plus matters such as the general get up of the characters, scenic effects and the like'.[299] However, the Court of Appeal reversed the decision, stating the performing right under the 1833 Act applied only to printed text, namely, books and other written compositions.[300] Elements of the sketch apart from the words were not protected.[301] Kennedy LJ remarked that for the purposes of the 1833 a 'dramatic piece' could not 'exist without words'.[302]

A text-centric approach is also visible in the subsequent ruling in *Scholtz v Amasis & Fenn*[303] which confirmed that the dramatic piece as protected by UK copyright law was equivalent to its literal text, not the other key elements that formed part of the performed work.[304] The case concerned a comic opera written by the defendant that featured several elements – such as characters, plot, setting, etc – common to an earlier work written by the plaintiff. Rejecting the infringement claim, the court stated:

> Unless the embodiment of the plot in words had to a substantial extent been appropriated, the plaintiff's case must break down. The fact that plot and scenic effects had been obviously borrowed by one dramatist from another was only evidence of *animus furandi*.[305]

The above makes clear that following the enactment of the Statute of Anne[306] in 1710 a text-centric model of copyright emerged and flourished during the eighteenth and nineteenth centuries. Initially judges focused on whether the 'book' in question had been reprinted by the defendant; later they focused on the literal 'text' even when performed as a dramatic piece. The reluctance to extend copyright protection beyond literal textual boundaries demonstrates some 'inherent judicial conservatism'.[307] As Lee notes, the courts in the 1700s and 1800s were willing to construe the statutory language of 'printing' of copies to include 'partial copies' of text as constituting infringement, but rights of dramatisation (of eg novels) were not yet established.[308] In chapter four I discuss the nature of nineteenth century

[299] ibid, 829.
[300] ibid, 830. I reflect on dramatic plagiarism in ch 4 on copyright infringement.
[301] ibid, 830 and 833.
[302] ibid, 834.
[303] *Scholtz v Amasis & Fenn* [1905–10] MacG. C.C. 216.
[304] Cooper (n 3) 107–09, demonstrating that the relationship between the physical and the intangible was an elusive question not only in textual works in the nineteenth century, but also regards copyright in paintings (ie, the painting as intangible work of an artist and the painting as a valuable physical canvas).
[305] *Scholtz v Amasis & Fenn* [1905–10] MacG. C.C. 216, at 218.
[306] Section 2 of the Statute of Anne 1710.
[307] Lee (n 247).
[308] ibid.

plagiarism and copyright infringement in greater detail as part of my overall assessment of infringement in contemporary theatre.

For now, one final aspect of infringement that is worth noting: in the case of theatrical texts the use of a scene/scenario began in the Victorian era to be the subject of infringement claims in other jurisdictions, particularly in the US.[309]

US Comparison under the 1856 US Copyright Act

For comparative value, it is worth considering the 1868 case of *Daly v Palmer* in the United States of America.[310] The case involved a dispute under the US 1856 Copyright Act over the play *Under the Gaslight* by the American playwright Augustin Daly.[311] The play contains a then-innovative (now cliched) scene set on a railroad, whereby a character is tied to the track as a train approaches and is rescued just in time by another character. When a similar scene appeared in a play *After Dark* by the Irish playwright Dionysius Lardner 'Dion' Boucicault the plaintiff took action. Even though there were no elements of dialogue common to the two works, Blatchford J held that the second work infringed the first based on the similarity in the scenario, movements and sequence of events, because these formed 'part' of the work. Further, the court accepted that copyright could protect a piece of drama even if it featured no spoken words.[312] Blatchford J opined:

> The 'railroad scene', in the plaintiff's play, is undoubtedly a dramatic composition. Those parts of it represented by motion or gesture, without language, are quite as much a dramatic composition, as those parts of it which are represented by voice … Indeed, on an analysis of the two scenes in the two plays, it is manifest that the most interesting and attractive dramatic effect in each is produced by what is done by movement and gesture, entirely irrespective of anything that is spoken.[313]

An injunction was granted and as a consequence, the defendants changed the railroad scene in *After Dark* to avoid infringing upon the earlier play.[314] Despite some strained reasoning, this decision moved US law definitively ahead of its UK counterpart in accepting that dramatic copyright needed to be open to *non-literal* elements. It has therefore been cited as a ruling that established property rights in incidents, a topic I return to in chapter four.[315]

[309] Miller (n 3).
[310] *Daly v Palmer* 6 F. Cas. 1132, 1136 (S.D.N.Y., 1868).
[311] U.S. Copyright Act 1831, 21st Cong., 2d. Sess., 4 Stat. 436 and U.S. Copyright Amendment Act 1856, 11 Stat. 138.
[312] *Daly v Palmer* 6 F. Cas. 1132, 1136 (S.D.N.Y., 1868).
[313] ibid. Miller (n 3) 77–83.
[314] Lee (n 247) 40.
[315] See also TW Clarke, 'Circuit Court of the United States for the Southern District of New York: Augustin Daly v Henry D Palmer and Henry C Jarrett' (1868) 3 *American Law Register* 453. See also JA Morgan, *The Law of Literature: Volume II* (New York: James Cockcroft & Co, 1875) 322; *Kalem v*

International Copyright: The Berne Convention 1886

The birth of international copyright has been explored exhaustively by several prominent scholars;[316] it is not my intention to probe this history in detail. All that is necessary for present purposes is to note a number of key aspects of the 1886 Berne Convention, which made solid the copyright work concept in the international legal context.

The Convention arose in part due to advocacy of international protection of copyright by major literary figures such as Victor Hugo and Charles Dickens who were frustrated that 'pirate' version of their works were on sale outside of their national jurisdictions.[317] Notably, the Berne Convention protects 'literary and artistic works' including works of drama and 'dramatico-musical works', but no further definition is given.[318] National jurisdictions therefore have a great deal of freedom in defining these works.[319] Furthermore, the Berne Convention does not expressly state

Harper Brothers 222 U.S. 55, 61 (1911); *Chappell v Fields* 210 F. 864, 865 (2d. Cir., 1914); *International Film Service v Affiliated Distributors* 283 F. 229, 234 (S.D.N.Y. 1922); *Sheldon v Metro-Goldwyn Pictures* 81 F. 2d. 49, 55 (2d. Cir. 1936); *Shipman v RKO Radio Pictures* 100 F. 2d. 533, 535–536 (2d. Cir., 1938); MB Nimmer, 'The Subject Matter of Copyright under the Act of 1976' (1977) 24 *UCLA Law Review* 978, 1011.

[316] C Seville, *The Internationalisation of Copyright Law: Books, Buccaneers and the Black Flag in the Nineteenth Century* (Cambridge: Cambridge University Press, 2006) and S Ricketson and JC Ginsburg, *International Copyright and Neighbouring Rights – The Berne Convention and Beyond*, 2nd edn (Oxford: Oxford University Press, 2006).

[317] Berne Convention for the Protection of Literary and Artistic Works (September 9, 1886; revised 1896 (Paris), 1908 (Berlin), 1914 (Additional Protocol), 1928 (Rome), 1948 (Brussels), 1967 (Stockholm), 1971 (Paris) – as amended 1979) hereafter referred to as Berne Convention; available at www.wipo.int/treaties/en/ip/berne/trtdocs_wo001.html. The Universal Copyright Convention 1952 was enacted to provide international protection standards for countries that were unwilling to accept certain terms of the Berne Convention. Today the Universal Copyright Convention is less relevant due to the requirement that countries accede to the TRIPS agreement for WTO membership. Both the Geneva (1952) and the Paris (1971) texts are available at www.unesco.org/new/en/culture/themes/creativity/creative-industries/copyright/universal-copyright-convention/. The later 'Rome Convention' was enacted to provide protection for other rights such as rights over sound recording and performers' rights. International Convention for the Protection of Performers, Producers of Phonograms and Broadcasting Organizations of 1961 (Rome Convention) with a link to https://www.wipo.int/export/sites/www/treaties/en/documents/pdf/rome.pdf. See also WIPO Performances and Phonograms Treaty of 1996 – https://www.wipo.int/treaties/en/ip/wppt/. The terms of Berne were largely copied over into the Agreement on Trade-Related Aspects of Intellectual Property Rights, Annex 1C of the Marrakesh Agreement Establishing the World Trade Organization (1994) (hereafter referred to as TRIPS), available at www.wto.org/english/docs_e/legal_e/27-trips_01_e.htm. The WIPO Copyright Treaty 1996 (hereafter referred to as the WCT) exists in compliance with Article 20 of the 'Berne Convention' and it complies with the Berne definition of 'literary and artistic works'. The WCT was enacted primarily to address the issues surrounding copyright and digital technology, available at www.wipo.int/treaties/en/ip/wct/trtdocs_wo033.html#P51_3806.

[318] Berne Convention, Article 2(1).

[319] However, the Berne Convention only covers 'literary and artistic works'. Ricketson and Ginsburg (n 316) 406–7. Ricketson and Ginsburg note that the Berne Convention in fact covers a number of works which may not always be classed as 'literary or artistic works'. Thus, the scope of this expression is wide. See United States Copyright Act 1976, s 102(a)(2), available at www.law.cornell.edu/copyright/copyright.act.chapt1a.html#17usc102.

that there is a requirement of 'originality'.[320] Nonetheless, Ricketson and Ginsburg state that there is 'a clear indication' that the notion of original intellectual creation is 'implicit in the conception of a literary or artistic work'.[321] When the Berne Convention was revised in 1908 it was decided that copyright should arise automatically, that is, that there should be no need for reservation.[322] It was also agreed that the minimum term should be 50 years after the life of the author.[323] As discussed further below, in 1911 these standards were brought into law in the UK.

The Imperial Copyright Act 1911

The Copyright Act 1911 was a piece of imperial legislation applying to the then United Kingdom of Great Britain and Ireland as well as to the wider British Empire. The Act stated that 'copyright shall subsist throughout the parts of His Majesty's dominions to which this Act extends for the time mentioned in every original literary dramatic musical and artistic work'.[324]

As noted earlier, the Copyright Act of 1911[325] brought the Berne Convention standards on matters such as duration of copyright term into UK law. Crucially, in the 1911 Copyright Act the protected subject-matter was defined for the first time via the more abstract concept of the 'work' as opposed to the 'book'.[326] This brought together under a central 'work' concept the literary (protected under the 1842 Act) and the dramatic (performances of which were protected under the 1833 Act). This took account of the changing nature of the jurisprudence in the copyright field – and it enabled judges in subsequent cases to focus more on the abstract or dematerialised subject of protection beyond the text, something particularly important in theatrical works.[327] Griffiths remarks that this 'represented a very important step away from a system under which rights were described in a manner that linked them closely with the material artefacts within which they were first recorded and towards a more abstract conception of the protected form'.[328]

[320] Ricketson and Ginsburg (n 316) 402–3.

[321] Berne Convention, Article 2(5). See also Ricketson and Ginsburg (n 316) 402–3, noting that the preparatory documents for the Brussels Revision Conference appear to acknowledge that the expression 'literary and artistic works' encompassed a notion of 'intellectual creation'.

[322] Convention for the Protection of Literary and Artistic Works 1908, Article 4 (hereafter referred to as Berlin Act), available at http://en.wikisource.org/wiki/Convention_for_the_Protection_of_Literary_and_Artistic_Works_(Berlin_Act,_1908).

[323] Berlin Act, Article 7.

[324] Copyright Act 1911, s 1(1) (hereafter referred to as CA 1911), available at www.opsi.gov.uk/RevisedStatutes/Acts/ukpga/1911/cukpga_19110046_en_1.

[325] ibid.

[326] ibid.

[327] YH Lee, 'The persistence of the text: the concept of the work in copyright law – Part II' (2018) *Intellectual Property Quarterly* 107, 108.

[328] J Griffiths, 'Dematerialization, Pragmatism and the European Copyright Revolution' (2013) 33 *Oxford Journal of Legal Studies* 767, 769.

With the 1911 Act copyright truly became a bundle of rights.[329] Specifically, the 1911 Act gave protections to the rights 'to produce or reproduce the work or any substantial part thereof in any material form whatsoever'; to 'perform … the work or any substantial part thereof in public'; to make adaptations including translations and dramatisations including 'any record, perforated roll, cinematograph film, or other contrivance by means of which the work may be mechanically performed or delivered'.[330] Reference to 'substantial part' made clear that infringement of the protected work could take place even if only a portion had been copied.[331] The 1911 Act also made clear that copyright encompassed the right to make translations and adaptations – not mere unauthorised publication of the literal text. The tortuous debates – first over performance and later over the right to make theatrical adaptations – were seemingly over.[332] In the chapters that follow I explore how the concepts of authorship/joint authorship (chapter three) and infringement (chapter four) have been developed in post-1911 copyright jurisprudence via the work concept; but it is notable that traces of the pre-1911 reasoning on common design (in joint authorship cases) and the literal text (in infringement cases) remain evident in contemporary copyright jurisprudence.

Conclusion

Over the course of this chapter I have demonstrated that the boundaries of what we now conceive of as 'the work of authorship' shifted continually in theatre practice and law during the period 1558–1911.[333] The period saw the rise of two separate property objects and sources of value – the print-text commodity (including partial reproduction of text) and the performance commodity – which would eventually be subsumed into the legal concept of the copyright work.[334] By 1911 the playwright as author owned the entirety of the property rights encompassed by the work. The commodification of the theatrical play – its transformation via law into an apparently stable object of property – during this period provides an example of how 'legal procedures invent the tradition which they purport only to continue'.[335] In the Elizabethan and Jacobean eras writers lacked ownership of either of these commodities, with the Stationers possessing legally enforceable printing monopolies and theatre companies holding a type of informal ownership of plays as performance texts.

Here, we should be in no doubt that the polyvocal creativity of Elizabethan drama – a radical form of 'shared writing' – poses a challenge to modern

[329] ibid.
[330] Copyright Act 1911, s 1(2).
[331] Sherman and Bently (n 179) 173–76.
[332] Lee (n 327) 108.
[333] Bently and Biron (n 18) 270–76.
[334] Miller (n 3).
[335] A Pottage, 'Introduction: Fabricating persons and things' in A Pottage and M Mundy (eds), *Law, Anthropology, and the Constitution of the Social – Making Persons and Things* (Cambridge: Cambridge University Press, 2004) 1, 6.

assumptions abouts authors and texts. It can be difficult for us as readers and audience members in the twenty-first century to move past 'the Enlightenment legacy of that necessary individual' but it is necessary that we try to do so.[336] By understanding theatrical creativity and industry we can trace theatre's influence on the development of copyright law, as well as the impact of law on theatrical practices.

So essential was polyvocal creativity in theatre that for the period 1558–1625 Masten even challenges Foucault's idea of the existence of a post-authorial 'constraining figure'.[337] He argues that the Jacobean text *The Knight of the Burning Pestle* (ascribed to Beaumont) 'defies even the ideally liberal constraint Foucault imagines' as fiction 'passing through something like a necessary or constraining figure'.[338] A similar argument could be made about *The Spanish Tragedy*.[339] By contrast, an unstable text such as *The Taming of The Shrew* could be viewed as passing through the constraining figure of Shakespeare while still accepting the input of others in the Lord Chamberlain's Men.[340] Yet, it is Ben Jonson, more than Shakespeare, who stands out as a self-conscious 'possessive' author in theatre at this time, aware of the value of what he contributed as a writer (to the print and performance commodities) and thus cognisant of the need to assert his voice as author-figure in print and on stage.[341] Jonson, along with posthumous appreciation of Shakespeare, helped lay the groundwork for the idea of individualist authority to come to prominence in theatre after the Restoration in 1660. Nonetheless, the Elizabethan/Jacobean periods demonstrate that it is possible for a collaborative product – the play – to be created successfully in an environment that does not prize, or reward, individual authorship through property rights.

Post-Restoration, someone akin to that author-figure emerged gradually in widespread theatrical practice and, eventually, in legal personhood (author) and property objecthood (copyright work). Thus, Loewenstein argues that the gradual development of the 'abstract notion of the copyright work' from the seventeenth century to the twentieth century began with the 'expansion of authorial rights within the seventeenth-century literary market'.[342] By the time of the Statute of Anne 1710, the dramatist had grown in esteem and authorial attribution of plays in print and in stage playbills had become the norm. Although the primary immediate beneficiaries of the 1710 Act were publishers, the Statute referred to 'authors' and over the eighteenth century it enabled writers to become increasingly assertive of their rights in the legal sphere at the Courts of Chancery and the Kings' Bench.

Copyright scholarship has long grappled with the consequences of legal authorship post-1710, with the Romanticism of the late eighteenth century and early-to-mid nineteenth century seen as providing the intellectual justification

[336] Masten (n 12) 352.
[337] Foucault (n 11).
[338] Masten (n 12) 352.
[339] Smith (n 100).
[340] Marino (n 56).
[341] Loewenstein (n 75).
[342] Loewenstein (n 47) 102.

for individual ownership rights. Nonetheless, an author-figure began to emerge in theatrical practice and in law well before the 'Romantic' era. Romanticism may have helped cement the concept of authorial ownership but it did not originate it.

Certainly, the Romantic conception of authorship appears to have influenced the law and, consequently, ideas of ownership of texts.[343] Bently argues there is a 'complimentary and reinforcing connection' between the 'emergence of the proprietary author at the end of the eighteenth century' and the 'growth of the powerful, modern, romantic conception of authorship'.[344]

Yet, even if the connection is not causative, but merely 'reinforcing', it remains worth examining, since enforcement at law fortifies the author function at the economic, societal and cultural levels.

We can trace individualist notions of authorship and ownership as the law evolved from the Statute of Anne through subsequent case law over performance rights. This culminated in nineteenth century reform legislation in 1833 and 1842, whereby the law moved from the mere protection of playbooks (from unauthorised printing and reprinting), to preventing unlicensed performances of play-texts.[345] These threads were joined together by the 1911 Copyright Act, which for the first time in UK law protected not 'books' or 'dramatic pieces' as separate entities, but dramatic works – property-objects encompassing a bundle of rights.

Along with collaboration, a notable recurring theme throughout the history of English theatre is the significance of informal norms. In the Elizabethan era, normative cooperation ensured different companies did not compete to perform each other's plays.[346] In the period 1770–1800 the London patent theatres cooperated to ensure unpublished plays such as *The School for Scandal* were performed at only one venue.[347] This provides one more link between theatre in history and today's theatre world, where the norms of theatre practice remain of great importance, as I outline in chapter three.

However, before I turn to analysis of present day copyright law in the next chapter, it is worth contemplating copyright law's underlying philosophy. As legal property, copyright is at the core of a system that perpetuates individualist notions of authorship. Ownership of property rights is more straightforward – and transactions easier to complete – when there are fewer owners. Royalties and licence fees may be seen in this context as the supposed 'return' on capital investment in the author function.

Here we are haunted by the questions raised by post-modernism: Barthes envisaged that once published the text cannot be controlled by the author and can only be understood through mediation between reader and other texts; Foucault asked us to imagine texts circulating without the need of an author-figure.[348] Yet, Masten

[343] Bently (n 52) 973, referring to the claim of Foucault that the modern author was born in the 1700s.
[344] ibid, 978.
[345] Miller (n 3).
[346] Lauriat (n 61).
[347] Gerland (n 232).
[348] Bently (n 52) 973. See also Foucault (n 11) and Barthes (n 11).

states that even Foucault must admit that it is, ironically enough, a form of 'pure romanticism' to imagine a culture devoid of all such mechanisms.[349] Some version of the author-figure is an inevitability. Redefining the Beckett/Foucault point, Masten finally asks: 'What, or rather how, does it matter who are speaking?'[350]

One answer is that the 'what' and the 'how' matter *in law* when parties are in dispute.[351] What does it matter who is the author-figure? How was the work created? These questions matter because that author-figure who created the work is in law the owner, in the first instance, of the dramatic work as an object of property. Latour and Lowe acknowledge this reality with their quip that 'the notion of the author' has become 'fuzzy' which complicates the issue of 'what happens to copyright royalties'.[352] This question – what happens to ownership in an era when authorship has been thoroughly deconstructed – demands to be answered.

Thus, in theatre when parties are in dispute over such questions lawyers and courts are given the difficult task of answering questions of authorship and ownership in a way that does justice to the parties (and, arguably, the wider theatre culture). This task begets its own questions regarding how modern drama typically gets created in the twenty-first century, and who typically claims the role of author (or joint author). When collaboration proceeds smoothly, certain parties (actors, directors, producers) may not need the property rights typified by authorial copyright; but when disputes occur, such rights can offer leverage to one party over another.

Can we as copyright lawyers define the author and the work in a way that complements Barthes' and Foucault's critical literary approach; or are law and theatre studies two different systems, incapable of communicating with one another?[353] How much attention should judges pay to literary or aesthetic matters?

Having undertaken analysis of the period 1558–1911, I now turn to how it may aid the recognition of authorship in the present. In the chapter that follows, I explore how authorship is performed in modern theatre (referring to empirical research); I consider how copyright law responds when disputes arise; and finally I query whether legal reform is required to better take account of theatrical practice.

[349] Masten (n 12) 351.
[350] ibid, 352.
[351] See generally M Rose, *Authors in Court: Scenes From the Theater of Copyright* (Cambridge, MA: Harvard University Press, 2016).
[352] B Latour and A Lowe, 'The migration of the aura, or how to explore the original through its fac similes' 1, 5–6, available at www.bruno-latour.fr/sites/default/files/108-ADAM-FACSIMILES-GB.pdf – originally published in T Bartscherer (ed), *Switching Codes: Thinking Through Digital Technology in the Humanities and the Arts* (Chicago: University of Chicago Press, 2010) 275.
[353] N Luhmann, *Law as a Social System* (Oxford: Oxford University Press, 2004).

3

Copyright Law and Performing Authorship in Theatre – Exploring the Contrasting Roles of the Playwright, Director and Performers

Introduction

Duncan Wu observes that 'all literary processes are collaborative, but theatre is more so than any other'.[1] This was true in the Elizabethan period and it remains true now. Yet, the precise context of that collaboration and the relationship between the parties matters greatly. Having examined the intertwined history of copyright law, authorship and the dramatic work in print and on stage from 1558–1911 in chapter two, in this chapter I move on to the modern age, with theatre competing with cinema, television, radio and other media for the public's attention. I explore the way that contemporary works of theatre are created and evaluate the question of how the law should recognise the authors and owners of such works. The very nature of dramatic works makes this exploration a challenge:

> As the text is translated into stage action it may acquire qualities entirely dependent on the collision of talents, the precise nature of which remains incalculable.[2]

In surveying contemporary theatre my focus is on a wide range of plays, from those that resemble single-author texts (by Samuel Beckett, Harold Pinter, Martin McDonagh, etc.) to works that feature substantial revision through workshops (by Caryl Churchill, David Edgar, Marie Jones, etc.) to highly collaborative 'devised'

[1] D Wu (ed), *Making Plays: Interviews with Contemporary British Dramatists* (Basingstoke: Macmillan Press Ltd, 2000) 9.

[2] ibid. See also B Salter, 'Taming the trojan horse: an Australian perspective of dramatic authorship' (2009) 56 *Journal of The Copyright Society of The USA* 789; B Salter and K Bowrey, 'Dramatic copyright and the "Disneyfication" of theatre space' in K Bowrey and M Handler, *Law and Creativity in the age of the Entertainment Franchise* (Cambridge: Cambridge University Press, 2017) 123 D Simone, *Copyright and Collective Authorship: Locating the Authors of Collaborative Work* (Cambridge: Cambridge University Press, 2019); YH Lee, 'The persistence of the text: the concept of the work in copyright law – Part I' (2018) *Intellectual Property Quarterly* 22 and J Griffiths, 'Dematerialization, Pragmatism and the European Copyright Revolution' (2013) 33 *Oxford Journal of Legal Studies* 767, 787–90.

pieces (by Complicité, Frantic Assembly, Forced Entertainment, etc.).[3] UK theatre finds remarkably varied ways to accommodate different forms of creativity. If legal and humanities scholars have attempted to deconstruct the author in the abstract, theatre participants have put such theories into their practice. As we shall see, the development of 'devised' theatre from the 1970s onward can be viewed as an example of this radical challenge to individualist or Romantic authorship.

In order to assess theatrical authorship, in the first part of this chapter I assess the current law on: (i) the copyright work, (ii) originality and (iii) authorship and joint authorship of plays. I explore twentieth century and twenty-first century legislation and case law in the UK jurisdiction on the question of how to define works of drama in light of the concept of originality, making comparative reference to relevant rules and case law approaches in common law jurisdictions such as the US, Canada, Australia and India. The analysis of the original dramatic work in this chapter builds upon recent discussions of the work concept undertaken by scholars such as Griffiths and Sherman.[4] I examine the work's material and immaterial boundaries in the context of theatre.[5]

In the second part of this chapter I explore theatre studies literature concerning the way works of drama are created, referring to insights from the 20 empirical interviews I undertook between 2011–13 with UK theatre participants. On the question of how dramatic works are authored I keep in mind Masten's point that even post-modern collaboration is often viewed 'as a mere subset or aberrant kind of individual authorship'.[6] I aim to show that in contemporary theatre, collaboration is far from aberrant – it is, in fact, the norm. Individual authors sometimes do provide dramatic works to theatre companies that are 'fully-formed'; yet in the case of revised works, collaboration via the workshop and rehearsal process can alter the play before it becomes a final text. In devised theatre the final play as performed is constitutive of a highly collaborative process. In light of this, I consider questions of credit and ownership.[7] I reflect on how authorship relates to ownership, as well as the way plays are licensed and how revenues are distributed.[8] The chapter concludes by considering whether copyright law, as currently legislated, can take account of the above processes, and what reforms, if any, might better facilitate the creative processes of theatre.

[3] S Shepherd and M Wallis, *Drama/Theatre/Performance* (London: Routledge, 2004) 1–8. See also A Field, 'All Theatre is Devised and Text-based' *The Guardian* (April 21 2009), available at www.guardian.co.uk/stage/theatreblog/2009/apr/21/theatre-devised-text-based.

[4] Griffiths (n 2). See also B Sherman, 'What is a work?' (2011) 12 *Theoretical Inquiries in Law* 99.

[5] L McDonagh, 'Plays, Performances and Power Struggles – Examining Copyright's Integrity in the Field of Theatre' (2014) 77 *The Modern Law Review* 533.

[6] J Masten, 'Beaumont and/or Fletcher: Collaboration and the Interpretation of Renaissance Drama' (1992) 52 *English Literary History* 337, 341.

[7] E Cooper, 'Joint authorship and copyright in comparative perspective: the emergence of divergence in the UK and USA' (2015) 62 *Journal of the Copyright Society of the USA* 245.

[8] The 2015 Writers Agreement negotiated by the Writers' Guild of Great Britain aims to deal with such disputes in advance, see https://writersguild.org.uk/wp-content/uploads/2015/02/WGGB_booklet_jun12_contracts_i.pdf. For data on theatre sales see https://uktheatre.org/theatre-industry/news/2018-sales-data-released-uk-theatre-and-society-of-london-theatre/. For the Society for Theatre Research see www.str.org.uk/publications/annual-publications/. For Theatre collecting societies see www.concordtheatricals.co.uk/resources/intro-to-licensing.

Understanding the Work in Modern Copyright Law

Turning to the work concept, I outlined in chapter two that the legal rights over plays changed over time during the eighteenth and nineteenth centuries. Initially only the printed text was protected, but by the time of the Copyright Act 1911 it was accepted that copyright ought to be a bundle of rights, protecting texts in print, performances of plays and dramatic adaptations of literary texts such as novels. Here I undertake an in-depth exploration of how copyright law defines and protects the *work*, referring to twentieth and twenty-first century case law in the UK, including relevant EU law aspects. I outline how, despite a range of case law since 1911, the modern work concept remains a conceptually under-developed one within copyright jurisprudence.[9] On this, Sherman argues that the work under copyright is an uncertain, 'fabricated' concept; while Pila states it is 'ontologically unstable'.[10] It may be that this conceptual vagueness stems from a belief on the part of judges that the concept ought to be kept flexible in order to allow various different types of original creativity to be protected. However, this under-development results in a great deal of uncertainty – particularly so in light of recent decisions at the CJEU level concerning originality, as I explore later on.[11] It is clear, however, that although the material boundaries of the work embody the original creation of the author, what is protected by copyright is not limited by this material form. For a performative work such as a play this seems particularly evident.[12]

I begin by examining the law's conception of the dramatic work, making comparative analysis of the musical work (like drama, a performative work) and the work of literature (which resembles a dramatic work in the textual sense).

Original Dramatic Works under the Copyright, Designs and Patents Act (CDPA) 1988

Under UK copyright doctrine, copyright arises upon the fixation of an original expression, in this case the dramatic work.[13] There is little guidance in the

[9] Copyright Act 1911 and Copyright Act 1956. See also Dramatic and Musical Performers Protection Act 1925 and Dramatic and Musical Performers Protection Act 1958.

[10] Sherman (n 4) 120, noting that the work is a 'fabricated concept' and J Pila, 'Copyright and its categories of original works' (2010) 30 *Oxford Journal of Legal Studies* 229, 236–37, noting that the work concept may be 'ontologically unstable'. See also J Pila, *The Subject Matter of Intellectual Property* (Oxford: Oxford University Press, 2017); A Pottage, 'Introduction: The Fabrication of Persons and Things' in A Pottage and M Mundy (eds), *Law, Anthropology and the Constitution of the Social – Making Persons and Things* (Cambridge: Cambridge University Press, 2004) 1 and M Foucault, 'What Is an Author?' in JM Marsh, JD Caputo and M Westphal (eds), *Modernity and its Discontents* (New York: Fordham University Press, 1992) 299.

[11] The work concept remains open to claims of copyright over unusual objects eg the ineffable taste of cheese even if such claims rarely succeed – Case C-310/17 *Levola Hengelo BV v Smilde Foods BV* [2018] Bus LR 2442.

[12] Griffiths (n 2). It is possible for a work to fall into more than one category eg in *Norowzian v Arks Ltd (No.2)* [2000] EMLR 67 it was held that a film can also be a dramatic work. Thus, a literary work such as a novel that is later read out (performed) on stage could be considered as a dramatic work in that context as well as being a literary one in its original form/context.

[13] Copyright Designs and Patents Act 1988 (CDPA), ss 1(1)(a) and 3(2), available at www.legislation.gov.uk/ukpga/1988/48/contents. Regarding the standard of originality see Case C-5/08 *Infopaq*

Berne Convention[14] or the TRIPS[15] agreement on defining dramatic works.[16] National jurisdictions therefore have a significant amount of discretion as to how to define the work of drama. Yet, the CDPA 1988 does not provide a full definition of 'dramatic work' – although it is stated that a dramatic work includes a work of dance or mime.[17] The courts have deepened the concept, emphasising that the key element is that a dramatic work must be capable of performance.[18] This means that such a work must have sufficient unity and coherence that would allow it to be performed, as in the case of a scripted work, as held by the Judicial Committee of the Privy Council in the case of *Green v Broadcasting Corp of New Zealand*.[19]

There is no doubt that in theatre the work is originated with performance in mind. In the case of a play, what is protected by the law – the script – must be viewed through this allographic lens, as a work which is intended to be realised via performance, typically by people other than the author.[20] Moreover, as I explore over the latter part of this chapter, the dramatic work is often developed, at least in part, via workshops and rehearsals, with directors, actors and producers making contributions.[21] In its early stages a work of theatre is therefore in

International A/S v Danske Dagblades Forening [2009] ECR I-6569; Case C–393/09 *Bezpecˇnostnı' Softwarova' Asociace-Svaz Softwarove' Ochrany v Ministerstvo Kultury* [2010] ECR I-1397; Case C-403/08 *Football Association Premier League and Others v QC Leisure and Other* [2011] ECR I-9083; Case C-429/08 *Karen Murphy v Media Protection Services Ltd* [2011] ECR I-0000; Case C-145/10 *Painer v Standard Verlags GmbH* [2011] ECR I-0000 and Case C-604/10 *Football Dataco Ltd v Yahoo!* UK Ltd [2012] ECR I-0000. See also *Newspaper Licensing Agency v Meltwater* [2010] EWHC 3099 (Ch); [2011] RPC 7; *Newspaper Licensing Agency v Meltwater* [2011] EWCA Civ 890; [2012] Bus LR 53 and *Public Relations Consultants Association Limited v The Newspaper Licensing Agency Limited and Others* [2013] UKSC 18. For analysis of the standard see J Davis and A Durant, 'To protect or not to protect? The Eligibility of commercially used short verbal texts for copyright and trade mark protection' (2011) *Intellectual Property Quarterly* 345 and A Rahmatian, 'Originality in UK Copyright Law: The Old "Skill and Labour" Doctrine Under Pressure' (2013) 44 *IIC* 4.

[14] Berne Convention for the Protection of Literary and Artistic Works (September 9, 1886; revised 1896 (Paris), 1908 (Berlin), 1914 (Additional Protocol), 1928 (Rome), 1948 (Brussels), 1967 (Stockholm), 1971 (Paris) – as amended 1979) hereafter referred to as Berne Convention; available at www.wipo.int/treaties/en/ip/berne/trtdocs_wo001.html.

[15] Agreement on Trade-Related Aspects of Intellectual Property Rights, Annex 1C of the Marrakesh Agreement Establishing the World Trade Organization (1994) (hereafter referred to as TRIPS); available at www.wto.org/english/docs_e/legal_e/27-trips_01_e.htm.

[16] S Ricketson and J Ginsburg, *International Copyright and Neighbouring Rights – The Berne Convention and Beyond*, 2nd edn (Oxford: Oxford University Press, 2006) 406–7. Rickenson and Ginsburg noted that the Berne Convention in fact covers a number of works which may not always be classed as 'literary or artistic works'. Thus, the scope of this expression is wide.

[17] CDPA 1988, s 3(1). See also C Waelde and P Schlesinger, 'Music and Dance – beyond copyright text?' (2011) 8 *SCRIPT-ed* 257.

[18] *Norowzian v Arks Ltd (No 2)* [2000] FSR 363, noting that a film can be a dramatic work. See also P Kamina, *Film Copyright in the European Union*, 2nd edn (Cambridge: Cambridge University Press, 2016) 78 and Simone (n 2) 186 on whether some element akin to a 'story' is required. See also *Nova Games Ltd v Mazooma Productions Ltd* [2007] RPC 589.

[19] *Green v Broadcasting Corp of New Zealand* [1989] 2 All ER 1056. See also *Banner Universal Motion Pictures Ltd v Endemol Shine Group Ltd and Others* [2017] EWHC 2600 (Ch).

[20] N Goodman, *Languages of Art* (Indianapolis: Hackett Publishing Co Inc, 1976) 99–123.

[21] CDPA 1988, s 3(2). See also *Brighton and Dubbeljoint v Jones* [2004] EWHC 1157 (Ch); [2004] EMLR 507.

a profound state of flux. Indeed, even some 'finished' dramatic works do not appear to be stable, singular objects of property; subsequent interpretations may push against their boundaries.[22] The work concept can thus fail to provide legal certainty in theatre where there is an *iterative* concept of the work at play. While copyright can take account of this via licensing of adaptations or derivative works (to use US parlance), this can be impractical, and it can necessitate the imposition of legal fictions (such as the finding of implied licences based on the prior behaviour of the parties).[23] On fixation, it is worth taking note of how easy it is to record the work with modern technology – iterative works such as plays can exist in multiple 'fixed' versions (written down by hand, typed into documents stored digitally, or recorded via camera or even smartphone) all of which may have evidentiary usefulness for establishing how the work came to be created, and who contributed to it.

The uncertain nature of the dramatic work can be observed by analysing the 2019 ruling in *Kogan v Martin*. Here, the Court of Appeal held that in the case of a dramatic work that goes through several drafts – in this case the screenplay for the film *Florence Foster Jenkins* – the final version of the screenplay should be considered as the culmination of those drafts, not as several separate adaptations (each with its own, albeit derivative, copyright).[24] Simone argues that the Court of Appeal approach has the advantage 'of being truer to life compared to the alternative, which would require salami-slicing the work in a way that is likely to seem unreal to its creators'.[25] For large scale collaborations such as Wikipedia it is evident that 'salami-slicing' creates complications; if each contribution to Wikipedia creates a separate work the result is a 'millefeuille' of adapted (derivative) copyright works (assuming they are sufficiently original to be protected).[26] Yet, the bond between Wikipedia editors is likely to be less strong than between the various contributors to a play (there will also likely be far fewer contributors to the play). Furthermore, the *Kogan* decision appears to depart from the 2004 High Court decision in *Brighton v Jones* where an initial short scenario – written by the director and used by the playwright as inspiration for her first draft of the play – appeared to be considered a separate dramatic work in its own right

[22] K Wyver, 'Not waiting for Godot: new show tackles Beckett's ban on women' *The Guardian* (18 October 2020), available at www.theguardian.com/stage/2020/oct/18/not-waiting-for-godot-new-show-tackles-becketts-ban-on-women.

[23] L McDonagh, 'Rearranging the Roles of the Performer and the Composer in the Music Industry – the Potential Significance of Fisher v Brooker' (2012) *Intellectual Property Quarterly* 64. See also CL Fisk, 'Will Work for Screen Credit: Labour and the Law in Hollywood' in P McDonald, E Carman, E Hoyt and P Drake (eds), *Hollywood and the Law* (London: Palgrave, 2015) 235; N Shemtov, *Beyond the Code: Protection of Non-Textual Features of Software* (Oxford: Oxford University Press, 2017) and L McDonagh, 'Protecting traditional music under copyright (and choosing not to do enforce it)' in E Bonadio and N Lucchi (eds), *Non-Conventional Copyright – Do New and Atypical Works Deserve Protection?* (Cheltenham: Edward Elgar, 2018) 151.

[24] *Kogan v Martin* [2019] EWCA Civ 1645. D Simone, 'Kogan v Martin: A New Framework for Joint Authorship in Copyright Law' (2020) 83 *The Modern Law Review* 877. See also the subsequent IPEC ruling – *Martin v Kogan* [2021] EWHC 24 (Ch).

[25] ibid, 881.

[26] Simone (n 2) 88–89.

from the play, and thus requiring a licence.[27] The fact that in the *Brighton* case the director and playwright had not begun the process with the explicit mutual intention to collaborate in *writing* a final joint dramatic work together may be a key distinction between *Kogan* and *Brighton*, explaining the different approaches taken to the work concept. In *Kogan*, by refusing to engage in 'salami-slicing' of the various drafts of the *Florence Foster Jenkins* script, the court could focus on the *collaboration* aspect of the joint authorship test with respect to the iterative work; whereas in *Brighton* the court focused less on collaboration and maintained a strict separation between two works – Brighton's early scenario (faxed to Jones) and Jones' final script (produced post-workshops). I reflect on this further below on the joint authorship test.

Original Musical Works

Musical works offer a useful counterpoint because, like dramatic works, they are capable of performance and are often authored collaboratively. In the key UK case on musical works – *Sawkins v Hyperion* – Mummery LJ drew attention to similarities between collaborators working towards musical works and dramatic works:

> In principle, there is no reason for regarding the actual notes of music as the only matter covered by musical copyright, any more than, in the case of a dramatic work, only the words to be spoken by the actors are covered by dramatic copyright. Added stage directions may affect the performance of the play on the stage or on the screen and have an impact on the performance seen by the audience. *Stage directions are as much part of a dramatic work as plot, character and dialogue.*[28] (emphasis added)

Although the case is often cited for its definition of music under copyright, these comments about drama are highly relevant, confirming that along with the dialogue and characters, stage directions can be protected by copyright.[29] In addition, although musical arrangements of public domain works were at issue, the ruling in *Sawkins* gives weight to the argument that if an author creates a new adaptation of a public domain dramatic work the new version will be protected by copyright to the extent of its new originality (any new dialogue, plot, stage directions, etc).[30] On this Marowitz argues that such adaptations 'should be entitled

[27] *Brighton and Dubbeljoint v Jones* [2004] EWHC 1157 (Ch); [2004] EMLR 507.

[28] *Sawkins v Hyperion* [2005] EWCA Civ 565; [2005] 1 WLR 3281.

[29] *Corelli v Gray* [1913] TLR 570.

[30] DS Stein, 'Every Move That She Makes: Copyright Protection for Stage Directions and the Fictional Character Standard' (2012–2013) 34 *Cardozo L. Rev.* 1571 noting that no US court has as yet upheld a copyright claim over stage directions. See also L Temme, 'To Be, or Not To Be: The Potential Consequences of Granting Copyright Protection for Stage Directions' (2018) 9 *Cybaris, An Intellectual Property Review* 1; M Livingston, 'Inspiration or Imitation: Copyright Protection for Stage Directions' (2009) 50 *B.C.L. Rev.* 427 and D Leichtman, 'Most Unhappy Collaborators: An Argument Against

to copyright protection because they are the original outgrowth of a director's imagination'.[31]

On the issue of joint authorship musical cases provide useful precedents relevant to drama. On viewing drafts of a joint work cumulatively, the approach taken by the Court of Appeal in *Kogan* (to dramatic works) can be contrasted with that of the view of the Court of Appeal in its 2008 decision in *Fisher v Brooker* (on musical works).[32] In *Fisher* the court regarded the early demo version of 'A Whiter Shade of Pale' composed and recorded by Gary Brooker by himself alone on piano, to be a separate musical work from its later hit arrangement, featuring the famous organ part (and thus, as in *Brighton*, the finding of an implied licence was required for legal use of the first work in the second).[33] The divergence between *Kogan* and *Fisher* may indicate that the question of how to assess works of joint authorship will be framed differently in the case of collaborators who begin a project together with the intention to create a jointly authored work (as occurred with the various drafts of the screenplay for *Florence Foster Jenkins*), than for a project that begins with a single author, with later collaborators adding key elements subsequently (as happened with the hit arrangement of 'A Whiter Shade of Pale').

Original Literary Works

Although plays are sometimes read as literature, dramatic works are not the same as literary works in UK law: literary works are not required to possess a performative quality.[34] This chimes with the view of scholars of literature and theatre such as Masten, who notes that, for example, a poem is clearly a text designed to be read; whereas a play is not limited to a communication between author and reader, and encompasses a representation of a theatrical experience.[35] Yet, due to the textual similarities between the dramatic and the literary, the way copyright protects works of literature is worth evaluating.

Under the CDPA original pieces of literature can be protected as 'literary works' as long as they are fixed in some medium.[36] There is no specific statutory definition of literariness; nor is there a legislative limit on the length a literary work

the Recognition of Property Ownership in Stage Directions' (1996) 20 *Colum.-VLA J.L. & Arts* 683. See also *Wood v Boosey* (1868) LR 3 QB 223 and *Redwood Music v Chappell* [1982] RPC 109.

[31] C Marowitz, 'Letter to the Editor, Stage Copyrights; What the Director Brings' *The New York Times* (5 February 2006).

[32] *Fisher v Brooker* [2008] EWCA Civ 287. See also *Fisher v Brooker* [2009] UKHL 41.

[33] This can be contrasted with the earlier High Court decision where the court viewed the early version as a 'sketch' – *Fisher v Brooker* [2006] EWHC 3239 (Ch); [2007] EMLR 256.

[34] CDPA 1988, s 3. That HH Judge Hacon appeared to treat the script as a literary work, rather than a dramatic work, was a crucial error in the first instance decision in *Martin v Kogan* [2017] EWHC 2927 (IPEC) at para 45.

[35] Masten (n 6) 341.

[36] CDPA 1988, s 3(2). See *Merchandising Corporation of America Inc v Harpbond Inc* [1983] FSR 32.

might be.[37] This has caused a debate within copyright discourse over whether copyright protection applies to very short pieces of text. This has relevance not only for literature but also for dramatic works, given that some *avant garde* plays can feature few words and may be made up mostly of stage directions.[38] The traditional view in UK copyright jurisprudence is that no matter how few or how many words it may contain, to be protected a work must be both sufficiently 'literary' and 'original'.[39] Literariness in this context is not a high standard – it merely means the work should convey some literary meaning. It is clear from the 1982 case of *Exxon* that an original, invented word such as Exxon fails on this count: rather than affording 'information, instruction or pleasure' the word Exxon signifies nothing, and therefore cannot be protected.[40]

Up until recently, very short pieces of text – such as headlines and titles – were generally perceived as falling outside the scope of legal protection in the UK.[41] However, rulings at the EU level over the past decade on originality give credence to the claim that headlines and titles are in fact separate 'original' copyright works to the works which they represent, and are therefore worthy of protection in their own right.[42] In fact, in EU law originality has come to be the main criterion by which to define the work concept.[43]

[37] Pila (n 10) 236–37, noting that the concept of the copyright work may be inherently ontologically unstable. Furthermore, in light of Case C-393/09 *Bezpečnostní softwarová asociace – Svaz softwarové ochrany v Ministry of Culture of the Czech Republic* [2010] ECR I-1397 (hereafter referred to as BSA), it may no longer be the case that the UK subject-matter categories are valid under (post-Brexit retained) EU law, a point in line with E Rosati, 'Originality in a Work, or a Work of Originality: The effects of the infopaq decision' (2011) 33 *EIPR* 746.

[38] See J Davis and A Durant (n 13); C Moran, 'How much is too much? Copyright protection of short portions of text in the United States and European Union after Infopaq International A/S v. Danske Dagblades' (2011) 6 *Washington Journal of Law, Technology and Arts* 247 and D Vaver, 'Intellectual Property: Still a Bargain?' (2012) 34 *EIPR* 579, 583–84. From the philosophical perspective of 'author's rights', copyright is laid down to protect the rights inherent in authorship itself. For further analysis of the justifications of intellectual property see M Spence, *Intellectual Property* (Oxford: Oxford University Press, 2007) 43–68 and J Waldron, 'From Authors to Copiers: Individual Rights and Social Values in Intellectual Property' (1993) 68 *Chicago-Kent Law Review* 841; J Litman, 'The Public Domain' (1990) 39 *Emory LJ* 965, 969 and T Parks, 'Does Copyright Matter?' *New York Review of Books Blog* (August 2012); available at www.nybooks.com/blogs/nyrblog/2012/aug/14/does-copyright-matter/.

[39] *Exxon Corporation v Exxon Insurance Consultants International Limited* [1982] Ch 119. See also *Baigent and Leigh v The Random House Group* [2007] EWCA Civ 247. The first instance decision was *Baigent and Leigh v The Random House Group* [2006] EWHC 719 (Ch).

[40] ibid.

[41] Vaver (n 38) 583–84. CDPA 1988, s 16(3)(a); available at www.legislation.gov.uk/ukpga/1988/48/contents. *Francis Day & Hunter Limited v Twentieth Century Fox Corp Limited* [1940] AC 112; *Ladbroke (Football) Ltd v William Hill (Football) Ltd* [1964] 1 WLR 273; *Exxon Corporation v Exxon Insurance Consultants International Limited* [1982] Ch 119; Case C-5/08 *Infopaq International A/S v Danske Dagblades Forening* [2009] ECR I-6569 ('*Infopaq*'); *Newspaper Licensing Agency v Meltwater* [2010] EWHC 3099 (Ch) ('*Meltwater*').

[42] *Infopaq* and *Meltwater* (n 41).

[43] Rosati (n 37).

Original Works in EU Copyright Law – Assessing the 'Dematerialised' Work of Originality

The UK CDPA in sections 3–8 specifies a limited number of 'closed' categories of work. To be protected an expression must meet the requirements of a specific type, that is, literary, musical, dramatic, artistic, etc. As outlined earlier, dramatic works must be performative in nature and must have sufficient unity to be performed.[44] One effect of EU jurisprudence has been to accelerate copyright law's shift from a focus on the form in which the protected subject-matter is embodied to the 'intangible essence contained within that form'.[45] In the same vein, European decisions over the past decade indicate that the UK's traditional work/fixation concepts are no longer tenable within the EU courts' broad, 'dematerialized' requirement of originality, which is founded upon the 'author's intellectual creation'.[46] As I explore here, although originality has always been required of works, it is now entwined with the work concept itself.

The 2009 CJEU ruling in *Infopaq* established 'intellectual creation' as the standard of originality for all works in the EU.[47] Subsequent CJEU rulings indicate that this can be evidenced by the author making 'free and creative choices' (Joined Cases C-403/08 and C-429/08 *Football Association Premier League/Murphy*) or showing a 'personal touch' (Case C-145/10 *Painer*).[48] In the same vein, the CJEU in Case C-469/17 *Funke Medien* remarked:

> [I]t is for the national court to ascertain whether […] the author was able to make free and creative choices capable of conveying to the reader the originality of the subject matter at issue, the originality of which arises from the choice, sequence and combination of the words by which the author expressed his or her creativity in an original manner and achieved a result which is an intellectual creation […], whereas the mere intellectual effort and skill [is] not relevant in that regard […].[49]

UK case law prior to *Infopaq* had not required creativity as such, but rather 'skill, labour and judgement'.[50] The UK courts accepted 'intellectual creation' as the new originality standard in *Newspaper Licensing Agency v Meltwater*[51] and *SAS Institute*

[44] C Handig 'Infopaq International a/S v Danske Dagblades Forening: is the term "work" of the CDPA 1988 in line with the European Directives?' (2010) 32 *EIPR* 53.

[45] YH Lee, 'The persistence of the text: the concept of the work in copyright law – Part II' (2018) *Intellectual Property Quarterly* 107, 108.

[46] Griffiths (n 2) 787–90.

[47] ibid.

[48] Joined Cases C-403/08 and C-429/08 *Football Association Premier League Ltd & Others v QC Leisure & Others; Karen Murphy v Media Protection Services Ltd* [2011] ECR I-9083; [2012] Bus LR 1321 ('Murphy') and Case C-145/10 *Eva Marie Painer v Standard VerlagsGmbH et. al* [2012] ECDR 6 ('Painer').

[49] Case C-469/17 *Funke Medien NRW GmbH v Bundesrepublik Deutschland* EU:C:2019:623.

[50] *Sawkins v Hyperion* [2005] EWCA Civ 565; [2005] 1 WLR 3281. *Ladbroke (Football) Ltd v William Hill (Football) Ltd* [1964] 1 WLR 273. See also *University of London Press Ltd v University Tutorial Press Ltd* [1916] 2 Ch D 601.

[51] *Meltwater* (n 41).

v World Programming.[52] Yet, in UK law it remains unclear whether the originality standard is now higher post-*Infopaq*[53] (intellectual creation) than it was before (skill, labour and judgement) as the cases that have arisen since *Infopaq* involve creative works that would have satisfied either standard.[54]

Further to this dictum on originality, in Case C-310/17 *Levola Hengelo* the CJEU stated that the notion of 'work' is an autonomous concept of EU law, meaning it must be applied by national courts in a uniform fashion, and no requirement of aesthetic or artistic value may be applied.[55] It is not entirely clear as to what limitations on the autonomous work concept exist, apart from the fact that a work must be the author's own intellectual creation.[56] Case law indicates there are some boundaries – in *Murphy* the CJEU emphasised that a football match cannot be a work of intellectual creation, a point perfectly in line with UK case law on dramatic works.[57] In *Levola* the claim for copyright in the taste of cheese was also denied for being ineffable and lacking sufficient permanence – also in tune with prior UK doctrine.[58] Nonetheless, as Griffiths argues, the shift to a general 'work' concept since *Infopaq* indicates that the UK's closed categories are no longer strictly tenable.[59] Arnold J (as he then was) in *SAS Institute Inc v World Programming Ltd* remarked:

> In the light of a number of recent judgments of the CJEU, it may be arguable that it is not a fatal objection to a claim that copyright subsists in a particular work that the work is not one of the kinds of work listed in section 1(1)(a) of the Copyright, Designs and Patents 1988 and defined elsewhere in that Act. Nevertheless, it remains clear that the putative copyright work must be a literary or artistic work within the meaning of Article 2(1) of the Berne Convention.[60]

On the work concept in UK doctrine, it is notable that the High Court in *Meltwater* held that in light of *Infopaq* a single newspaper headline could amount to an original literary work in its own right, that is, apart from the article which it represents, provided that it is the author's intellectual creation.[61] Proudman J apparently

[52] *SAS Institute Inc v World Programming Ltd* [2013] EWHC 69 (Ch).

[53] *Public Relations Consultants Association Limited v The Newspaper Licensing Agency Limited and Others* [2013] UKSC 18.

[54] Rosati (n 37).

[55] Case C-310/17 *Levola Hengelo BV v Smilde Foods BV* (n 11).

[56] *Infopaq* (n 41).

[57] *Murphy* (n 48).

[58] Case C-310/17 *Levola Hengelo BV v Smilde Foods BV* (n 11).

[59] Griffiths (n 2).

[60] *SAS Institute Inc v World Programming Ltd* [2010] EWHC 1829 (Ch).

[61] *Meltwater* (n 41), Proudman J at [61] (see also [62]–[67]). Proudman J referred to *Lamb v Evans* [1893] 1 Ch 218; *Francis Day & Hunter Limited v Twentieth Century Fox Corp Limited* [1940] AC 112; *Ladbroke (Football) Ltd v William Hill (Football) Ltd* [1964] 1 WLR 273; *Exxon Corporation v Exxon Insurance Consultants International Limited* [1982] Ch 119; [1982] RPC 69; *Shetland Times Limited v Wills*

accepted that a headline can be sufficiently literary.[62] Notably, Proudman J did not give much consideration to the idea that something could be original and literary but not a 'work'.[63] It is possible that in future, courts may give more credence to this notion.[64]

The overall effect of *Infopaq/Meltwater* is that headlines and titles can be protected separately under copyright if they are sufficiently 'original' and 'literary'.[65] Yet there is little guidance as to when a very short work will be sufficiently original[66] and literary and when it will not be.[67] Brexit means that from 2021 UK courts will no longer be obliged to follow CJEU decisions in this regard, though to the extent EU copyright principles have become part of the common law they will remain in place until legislative changes are made or the UK courts alter the doctrine. For present purposes – and in the absence of a UK precedent stating otherwise – I proceed on the basis that the elements of dramatic work identified by the UK courts, such as performativity, are still relevant to assessing whether a work of copyright exists in the context of theatre.[68]

Original Works – Comparative Insights

There is comparative value in considering the US position on originality of works of drama.[69] Section 102 of the US Copyright Act 1976 provides that original

[1997] EMLR 277 and *IceTV Pty Limited v Nine Network Australia Pty Limited* ('*IceTV*') (2009) 239 CLR 458 and the Federal Court of Australia in *Fairfax Media Publications Pty Limited v Reed International Books Australia Pty Limited* [2010] FCA 984 ('*Fairfax*') at [28]–[50].

[62] Pila (n 10). See also M Husovec, 'Intellectual Property Rights and Integration by Conflict: The Past, Present and Future' (2016) 18 *Cambridge Yearbook of European Legal Studies* 239, 261; J Griffiths, 'Constitutionalising or Harmonising? – The Court of Justice, the Right to Property and European Copyright Law' (2013) 38 *European Law Review* 65 and M Mimler, 'The Court of Justice of the European Union finds that copyright does not subsist in the taste of cheese spread (Levola Hengelo BV v Smilde Foods BV (Case C-310/17))' (2019) 115 *Intellectual Property Forum* 96.

[63] For an assessment of the notion of 'the work' see Sherman (n 4).

[64] *SAS Institute Inc v World Programming Ltd.* [2013] EWHC 69 (Ch) at [34] noting that something which is considered a 'language' is not a copyright work.

[65] Davis and Durant (n 13). J McCutcheon, 'Levola Hengelo BV v Smilde Foods BV: The Hard Work of Defining a Copyright Work' (2019) 82 *The Modern Law Review* 936.

[66] *Meltwater* (n 41), Proudman J at [63]–[72].

[67] On the 'literary' aspect of the analysis Proudman J clearly saw the headline as being a separate work from the underlying article. This point is significant because it arguably veers away from the dicta of Laddie J laid down in the case of *Hyperion v Warner*, where he stated that collapsing one copyright work into several different independent works was not a proper application of the law. Proudman J did not refer to the *Hyperion v Warner* case, but in any event she seemed satisfied that an original headline would be a separate work to the underlying article. *Hyperion Records Ltd v Warner Music* (UK) Ltd 19 May 1991, Ch D, unreported.

[68] Lee (n 2) 44.

[69] US Copyright Act 1976, 17 U.S.C. §§ 101–102. Fixation should be 'sufficiently permanent or stable' and thus 'perceived, reproduced or otherwise communicated' for a non-transitory period.

works of authorship are protected, but the definition of originality is left up to the courts.[70] In *Feist Publications v Rural Telephone Service Co*, the Supreme Court of the United States (SCOTUS) emphasised independent creation of a work with a 'minimal degree of creativity'. The decision in *Feist* that a telephone book was not protected was based on the view that a copyright work must have some creativity; whereas, an alphabetically arranged list of names lacked a creative spark or intellectual stamp.[71] Woodmansee reflects that in this narrow sense judges in the US are willing to entertain aesthetic requirements.[72] The US position is therefore not far away from the decisions in cases such as *Infopaq* on originality in the EU (and at present, in the UK post-*Meltwater/SAS*). In the US the categorisation of works is not based on closed categories – in section 102 dramatic works are, however, cited as one type of work that is protected. Dramatisations and adaptations are given specific recognition under section 101.[73] In the 1938 US case of *Seltzer v Sunbrock* the court held this type of work must feature some story elements, such as a simple plot or narrative, or the repetition of some action, speech, or character.[74] It is likely the US protection of dramatic works is comparable with the way UK law protects such works with respect to scripted dialogue, identifiable characters and detailed plot scenarios.[75] Moreover, although it has not yet been made explicit in US case law, Livingston argues that the straightforward application of key copyright principles 'would dictate that stage directions are subject to copyright protection'.[76]

The Supreme Court of Canada (SCC) in *CCH Canadian Ltd v Law Society of Upper Canada*[77] held that the Canadian originality standard is 'skill and judgment'.[78] While ruling that the US *Feist* standard was too high a threshold,

[70] I explore the idea/expression dichotomy in ch 4. See, eg *Baker v Selden*, 101 U.S. 99 (1880) 25 L. Ed. 841.

[71] *Feist Publications Inc v Rural Telephone Service Co Inc* 499 US 340 (1991). See also L Bently, 'Copyright and the Death of the Author in Literature and Law' (1994) 57 *The Modern Law Review* 973, 977.

[72] M Woodmansee, 'The Genius and the Copyright: Economic and Legal Conditions of the Emergence of the "Author"' (1984) 17 *Eighteenth Century Studies* 425, 440.

[73] It appears US courts rarely go beyond the categories and works analogous to the UK's categories – see eg *NBA v Motorola* 105 F. 3d. 841 (2nd Cir. 1997) holding that a basketball game is not a work of authorship).

[74] *Seltzer v Sunbrock* 22 F. Supp 621 (S.D. Cal. 1938).

[75] *Nichols v Universal Pictures Corporation*, 45 F.2d. 119 (2d. Cir. 1930); *Thomson v Larson* 147 F.3d. 195 (2d. Cir. 1998) 203–204 requiring objective indicia of the intent to be joint authors of the musical Rent. See also 'Recent Case, Copyright – Joint Authorship – Second Circuit Holds That Dramaturg's Contributions to the Musical Rent Did Not Establish Joint Authorship with Playwright-Composer – Thomson v. Larson' 147 F.3d. 195 (2d. Cir. 1998) (1999) 112 *Harv. L. Rev.* 964, 968–969.

[76] M. Livingston, 'Inspiration or Imitation: Copyright Protection for Stage Directions' (2009) 50 *B.C. L. Rev.* 427. 486. See, however, *Garcia v Google* 786 F.3d. 733 (9th Cir. 2015) (en banc) on performances and copyright works.

[77] *CCH Canadian v Law Society of Upper Canada* [2004] SCC 13. See also *Robertson v Thomson Corp* (2006) SCC 43.

[78] As noted earlier, the closest comparator with the UK is Ireland, but there is a lack of case law on point. Certainly, there is no reason to believe that at present the Irish standard of originality is different to the UK standard since both are under the umbrella of EU law's 'intellectual creation' threshold. The originality standard in Ireland under the CRRA 2000 would therefore be 'intellectual creation'.

the court also rejected the idea that pure 'sweat of the brow' labour was sufficient – this indicates that the Canadian standard is somewhere between the traditional UK 'skill, labour and judgement' up to 2010 (pre-*Infopaq/Meltwater*) and the US *Feist* standard of creativity.[79] This Canadian standard was cited with approval in the Indian Supreme Court case of *Eastern Book Company v DB Modak*[80] when assessing the literary work concept in the context of compilations.[81] In Ireland the originality standard appears to be in line with *Infopaq* and the subsequent UK case law.[82]

Canada utilises a closed list of categories in section 5(1) of its Copyright Act, including the specific category of dramatic works, in line with the UK approach.[83] However, Canada provides a more detailed definition. Section 2 of the Canadian Copyright Act (1985) defines 'dramatic work' to include 'any piece for recitation, choreographic work or mime, the scenic arrangement or acting form of which is fixed in writing or otherwise'.[84] This captures that the dramatic work as a whole need not be fixed in a static form (presumably because, by its nature, it cannot be) in order to be sufficiently fixed for copyright to arise. The term 'acting form' is not defined, but it likely includes stage directions, etc. as part of the essential (fixed) elements of the dramatic work. The SCC decision in *Cinar v Robinson* (2013) is relevant to the definition of a dramatic work, insofar as it is about a story board, characters and settings for a proposed TV series.[85] The court noted that the overall architecture, the characters and their interactions, etc. constituted the protected elements when they were the result of skill and judgement.[86] The earlier Canadian case of *Hutton v Canadian Broadcasting Corp.* (1989) (Alba. Q.B.) is also instructive on the 'dramatic' character of this kind of work – the court held that a TV show of music videos was not 'dramatic' because there was no story-line, no dramatic 'conceit' and no dramatic incident.[87]

This similarity between UK and Irish standards may change post-Brexit, as the UK will no longer be bound by the EU standard, and may choose to diverge. See L McDonagh and M Mimler, 'Intellectual Property Law and Brexit: A Retreat or a Reaffirmation of Jurisdiction?' in M Dougan (ed), *The UK After Brexit: Legal and Policy Challenges* (Cambridge: Intersentia, 2017) 159.

[79] CJ Craig, 'Resisting Sweat and Refusing Feist: Rethinking Originality After CCH' (2007) 40 *University of British Columbia Law Review* 69.

[80] *Eastern Book Company v DB Modak* (2008) 1 SCC 112.

[81] Copyright Act 1957, s 13 confers protection on literary works, dramatic works, musical works, and artistic works.

[82] The Irish case *Gormley v EMI Records (Ire) Ltd* [2000] 1 IR 74 remains the leading statement on originality in Irish copyright law, with the court alluding to some aspect of creativity being part of the requirement, a point in line with the later CJEU decisions. The specific topic of the 'author's intellectual creation' was not analysed explicitly in the more recent cases *Phonographic Performance (Ireland) Ltd v Foyle* [2015] IEHC 778 and *Sony Music Entertainment Ireland Ltd v UPC Communications Ireland Ltd* [2016] IECA 231 but there is no reason to believe the Irish threshold is not in line with the EU standard.

[83] Copyright Act, R.S.C. 1985, c. C-42, s 5(1).

[84] ibid, s 2.

[85] *Cinar Corp v Robinson* [2013] 3 SCR 1168.

[86] ibid, at [43]–[46].

[87] *Hutton v Canadian Broadcasting Corp.* [1989] A.J. No. 1193 (Alta. Q.B.) and *Cummings v Global Television Network Quebec, Limited Partnership* [2005] Q.J. No. 6707 (Que. S.C). The court cited the above US case of *Seltzer v Sunbrock* (n 74).

In Australia, like Canada, copyright law bears the strong influence of the UK system, with a closed list of works and a traditional standard of 'skill, labour and judgement'.[88] Yet, the case of *IceTV* indicates that some element of intellectual creativity forms part of the originality threshold, casting doubt on whether fact-based works can be protected.[89,90] In *IceTV* the court stated that 'original works emanate from authors' and such works should be the product of 'intellectual effort'.[91] The *IceTV* originality standard is thus broadly comparable with the *Infopaq/Meltwater* threshold. As in the UK, a performativity is a necessary quality of dramatic works in Australia.[92] Crucially, the specific issue of very short works – in this case a newspaper headline – was at issue in *Fairfax Media Publications Pty Limited v Reed International Books Australia Pty Limited* in 2010.[93] Unlike in the UK/EU, Bennett J stated that it was unlikely that copyright could subsist in a headline or title:

> Headlines generally are, like titles, simply too insubstantial and too short to qualify for copyright protection as literary works.[94]

Bennett J also made some important comments on the need for a 'work' to exist:

> There may well be writings of original words or phrases that simply do not reach the level of constituting a 'work', regardless of literary merit. This is not just because they are short, as a deal of skill and effort can go into producing, for example, a line of exquisite poetry. It is because, on its face and in the absence of evidence justifying its description as a literary 'work', the writing does not, qualitatively or quantitatively, justify that description.[95]

In Bennett J's view, three requirements exist for copyright to arise – there must be something which is 'original', which is 'literary' and which can be properly described as a 'work' – and broadly in line with UK case law particularly the view expressed by Arnold J in *SAS*.[96] Nonetheless, although the court in *Fairfax* recognised that in most cases headlines were too trivial, Bennett J stated that it was not impossible that a headline or a title could amount to a copyright work. In this regard, the case can be said to be broadly in line with UK authority up to 2010.

[88] Copyright Act 1968, s 10.
[89] *IceTV* (n 61).
[90] J McCutcheon, 'When Sweat Turns to Ice: The Originality Threshold for Compilations Following IceTV and Phone Directories' (2011) 22 *Australian Intellectual Property Journal* 87; M Davison, 'Copyright Protection for Compilations: Australia Does a U- Turn' (2010) 32 *European Intellectual Property Review* 457.
[91] *IceTV* (n 61) 493–94 at [95]–[96] and 474.
[92] *Nine Network Australia Pty Ltd v Australian Broadcasting Corporation* (1999) 48 IPR 33. The case of *Green v Broadcasting Corp of New Zealand* [1989] 2 All ER 1056 came to the Privy Council from an appeal from a case in New Zealand.
[93] *Fairfax* (n 61).
[94] ibid at [44].
[95] ibid at [45]. See also *IceTV* (n 61).
[96] Proudman J in *Meltwater* lacked analysis of the 'work' factor.

Summary of the UK Position on Originality of Dramatic Works

Until 2010, the potential for copyright in the UK to apply to very short literary or dramatic works tended to be discussed in hypothetical, speculative, and even sometimes negative, terms.[97] While it had never been ruled in the UK that a single headline or title could never be a copyright work, in *Meltwater* it was stated definitively that 'some of the headlines are independent literary works'.[98] The overriding focus in *Infopaq* and *Meltwater* on originality over work-form may mean that the concept of originality under UK law is now a 'dematerialised' one – one that has been stripped of almost any material limitations set by the boundaries of, for example, literariness.[99] If this is the case, then what the law ultimately protects is a dematerialised expression of originality defined by the author's intellectual creativity. On the other hand, that a headline could be said to be sufficiently literary to be original fits the *Exxon* requirement that a literary work should convey some meaning. Moreover, in *Kogan*, the form of the dramatic work was important to considering whether Julia Kogan had contributed sufficient originality to be a joint author, as detailed below on joint authorship.

In the theatrical context it is likely that a very short play with, for example, 11 words could be protected as a work of copyright. This ought not to be thought of as unusual (or unwelcome) – some avant-garde works can be mostly made up of stage directions (see Samuel Beckett).[100] Many in theatre would no doubt view this as a positive aspect of the law.[101]

Yet, for playwrights who appreciate the ability to quote liberally from other works, or even to refer to the titles of books or everyday newspaper headlines in their plays, copyright law may prove disruptive to such practices. If this is borne out in future cases it could eventually have a considerable negative effect on the ability of literary and dramatic artists involved in 'intellectual creation' to make

[97] Vaver (n 38). See also L McDonagh, 'Headlines and Hyperlinks: UK Copyright Law post-Infopaq' (2011) 1 *Queen Mary Journal of Intellectual Property* 184 and E Bonadio and L McDonagh, 'Artificial Intelligence as Producer and Consumer of Copyright Works: Evaluating the Consequences of Algorithmic Creativity' (2020) *Intellectual Property Quarterly* 112.

[98] *Meltwater* (n 41), Proudman J at [72] (referred to with approval in [22] of the Court of Appeal judgment).

[99] Griffiths (n 2). For discussion of music cases in light of CJEU decisions on originality see L McDonagh, 'Is Creative use of Musical Works without a licence acceptable under Copyright?' (2012) 43 *International Review of Intellectual Property and Competition Law (IIC)* 401.

[100] S Beckett, 'Act Without Words I' in *The Complete Works of Samuel Beckett* (London: Faber & Faber, 2006).

[101] ZK Said, 'Copyright's Illogical Exclusion of Conceptual Art That Changes over Time' (2016) 39 *Colum.-VLA J.L. & Arts* 335.

use of very short works in the development of new works.[102] This issue of infringement is explored further in chapter four.[103]

Authorship and Ownership of the Economic Rights

Legislation has surprisingly little to say about authorship. Academics, however, are fascinated by it.[104] The CDPA merely outlines[105] that the author is the person who creates the work and who is the first owner of the copyright.[106] The economic rights accruing to the author under the CDPA include the exclusive right to, for example, license and assign the work, copy the work, adapt the work, and perform it.[107] Thus, when a theatre company wishes to perform a play which is protected by copyright, the theatre company will attempt to get a licence from the author, or a representative, typically an agent such as Concord (Samuel French).[108] Depending on the circumstances, this licence may cover a single performance or an entire initial run of the play.[109] In practical terms the ownership of a copyright work can be agreed through contractual terms.[110]

[102] Directive 2001/29/EC of the European Parliament and of the Council of 22 May 2001 on the harmonisation of certain aspects of copyright and related rights in the information society – available at http://eur-lex.europa.eu/LexUriServ/LexUriServ.do?uri=CELEX:32001L0029:EN:HTML See also Directive (EU) 2019/790 of the European Parliament and of the Council of 17 April 2019 on copyright and related rights in the Digital Single Market and amending Directives 96/9/EC and 2001/29/EC (Text with EEA relevance.), OJ L 130, 17.5.2019.

[103] As I reflect upon later on in ch 4, this may require a creative interpretation of the fair dealing exceptions such as 'quotation'. See however, the view of J Parkin, 'The copyright quotation exception: not fair use by another name' (2019) 19 *Oxford University Commonwealth Law Journal* 55.

[104] See, eg P Jaszi, 'Towards a Theory of Copyright: The Metamorphoses of Authorship' (1991) 2 *Duke L.J.* 455; D Saunders, *Authorship and Copyright* (London: Routledge, 1992); M Woomansee and P Jaszi (eds), *The Construction of Authorship: Textual Appropriation in Law and Literature* (Durham, NC: Duke University Press, 1999); L Zemer, *The Idea of Authorship in Copyright* (Ashgate Publishing, Ltd, 2007); CJ Craig, 'Reconstructing the Author-Self: Some Feminist Lessons for Copyright Law' (2007) 15 *Journal of Gender, Social Policy and the Law* 207; G D'Agostino, *Copyright, Contracts, Creators, New Media, New Rules* (Cheltenham: Edward Elgar, 2010); M Van Eechoud (ed), *The Work of Authorship* (Amsterdam: Amsterdam University Press, 2014); C Buccafusco, 'A Theory of Copyright Authorship' (2016) 102 *Virginia L. Rev.* 1229.

[105] CDPA 1988, s 3(2).

[106] CDPA 1988, s 9(1) and ss 77–79.

[107] CDPA 1988, s 2(1) and ss 16–27. For a discussion of the meaning of public performance see *Bamgboye v Reed* [2004] EMLR 61.

[108] The UK Writers' Workshop offers advice to authors on finding an agent, see www.writersworkshop.co.uk/literary-agents.html.

[109] M Rimmer, 'Heretic – Copyright Law and Dramatic Works' (2002) 2 *Queensland University of Technology Law and Justice Journal* 131, 133, noting that a negotiation typically occurs before this licence is granted in which the author-playwright, as copyright owner, may seek to restrict the making of changes to the play, such as textual edits, subtractions or additions, in advance of the envisaged performance.

[110] The Writers Agreement and *The Working Playwright* (Writers' Guild of Great Britain, 2019) aims to deal with such disputes in advance, see https://writersguild.org.uk/wp-content/uploads/2015/02/WGGB_booklet_jun12_contracts_i.pdfandhttps://writersguild.org.uk/wp-content/uploads/2019/08/WGGB-Working-Playwright-Agreements-and-Contracts-1.pdf.

In the UK, copyright in the work lasts for 70 years after the end of the life of the author; subsequent to this, the work falls into the public domain.[111] As noted later on, duration is an important factor in the trajectory of theatrical works. Classic works by luminaries such as Sophocles, Shakespeare and Chekhov are in the 'public domain'.[112] This has a number of consequences. Performances of these plays do not require the payment of royalties; nor does the playwright (long dead) need to be consulted about making radical changes to the play. By contrast, many works by dead playwrights such as Samuel Beckett, Brian Friel, Agatha Christie and Harold Pinter remain in copyright, as do works by notable playwrights who are very much still alive at time of writing, such as Tom Stoppard, Martin McDonagh, Caryl Churchill and Alan Bennett.

Overview of Joint Authorship

Later in this chapter I use empirical insights to explore the way that the dramatic work is authored via a collaborative workshop process, with several participants – the playwright, the director, the actors – making creative contributions. Before undertaking this examination, I must first outline the law of joint authorship.[113] The CDPA provides in s.10 for 'joint authorship' of a copyright work as 'a work produced by the collaboration of two or more authors in which the contribution of each author is not distinct from that of the other author or authors'.[114] Case law shows that in the UK work of joint authorship must be made in line with a common design and the contributions of the purported joint authors must meet the threshold of originality.[115]

Joint Authorship of Dramatic Works in the UK

Prior to the CDPA 1988 the most significant case involving joint authorship of a dramatic work (considered under the 1956 Act) was the 1985 case of *Wiseman v George Weidenfeld and Nicholson Ltd.*[116] The case involved a play – *The English*

[111] CDPA 1988, s 12. Under the transitional provisions in Schedule 1 of the CDPA some very old unpublished works remain protected in the UK until 2039 – this potentially includes unpublished works by playwrights whose published works are now in the public domain. See also Directive 93/98/EEC of 29 October 1993 harmonizing the term of protection of copyright and certain related rights OJ L 290, 24.11.1993 and Directive 2006/116/EC of the European Parliament and of the Council of 12 December 2006 on the term of protection of copyright and certain related rights OJ L 372/12, 27.12.2006.
[112] J Boyle, *The Public Domain* (New Haven, CT: Yale University Press, 2009).
[113] Simone (n 2).
[114] CDPA 1988, s 10.
[115] *Fisher v Brooker* [2006] EWHC 3239 (Ch); [2007] EMLR 256; [2007] FSR 12; [2008] EWCA Civ 287; [2009] UKHL 41.
[116] *Wiseman v George Weidenfeld and Nicholson Ltd* [1985] FSR 525.

Way of Doing Things – the text of which was written by William Donaldson (based on his novel). The claimant Wiseman had suggested to Donaldson that he adapt the novel into a play, and Wiseman also provided advice and editorial criticism during the script-writing process. Wiseman claimed this entitled him to a share of joint authorship. The court disagreed, holding that even if Wiseman had offered useful advice and constructive criticism, this did not equate to authorial writing.

There are not many twenty-first century cases involving dramatic works in the UK. We have one significant High Court decision on a stage play (*Brighton v Jones*) as well as a major Court of Appeal decision on a screenplay (*Kogan v Martin*). Apart from that, musical joint authorship cases, and particularly the key case of *Fisher v Brooker*, provide comparative value.

The 2004 case of *Brighton v Jones* concerned the authorship of the commercially successful play *Stones in His Pockets*.[117] This was primarily a dispute between the director of the initial production of the play (Brighton) and the playwright (Jones). *Stones in his Pockets* was first staged by the Dubbeljoint Theatre Company in Belfast in 1996. It was fairly successful in its initial run, but did not become a commercial success immediately. During the late 1990s, the playwright re-wrote the play extensively by herself. This revised version of the play went on to become very popular in the West End and on Broadway.[118] Consequently, it generated large amounts of royalty revenue which accrued to Jones (the playwright), that is, the author/owner of the dramatic work. Following the success of the revised version of the play Brighton and the Dubbeljoint Theatre Company took a High Court copyright case against Jones. Brighton claimed a joint share in the dramatic work, and a proportionate share of royalties. The theatre's claim was based on a contract agreed with Jones at the time of the first production, that the theatre would receive a proportion of later royalties and credit as the first theatre to stage it.

Regarding the main claims, the court in *Brighton* rejected suggestions that the comments and edits provided by the director during the development of the script via the workshop/rehearsal process amounted to a joint authorship contribution of sufficient originality for a share in the work to arise. Due to the fact the court hearing took place almost a decade after the workshop/rehearsal process had concluded, the parties' memories of which person had contributed what were vague. In the face of unclear recollections, the court concluded that Pamela Brighton was merely doing what any director would do in the circumstances of preparing the play to be staged. The court also emphasised the existence of a contract between the Dubbeljoint Theatre Company and the writer, which stated that Jones would receive the resulting copyright.[119]

[117] *Brighton & Dubbeljoint v Jones* [2004] EWHC 1157 (Ch); [2004] EMLR 507.

[118] See for instance this 2011 review of a London performance, available at www.guardian.co.uk/stage/2011/dec/20/stones-in-his-pockets-review.

[119] This is broadly in line with the terms of standard contracts, as noted in *The Working Playwright* (Writers' Guild of Great Britain, 2019) which aims to deal with such disputes in advance: see https://writersguild.org.uk/wp-content/uploads/2019/08/WGGB-Working-Playwright-Agreements-and-Contracts-1.pdf.

Nonetheless, there was an additional claim. The provision of written instructions, including character and basic scenario details, was capable of creating an authorship interest. In this case the director had faxed written instructions to the writer to try to encourage her to begin work on the play, which was somewhat behind schedule. The director, Pamela Brighton, kept a copy of these written notes and produced them at trial. At the trial Marie Jones admitted that the first scene of the play contained a scenario and characters recognisable from these written notes. In this context, where the play that Jones had written, and subsequently revised, was derivative of the instructions given to Jones by Brighton, the court held that Brighton did have a copyright interest under the law. The court considered the play to be in part an adaptation of the (separate) earlier 'work' created by Brighton and faxed to Jones.

It is notable, and arguably unfortunate, that the court emphasised writing over other forms of creative input, stressing that Jones typed up the script on her laptop.[120] On this, however, it must be remembered that courts inevitably require evidence in order to make their determinations, and clear written evidence tends to persuade judges more readily than vague oral remembrances.

In the 2019 ruling in *Kogan v Martin* the Court of Appeal specified four elements of joint authorship: (a) collaboration, (b) authorship, (c) contribution and (d) non-distinctness of contribution.[121] Here the Court of Appeal of England and Wales overturned a decision of the Intellectual Property Enterprise Court (IPEC) concerning the authorship of screenplay for Stephen Frears' 2016 film, *Florence Foster Jenkins*.[122] Nicholas Martin was attributed as its writer upon the film's release, and in 2017 his sole authorship claim was upheld by the IPEC.[123] The Court of Appeal, however, decided that the IPEC had not properly applied the criteria of joint authorship in considering whether the appellant – Julia Kogan – had made the right sort of 'authorial' contributions to the screenplay to be considered a joint author of the final work. In paragraph 33 the Court of Appeal provided a remarkably clear-headed statement of the law on joint authorship, even drawing an interesting analogy between the working relationship between TS Eliot and Ezra Pound on the important question of when authorship ends, and 'mere' editing begins:

> A striking illustration is the contribution made by Ezra Pound to *The Waste Land*. When T.S. Eliot showed him the original draft, Pound proposed very extensive deletions and revisions, with considerable consequences for the poem as published (indeed he became its dedicatee). But neither poet ever considered it a work of joint authorship, and it has not been regarded as such in the century since it was published, even though Pound's contribution is now widely known. This is because he was acting as a friend and critic and not a collaborator in a common design. By contrast, a collaborator may

[120] *Brighton & Dubbeljoint v Jones* [2004] EWHC 1157 (Ch) at [42].
[121] *Kogan v Martin* [2019] EWCA 1645.
[122] ibid. Following the subsequent IPEC retrial, Kogan was awarded a 20% ownership share of the copyright in the dramatic work – *Martin v Kogan* [2021] EWHC 24 (Ch).
[123] [2017] EWHC 2927 (IPEC).

> become a joint author after an apparently lesser contribution than Pound's. Take, for example, *Beckingham v Hodgens* (cited above) where a successful claim for joint authorship was made by a session musician who contributed a distinctive four-bar riff to a pop song that had been substantially conceived before he was hired. These examples show the importance of identifying the true nature of the interaction between the parties in relation to the work, an assessment that provides the essential context for consideration of questions of authorship and contribution.[124]

This contextual approach taken by the Court of Appeal is laudable and demonstrates how far the critique of singular authorship has penetrated copyright jurisprudence.[125] The case law prior to *Kogan* tended to focus overwhelmingly on the 'authorship' limb of the joint authorship test and thus neglected the requirement for collaboration even though the latter is an express requirement in the CDPA.[126] The *Kogan* ruling puts collaboration front and centre in analysis of joint authorship; it encourages courts to consider the precise context of the collaboration and that authorial, original contributions can be made in varied ways – not just 'writing'. As I discuss later on with respect to the empirical research, this opens up the possibility that the way plays are created eg via methods of 'revising' and 'devising' can be assessed fairly and properly by the courts.

A high-profile and bitter joint authorship row erupted in 2019 between Idris Elba, Kwame Kwei-Armah, Sarah Henley and Tori Allen-Martin over a newly created play – *Tree* – performed at the 2019 Manchester International Festival.[127] From 2013–18 Henley and Allen-Martin had worked with the actor and director Idris Elba on developing the embryonic dramatic work *Tree*, with the two participating in multiple drafts, workshops, and industry performances. However, in 2018 they were surprised to find that in a draft by Kwame Kwei-Armah and in subsequent publicity for the play their names were removed from the project, despite their work being clearly visible in Kwei-Armah's revised script:

> Kwame held onto our ideas and work including the premise, timelines and time-zones, most of our characters and their relationships to each other and many of the plot points.[128]

Henley and Allen-Martin did not take legal action after they had been ousted from the project, citing the costs and hassle. This is unfortunate as in light of *Kogan* the UK courts have now moved towards a more contextual analysis of joint authorship,

[124] *Kogan v Martin* [2019] EWCA 1645 at [33].

[125] AM Adler, 'Against Moral Rights' (2009) 97 *California Law Review* 263, 276, referring to R Badenhausen, *T.S. Eliot and the Art of Collaboration* (Cambridge: Cambridge University Press, 2004) 76. See also CJ Craig and I Kerr, 'The Death of the AI Author' (2019) *Osgoode Legal Studies Research Paper* 1.

[126] Simone (n 2) 251–56.

[127] M Brown, 'Writers claim being excluded after creating Idris Elba play' *The Guardian* (2 July 2019), available at www.theguardian.com/culture/2019/jul/02/writers-claim-being-excluded-after-creating-idris-elbas-play.

[128] S Henley and T Allen-Martin, 'Tree. A Story of Gender and Power in Theatre' *Medium* (2 June 2019), available at https://medium.com/@toriandsarahburnbright/tree-a-story-of-gender-and-power-in-theatre-23b8a2468224.

and the two aggrieved parties would likely have had a strong case. I explore this further below.[129]

Joint Authorship of Musical Works in the UK

On music, the at times contradictory nature of UK jurisprudence can be observed by considering two key music cases: *Hadley v Kemp* (1999)[130] and *Fisher v Brooker* (2006).[131] The courts' key question in both cases was: has the purported joint author has made the 'right kind' of creative contribution?[132] In *Hadley*, Park J held that the addition of a substantial saxophone solo by a band member – Steven Norman – was insufficient to award a share of joint authorship of the Spandau Ballet song 'True'.[133] This decision was controversial – the standard of 'significant and original'[134] as applied by Park J in relation to Norman's saxophone solo was so burdensome that 'Charlie Parker would have been struggling to come up with a saxophone solo which would have entitled him to be considered a joint author' alongside principal composer Gary Kemp.[135] However, this must now be considered in light of the subsequent ruling in *Fisher v Brooker* where the court held that the addition of the famous organ intro to 'A Whiter Shade of Pale' (originally written as a bare piano demo by Gary Brooker) was found to be sufficient to confer a share of authorship onto the organ player, Matthew Fisher. It is therefore

[129] Traditional forms of music provide a clear example where the iconic Western figure recognised by copyright – the individual composer – is largely absent. Historically, traditional music, whether European folk music, indigenous traditional music or jazz/blues, eg J Lind, *A History of European Folk Music* (Rochester, NY: University of Rochester Press, 1997); T Whyton, *Jazz Icons: Heroes, Myths and the Jazz Tradition* (Cambridge: Cambridge University Press, 2010); O Arewa, 'Copyright on Catfish Row: Musical Borrowing, Porgy and Bess, and Unfair Use' (2006) 37 *Rutgers L.J.* 277, 278–90; M Kuss, 'Performing Beliefs: Indigenous Peoples of South American, Central America and Mexico' in *Music in Latin America and the Caribbean: An Encyclopedic History* (Austin: University of Texas Press, 2010); P Malm, *Music Cultures of the Pacific, the Near East, and Asia* (Hoboken, NJ: Prentice Hall, 1996); H Kwabena Nketia, *The Music of Africa* (New York: WW Norton & Company, 1974); J Toynbee, 'Copyright, the Work and Phonographic Orality in Music' (2006) 15 *Social and Legal Studies* 77, 79–99. For an account of IP law informed by a critique of racial injustice see A Vats, *The Color of Creatorship: Intellectual Property, Race, and the Making of Americans* (Stanford, CA: Stanford University Press, 2020).

[130] *Hadley v Kemp* [1999] EMLR 589, 644–50.

[131] *Fisher v Brooker* [2006] EWHC 3239 (Ch); [2007] EMLR 9 at [36]. The case went to the Court of Appeal – *Fisher v Brooker* [2008] EWCA Civ 287; [2008] Bus LR 1123. On further appeal to the House of Lords, it was held that Fisher could receive a share of future royalties, despite the fact that he had waited almost 40 years before taking the case – *Fisher v Brooker* [2009] UKHL 41; [2009] 1 WLR 1764.

[132] *Cala Homes (South) Ltd v Alfred McAlpine Homes East Ltd* [1995] FSR 818. See also *Godfrey v Lees* [1995] EMLR 307, *Ray v Classic FM plc* [1998] FSR 622 and *Beckingham v Hodgens* [2003] EWCA Civ 143.

[133] *Hadley v Kemp* [1999] EMLR 589, 644–50.

[134] *Fylde Microsystems v Key Radio Systems Ltd* [1998] FSR 449.

[135] D Free, 'Beckingham v. Hodgens: The Session Musician's Claim to Music Copyright' (2002) 1 *Entertainment Law* 93, 97. See also A Barron, 'Harmony or Dissonance? Copyright Concepts and Musical Practice' (2006) 15 *Social and Legal Studies* 25 and GJ Fleet, 'What's in a Song? Copyright's Unfair Treatment of Record Producers and Side Musicians' (2008) 61 *Vanderbilt Law Review* 1235.

clear that a piece of music 'will often be a work of joint authorship between some or all of the musicians' performing and improvising together.[136]

It is worth considering comparative insights into the way that joint authorship is assessed in the US, Canada, Australia and India.

Joint Authorship – Comparative Insights

Like the UK, statutory copyright law in common law countries such as Ireland, Australia, India, Canada, etc provides expressly that joint authorship requires collaboration and (original) contributions from more than one party that are not 'distinct' from one another.[137] In Ireland, for instance, a work of 'joint authorship' is defined in precisely this way.[138]

In Australia, as noted earlier, original works must be the product of 'intellectual effort'.[139] This *IceTV* originality standard is thus what is expected of collaborative joint authors, working pursuant to a common design, for joint authorship of a work to arise. However, in Australia there is a lack of case law involving joint authorship of plays.[140] Generally, the rules applied to joint authorship regarding common design and original contribution follow the precedents established in the UK prior to *Kogan*. There has yet to be a court decision on joint authorship post-*Kogan* – and the Australian cases decided in recent years involve relatively prosaic works such as phone directories, health care info and software rather than creative works such as plays and film scripts.[141]

In India, an important decision on joint authorship is the 1989 Delhi High Court judgment in *Najma Hcptulla v Orient Longman Ltd*.[142] In the process of making the book *India Wins Freedom* in the late 1950s Maulana Azad had described his life's political experiences in Urdu, and on this basis Prof. Humayun Kabir had written up the draft of the work in English, which Azad then approved. Referring to UK case law, the court held that where the contributions made by two authors – Azad and Prof Kabir – towards a final work were towards a common design and not severable, the literary work created by the two individuals was a collaborative

[136] R Arnold, 'Reflections on "The Triumph of Music": Copyrights and Performers' Rights in Music' (2010) *Intellectual Property Quarterly* 153.

[137] Copyright Act 1968 (Cth) (Australia), s 10(1); Copyright Act, R.S.C. 1985 (Canada), c. C-42, s 2; CRRA 2000 (Ireland), s 22; Copyright Act 1957 (India), s 2(z). See also Cooper (n 7).

[138] CRRA, s 22(1). In Ireland, the law on joint authorship is likely to be interpreted in the same manner as the law in the UK. See eg *Gormley v EMI Records (Ire) Ltd* [2000] 1 IR 74.

[139] *IceTV* (n 61) 493–4 at [95]–[96] and 474. McCutcheon (n 90).

[140] Copyright Act 1968 (Cth), s 10(1).

[141] *Telstra Corporation Limited v Phone Directories Company Pty Ltd* [2010] FCA 44; *Primary Health Care Limited v Commissioner of Taxation* [2010] FCA 419; *Acohs Pty Ltd v UCorp Pty Ltd* [2010] FCA 577; *Career Step, LLC v TalentMed Pty Ltd (No 2)* [2018] FCA 132.

[142] *Najma Hcptulla v Orient Longman Ltd*, AIR 1989 Del 63; 14 IPLR 36 (1989). See also *Nav Sahitya Prakash and Ors v Anand Kumar and Ors*, AIR 1981 All 200 on co-ownership.

work of joint authorship.[143] The court recognised that in joint authorship cases contributions made by both authors ought to be not distinct in the final work, even if each author had contributed differently in the making of the work. However, the court did not lay down any particular standard to assess the degree of collaboration required to determine joint authorship.[144]

In Canada there is an important case on joint authorship of musical works – the 1999 case of *Neudorf v Nettwerk Productions Ltd*.[145] Here, the music producer Darryl Neudorf had produced some tracks with the popular music artist Sarah McLaughlan. Neudorf claimed to be a joint author because as producer he had suggested particular expressive elements (eg a melody line or a bridge to the chorus) that were integrated into the final arrangements of the songs as recorded. For some tracks, the court found his contributions to be insufficient, or held that they were only in the nature of ideas (as suggestions that McLachlan was free to accept or reject). Nevertheless, with respect to one song – 'Steaming' – Neudorf had made a substantial contribution to the vocal melody; but the absence of a shared *intent* to be a joint author was fatal to his claim. McLachlan did not consider herself to be co-writing the songs with Neudorf. The court also found that Neudorf was playing a supportive role in the creative process rather than an authorial one. In 2009 the Federal Court expressed doubt the approach of *Neudorf* but did not definitively hold against it.[146] A UK court, post-*Kogan*, might consider that in the context of the creative process that produced 'Steaming' Neudorf's contribution would entitle him to a share of joint authorship. At present, the Canadian judicial approach is somewhere between the UK and US approaches, influenced in particular by the US *Childress* case (discussed below).

The US Copyright Act 1976 defines a jointly authored work as 'a work prepared by two or more authors with the intention that their contributions be merged into inseparable or interdependent parts of a unitary whole'.[147] The US joint authorship doctrine – as exemplified by *Childress v Taylor* – thus requires both parties to *intend* to be joint authors; and in the absence of such shared intent, the party identified as the 'dominant author' will receive sole authorship/ownership.[148] In the subsequent case of *Aalmuhammed v Lee*, the intent requirement prevented the expert consultant – Jefri Aalmuhammed – from being a joint author of the film *Malcolm X* even though, as claimed, he had created two entire scenes with new

[143] The court referred to *Levy v Rutley* (1871) L.R. 6 C.P 523, *Walter v Lane* [1900] AC 539 *and Donoghue v Allied Newspapers Ltd* [1937] 3 All ER 503.

[144] A Sebastian, 'Joint Authorship in Cinematographic Films: The Conundrum of the Primary Director' (2014–2015) 7 *Indian J Intell Prop L* 69.

[145] *Neudorf v Nettwerk Productions Ltd., et al* [1999] B.C.J. No. 2831 (B.C.S.C). [2000] RPC 935.

[146] *Neugebauer v Labieniec* [2009] FC 666.

[147] 17 U.S.C. § 101. See also SC Brophy, 'Joint Authorship under the Copyright Law' (1994) 16 *Hastings Comm. & Ent. L.J.* 451.

[148] *Childress v Taylor*, 798 F. Supp. 981 (S.D.N.Y. 1992).

characters, and had re-drafted parts of the script relating to Malcolm X's historic Haj pilgrimage to Mecca.[149]

In the US the essential case on joint authorship of a work of drama involves the musical *Rent*. In *Thomson v Larson*, the dramaturge who had worked on *Rent*'s development for stage argued she should receive a share of joint authorship (and associated credit).[150] The court found that the writer of the musical had not intended that Thomson would be a joint author, and thus, in line with *Childress*, Thomson could not be recognised as such. Despite this, the court seemed open to the suggestion that what Thomson contributed could amount to a separate copyright interest (somewhat similar to the situation in the UK case of *Brighton* where Pamela Brighton was found to own the early draft scenario as a separate work). The case settled before this could be established. It is clear that in the US (and to some extent, Canada, post-*Neudorf*) joint authorship features an additional hurdle to that of the UK, Australia and India – each of the joint authors must intend to create a work of joint authorship and a joint authorship claim will fail if one purported joint author cannot establish this intention where there is a more plausible or 'dominant' single author.

In the US actors have made claims for authorship rights, at least in the context of films, though such claims do not relate to the underlying dramatic work (script).[151] There have also been several claims by directors in the US asserting a copyright interest in stage directions, but up to now there have been no definitive judicial rulings on the issue.[152] As a result it is not clear whether such stage directions would be part of the original dramatic work itself or whether they would constitute a separate copyright interest, similar to what was considered by the court in *Thomson v Larson*. In relation to the US, Weidman argues that awarding a joint authorship share to directors could create overlapping copyrights engendering problems for later interpreters.[153]

In the UK, since the result of joint authorship is *joint ownership*, the fragmentation of ownership means all joint authors must approve eg licensing of works.

[149] *Aalmuhammed v Lee* 202 F.3d. 1227 (9th Cir. 2000). See also *Richlin v Metro-Goldwyn-Mayer Pictures, Inc.* 531 F.3d. 962, 970 (9th Cir. 2008).

[150] *Thomson v Larson* 147 F.3d. 195 (2d. Cir. 1998) 203–204 requiring objective indicia of the intent to be joint authors of the musical Rent. See also 'Recent Case, Copyright – Joint Authorship – Second Circuit Holds That Dramaturg's Contributions to the Musical "Rent" Did Not Establish Joint Authorship with Playwright-Composer – Thomson v. Larson, 147 F.3d 195 (2d Cir. 1998)' (1999) 112 *Harv. L. Rev.* 964, 968–69. See also *Childress v Taylor*, 798 F. Supp. 981 (S.D.N.Y. 1992).

[151] *Garcia v Google, Inc.*, 786 F.3d. 733 (9th Cir. 2015). J Hughes, 'Actors as Authors in American Copyright Law' (2019) *Connecticut Law Review* 409, see https://opencommons.uconn.edu/law_review/409.

[152] *Gutierrez v DeSantis*, No. 95–1949 (S.D.N.Y. filed Mar. 22, 1995); *Mantello v Hall*, No. 97cv8196 (S.D. Fla. filed 21 March 1997); *Einhorn v Mergatroyd Productions* 426 F.Supp. 2d. 189 (S.D.N.Y. 2006).

[153] J Weidman, 'The Seventh Annual Media and Society Lecture: Protecting the American Playwright' (2007) 72 *Brook. L. Rev.* 641, 649.

Following a play's initial run, joint ownership rules could have an unpredictable impact on the playwright's ability to get the play performed by a different theatre, and could also affect licensing of adaptations.[154]

Beyond the Individual – Exploring Theatrical Authorship as a Social Practice

For much of the nineteenth and twentieth centuries, if not earlier, authorship was often linked with Western – typically male – individualism.[155] The post-modern 'death of the author' critique has made authorship a contested concept.[156] Scholars highlight historical studies that show that forms of co-writing have been common throughout literary and dramatic history 'even at the height of the cult of the solitary genius in romanticism'.[157] Taking this further, other commentators argue that the creative process ought not to be attributed just to individual 'genius';[158] rather, it should be acknowledged that authorship is often inherently social and collaborative.[159] Further critical views are put forward by Carys Craig and Daniela Simone: they call for courts to value the social elements

[154] McDonagh (n 23).

[155] See generally CJ Craig, *Copyright, Communication and Culture: Towards a Relational Theory of Copyright Law* (Cheltenham: Edward Elgar, 2011).

[156] R Barthes, 'The Death of the Author' in (R Howard, trans, 1967) 5/6 *Aspen: The Magazine in a Box* www.ubu.com/aspen/aspen5and6/index.html and M Foucault, 'What Is an Author?' in JM Marsh, JD Caputo and M Westphal (eds), *Modernity and its Discontents* (New York: Fordham University Press, 1992) 299, 305. See also Aristotle, *Poetics* (A Kenny ed, Oxford: Oxford University Press, 2013).

[157] M Krause, 'Practicing Authorship: The Case of Brecht's Plays' in C Calhoun and R Sennett (eds), *Practicing Culture* (Oxford: Routledge, 2007) 217. See also T Moi, *Sexual/Textual Politics* (London: Methuen, 1985); J Stillinger, *Multiple Authorship and the Myth of Solitary Genius* (New York: Oxford University Press, 1991); and CW Zhu, '"Copyleft" Reconsidered: Why Software Licensing Jurisprudence Needs Insights from Relational Contract Theory' (2013) 22 *Social & Legal Studies* 289.

[158] See, eg RJ Coombe, *The Cultural Life of Intellectual Properties: Authorship, Appropriation and the Law* (Durham, NC: Duke University Publishing, 1998); K Bowrey, 'Alternative Intellectual Property?: Indigenous Protocols, Copyleft and New Juridifications of Customary Practices' (2006) 6 *Macquarie Law Journal* 65; D Wassel, 'From Mbube to Wimoweh: African Folk Music in Dual Systems of Law' (2010) 20 *Fordham Intellectual Property, Media and Entertainment Law Journal* 289; L McDonagh, 'Protecting traditional music under copyright (and choosing not to do enforce it)' in Bonadio and Lucchi (eds) (n 22). See also E Ostrom, *Governing the Commons* (New York: New York University Press, 1990).

[159] S Stern, 'Copyright, Originality and the Public Domain in Eighteenth-Century England' in R McGinnis (ed), *Originality and Intellectual Property in the French and English Enlightenment* (New York: Routledge, 2009) 69, 71. For commentary on the nature of the literary work see J Pila, 'The Literary Work within Copyright Law: An Analysis of its Present and Future Status' (1999) 13 *Intellectual Property Journal* 133.

of authorship – what Craig deems 'relational authorship' – prioritising the active input of multiple parties within the creative process.[160]

In theatre these issues are ever-present. Collaboration is a constant, evident in the 1550s, through the Romantic period, and up to our present day.[161] But the nature of this collaboration is not static – Elizabethan polyvocal theatricality is not the same as contemporary devised theatre. In relation to the changing nature of collaborative creativity in theatre Masten asks:

> What does 'composition' include in such a context? (Re)writing? Copying? Staging? The addition of theatrical gestures? … When is (the writing, staging, printing of) a text complete?[162]

The turn away from focusing on singular authorship finds particular resonance in theatre because what is protected by the law is a performative work – one that is often developed in collaboration between the playwright, director and performers. As such the idea of an individual author 'genius' – so pervasive in romantic history and reflected in copyright theory – is unsettled by the very practices of theatre. Despite this, when one considers the deification of Shakespeare, discussed in the previous chapter, or singular, iconic modern and post-modern figures such as Brecht, Beckett, Pinter, Nottage or Stoppard, it appears the cult of the theatrical author endures. Collaboration may be inherent to the medium, but collaborators are not always given recognition. Krause places the blame on the 'institution of authorship' – represented by publishing, literary scholarship and biography – for acting as 'a real abstraction from the practices of production, which obliterates the role of the collaborators'.[163] Similarly, Smith states that journalists and critics often 'seek to identify the (singular) "author" of a piece of theatre' even where the actual creative practices suggest otherwise.[164]

However, it is not always the case that singular authorship is promoted within theatre practice. UK theatre finds remarkably varied ways to accommodate different forms of creativity. If legal and humanities scholars have attempted to deconstruct the author in the abstract, theatre participants have put such theories *into their practice*.[165] The development of 'devised' theatre from the 1970s onward encouraged actors to be creative, reflecting 'a commitment to breaking the authority of directors and, in some instances, to challenging the authorial voice of the

[160] CJ Craig, 'Reconstructing the Author Self: Some Feminist Lessons for Copyright Law' (2007) 15 *American University Journal of Gender, Social Policy and the Law* 207 and Simone (n 2).

[161] J Cox and D Kastan (eds), *A New History of Early English Drama* (New York: Columbia University Press, 1997).

[162] Masten (n 6) 340.

[163] Krause (n 157) 216–17.

[164] M Smith, *Processes and Rhetorics of Writing in Contemporary British Devising: Frantic Assembly and Forced Entertainment* (PhD thesis, University of York, 2013) 49–50, see http://etheses.whiterose.ac.uk/8379/1/Processes%20and%20Rhetorics%20of%20Writing%20in%20Contemporary%20British%20Devising%20-%20MARK%20SMITH.pdf.

[165] E Govan, H Nicholson and K Normington, *Making a Performance: Devising Histories and Contemporary Practices* (London: Routledge, 2007) 16–19 and 30–36. Of importance in this regard was the removal of state censorship of UK theatrical productions via the Theatres Act 1968.

playwright'.[166] Oddey thus views devised theatre as a challenge to literary or text-based theatre which she argues is co-dominated, often in a patriarchal fashion, by the playwright and director.[167] In contrast, Heddon and Milling argue against such a binary perspective, noting that the rise of the creative actor in devised theatre has at times worked alongside the roles of director and writer, with all playing a role in the creativity.[168] Indeed, as I explore below, rather than a stark opposition between text-based theatre and devised theatre, there are in fact a lot of shared practices between the two.[169] In this vein, Heddon and Milling argue that 'devised performance lies on a continuum with script work'.[170]

Perhaps the most famous early UK example of a company founded to develop texts collaboratively is the Joint Stock Company which was formed in 1973 by Max Stafford-Clark, David Hare and David Aukin.[171] The central idea was to use collectivist working methods to create new plays. Joint Stock's resultant work with the writer Caryl Churchill during the 1970s-80s was profound and truly collaborative.[172] In more recent years, devising companies like Complicité,[173] Frantic Assembly[174] and Forced Entertainment[175] emphasise dialogic collaboration – rather than singular composition – in the way they work and their internal structures.[176]

These kinds of formal structures can have an impact on how the works get created; but, as I describe in detail later on, they can also have an impact on the key legal questions of ownership, credit-sharing and royalty-sharing. Heddon and Milling comment that the problem of 'how collaborations work in practice' and the complexity of managing division of labour tend to be 'recurring issues for

[166] ibid, 16.

[167] A Oddey, *Devising Theatre: A Practical and Theoretical Handbook* (London: Routledge, 1994) 7–11.

[168] D Heddon and J Milling, *Devising Performance: A Critical History* (Basingstoke: Palgrave Macmillan, 2005) 7.

[169] ibid, 34–36.

[170] ibid, 36.

[171] R Ritchie, *The Joint Stock Book: The Making of a Theatre Collective* (London: Methuen, 1987) and T Shank, (ed), *Contemporary British Theatre* (Basingstoke: Palgrave Macmillan, 1996). In the context of Ireland/Northern Ireland see MJ Richtarik, *Acting Between the Lines: The Field Day Theatre Company and Irish Cultural Politics 1980–1984* (Oxford: Clarendon Press, 1994) and T. Eagleton, F. Jameson & E. Said, Nationalism, *Colonialism and Literature* (Minneapolis: University of Minnesota Press, 1990).

[172] C Churchill, *Cloud 9* (London: Methuen, 1984).

[173] H Freshwater, 'Physical Theatre: Complicite and the Question of Authority' in N Holdsworth and M Luckhurst (eds), *A Concise Companion to Contemporary British and Irish Drama* (Oxford: Blackwell, 2008) 171. See also 'Simon McBurney on Devised Theatre – it's absolutely petrifying' *The Telegraph* (3 August 2015) at www.telegraph.co.uk/theatre/actors/simon-mcburney-on-devised-theatre-absolutely-petrifying/; also www.complicite.org/media/1439372000Complicite_Teachers_pack.pdf and www.bl.uk/20th-century-literature/articles/theatre-de-complicite-and-storytelling.

[174] See www.franticassembly.co.uk/about; see also S Graham and S Hoggett, *The Frantic Assembly Book of Devising Theatre* (Abingdon: Routledge, 2009).

[175] See www.forcedentertainment.com/; see also H Freshwater, 'Delirium: In Rehearsal with theatre O' in A Mermikides and J Smart (eds), *Devising in Process* (Basingstoke: Palgrave Macmillan, 2010) 128 and A Frost and R Yarrow, *Improvisation in Drama*, 2nd edn (Basingstoke: Palgrave Macmillan, 2007).

[176] D Williams, 'Killing the Audience: Forced Entertainment's First Night' (2009) 54 *Australasian Drama Studies* 50. See also R Hornby, 'Forgetting the Text: Derrida and the "Liberation" of the Actor' (2002) 18 *New Theatre Quarterly* 355.

devising companies'.[177] Even in devising companies there will often be a 'constant' leader but also a 'tendency to work collaboratively within this hierarchical structure'.[178] For example, Sheffield-based company Forced Entertainment develops performances collaboratively – but artistic director Tim Etchells typically takes on the leadership role of director and writer.[179] Similarly, Simon McBurney is undoubtedly the lead figure in Complicité.

In order to examine the legal questions related to joint authorship, I must explore how the text of the script typically comes into being in theatre. This includes the issue of who contributes during workshops and rehearsals to the final version of the play; and the question of whether the law should take account of the unique aspects of theatre when disputes arise. I now turn to theatre studies and to my own empirical research in order to answer these questions.[180]

Evaluating the Original Dramatic Work as Theatrical Text – 'Fully Formed' or 'Devised/Revised'?

In light of the earlier examination of the dramatic work and originality under copyright law, it is worth considering here what the original dramatic work actually *is* in the context of theatre play-texts. Here I trace the play-text from its origins through to its first performances. My focus is on copyright law and questions of authorship and ownership, so the dramatic work remains the key guiding concept. For present purposes the boundaries of the dramatic work can be said to include all aspects of the theatrical text as performed – not only the dialogue, but also non-literal elements such as detailed plot, characters and stage directions.[181]

Property law may be about boundaries and fixation, but in contemporary theatre is there such a thing as 'the original' version of a play?[182] The allographic nature of dramatic works means that inevitably a different type of 'composition' occurs than in the case of the individual scribe working alone, originating a literary text.[183] Indeed, there is a view that theatre writing – in order to be 'reflective of actual practice among many playwrights' – ought not to be viewed as singular at all, but as 'dialogic'.[184]

[177] Heddon and Milling (n 168) 38.
[178] ibid, 213.
[179] ibid, 213.
[180] McDonagh (n 5).
[181] *Sawkins v Hyperion* [2005] EWCA Civ 565; [2005] 1 WLR 3281. See also *Kogan v Martin* [2019] EWCA Civ 1645.
[182] Sherman (n 4).
[183] Smith (n 164), referring to 'Interview with Sarah Kane: 3 November 1998'. Department of Drama and Theatre: Royal Holloway University of London (2009), see www.royalholloway.ac.uk/dramaandtheatre/research/researchgroups/contemporarybritishtheatreandpolitics/sarahkane.aspx.
[184] Smith (n 164) 49–50. G Rabkin, 'Is There a Text on This Stage? Theatre/Authorship/Interpretation' (1985) 9 *Performing Arts Journal* 142. See generally N Grene, and C Morash (eds), *The Oxford Handbook of Modern Irish Theatre* (Oxford: Oxford University Press, 2016).

From the available literature and my empirical interviews, it is clear there are, broadly, two principal ways by which new plays get created: the first, involves a playwright providing a relatively *fully-formed* text; whereas the second involves some element of the *devising* of a text through the workshop process or at least the major *revising* of a partially-formed text.[185]

With respect to the first method – whereby the play arrives to the theatre as an already fully-formed text – this is most common at established theatres, eg with commissioned work at The National Theatre. Here the model is more akin to the individual scribe working alone. Such a play may simply need a period of rehearsals before performance. The director Nicholas Hytner, speaking in the late 1990s, commented:

> I believe that Pinter just delivers a finished play with every comma in place, and I know for instance that in Kazan's autobiography he says quite unequivocally that the best plays he directed were those that arrived on his desk requiring little or no work: *Death of Salesman* and *Streetcar*. It may be that works as singularly revolutionary as *Death of a Salesman* and *Streetcar* do just arrive; but it's different every time. The play I did a year or so ago, *The Cripple of Inishmaan* by Martin McDonagh, was just that: it required nothing, a few little cuts, that was it.[186]

Thus, in the cases of Arthur Miller, Samuel Beckett or Martin McDonagh the question of joint authorship seems a moot one – singular authorship is the reality. Nonetheless, these are somewhat atypical cases within the diverse UK theatre realm. More common is the second way of creating a play-text, that which occurs at least in part either via conceptual devising or by 'workshopping' and revising the text.[187] This method is most common at smaller, medium-sized and fringe theatres (where the majority of new works are first staged). Devising typically takes place via the collective process of building up a play from scratch. Collective improvisation and radical experiments may provoke inspiration, but at some point a structure will need to be imposed on the process, typically by the 'leader' eg Tim Etchells or Simon McBurney, who will begin to put any creative fragments that have emerged into some form of partial text.[188]

If the writer provides a partial text at the beginning of the process, then it will be 'workshopped' and revised over several weeks (or more) in order to finalise it.

[185] See, eg S Sigal, 'Monstrous Regiment: The Gendered Politics of Collaboration, Writing, and Authorship in the UK from the 1970s Onwards' in K Syssoyeva and S Proudfit (eds), *Women, Collective Creation, and Devised Performance* (New York: Palgrave Macmillan, 2016) 177 and D Williams (ed), *Collaborative Theatre: The Théâtre du Soleil Sourcebook* (London: Routledge, 1999).

[186] Wu (ed) (n 1) 103–4.

[187] Oddey (n 167); A Mermikides, 'Brilliant Theatre-making at the National: Devising, Collective Creation and the Director's Brand' (2013) 33 *Studies in Theatre & Performance* 153; and G McAuley, *Not Magic But Work: An Ethnographic Account of a Rehearsal Process* (Manchester: Manchester University Press, 2012).

[188] A Mermikides, 'Forced Entertainment – The Travels (2002): the Anti-Theatrical Director' in J Harvie and A Lavender (eds), *Making Contemporary Theatre: International Rehearsal Processes* (Manchester: Manchester University Press, 2010) 101.

In either situation, there will be a collaborative, performative process, with the writer, director and actors all present (though not always at the same times).[189]

A play may begin its life, as in *Brighton v Jones*, as an outline scenario, for example, featuring two characters at a specific location, with a few lines of dialogue.[190] In that specific case, one party (the director) started off the process of creating the play *Stones in His Pockets* by writing an outline, which was then fleshed out by another party (the playwright) into a rough draft of the script. That partially-formed script was then probed and performed by the director and actors during several weeks of a workshop process, whereby several key edits and changes were made (with the input of all parties: writer, director, actors). The case demonstrates that even a play that begins its workshop process with a partially-formed script often undergoes major revisions, before materialising as a complete, performative work.

For this reason, the 20 interviewees were broadly in agreement that workshops are usually a necessity to get to a final text. One actor emphasised that the workshop is a 'collective process that goes beyond merely rehearsing a text' whereby the writer, director and actors, and potentially other creative parties such as dramaturges, build up the scenes, characters and dialogue of a play.[191] Another writer told me that 'workshopping the text' is important for allowing everybody 'to see what works and what doesn't'.[192]

In this vein, the legal scholar Susan Keller remarks that a workshop offers 'opportunities to work through the play's problems'.[193] Similarly, in an interview with Duncan Wu, the director Nicholas Hytner stated that in his experience the writer will provide a text in some form, but it will usually be in need of edits, cuts and additions, which he is happy to suggest.[194]

It is clear, therefore, that in the case of devised/revised theatre the text is in an 'unsettled' state during the workshop process. In fact, due to his experiences of workshops, one writer expressed to me his scepticism that there can ever be such a thing as a truly original 'ur-text' in theatre; he emphasised that it is common for theatrical works to pass through many 'filters' before they emerge on stage (or in published text, which generally follows the first staging of the play).[195] The writer Alan Bennett and the director Nicholas Hytner are on record as saying that the workshop process was crucial to their rewriting and reworking of the text of *The Madness of George III* – with Bennett noting:

> Well, there's a photograph of the table in the rehearsal room with all the rewrites hung up, and it looks like a load of laundry hanging up to dry, all these sheets that the

[189] See generally KM Syssoyeva and S Proudfit (eds), *Collective Creation in Contemporary Performance* (New York: Palgrave Macmillan, 2013).

[190] *Brighton & Dubbeljoint v Jones* [2004] EWHC 1157 (Ch).

[191] Anon 8.

[192] Anon 3.

[193] S Keller, 'Collaboration in Theater: Problems and Copyright Solutions' (1986) 33 *UCLA Law Review* 891, 908–9.

[194] Wu (n 1) 106.

[195] Anon 2.

> poor actors had to take away every day and learn. There was so much rewriting to be done.[196]

In an interview with Duncan Wu, the director Max-Stafford Clark stated that he found workshops essential to the work of Joint Stock during the 1970s–80s. Yet, he notes that the directors of the older generation, such as William Gaskill, came from an older tradition at the Royal Court whereby you 'rehearsed the script as it was written or you didn't do it at all'. For Stafford-Clark, however, a script was 'a starting-point' – whereas he stated that for the older generation 'it was a kind of inspirational Holy Grail'.[197]

In more recent decades, a younger generation of theatre-makers has embraced the workshop and the practices of devised theatre. Turner posits the workshop as a demiurgic model for theatrical authorship processes, with collaborators viewing a text as 'something to glance off' rather than as a refined singular work.[198] Successful examples of collaborative devising include the many acclaimed theatrical works produced by Forced Entertainment and Complicité[199] or the 2014 play *Blurred Lines* created by writer Nick Payne and the director Carrie Cracknell, peformed at The National Theatre.[200]

From a copyright perspective, the fact the play as text may exist in several distinct versions at different times adds complexities. The *Kogan* case suggests that where the purported joint authors have started the project together, the drafts could be considered together as a single, cumulative dramatic work – as opposed to 'salami-slicing' the work in to a set of separate adapted (or derivative) works.[201] On the other hand, *Brighton* and *Fisher* suggest that a work started by one party may end up being considered as separate from its later jointly authored adaptation or arrangement.[202] In any event, in order to consider the question of who owns the copyright in the dramatic work(s), it is necessary to evaluate all of the possible authorial contributions.

Joint Authorship: How Do Dramatic Works Get Created Via the Workshop Process?

As noted earlier, in the case of a playwright who delivers a fully-formed script, any workshop process may be very brief, or may not happen at all – the play may

[196] ibid, 82 (Bennett) and 106 (Hytner).
[197] ibid, 57.
[198] C Turner, 'Something to glance off: Writing Space' (2009) 2 *Journal of Writing in Creative Practice* 217; C Turner 'Writing for the contemporary theatre: towards a radically inclusive dramaturgy' (2010) 30 *Studies in Theatre and Performance* 75.
[199] One personal favourite is Complicité's *The Encounter* (2016), available at www.complicite.org/productions/theencounter.
[200] See https://www.curtisbrown.co.uk/client/nick-payne/work/blurred-lines.
[201] Simone (n 24) 877.
[202] McDonagh (n 23).

just go through a rehearsal process where little is edited or added before staging. The playwright would clearly be the author and owner of that dramatic work. It is therefore in the case of the second type of work – what I broadly define as the devised/revised text – that workshops become crucial and questions of joint authorship arise.[203]

From my interviews and from theatrical scholarship, it is clear the devising/revising processes of the workshop are quite varied (and to some extent depend on whether the starting point is a theatrical concept or an actual draft text).[204] During a workshop a writer or director may suggest a generalised situation or an emotional scenario to be acted out and improvised, for example, 'an angry man seeking revenge'; a director may suggest, or even dictate, changes to characters or entire lines of dialogue; or actors may be encouraged to improvise dialogue eg 'to play with the characters' as one actor put it to me.[205] The writer will seek to embody any new characters or dialogue additions in the writing up of new versions of the script. The play as eventually performed may end up differing substantially from the original concept (and from the initial or partial script).[206] Thus, there may be several parties making *original contributions* to the play sufficient to create a joint authorship interest.

For example, one actor told me during an interview that in one recent play she had enjoyed the 'free-form' workshop improvisation that had led her to come up with several lines of dialogue for her character; she noted that the writer had then 'gone away' to do some further writing, using the actor's familiar 'speech patterns' to write the majority of the remainder of her character's dialogue.[207]

David Edgar has related how scene 6 of his play *Pentecost* – directed by Michael Attenborough – was devised almost from scratch, with the actors adding a 'tremendous amount' through 'improvisations':[208]

> It was a process of character-creation in which I was using the actors' perceptions in order to build characters in collaboration with those actors.[209]

Michael Attenborough has confirmed that the workshop transformed the play from its initial text:

> When we started rehearsals there was a whole scene yet to be written … The text was so mutable at that point that it would have been impossible to try and get a printed text out for the first performance.[210]

[203] There are of course many different forms of devising – I use the term broadly here to encompass not only devising from scratch but also undertaking major revisions of a draft text – for a thorough overview see D Radosavljević, *Theatre-Making: Interplay Between Text and Performance in the 21st Century* (Basingstoke: Palgrave Macmillan, 2013).

[204] A Dickson, 'The drama factory: how theatre scripts reach the stage' *The Guardian* (16 Dec 2009), see www.theguardian.com/stage/2009/dec/16/new-writing-theatre-slush-pile.

[205] Anon 7.

[206] C Wilkinson, 'Noises off: Must directors stick to the script?' *The Guardian* (23 Aug 2008), see www.theguardian.com/stage/theatreblog/2008/aug/23/noisesoffmustdirectorssticktothescript.

[207] Anon 7. See also Freshwater (n 173).

[208] Wu (n 1) 138.

[209] ibid, 143.

[210] ibid, 148.

Workshops tend to involve short scenes of improvisation involving manipulating clichés and making leaps, starting out with scenarios going from eg A to B, and then, more drastically, from eg A to K – these are processes which are very useful for developing some texts, but less so with others.[211] On this, the playwright Howard Brenton has remarked:

> You could never workshop a Pinter play because he goes from A to K all the time. It would just collapse; you couldn't do it.[212]

As noted earlier, such fully-formed texts will not go through the workshop process; they will just be rehearsed and staged. David Hare is best known as a playwright but he has also directed several plays, including *Heartbreak House*, written by George Bernard Shaw. In an interview with Duncan Wu, Hare emphasised that Shaw's is a text that must be performed as written:

> … Shaw is very specific … everything's in a puppet-theatre in his mind, and that if you don't crudely obey his instructions, which are very, very detailed, about the physical layout, you get yourself into terrible trouble … So there's freedom but there's only freedom if you accept his rules. I don't know another writer so resistant to directorial adaptation.[213]

The same is true of Beckett, another precise playwright prone to working from a highly specified and authored text.[214] By contrast, Brecht (working largely in Germany) made comprehensive use of the workshop process to devise a final text.[215] Indeed, Brecht's workshops can be described as 'an extreme case of sustained collective production'.[216] Shared practices included the collection of material, the translation of original sources, the organisation of rehearsals, and the making of text edits.[217] The playwright Howard Brenton has commented that Brecht appropriated original contributions made by his collaborators:

> Brecht used to write with a big long table, and often in the rehearsal room. There'd be new stuff on the table in the morning. Indeed, anyone who had a bright idea would find their bright idea in the text before they knew it. There was a hoovering sort of method about the way Brecht thought, and he always wanted it to be collective – though of course he always dominated it.[218]

One key Brecht collaborator was Elizabeth Hauptmann, who made important contributions to several key works including *Man Equals Man* and *Saint Joan of the Stockyards*.[219] Hauptmann worked intensely with Brecht, taking up his ideas

[211] ibid, 44.
[212] ibid, 44.
[213] ibid, 192.
[214] J Fletcher, *Beckett – The Playwright and his Work*, 2nd edn (London: Faber & Faber, 2006).
[215] Krause (n 157).
[216] ibid.
[217] ibid, 220. Key parties in Brecht's circle were the composers Hanns Eisler and Kurt Weill, the writers Hermann Borchart, Emil Hesse-Burri, and Hella Wuolijoki, and the directors Bernard Reich and Slatan Dudow.
[218] Wu (n 1) 44.
[219] P Hanssen, *Elisabeth Hauptmann: Brecht's Silent Collaborator* (New York: Peter Lang, 1995).

and working them through dramaturgically.[220] The work *Man Equals Man* existed only as a very rough sketch until Hauptmann came into the process. It was she who offered the solution to the plot's key problem: the motivation for the main character's involvement with three soldiers, which ended up centring on a discussion between the characters concerning an elephant.[221] Similarly, for the works *Saint Joan of the Stockyards* and *Happy End* several key story elements and characters originated with Hauptmann.[222] Knopf states:

> One can conclude from the material that Emil Hesse-Burri and Elisabeth Hauptmann did most of the initial work, including the writing and they provided the structure of the fable; Brecht's work consisted mostly in checking the proposals, editing the texts and expanding them.[223]

Indeed, from my interviews, and from theatre scholarship, it is clear that the creative participants involved (writers, directors and actors) realise not only that collaboration occurs during the workshop, but that different collaborators contribute in original and profound ways to the final text, often altering it significantly.[224] Yet, such contributions often go unrecognised. Later on, I discuss the issues of credit and ownership in detail. For now, it is sufficient to note that many of these examples of collaborative authorship appear to meet the test for joint authorship outlined above – the contributions are likely to be considered sufficiently original; not distinct but essential to the final work; and aimed towards a common design as part of a collaboration. Before focusing on the legal issues arising from these processes, it is necessary to analyse what the typical contributions made by the writer, director and actors are in practice.

The Role of the Writer

Despite the multifaceted nature of collaboration – or perhaps, because of it – in my interviews I encountered universal respect from all parties for the role of the writer in 'shaping the play'. Moreover, writers tend to feel a sense of duty towards the text from the very beginning of the process. One playwright told me in an interview that during workshops even though he is open to suggestions, he nevertheless feels a need to 'protect' the script to ensure the intended meaning is not lost.[225] The need to do this can be heightened as the process goes on. Another playwright told me that he felt his power to influence the text was strong at the beginning and middle of the process, but was comparatively 'weak' by the end of

[220] ibid, 19.
[221] ibid, 21–22.
[222] ibid, 50–58.
[223] Krause (n 157) 222.
[224] A Field, 'All theatre is devised and text-based' *The Guardian* (21 April 2009), see www.theguardian.com/stage/theatreblog/2009/apr/21/theatre-devised-text-based.
[225] Anon 1.

the workshop; that he started out 'as the important figure' but by the end he felt the director had 'taken over' – something he ultimately felt was necessary to the final task of getting the play into a workable form for staging.[226]

The director Max Stafford-Clark drew on insights from his experiences working with the playwrights Howard Brenton, David Hare and Caryl Churchill as part of Joint Stock, opining:[227]

> What I'm saying is that respect for the writer, handing the material back to the writer, and the kind of acceptance that the writer is the senior collaborator, is very much a part of Joint Stock's success …[228]

Commenting on this, the playwright Howard Brenton has stated that although several important changes were made to the scripts during workshops with Stafford-Clark for the plays *Bloody Poetry* and *Epsom Downs*,[229] he nonetheless stated that in each case 'I always felt it was my play'.[230]

Likewise, there can be boundaries directors will not cross – the director Michael Attenborough has emphasised that in a workshop he would not add a line to the play without the writer's consent; but he would make suggestions, sometimes even being 'utterly perverse with the text'.[231]

The director Michael Blakemore, commenting on his experiences of workshops with the writer Michael Frayn, has stated that on the final text he would always defer to Frayn as writer:

> But he also knows that if he says, 'No I don't like that', there's a point beyond which I won't argue: he wrote the play and I *must* accept his authority.[232]

In devised theatre, the role of the writer may also be played by a leader figure who is not viewed primarily as a playwright as such. Mermikides relates that Tim Etchells does this job in Forced Entertainment, commenting that:

> … the work as a whole is composite and fragmented. However, once Etchells begins to craft this material into a script, once dramaturgical and aesthetic criteria are applied, then we might ask whether this constitutes the imposition of individual authorship […] After all, the act of writing is the quintessential expression of authorship: a solitary creative act that commits to paper.[233]

[226] Anon 3.
[227] Smith (n 164) 44 and 58, arguing that it is necessary to weigh up critically the grander polemical claims for the egalitarian structure of the company in light of the power-struggle dynamic. This becomes even more crucial in the context of the 'MeToo' scandal that forced Stafford-Clark to depart his most recent theatrical role – A Topping, 'Theatre director Max Stafford-Clark was ousted over inappropriate behaviour' *The Guardian* (20 October 2017) at www.theguardian.com/stage/2017/oct/20/theatre-director-max-stafford-clark-was-ousted-over-inappropriate-behaviour.
[228] Wu (n 1) 57–58.
[229] ibid, 32.
[230] ibid, 46.
[231] ibid, 154.
[232] ibid, 234.
[233] Mermikides (n 188) 115.

The Role of the Director

Respect for the director's influence came across strongly in my interviews. Several interviewees stated that in theatre workshops the director is the 'editor' of the text, but there was acknowledgement that the director's role can go beyond mere edits.[234] This view seems widely held within theatre circles. For instance, the playwright Tom Stoppard has acknowledged the importance of the contributions to his plays by his long-time collaborator, the director Peter Wood, in terms of original development and staging.[235] The writer Alan Bennett has remarked that for the play *Habeas Corpus* the director Ronald Eyre was essential to the play's completion – Eyre's task was to work at 'slimming the text down, seeing what one didn't need'.[236] In a similar vein, with respect to his work with the playwright Michael Frayn, the director Michael Blakemore has asserted:

> I've had quite a big editorial contribution. That was true of *Noises Off*.[237]

More generally, the director Charles Marowitz opines that directorial conception 'adds an entirely new dimension to a dramatist's work'.[238] In relation to the text, Wu argues the director is 'helping to bring it to completion, as he takes practical control of it, mediating it to those involved in its production'.[239] For this reason Wu opines that a director who contributes to a dramatic work in this way during a workshop becomes more than an editor and is 'very nearly a co-author'.[240] Three of the interview participants I spoke with who had worked as directors referred to a sense of co-creation or co-authorship in achieving the final staged work.[241]

A highly specific contribution may create a particularly heightened sense of joint authorship. On this, the director Michael Attenborough has spoken of the significant contributions he has made to plays, including major alterations to characters.[242] The same is true of the director Richard Eyre, who has commented that in the process of the text's evolution, he sometimes has to make important cuts.[243] In fact, Eyre did exactly this when working with the playwright David Hare, stating:

> Actually, the first thing that I did at the end was cut the last line.[244]

[234] Anon 1–6, 15, and 20.
[235] ED Lyman, 'The Page Refigured' (2002) 7 *Performance Research* 90, 100. See also 'Peter Wood: Obituary' *The Guardian* (18 Feb 2016) at www.theguardian.com/stage/2016/feb/18/peter-wood-obituary.
[236] Wu (n 1) 80.
[237] ibid, 234.
[238] Marowitz (n 31).
[239] ibid, 9 and 86.
[240] Wu (n 1) 205.
[241] Anon 9–11.
[242] ibid, 149.
[243] ibid, 181 and 202.
[244] ibid, 203.

Summing up the unsung status of the director's contributions, the writer Michael Frayn has commented on the director Michael Blakemore:

> If you want to make your reputation as a director, you need to direct the classics, because if you direct a play everyone has seen before, everyone can see what you've done. If there's a production of *Hamlet* and everyone's going around on roller-skates, they know that's the director's idea … So the director gets the credit or the blame for this idea. If you do a new play, no one has the faintest idea what was the director's idea and what was the writer's idea, or what the actors suggested in the rehearsal room … But what a good director does with a new play (and what Michael's always done with me) is to work with the writer first of all, both to get the text right and to make sure he's understood the play – which is quite difficult with a new text, it's not at all obvious. With *Noises Off*, for instance, Michael persuaded me to rewrite great slabs of the play, because they were not clear. He also put forward a lot of ideas of his own which I incorporated into the play, but he doesn't get the best director prizes because no one can see the work that's gone on.[245]

Stage directions are another specific addition that directors often make to a text. Alan Bennett remarked that Ronald Eyre's stage directions for *Habeas Corpus* were essential to its success, so much so that 'it can only be staged in the way he staged it; there isn't enough dialogue to do it any other way'.[246]

The distinction between the play-text and a director's staging flourish can be observed from this description by Duncan Wu of a performance of *The Secret Rapture*, written by David Hare and directed by Howard Davies, at the National Theatre in 1987:

> With the female protagonist (Isobel) dead, her sister Marion stood in the garden of Isobel's country house, and spoke the final line of the play: 'Isobel, where are you? Isobel, why don't you come home?'. The published text ended there. But Davies had an audacious touch up his sleeve. At that moment, the actress who had played Isobel appeared at the back of the stage, very dimly seen, behind layer upon layer of stage gauze. The 'ghost' was barely present, barely perceptible, and, almost before it had registered on the mind's eye, the curtain descended. The image resonates whenever I recall that production.[247]

We know from *Sawkins* that stage directions can be protected as part of the dramatic work – but the question of who exactly would own such directions has never come to court in the UK. I reflect further on this ownership question later on.

The Role of the Actors (Performers)

Actors can influence the final performative text in significant ways. I have already referred to one of my interviewees – an actor – who contributed several lines for

[245] ibid, 225–26.
[246] ibid, 80.
[247] ibid, 3.

her character via improvisation during the workshop that ended up in the final version of the text.[248] It is also the case that actors can suggest cuts – Alan Bennett has stated that the actor Nigel Hawthorne insisted on the removal of a key scene at the end of the play, *The Madness of George III*, where the King takes off his crown and discusses his illness with the Queen.[249]

There is also the addition of new material improvised by actors. The director Michael Attenborough, concerning the improvisation by actors (with the writer David Edgar) that led to Scene 6 of *Pentecost* being created, has commented:

> Basically, what they improvised was storytelling, and means of communication. We were just waiting for that moment when David would say 'Okay, I've got enough in my head. Now I'll go away and write the scene.' Of course, one of the difficult things about this (and you have to break it to the actors) is that what comes back is not their scene. They think they have created it – and of course they feel proprietorial to a degree – but what they did was *enable* David to write it, and it is *his* scene. And there was, to a degree, an element of 'But when we improvised we did this, this and this'; and he had to say, 'Yes you did, but that isn't how I've written it; I've written it differently.'[250]

For Scene 6 of *Pentecost*, even if Edgar had 'written it differently' the original contributions of the actors could still be visible in the text, and thus form part of the final work. After all, in *Brighton v Jones*, the director Pamela Brighton's outline scenario was still visible in the final work, and as such her copyright interest in that early scene was protected. So the question of ownership is not as straightforward as claimed by Attenborough here.

The Final 'Transcendent' Work

In light of the above it is possible to argue – per Pierre Bourdieu – that creativity in the theatrical context is a social practice involving power struggles between the various agents active in the field of theatre, such as playwrights, directors and actors.[251] Resolving such power struggles successfully is crucial to the creative process of theatre. Where the workshop process fails, and the collaboration breaks down, the work may fail to materialise. Conversely, from the interviews I conducted it is clear that when the process works it is because there is mutual respect from all parties for each other's roles. As one director said to me, the writer is 'in charge' of the text; the director is 'in charge' of the staging; and the actors must be given the 'freedom to inhabit the roles', which may require improvisation.[252]

[248] Anon 7.
[249] ibid, 85.
[250] ibid, 154.
[251] P Bourdieu, *The State Nobility: Elite Schools in the Fields of Power* (Stanford CA: Stanford University Press, 1996), 264–74. See also generally P Bourdieu, *The Logic of Practice* (Stanford CA: Stanford University Press, 1990).
[252] Anon 10.

When it succeeds, the eventual work transcends the workshop 'struggle', becoming a true 'amalgam of all these elements'.[253] Thus, the director Michael Attenborough has remarked:

> In the end, something happens on stage which transcends that; something like a spirit rises out of the theatrical event which just sweeps everybody along … If you can't collaborate, making those practical decisions, I don't think you get to the higher plane, you don't get to that subsequent transcendent stage.[254]

Given the profound nature of this collaboration, and the examples described above of specific contributions made by the writer, director and actors to the text, it is now necessary to unpack the legal relationship between all parties to the eventual dramatic work, including joint authorship, credit and ownership.

Is the 'Workshopped' Play a Work of Joint Authorship?

The collaborative model of creativity at work in theatre devising/revising via workshops – featuring an unsettled text and multiple creative contributors, as evidenced by the above examples – does not lend itself easily to the traditional way copyright recognises authorship or joint authorship.[255] As Smith states, the attribution of authorship is complicated here by the 'multiple collaborations' at the centre of these creative processes.[256]

With respect to the law, copyright lawyers tend to merely ask: who wrote the play? In a case of disputed authorship, a court will usually ascribe economic and moral rights in the dramatic work to the playwright only. The unsettled nature of the text during workshops, as well as the multifaceted nature of the collaboration, creates a situation where it is difficult for the court to distinguish between, for example, the competing claims of the writer and director. In such a dispute, the court tends to hold in favour of the status quo, that the writer should own the dramatic work, as occurred in *Brighton v Jones*.

Nevertheless, a careful application of copyright doctrine may well identify many more co-authors than are typically acknowledged. Multiple parties may have contributed significant, fixed, original expressions to the dramatic work as it evolved. In the UK, Ireland and other common law territories, cases such

[253] Wu (n 1) 233.

[254] ibid, 151–52.

[255] On the point of attribution, an issue I explore in more detail in ch 5, it is important to note that in the theatre world everybody tends to get some form of credit, from the writer and director to the actors and production staff, in the programme. Often, when a new play is published, the original cast of actors will be named at the beginning of the text – all the actors I interviewed found this gesture on the part of the writer to be very favourable as a means of recognition. See a number of examples of the original cast or actors being credited in S Beckett, *The Complete Dramatic Works* (New York: Faber and Faber, 2006).

[256] Smith (n 164) 49–50.

as *Kogan v Martin* and *Fisher v Brooker* offer hope.[257] UK courts can recognise significant original contributions and joint labouring towards a common design, and thus correctly attribute copyright to multiple collaborators in the workshop context. Conversely, this acknowledgment also reveals how the US/Canadian *Childress/Neudorf* requirement of shared intent can sustain the status quo – such contributors are viewed within a non-authorial prism and the law effectively keeps them there. This reveals the extent to which the established expectations of copyright jurists can hold a powerful sway over the practical ordering of the creative relationships.

There may be other factors at play that make it difficult to reward collaborators. Krause argues the institutional requirements of authorship – specifically, the intention to create an attractive singular marketable 'brand' – have meant that in the case of the Brecht-Hauptmann collaborations 'everything work-related became labelled as "Brecht"' while Hauptmann became 'invisible' as a writer.[258] As Krause laments, the impact of this can be seen as both symbolic and material:

> The collaborators are alienated from themselves and each other, from their texts and the material and symbolic recognition for those texts. Authorship comes to stand between them and between Brecht and them. Hauptmann sometimes received credit as a translator – she received 12.5 per cent of proceeds from The Threepenny Opera. Her name appears as a co-author on several of the plays … Most of the time, though, once a piece was published under Brecht's name – even as the result of a consensual strategy – the royalties would automatically go to Brecht's account.[259]

Thus, by giving one of the agents in the field – the author-playwright – a kind of economic capital in the form of the copyright, the law empowers writers, potentially at the expense of other collaborators.[260] Historically, the courts have tended to enforce the 'author function' in a singular form. Yet, as noted earlier, there has been a welcome shift towards taking a contextual view of creativity in recent UK case law on joint authorship.[261]

Out of 20 interviewees, six participants I spoke to shared experiences involving acting or directing where they ended up feeling aggrieved at a lack of recognition for their contributions to the dramatic work; in these cases they considered that due to contributions they made during the collective creation of the play they deserved a share of the copyright via credit (attribution) and/or via proportionate revenue-sharing (ownership).[262]

[257] *Kogan v Martin* (n 24) and *Fisher v Brooker* (n 131).

[258] Krause (n 157) 11–12.

[259] ibid, 14.

[260] See generally, K Pistor, *The Code of Capital: How the Law Creates Wealth and Inequality* (Princeton, NJ: Princeton University Press, 2019).

[261] *Kogan v Martin* (n 24). Craig and Kerr (n 125). See also MT Sundara Rajan, 'Moral rights: the future of copyright law?' (2019) 14 *Journal of Intellectual Property Law & Practice* 257.

[262] Anon 7, 10–11, 13–14, 16.

As in *Brighton v Jones*, proving such cases in court can be difficult.[263] Only four of the 20 interviewees had heard of the legal dispute over *Stones in his Pockets*, and overall, their understanding of copyright law tended to be scattered at best. Furthermore, none of the six aggrieved participants had seriously considered taking legal proceedings against the author-playwright. The reasons given for this included the purported costs of engaging in legal action, as well as the common concern that it would be a 'waste of creative energy', as one director put it.[264] There may also be reputational harm caused within the community from having breached informal norms, which form an important part of how the theatrical community regulates itself.[265]

Indeed, the issue of joint authorship of plays during the early stages of the play's life very rarely results in a court case in the UK. Nonetheless, there have been high profile disputes in recent years, especially in the case of *Tree* in 2019.[266] Notably in that dispute, despite having a plausible argument that they were joint authors of early drafts of the dramatic work, the two purported joint authors decided not to pursue legal action, citing the financial cost involved; instead, they made their complaint in the media.[267] This reluctance to take legal action, even when possessing a relatively strong case, chimes with the experiences of the interviewees I spoke with.

The actor/dramaturge I interviewed stated very clearly that if a lot of improvisation has gone on via the workshop process, then 'credit should be given'. This potentially includes 'a share of ownership' and related revenues being provided to the person who made the contribution. When I asked her if she could quantify when such a contribution would reach the point where shared ownership would become justifiable, she replied by stating that it was a difficult question to answer in the abstract, but that it would have to be 'more than adding a few lines'.[268]

The director Michael Blakemore has spoken of not being credited for his contributions to plays, noting that that 'moments of invention that I'm particularly proud of have been credited to the authors'.[269] Blakemore stated that, despite tensions arising, he come to terms with the writer's pre-eminence as part of the theatrical bargain:

> There is a certain antagonism, I think, between writers and directors, built into the job, because the director *has* to accept that the play is, as it were, the first cause. There would be no production without it, and his artistic vision is at the service of someone else's … I had a successful collaboration with Peter Nichols earlier in my career, but it really did

[263] *Brighton v Jones* (n 20).
[264] Anon 11.
[265] Anon 7 and 11.
[266] M Brown, 'Writers claim being excluded after creating Idris Elba play' *The Guardian* (July 2019), see www.theguardian.com/culture/2019/jul/02/writers-claim-being-excluded-after-creating-idris-elbas-play.
[267] Henley and Allen-Martin (n 127).
[268] Anon 14.
[269] Wu (n 1) 233.

> break down after about three shows … Peter was a little bit resentful of the contribution that I made, and I suppose I was resentful because he wasn't quite acknowledging that contribution … The human mind is extraordinarily proprietorial and protective of the things it invents, the things that it adds to the universe.[270]

One interesting aspect of this comment is that despite a feeling of 'antagonism' Blakemore accepted that a lack of authorial recognition for directors is 'built into' the community architecture of theatre; he did not express a desire to alter this structure. Yet, others are not so sanguine. In our conversations the six interviewees who had gone through a negative experience regarding a lack of credit and ownership indicated a hope that the community structure would become more accepting of their contributions.

The Importance of Contracts

All the interviewees I spoke with acknowledged that it would be preferable to specify at the beginning of the creative process what the credit and ownership rights situation will be at the end of the project. Yet, they universally agreed that this did not always happen.[271] This not surprising – the focus when starting a new project is, inevitably, on getting the artistic part of the collaboration up and running, rather than dealing with contractual practicalities.

Nonetheless, a failure to agree credit and rights issues beforehand can have important consequences. In the (admittedly rare) case that the devised/revised play starts to generate a lot of revenue, multiple claims could arise. This occurred in *Brighton v Jones*, a case which arose largely because the relevant work – a revised 'workshopped play – had, unexpectedly, become a big hit, with productions on Broadway and in the West End.[272] In the case of *Brighton v Jones*, the dispute over *Tree*, and the six examples given by my interviewees, parties were left feeling aggrieved when their contributions went unrecognised.

Some clarity is brought to the situation by *The Working Playwright*'s outline of the agreement between the Writers' Guild of Great Britain and the major UK theatres. It provides for standard contractual terms and standard fees for writers. Furthermore, it specifies that the copyright in the final work should belong to the writer, even if other contributors add substantially to the text during the workshop:[273]

> Crucially, the definition of 'writer' includes 'writer of a play created wholly or partly by improvisation', and the 'play' includes any changes made in the text.

[270] ibid, 246.
[271] Anon 1–20.
[272] *Brighton v Jones* (n 27).
[273] The 2015 Writers Agreement and *The Working Playwright* (Writers' Guild of Great Britain, 2019) aims to deal with such disputes in advance, see https://writersguild.org.uk/wp-content/uploads/2015/02/WGGB_booklet_jun12_contracts_i.pdf; https://writersguild.org.uk/wp-content/uploads/2019/08/WGGB-Working-Playwright-Agreements-and-Contracts-1.pdf.

> This means that the writer alone owns the copyright of the play, whether or not others have contributed to its creation or final form. The play includes the stage directions.

In other words, contracts agreed with The Writers' Guild of Great Britain specify that the writer owns copyright in the play regardless of whether other parties make original contributions (including stage directions) sufficient to create a copyright interest.[274] Thus, as a common term of agreement between writers and theatres, playwrights usually obtain the copyright in the dramatic work at the end of the process, regardless of how much collective devising/revising has occurred. These contracts do not, however, apply to all theatres in the UK.[275] Nor would such agreements deal with the scenario that arose in *Tree*, a collaboration involving an actor and several writers/devisers working together. Moreover, even where contracts exist, disputes may yet occur if a non-writer makes an unexpectedly substantial contribution. There was a contract in place in *Brighton v Jones*, and it was ultimately relevant to the outcome in Jones' favour; but it did not preclude the legal claim for joint authorship under copyright from coming to court.[276]

The Working Playwright is a laudable attempt to bring legal certainty to a complex situation. The Writers' Guild of Great Britain, and especially the playwright David Edgar as the (now former) Theatre Committees Co-Chair, deserve praise for developing an accessible summary of the legal agreements. Yet, the attempt to create legal certainty for the writer arguably comes at the cost of recognising the *value* of the original, collaborative contributions of the other creative parties (indeed it attempts to pre-empt such claims).

This brings up a question of fairness: what *should* the law protect in such scenarios? Consider the six interviewees (out of 20) who shared experiences with me where they considered it would have been just to share attribution and ownership rights.[277] *The Working Playwright* and associated agreements would not provide a solution for them. They, as per Michael Blakemore,[278] are expected to accept that the structures of theatre priortise the writer in this way. Not everybody in UK theatre shares this deference to this 'accepted' norm. Companies like Frantic Assembly and Forced Entertainment show a keen awareness of the way that their practices 'do not fit neatly into the institutional constraints and expected structures of copyright, royalties, marketing, and programming'.[279] In the US context, Shechtman remarks:

> If it's truly a collaborative art form, then why is it only the author who participates in the subsidiary rights that flow from a successful New York production? The appropriate resolution is to give fair credit to all the artists' contributions. One day, it may end up

[274] ibid.

[275] The agreements are broken into three separate ones – one for The National Theatre, the Royal Shakespeare Company and the Royal Court; one for repertory theatres and several other UK theatres that receive public subsidies; and a final one covering some independent theatres.

[276] *Brighton v Jones* (n 20).

[277] Admittedly, this was a minority of those I interviewed, though not an insignificant minority.

[278] Wu (n 1) 233.

[279] Smith (n 164) 49–50.

> that the author gets eighty percent, the director ten percent, the original cast X and the designers Z. Because, at bottom, this is all about money.[280]

Even if the Writers' Guild of Great Britain-agreed contract specifies that the writer owns the copyright in the final work, can this be changed if circumstances warrant it? The answer is, of course, yes. If all parties agree, a new contract can be drawn up to share credit and ownership, including royalties. As noted earlier, a recent example of shared credit and ownership by contractual agreement concerns the play *Blurred Lines*, first staged at the National Theatre in 2014, with both writer Payne and director Cracknell sharing the copyright ownership in the dramatic work, and other parties given credit for eg contributing poetry.[281]

One point which came out clearly from the interviews is that, in practice the question of when credit and royalty-sharing actually occurs tends to depend on the playwright's consent as 'default' copyright owner (as envisaged by *The Working Playwright*).[282] In particular, it seems that only in a small number of cases does royalty sharing occur in practice, and whether this occurs tends to depend on the writer's decision. In the case of *Tree*, however, it was the two initial writers – Henley and Allen-Martin – who ended up with neither credit nor ownership/royalties.[283]

On credit, Tony Kushner gave attribution – thought not authorial credit as such – to six separate casts in the first book publication of *Angels in America*, lauding the first cast in particular for having 'transformed' the play during its early workshops.[284] My interviewees generally expressed support for attribution of the original cast of a new play in the published version, and it can offer solace to the actors and director even where this attribution is not specifically authorial. However, there may be cases where attribution may not suffice. The work *A Mouthful of Birds* (1986) was created as an innovative 'play with dance' via a collaboration between Caryl Churchill, the director-playwright David Lan, the choreographer Ian Spink and the artistic director Les Waters.[285] Spink, who had contributed choreography, and was attributed as choreographer, did not receive a share in the copyright ownership of the resulting text, which accrued only to Churchill and Lan. He later stated that it 'did feel very strange' that only Churchill and Lan received royalties for licensing of the play.[286]

[280] J Green, 'Exit, Pursued by a Lawyer' *The New York Times* (29 Jan 2006).

[281] Contemporary reviews commented on the profound nature of their collaboration, see www.curtisbrown.co.uk/news/3237. The credits are shown in this official National Theatre excerpt: https://d1hsr9wh84jepr.cloudfront.net/newviews-excerpt4-blurredlines-2014-15.pdf.

[282] The 2015 Writers Agreement and *The Working Playwright* (Writers' Guild of Great Britain, 2019) aims to deal with such disputes in advance, see https://writersguild.org.uk/wp-content/uploads/2015/02/WGGB_booklet_jun12_contracts_i.pdf; https://writersguild.org.uk/wp-content/uploads/2019/08/WGGB-Working-Playwright-Agreements-and-Contracts-1.pdf.

[283] Henley and Allen-Martin (n 128).

[284] T Kushner, *Angels in America – A Gay Fantasia on National Themes* (New York: Theatre Communications Group, 1995).

[285] DR Gobert, *The Theatre of Caryl Churchill* (London: Methuen, 2014) 52–53. Gobert relates that although Caryl Churchill did participate in Joint Stock productions, by the early 1980s she had formed 'Caryl Churchill Ltd' to manage her copyrights.

[286] ibid.

On royalties, Lin-Manuel Miranda and producer Jeffrey Seller decided to share royalties – but not authorial credit as such – with the original cast of *Hamilton* in recognition of the contributions made by those actors in the early stages and workshops.[287] The *New York Times* reported:[288]

> Last fall, it was reported that members of the cast asked Seller for a share of the gross, though they are not owed that by contract. 'They are the ones bringing this show to life,' he told me. 'It was a powerful argument they made; it was gut-wrenching for me, and I took it seriously.' (He would not give specifics but said that he had reached an agreement and that the matter was resolved, at least for now.)

As noted earlier, six of my interviewees expressed some discontent about not being credited or rewarded adequately for their creative contributions to particular works. Two other interviewees – both of whom had written works for the stage – shared examples where they *had* agreed to sharing of credit and ownership in a play with another party. The actor/director/writer spoke of an example in his own career when 'I elected to share credit and ownership' with another actor who had 'worked in collaboration' with him.[289] This had not been the initial plan, but after the process had ended, he realised that the contributions made by the actor were 'sufficiently weighty' for it to be the fair thing to do.[290] The other of the two – a writer – stated that one collaborative project he had undertaken with an actor resulted in such a profoundly co-authored work that 'it would have been wrong for me to claim sole credit and ownership'.[291]

Nonetheless, several of the remaining interviewees had not experienced this, with the rest of the writers in particular opposing authorship-sharing. One writer told me very clearly that he would not 'share credit or ownership in almost any circumstance' because even if a suggestion made by another party, for example, an actor, found its way into the play, 'I am still the person putting that suggestion into expression'.[292] Another playwright stressed that it ought to be the case that 'the writer should always hold the power' to decide whether or not to share credit/ownership with others.[293] The same writer also said that the economic model of theatre had influenced his views on this. In this regard, he told me that writers tended to earn 'very little from their upfront labour', that is, they received a small payment to cover the licensing of the play for its initial theatrical run. In this context, he saw the retention of copyright in the play, in the event that it did go

[287] R Morgan, 'How Hamilton's Cast Got Broadway's Best Deal' *Bloomberg* (28 September 2016), available at www.bloomberg.com/features/2016-hamilton-broadway-profit/. A similar agreement was reached with the writers and producers of another popular musical – *The Book of Mormon*. See P Boroff, 'Mormon Pays Millions to Workshop Cast as Actors Developing New Shows Find Royalties in Short Supply' *Broadway Journal* (15 April 2016), available at http://broadwayjournal.com/mormon-pays-millions-to-workshop-cast-as-actors-lament-rise-of-royalty-free-developmental-labs/.

[288] M Sokolove, 'The C.E.O. of 'Hamilton' Inc.' (5 April 2016), available at www.nytimes.com/2016/04/10/magazine/the-ceo-of-hamilton-inc.html.

[289] Anon 15.

[290] ibid.

[291] Anon 1.

[292] Anon 4.

[293] Anon 2.

on to generate lots of revenue, as the writer's 'reward'.[294] Of course, directors and actors can also be low paid, so this is not an irrefutable argument.[295] Intriguingly, the same interviewee stated that he would be more open to sharing authorship if the structures of theatre were set up differently, and if his position – particularly in terms of economic support and revenue – was more secure.

Weidman makes a distinction between professionalised TV/film-writing, and writing for the stage. He argues TV and film writers tend to be reasonably well paid in comparison with playwrights; but they often have to cede final control over production and story to the companies they are employed by or that they contract with.[296] By contrast, Weidman calls theatre 'a writer's medium' with ownership of the copyright in the play providing a 'legal firewall guaranteeing that it will remain that way'.[297] Weidman resists calls to allow non-writers such as directors a share in the copyright.

On ownership, the playwright David Edgar has stated that even in the case of Scene 6 of *Pentecost*, where the actors had added substantially to the text, it was still right that he retained full ownership:

> It wasn't like they were playing themselves … they weren't their own creation. In fact, two-thirds of all of the parts were there already. To that extent they were being fantastically helpful, but they weren't producing something which was exclusively theirs – so in this case I didn't see it as a problem. There are certain moral issues about things being created, but artistically I didn't regard that as a problem.[298]

Yet, if it is true that the actors 'weren't producing something which was exclusively theirs' then it is also true that Edgar was not producing something that was *exclusively his*. Edgar's presumption that he should own the resulting text is, of course, not surprising; as noted earlier, he was one of the driving forces behind *The Working Playwright*, which prioritises the writer's ownership.

Overall, the normative presumption of the writers' ownership of copyright seems strong in the theatre community, even if not universally popular. In the field of stand-up comedy, Oliar and Sprigman argue that social norms are the main way by which comedians regulate cases against possible joint authorship, with litigation a rare occurrence. Oliar and Sprigman show that the key norm is that the comedian who comes up with the central premise owns the joke, regardless of whether any other party provided additional input.[299] This seems close to the scenario envisaged by *The Working Playwright*, which states that the writer should own the copyright regardless of who else has made original contributions.[300]

[294] Anon 2.

[295] R Swain, 'Low Pay, No Pay, Fringe Theatre' *The Guardian* (11 June 2013), see www.guardian.co.uk/culture-professionals-network/culture-professionals-blog/2013/jun/11/low-pay-no-pay-fringe-theatre.

[296] Weidman (n 153) 641. See also Fisk (n 23).

[297] Weidman (n 153) 642.

[298] Wu (n 1) 143.

[299] D Oliar and C Sprigman, 'There's No Free Laugh (Anymore): The Emergence of Intellectual Property Norms and the Transformation of Stand-Up Comedy' (2008) 94 *VA. L. Rev.* 1787, 1825. See also G Pate, *Enter the Undead Author: Intellectual Property, the Ideology of Authorship, and Performance Practices Since the 1960s* (Lanham, Maryland: The Rowman & Littlefield Publishing Group, 2019).

[300] The 2015 Writers Agreement and *The Working Playwright* (Writers' Guild of Great Britain, 2019) aims to deal with such disputes in advance, see https://writersguild.org.uk/wp-content/uploads/2015/02/

Yet in the theatrical realm, the lingering impression is of a contradiction: theatre as a field that encourages joint labour to be realized in the form of a collaborative product (the dramatic work), and yet which fails to recognise the authorial nature of those collaborative contributions.[301]

Assessing the Legal Problems that can Arise from Sharing Ownership

Splitting authorship and ownership can be a fair solution – but it does have significant practical consequences.[302] Weidman argues that awarding, for example, directors a share of ownership will produce complications and could encourage litigation.[303] Similarly, Bently describes the complexities than can result when authorship is split in UK law:

> Because a single property owner means that assignments and licences of copyright are easier and cheaper to effect, copyright law prefers to minimise the number of authorial contributions it is prepared to acknowledge rather than reflect the 'realities' of collaborative authorship. To simplify ownership in this way may privilege certain contributions over others, but it provides a property nexus around which contractual arrangements can be made recognising the value of those other contributions.[304]

Nevertheless, Simone argues persuasively that contractual arrangements will be far more effective if all the relevant authors have a 'bargaining chip' since contractual bargaining occurs in the 'shadow' of the law.[305]

An example of the complications that can arise from shared ownership is the playwright Mike Kenny's work at the Leeds Playhouse Theatre. Kenny agreed to collaborative 'devising' which was 'deliberately egalitarian'.[306] With respect to the pieces created, ownership was shared equally between each individual in the Playhouse – even the stage manager and administrator, who Kenny noted were 'people who hadn't been actively involved in putting the words on the paper'.[307] Due to this, Kenny lamented that subsequent productions were 'administratively difficult' to put on – and the copyright royalties ended up being 'split thinly' between 'the nine or so people involved'.[308] Kenny also remarked that 'towards the end of that period it started to feel egalitarian but inequitable' because of the fact that 'some people were much more at the heart of creation than others' yet

WGGB_booklet_jun12_contracts_i.pdf;https://writersguild.org.uk/wp-content/uploads/2019/08/WGGB-Working-Playwright-Agreements-and-Contracts-1.pdf.

[301] Gobert (n 285).

[302] See generally MA Heller, 'The Tragedy of the anti-commons: Property in the transition from Marx to Markets' (1998) 111 *Harvard Law Review* 621.

[303] Weidman (n 153) 651.

[304] Bently (n 71) 981–82, citing *Wiseman v Wiedenfeld* [1985] FSR 525.

[305] Simone (n 2) 249–50.

[306] Smith (n 164) 44, referring to an interview he undertook with Mike Kenny in March 2011.

[307] ibid.

[308] ibid.

everyone received the same share.[309] Thus, it must be acknowledged that recognising collaboration and shared ownership does not always work as well as hoped.[310] Some individuals sometimes end up shouldering more of the burden and may feel aggrieved if credit and ownership are shared equally. Nancy Meckler, director of The Freehold – a pioneering theatre collective in the UK active in the late 1960s until the mid-1970s – has commented to this effect.[311]

Conclusion

As Stern remarks, 'we do not, even now, have a standard approach to the concept of the dramatic author'.[312] Nor should we, given the intense variety of ways plays get created, as I have outlined in this chapter. Although there are situations where fully-formed texts are submitted to theatres, in most cases theatrical authorship is profoundly social and centred on devising/revising. There are various creative agents – playwrights, directors and actors – making contributions and the eventual performance on stage is constitutive of the creative acts of all the collaborating parties.[313] Workshop processes are iterative with the play going through several different versions before emerging as the final work. The eventual output of the theatrical workshop – embodied by the script – provides an example of how 'the spontaneity of mental creativity has to be materialised before it can constitute property'.[314]

Despite this, and more than 50 years after the work of Foucault and Barthes, the myths of singular authorship endure; collective processes still struggle for visibility and legal recognition.[315] Given the practical realities of collaboration in theatre, why is there still a preference, whether among readers, audiences or courts, for single authors? Hirschfield offers one answer: that post-Barthes/Foucault, some scholars have begun to resuscitate 'ideas of authorship and of its purposes and agencies; to clarify investments and stakes in the "author function"; and to attend to authorial activities of production and consumption in what Pierre Bourdieu calls "the field of cultural production"'.[316] As in chapter two, this brings to mind

[309] Smith (n 164).

[310] Wu (n 1).

[311] D Heddon and J Milling, *Devising Performance: A Critical History* (Basingstoke: Palgrave Macmillan, 2006) 47.

[312] T Stern, 'Review of Authorship and Appropriation: Writing for the Stage in England, 1660–1710' (2002) *The Scriblerian* 73, 74.

[313] P Bourdieu, *The State Nobility: Elite Schools in the Fields of Power* (Stanford CA: Stanford University Press, 1996) 264–74. See also generally P Bourdieu, *The Logic of Practice* (Stanford CA: Stanford University Press, 1990).

[314] A Pottage and M Mundy (eds), *Law, Anthropology, and the Constitution of the Social – Making Persons and Things* (Cambridge: Cambridge University Press, 2004), 1, 9.

[315] Krause (n 157) 219.

[316] H Hirschfeld, 'Early Modern Collaboration and Theories of Authorship' (2001) 116 *Theories and Methodologies* 609, 619–20.

the idea that the theatrical text is not just a text – it is a copyright work, a multi-faceted commodity potentially underpinning value in print, performance and adaptation. This puts the issue of ownership to the fore.

As legal property, copyright is at the core of this institutional system that perpetuates individualist notions of authorship. The way that works of theatre are created today is a collaborative reality that copyright law does not easily acknowledge.[317] Publishers and courts have a tendency to prefer singular authors because ownership of property rights is more straightforward – and transactions easier to complete – when there are fewer owners.[318] Creative collaboration is often underplayed and 'almost always flies under the banner of single authorship'.[319] Royalties and licence fees become the supposed 'return' on the investment in the author function. Indeed, for marketing purposes, it can be easier to sell, for example, the works of Brecht's workshop under the singular brand name of 'Brecht' rather than deal with the fractured, collective voices who contributed to the plays. Traditionally, when judges are faced with assessing claims of copyright law, such as in *Brighton*, they tend to focus more on maintaining legal coherence and continuity of ownership than on contextual analysis of fluid creative practices.[320]

Copyright law can thus refuse to recognise important contributions to the play during the workshop where these are classed as mere 'ideas'. Copyright scholars critique this and argue for the law to be more open to the actual creative practices of authorship.[321] At the same time, as Salter relates, there is a danger that legal reform may disrupt informal theatrical practices.[322]

On this, it is worth recognising that legislative reform may not actually be necessary because the courts in the UK have already begun to revise the joint authorship test – the contextual approach taken in the *Kogan v Martin* case is a step in the right direction.[323] Fairness demands that when deciding questions of authorship and ownership, the courts must continue this recent trend of being open to contextual evidence, weighing up the claims in light of the complexities of the creative field within which the work emerged.[324]

[317] Bently (n 71) 981. Examples include how entrepreneurial works can be protected, eg films and sound recordings under the CDPA and of course, for computer-generated works.

[318] J Bellido and F MacMillan, 'Music Copyright after Collectivisation' (2016) *Intellectual Property Quarterly* 231. Concord Theatricals (Samuel French) is the agency that licenses the works of Pinter, Bennett, Beckett, Churchill, Ayckbourn etc for performance. Of importance is the Authors' Licensing and Collecting Society (ALCS) which collects and distributes royalties to authors for print sale/use, see www.alcs.co.uk.

[319] A Lunsford and L Ede in 'Collaborative Authorship and the Teaching of Writing' in M Woodmansee and P Jaszi (eds), *The Construction Of Authorship: Textual Appropriation In Law and Literature* (Durham, NC: Duke University Press, 1994) 418.

[320] Bently (n 71) 980.

[321] L Bently and L Biron, 'Discontinuities between legal conceptions of authorship and social practices: What, if anything, is to be done?' in M van Eechoud (ed), *The Work of Authorship* (Amsterdam: Amsterdam University Press, 2018) 237, 270–76.

[322] Salter (n 2) 891.

[323] Simone (n 24).

[324] Simone (n 2).

Nevertheless, the costs of litigation – both in monetary terms and in terms of time wasted – remain such that most theatre participants tend to avoid litigation. The recent dispute over the play *Tree* is an example of this – it went unresolved by law and played out instead in the media (and within the theatre community).[325] As such, although the courts should maintain conceptual openness when it comes to joint authorship, we as lawyers cannot expect this alone to suffice. Copyright law is not the be-all and end-all; it remains in many instances a tool of the powerful; but there are times when for unsung parties it can prove to be a powerful tool, the impact of which may be felt outside of the legal system.[326] For instance, it may be the case that a precedent like *Kogan* encourages more joint authorship claims within the theatre field; by contrast, the earlier precedent of *Brighton* may well have discouraged the pursuit of such claims, even within the theatrical community.[327] Many of the new 'disputes' may not actually come to court – they may simply be resolved amicably between the parties, such as when the two interviewees I spoke with agreed to share credit and ownership via contract with their respective co-authors. This is encouraging, as is the sharing of copyright in the play *Blurred Lines* created by the writer Nick Payne and the director Carrie Cracknell.[328] Even if it can make licensing of rights more complex, the argument that credit and ownership should be shared proportionately based on what each contributor has added to the work remains compelling.[329]

[325] Henley and Allen-Martin (n 128). Even the costs of litigation at the Intellectual Property Enterprise Court – where recoverable costs are capped at £50,000 – can be off-putting to theatre artists.

[326] M Iljadica, *Copyright Beyond Law: Regulating Creativity in the Graffiti Subculture* (Oxford: Hart, 2016) 289.

[327] RH Mnookin and L Korhauser, 'Bargaining in the Shadow of the Law: The case of divorce' (1979) 88 *Yale LRev* 950.

[328] See https://www.curtisbrown.co.uk/client/nick-payne/work/blurred-lines.

[329] A George, *Constructing Intellectual Property* (Cambridge: Cambridge University Press, 2012) 177.

4

When Does Copyright Infringement Occur on 'The Haunted Stage'?

Introduction

Theatrical ghosts are varied – the Senecan, the Shakespearean, the Ibsenian – and they interact, inevitably, with the ghosts, memories and traumas we as an audience bring to our attendance of plays.[1] For this reason Carlson puts forward the idea that that theatre is a 'haunted stage', with new performances regularly stimulating the spectators' recollections, conjuring up the ghosts of previous plays and productions.[2] Carlson's notion raises an important issue at the heart of all that is haunting about drama; namely that theatre is a medium that builds upon prior existing works, tropes, themes and quotations. Throughout dramatic history, virtually every aspect of stage production has been recycled. How does the idea of copyright infringement operate in this theatrical context?[3]

There is little contemporary case law on infringement of dramatic works, which means that analogies must be drawn from cases involving literature and music. The verbatim copying of dialogue, or the taking of a small amount of text from one work and using it in another, is likely to amount to copyright infringement.[4] Dialogue and text aside, the more difficult question is where to draw the boundary between copyright infringement and the creative re-use of theatrical tropes, characters and scenarios. How can copyright law draw a line between the acceptable 'evoking' of another writer's work and infringing 'substantial' taking from the work itself?

[1] C Perry, *Shakespeare and Senecan Tragedy* (Cambridge: Cambridge University Press, 2020); W Shakespeare, *The Oxford Shakespeare: Hamlet* (S Wells ed, Oxford: Oxford University Press, 2008); H Ibsen, *Four Major Plays (Doll's House; Ghosts; Hedda Gabler; and The Master Builder)* (J McFarlane and J Arup tr, Oxford: Oxford University Press, 2008).

[2] M Carlson, *The Haunted Stage: The Theatre as Memory Machine* (Ann Arbor, MI: Michigan University Press, 2001).

[3] D Miller, *Copyright and the Value of Performance, 1770–1911* (Cambridge: Cambridge University Press, 2018). See also MH Birkhold, *Characters Before Copyright: The Rise and Regulation of Fan Fiction in Eighteenth-Century Germany* (Oxford: Oxford University Press, 2019). See generally A Schwarbach, *Fan Fiction and Copyright: Outsider Works and Intellectual Property Protection* (Farnham: Ashgate, 2011).

[4] Case C-5/08 *Infopaq International A/S v Danske Dagblades Forening* [2009] ECR I-6569 ('*Infopaq*'). *Newspaper Licensing Agency v Meltwater* [2010] EWHC 3099 (Ch) ('*Meltwater*'). See also on appeal [2011] EWCA Civ 890 and [2013] UKSC 18.

In this chapter I examine the doctrine of copyright infringement and the various fair dealing exceptions/limitations under UK law, with comparative insights drawn from jurisdictions such as the US, Canada, Australia and India. Relying on literature from theatrical studies, as well as the empirical case study, this chapter reveals insights about the way theatrical participants (directors, playwrights, actors, producers) regulate – or choose not to regulate – disputes about copying, allegations of plagiarism and cases of infringement.

The empirical interview data show that re-interpretation, and even copying, is a common-place 'natural' part of the theatrical creative process. Litigation is rare. Moreover, participants possess divergent views on the rights and wrongs of copying. At times, UK theatre participants appear to regulate themselves – this regulation appears to be *normative* but not legal, with resolutions found outside of the mechanisms of copyright law. Even in relatively clear cases of copying, artists are wary of entering the arena of law, fearing both the costs of litigation and that the ultimate result could be a 'bad precedent' that restricts the overall freedom to create.[5] The chapter concludes by reflecting on the legal ramifications of the theatrical creative process and assessing the social norms at play in the theatrical context.[6]

Claims of Plagiarism and Infringement in Theatre in Historical Perspective 1709–1911

In chapter two I considered the dramatic texts in the context of early modern theatre, from the Elizabethan period up to the dawn of the twentieth century. As discussed, it was common in the sixteenth and seventeenth centuries for writers to make use of entire plots and characters from ancient and contemporary plays in their own new texts.[7] Playwrights of the time did not shy away from this; nor did they have any reason to hide it.[8] Copyright law as we know it did not yet exist and while there were formal and informal ways of regulating theatrical practice,

[5] See generally R Tushnet, 'Free to Be You and Me? Copyright and Constraint' (2015) 128 *Harvard Law Review Forum* 125; R Tushnet, 'My Fair Ladies: Sex, Gender, and Fair Use in Copyright' (2006) 15 *American University Journal of Gender, Social Policy, and Law* 273 and A Chander and M Sunder, 'Everyone's a Superhero: A Cultural Theory of Mary Sue Fan Fiction as Fair Use' (2007) 95 *California Law Review* 597.

[6] E Fauchart and E Von Hippel, 'Norms-Based Intellectual Property Systems: The Case of French Chefs' (2008) 19 *Organization Science* 187; D Oliar and C Sprigman, 'There's No Free Laugh (Anymore): The Emergence of Intellectual Property Norms and the Transformation of Stand-Up Comedy' (2008) 94 *Virginia Law Review* 1787; D Fagundes, 'Talk Derby to Me: Intellectual Property Norms Governing Roller Derby Pseudonyms' (2011) 90 *Texas Law Review* 1093 and E Sarid, 'Don't Be a Drag, Just Be a Queen-How Drag Queens Protect their Intellectual Property without Law' (2014) 10 *FIU Law Review* 133.

[7] See generally L Erne, *Shakespeare as Literary Dramatist*, 2nd edn (Cambridge: Cambridge University Press, 2013).

[8] See generally P Kewes, *Authorship and Appropriation: Writing for the Stage in England, 1660–1710* (Oxford: Clarendon Press, 1998). See also P Kewes (ed), *Plagiarism in Early Modern England* (London: Palgrave MacMillan, 2003).

there was nothing akin to what we know as copyright infringement litigation.[9] Re-using another playwright's plot, or even their dialogue, on stage was not a matter for copyright: only *print* mattered in law and print was in the hands of the Stationers' Company.

Kewes notes that towards the end of the seventeenth century the practices of theatrical appropriation changed as 'demand for the explicit acknowledgement of sources intensified'.[10] The ever-expanding market for printed playbooks 'prompted an enquiry into the licence of authors to appropriate older texts'.[11] As discussed in chapter two, the shift towards recognising individual authorship grew in significance from the Statute of Anne 1710 onward, along with a presumption of originality on the part of the writer (as author) that was perfectly in line with the ethos of the new emerging copyright law.[12] At the time of the Statute of Anne, infringement meant printing without the permission of the copyright owner.[13] What was protected was the 'book as a physical entity'.[14] As discussed in chapter two, by the mid-eighteenth century the courts began to view the right as applying to an immaterial text beyond the physical book, though one limited to the words on the page, as opposed to the incidents described therein.[15]

The possible consequences of the protection of the immaterial text did not go unnoticed. The 1762 book *An Enquiry in the Nature and Origin of Literary Property* contains a prescient lamentation over what could occur under the rapidly expanding law of copyright:

> Poet would commence his Action against Poet, and Historian against Historian, complaining of literary Trespasses. Juries would be puzzled, what Damage to give for the pilfering of an Anecdote, or purloining the Fable of a Play.[16]

Nonetheless, theatrical plagiarism was commonplace in the eighteenth century.[17] It was not until the nineteenth century that the prominence of theatre

[9] B Lauriat, 'Literary and Dramatic Disputes in Shakespeare's Time' (2018) 9 *Journal of International Dispute Settlement* 45.
[10] Kewes (n 8).
[11] ibid.
[12] ibid.
[13] Section 1 of An Act for the Encouragement of Learning by Vesting the Copies of Printed Books in the Authors or Purchasers of Such Copies during the Times Therein Mentioned 1709 (Imp) 8 Anne, c 19 – The Statute of Anne stated that the owner of the book's 'Copy' possessed 'the sole liberty of printing and reprinting' it and any infringer would be liable to 'forfeit such Book or Books, and all and every Sheet or Sheets' giving the owner the right to 'forthwith Damask and make Waste Paper of them'.
[14] B Kaplan, *An Unhurried View of Copyright* (New York: Columbia University Press, 1967) 9.
[15] *Pope v Curl* [1741] EngR 500; (1741) 2 Atk 342; 26 ER 608 and *Millar v Taylor* [1769] EngR 44; (1769) 4 Burr 2303, 2396; [1769] EngR 44; 98 ER 201, 251 (Lord Mansfield). See also B Sherman and A Strowel (eds), *Of Authors and Origins: Essays on Copyright Law* (Oxford: Clarendon Press, 1994).
[16] W Warburton, *An Enquiry in the Nature and Origin of Literary Property* (London: William Flexney, 1762).
[17] LJ Rosenthal, *Playwrights and Plagiarists in Early Modern England* (Ithaca: Cornell University Press, 1996). There is some evidence that literary and dramatic characters were viewed as 'common property' by the public, with unauthorised 'sequels' circulating within the literary market during the 18th century – see generally DA Brewer, *The Afterlife of Character 1726–1825* (Philadelphia: University of Pennsylvania, 2005).

as a public art forum led to several key copyright case precedents arising on the concept of infringement relevant to theatre. As described in chapter two, claims of infringement of works of theatre increased both in number and in breadth of claim at this time.[18] This included claims over the right to perform (rather than print) the work;[19] to make adaptations/dramatisations;[20] and, eventually, for protection of particular dramatic scenarios/scenes (rather than dialogue).[21] These latter 'scenario' claims were generally not successful in the UK in the nineteenth century, as copyright in dramatic pieces was associated with the text itself (*Scholtz v Amasis & Fenn*).[22] However, as mentioned in chapter two, the situation was different in the US where the 1868 case of *Daly v Palmer* established copyright in an incident or scenario; specifically, the 'oncoming train' scene in Daly's play was held to be infringed by the defendant's use of a very similar scene in another work (even where the precise dialogue was not copied).[23]

Even if UK law did not yet clearly protect against such non-literal copying, by the end of the nineteenth century the contemporary commentator Augustine Birrell anticipated that it was only a matter of time before such claims were successful, lamenting that asking judges to make determinations about whether 'plots' or 'scenes' had been copied without permission was a near impossible task:

> Plots, situations, and scenes have been the common property, both of novelists and dramatists, for so long a time that to attempt to set them out now by metes and bounds … would tax even the lettered intellect of a judge of the Chancery Division.[24]

As I explore below, from 1911 onwards the UK courts have indeed attempted to deal with this 'taxing' issue.

[18] Several amendments to the law were made by legislation with the Dramatic Copyright Act 1833 and the Copyright Act 1842 being the most important – Engraving Copyright Act 1734 (Imp) 8 Geo 2, c 13; Engraving Copyright Act 1767 (Imp) 7 Geo 3, c 38; Copyright Act 1775 (Imp) 15 Geo 3, c 53; Prints Copyright Act 1777 (Imp) 17 Geo 3, c 57; Sculpture Copyright Act 1814 (UK) 54 Geo 3, c 56; Dramatic Copyright Act 1833 (UK) 3 & 4 Wm 4, c 15; Lectures Copyright Act 1835 (UK) 5 & 6 Wm 4, c 65; Prints and Engraving Copyright (Ireland) Act 1836 (UK) 6 & 7 Wm 4, c 59; Copyright Act 1836 (UK) 6 & 7 Wm 4, c 110; Copyright Act 1842 (UK) 5 & 6 Vict, c 45.

[19] *Longman v Winchester* (1809) 16 Ves Jr 269 – where a second work had been based on an original work, with the second work featuring the addition of significant new material by the subsequent author, the second work nonetheless amounted to infringement of the first work. *West v Francis* (1822) B & Ald 738, 743 – describing a copy as creating the impression of the original. See also E Cutler, *The Law of Musical and Dramatic Copyright* (London: Cassell & Co, 1892) 14–17.

[20] *Reade v Conquest* (1861) 142 Eng. Rep. 297 (CPD), *Tinsley v Lacy* (1863) 1 Hem. & M. 747 at [751] – [752] and *Toole v Young* (1874) 9 LR 523. *Warne & Co v Seebohm* (1888) 39 Ch D 73 Ch D at [78]–[79].

[21] *Daly v Palmer*, 6 Fed Cas 1132 (S.D.N.Y. 1868). See also *Holmes v Hurst* 174 US 82 (1899).

[22] *Scholtz v Amasis & Fenn* [1905–10] MacG CC 216.

[23] *Daly v Palmer*, 6 Fed Cas 1132 (S.D.N.Y. 1868).

[24] A Birrell, *Seven Lectures on the Law and History of Copyright in Books* (New York: GP Putnam's Sons, 1899) 157. See generally R McFarlane, *Original Copy: Plagiarism and Originality in Nineteenth-Century Literature* (Oxford: Oxford University Press, 2007), TJ Mazzeo, *Plagiarism and Literary Property in the Romantic Period* (Philadelphia: University of Pennsylvania Press, 2007), D Worrell, *Theatric Revolution: Drama, Censorship, and Romantic Period Subcultures 1773–1832* (Oxford: Oxford University Press, 2006), C Pettitt, *Patent Inventions: Intellectual Property and the Victorian Novel* (Oxford: Oxford University Press, 2004) and K Temple, *Scandal Nation: Law and Authorship in Britain, 1750–1832* (Ithaca: Cornell University Press, 2003).

Infringement of Copyright under the 1911 Act and the 1956 Act

As noted in chapter two, the Imperial Copyright Act 1911 set the terms of modern copyright infringement in the UK and the common law world.[25] Section 1(2) of the 1911 Act provided that copyright included the right to 'produce or reproduce the work or any substantial part thereof in any material form whatsoever' as well as the exclusive reproduction right, which included for example dramatisation of the work. The 1911 Act thus paved the way for claims of non-literal copying (akin to the *Daly v Palmer* decision in the US). This became clear with the post-1911 Act ruling of the Court of Appeal in *Rees v Melville*:[26]

> In order to constitute an infringement it was not necessary that the words of the dialogue should be the same, the situations and incidents, the mode in which the ideas were worked out and presented might constitute a material portion of the whole play, and the Court must have regard to the dramatic value and importance of what if anything was taken, even though the portion might in fact be small and the actual language not copied.[27]

Thus, in *Rees v Melville* the 'dramatic value and importance' of the scene was taken into account when considering whether it was 'substantial'.[28] That the post-1911 dramatic work included the protection of incidents, situations, scenarios and scenes – not merely the words on the page – was also acknowledged in *Corelli v Gray*.[29] According to Cozens-Hardy MR the 1911 Act had made a significant change:

> The taking for the purposes of a dramatic work of any substantial part of the combination of incidents in a copyright novel, even although none of the words were taken, was now an infringement.[30]

This idea of protection beyond the work's formal, textual boundaries may have been influenced by economic considerations that valued the work as an 'closed and secure entity', that is, a stable object of property.[31] Yet, Lee argues that even post-1911, analysis of the text has remained a significant factor in 'the co-existence of two contradictory models' of the work: on one hand, a theoretically 'abstract' entity; and on the other hand, a work 'frequently treated as being essentially textual in nature for the purposes of doctrinal decision-making'.[32] Indeed, the

[25] (UK) 1 & 2 Geo 5, c 46.
[26] *Rees v Melville* [1911–1916] MacG CC 168, 174 (Swinfen Eady LJ).
[27] ibid.
[28] ibid.
[29] *Corelli v Gray* [1913] TLR 570, 571.
[30] ibid, 574.
[31] B Sherman and L Bently, *The Making of Modern Intellectual Property Law* (Cambridge: Cambridge University Press, 1999) 173–76. See also J Waldron, 'From Authors to Copiers' (1988) 68 *Chicago-Kent Law Review* 841.
[32] YH Lee, 'The persistence of the text: the concept of the work in copyright law – Part II' (2018) *Intellectual Property Quarterly* 107, 108.

UK test for infringement has remained relatively consistent from the 1911 Act through to the current law. In a musical case decided under the 1911 Act – *Hawkes v Paramount*[33] – a 20 second portion of the popular tune 'Colonel Bogey' was used in a newsreel. The court made a qualitative determination that this portion amounted to a 'substantial part' of the work. As I discuss later on, this decision would likely be made in the same way, with the same result, today. Nevertheless, the question of where to draw the boundaries of the work remained (and remains) uncertain. In the 1916 case of *Glyn v Weston Feature Film Co* it was even suggested that taking inspiration from a work was acceptable as long as the new work was sufficiently original and not a mere copy of the first work:

> ... that no infringement of the plaintiff's rights takes place where a defendant has bestowed such mental labour upon what he has taken and has subjected it to such revision and alteration as to produce an original result.[34]

Despite this ambiguous statement, the post-1911 case law did lead to the development of some stable norms. As noted earlier, in addition to textual copying, it became established law that the detailed plot of a play or novel – the use of scenes and incidents without words – can constitute a 'substantial part' of a work for the purposes of infringement.[35] On whether a specific character can be protected in itself, Maugham J in *Kelly v Cinema Houses* appeared to reject the idea:

> If we found a modern playwright creating a character as distinctive and remarkable as Falstaff, or as Tartuffe, or Sherlock Holmes, would it be an infringement if another writer, one of the servile flock of imitators, were to borrow the idea and to make use of an obvious copy of the original? I should hesitate a long time before I came to such a conclusion ... One might almost as well claim a monopoly for a brave and handsome hero, a lovely blonde heroine or an unprepossessing villain with dark moustaches.[36]

The Copyright Act of 1956[37] broadened the scope of copyright to include further rights in sound recordings, cinematographic works and broadcasts. The test for infringement remained relatively consistent. In the 1964 case of *Ladbroke v William Hill* Lord Reid emphasised that the issue of what amounts to a 'substantial part' of a work invariably depends on qualitative analysis rather than a quantitative test.[38] Broadly, the court's emphasis was on the quality of the part taken – and this central point regarding quality, not quantity, still holds in law today.

[33] *Hawkes and Sons (London) Ltd v Paramount Film Service Ltd* [1934] Ch 593.

[34] *Glyn v Weston Feature Film Co* [1916] 1 Ch 261, 268. *Milligan v Broadway Cinema Production* [1923] Scots Law Times 35; [1922–3] MCC 343, Court of Session – a Scottish case concerning the dramatic work's boundaries.

[35] See, eg *Kelly v Cinema Houses* [1928–35] MacG CC 362; *Bolton v British International Pictures* [1936–45] MacG CC 20; *Harman Pictures v Osborne* [1967] 1 WLR 723 ChD.

[36] *Kelly v Cinema Houses* [1928–35] MacG CC 362, 368. See also SC Isaacs, *The Law Relating to Theatres, Music Halls, and Other Public Entertainments, and to the Performers therein, including the Law of Musical and Dramatic Copyright* (London: Sevens &. Sons Ltd, 1927).

[37] Copyright Act 1956 ('CA 1956') available at www.opsi.gov.uk/acts/acts1956/pdf/ukpga_19560074_en.pdf.

[38] *Ladbroke (Football) Ltd v William Hill (Football) Ltd* [1964] 1 WLR 273 at 276. See also *Francis Day & Hunter v Bron* [1963] Ch 587, *Ravenscroft v Herbert* [1980] RPC 193 and *Ludlow Music v Robbie Williams* [2001] FSR 271.

Infringement of Copyright under the CDPA 1988

I now turn to the contemporary law in the UK. The CDPA 1988 gives the owner the right to control 'restricted acts' in relation to the work, including the right to copy, perform, broadcast or adapt the work.[39] The CDPA states:

> Copyright in a work is infringed by a person who without the licence of the copyright owner does, or authorises another to do, any of the acts restricted by the copyright.[40]

Primary infringement of a dramatic work can therefore occur by copying,[41] by publication (issue of copies to the public),[42] by performance (the showing or playing of the work in public),[43] by making an adaptation[44] or by broadcasting (or including the work in a cable programme service).[45] It is for the claimant to show that the allegedly 'infringing' work is derived from their copyright work.[46] The court will draw an inference of derivation where it can be shown that the defendant had access to or familiarity with the copyright work.[47] Importantly, infringement can be made in relation to a work 'as a whole' or to any 'substantial part' of it.[48] As I describe later on, it is this notion of 'substantiality' that has proven the most important in copyright case law in the UK – and in recent EU decisions.

How Much (or How Little) Needs to be Copied? The Meaning of 'Substantial Part'

The traditional infringement test in the UK is a qualitative assessment of whether a 'substantial part' of the original copyright work can be perceived in the context of the allegedly infringing work.[49] As Birrell expressed in 1899, it can be very difficult for courts to determine what amounts to a 'substantial part' in the context of an aesthetic, performative work.[50] Even in a case of literal copying, it is not clear exactly how much of the text needs to be copied for infringement to occur. The role of expert

[39] CDPA 1988, s 16–27; Copyright and Related Rights Act (CRRA) 2000, ss 37–43.
[40] CDPA 1998, s 16(2).
[41] CDPA 1998, s 17; CRRA 2000, s 39.
[42] CDPA 1998, s 18; CRRA 2000, s 41.
[43] CDPA 1998, s 19; CRRA 2000, s 40
[44] CDPA 1998, s 21; CRRA 2000, s 43.
[45] CDPA 1998, s 20; CRRA 2000, s 40.
[46] CDPA 1988, s 27(4); CRRA 2000, s 44(4). See *Autospin (Oil Seals) v Beehive Spinning* [1995] RPC 683 where there was a failure to show a causal connection and *Sawkins v Hyperion Records Ltd* [2005] EWCA Civ 565 at [30].
[47] *Designers Guild Ltd v Russell Williams* (*Textiles Ltd*) [2001] FSR 113.
[48] CDPA 1988, s 16(3); CRRA 2000, s 37(3).
[49] Post-*Infopaq*, the term 'part' may be used given that this is the CJEU's language, but for present purposes the term 'substantial part' remains relevant as it is the UK term of usage.
[50] JM Keyes, 'Musical Musings: The Case for Rethinking Music Copyright Protection' (2004) 10 *Michigan Telecommunications and Technology Law Review* 407, 433.

testimony in these kinds of cases is also of questionable value due to the problem of subjectivity.[51]

The courts have attempted to bring some clarity to the situation by emphasising the relative value of the particular part. From the 2001 case of *NLA v Marks and Spencer* we know that if a part is original enough to be protected in itself, then the unauthorised taking of it will be prohibited.[52] This emphasis on quality is a constant in UK case law, whether the dispute involves a textual analysis or a visual assessment.[53] The qualitative nature of the test is useful, given that a strict quantitative test would not be meaningful in all contexts of apparent infringement, such as in a case of copying of a small but memorable part of a work.[54]

In the past decade, UK infringement doctrine has taken account of the 2009 *Infopaq* judgment of the CJEU, where it was held that the unauthorised taking of 11 words could potentially amount to copyright infringement if these words reflect the 'author's intellectual creation'.[55] Though phrased differently, the *Infopaq* judgment advocates a very similar test to the UK's traditional 'qualitative' test for 'substantive part' – that a part of relative value ought to be protected, even if quantitatively small.

As outlined in chapter three, the importance of the *Infopaq* judgment on the doctrine of infringement was acknowledged in the subsequent UK cases of *Meltwater*[56] and *SAS*.[57] The effect of *Meltwater*, taken together with previous case law, indicates that titles and headlines can be protected separately under copyright if they are sufficiently 'original' and 'literary'.[58] Yet the courts give little guidance as to when a title will be sufficiently original and literary and when it will not be.[59] In *Meltwater* the court also noted that even a headline that does not amount to an independent literary work in its own right could still be described as forming part of the article which it headed. Therefore, with regard to claims of copyright infringement, a headline or title may in some cases amount to a 'substantial part' of

[51] ibid, 435.

[52] *Newspaper Licensing Agency v Marks & Spencer* [2001] UKHL 38; [2003] 1 AC 551.

[53] *Designers Guild Ltd v Russell Williams (Textiles Ltd)* [2001] FSR 113. See also *Temple Island Collections Ltd v New English Teas Ltd & another* [2012] EWPCC 1 and *Coffey v Warner/Chappell Music* [2005] FSR (34) 747.

[54] M Spence and T Endicott, 'Vagueness in the Scope of Copyright' (2005) 121 *Law Quarterly Review* 657, 663.

[55] *Infopaq* (n 4).

[56] *Meltwater* (n 4).

[57] *SAS Institute Inc v World Programming Ltd.* [2013] EWHC 69.

[58] J Davis and A Durant, 'To protect or not to protect? The Eligibility of commercially used short verbal texts for copyright and trade mark protection' (2011) *Intellectual Property Quarterly* 345.

[59] *Meltwater* (n 4); Proudman J at [63]–[72]. On the 'literary' aspect of the analysis Proudman J clearly saw the headline as being a separate work from the underlying article. This point is significant because it arguably veers away from the dicta of Laddie J laid down in the case of *Hyperion v Warner*, where he stated that collapsing one copyright work into several different independent works was not a proper application of the law. Proudman J did not refer to the *Hyperion v Warner* case, but in any event she seemed satisfied that an original headline would be a separate work to the underlying article – *Hyperion Records Ltd v Warner Music* (UK) Ltd 19 May 1991, Ch D, unreported.

the article. For dramatic works, this may mean that making use of short extracts of an existing copyright work in the development of a new work could be infringing (even the use of titles). This possibility makes the fair dealing requirements all the more important, as outlined later on in this chapter.

Assessing the Copying of Plots and Characters in Light of the Idea/Expression Dichotomy

Literal copying of short pieces of text is likely to amount to infringement. What about the non-literal? It is here that the notoriously elusive idea/expression dichotomy comes into play.[60] The general rule – that ideas cannot be protected, only expressions of those ideas – is an often unhelpful cliché. It is more accurate to say that insufficiently detailed ideas (eg, the love triangle plot) and generic expressions (eg, 'Oh my God!') cannot be protected.[61] Indeed, rather than grappling with the terms 'idea' and 'expression', the term 'stylistic convention' provides a more accurate descriptor of an expression of theatre/drama that is too generic to be protectable under copyright.[62] A stylistic convention – such as a stock character or genre trope – cannot be held to be part of the author's protectable, original input.[63] As a result, no infringement action would succeed if a mere stylistic convention is taken from one work and used in another. Such conventions are in the public domain.[64]

Perhaps the most important recent statement on dramatic copyright comes from a case involving a musical work. In *Sawkins* the court stated:

> The test of substantial reproduction is not a note-by-note textual comparison of the scores. It involves listening to and comparing the sounds of the copyright work and of the infringing work. So, it is possible to infringe the copyright in a musical work without taking the actual notes: see *Austin v Columbia Gramophone Co Ltd* [1917–23] MacG CC 398. In principle, there is no reason for regarding the actual notes of music as the only matter covered by musical copyright, *any more than, in the case of a dramatic work, only the words to be spoken by the actors are covered by dramatic copyright. Added stage directions may affect the performance of the play on the stage or on the screen and have*

[60] P Masiyakurima, 'The Futility of the Idea/Expression Dichotomy in UK Copyright Law' (2007) 38 *International Review of Intellectual Property and Competition Law (IIC)* 548.

[61] *Corelli v Gray* [1913] TLR 570. See also *Rees v Melville* [1911–16] MacG CC 168.

[62] Similarly, in music some chord progressions and generic musical phrases are too common to be protectable, as noted in S Vaidhayanathan, *Copyrights and Copywrongs: The Rise of Intellectual Property and How It Threatens Creativity* (New York: New York University Press, 2001) 117.

[63] On literary genres and copyright see O Rachum-Twaig, *Copyright Law and Derivative Works: Regulating Creativity* (London: Routledge, 2019); CR Miller, 'Genre as Social Action' (1984) 70 *Quarterly Journal of Speech* 151 and JC Lena, *Banding Together: How Communities Create Genres in Popular Music* (Princeton: Princeton University Press, 2012).

[64] L McDonagh, 'Is Creative use of Musical Works without a licence acceptable under Copyright?' (2012) 43 *International Review of Intellectual Property and Competition Law (IIC)* 401.

> *an impact on the performance seen by the audience. Stage directions are as much part of a dramatic work as plot, character and dialogue.* (My emphasis.)[65]

Given the court's acceptance that in addition to the text/dialogue, a play's plot, characters and stage directions may be protected, it is worth considering how infringement of these non-literal elements might occur in the theatrical context. In the UK the main precedent we have on idea/expression and literary works arose as a result of the 2006–7 copyright dispute in *Baigent v Random House*.[66] The case, concerning Dan Brown's novel *The Da Vinci Code*, centred on whether a 'substantial part' of the work had been copied from the claimants' earlier work *Holy Blood, Holy Grail*, or whether it was merely the earlier book's unprotectable ideas that had been used by Dan Brown.[67] The court stated that mere 'information, facts, ideas, theories and themes' cannot be given copyright protection because to do so could have the effect of monopolising historical research.[68] Brown had not copied any text and had only made use of thematic ideas. The court concluded that since such mere themes and facts cannot be said to form a 'substantial part' of a literary work, no case of infringement could be maintained.[69] In a similar vein, when JK Rowling was accused of copying the character of 'Harry Potter' from the earlier published character 'Willy the Wizard' the case ultimately failed.[70] Any common plot or character elements between the Harry Potter book series and Willy the Wizard were generic. On this, McCutcheon notes that there is no specific ruling in the UK that a literary or dramatic character is protected under copyright as a separate work in itself; instead, a detailed character would likely be protected as part of the key original content of the work.[71]

In determining when to give protection to plots and characters, Rebikoff suggests the law should be open to analysing storytelling patterns in the manner of literary theorists like Vladimir Propp.[72] In this view, a story is the mere chronology of events, and might not be protected; whereas a narrative involves the specific arrangement of scenes by an author, and may be original enough, by itself, to be

[65] *Sawkins* (n 46).

[66] *Baigent and Leigh v The Random House Group Ltd* [2007] EWCA Civ 247; [2007] FSR 579.

[67] ibid, Mummery LJ at [156].

[68] CDPA 1988, s 16(3). *Ladbroke (Football) Ltd* (n 38).

[69] *Baigent* (n 66). See also C Waelde and P Schlesinger, 'Music and Dance: Beyond Copyright Text' (2011) 8 *SCRIPTed* 257 and R Tushnet, 'Performance Anxiety: Copyright Embodied and Disembodied' (2013) 60 *J Copyright Soc'y USA* 209.

[70] *Paul Allen (trustee of Adrian Jacob, deceased) v Bloomsbury Publishing and JK Rowling* [2010] EWHC 2560 (Ch). See also R Casalini, 'Harry Potter, Scientology, and the Mysterious Realm of Copyright Infringement: Analyzing When Close is Too Close and When the Use is Fair' (2010) 26 *Touro L Rev* 313.

[71] J McCutcheon, 'Property in Literary Characters: protection under Australian Copyright Law' (2007) 29 *European Intellectual Property Review* 140. See also J Scharff, 'The Copyrightability of Fictional Characters: Why Harry Potter, Arya Stark, and Matrim Cauthon Are Copyrightable' (2020) 35 *Touro L Rev* 1291 and MW Carroll, 'Copyright's Creative Hierarchy in the Performing Arts' (2012) 14 *V and J Ent & Tech L* 797.

[72] S Rebikoff, 'Restructuring the Test for Copyright Infringement in Relation to Literary and Dramatic Plots' (2001) 25 *Melbourne University Law Review* 340.

protected. For Rebikoff, an example of a stable storytelling function would be 'St George kills the dragon' – which could fulfil the same 'heroic' storyteller function as 'Theseus traps the minotaur'; but only if the appropriate function of the trope is 'the hero triumphs over the villain'. By contrast, in another tale 'St George kills the dragon' could represent a negative function such as 'the helper is slain' if it were the case that the dragon was the hero of the story.[73] However, the usefulness of this approach will not always be obvious. Theatre works can vary considerably – a work like *Waiting for Godot* is framed by the precise absence of plot or story; by contrast *Rosencrantz and Guildenstern are Dead* subverts the story of *Hamlet*. Structuralist/formalist patterns may not always be identifiable or may be misleading. Nevertheless, courts should be open to the insights of literary scholars if they are relevant to the legal test in the context of a particular case.

New Adaptations of Public Domain Works

In addition to stylistic conventions, entire works may reside in the public domain. Where copyright protection has expired – as in the case of the works of Shakespeare, Ibsen or Chekhov – it is of course possible for creators to take and re-use whole works, and substantial parts of works, without restriction. It is one of the reasons these works are performed so frequently. When in 2012 James Joyce's works fell into the public domain, this prompted a plethora of theatrical stage and radio adaptations.[74]

In the case of a new adaptation of a public domain work that features original elements, such as adding new dialogue, scenes, characters, or settings to the existing work of Shakespeare or Chekhov, then a case of infringement could arise if these new elements were copied. For such a case to succeed, the court must be of the opinion that a work has been infringed through the 'taking' of the 'originality' from the copyright adaptation. To use the terms of the traditional UK test, an infringer must take a substantial part of the new adaptation itself, rather than merely the public domain material.[75]

There is a lack of UK case law on dramatic adaptations of public domain works. There are, however, a small number of musical cases of relevance. For instance, in *Austin v Columbia*[76] new musical arrangements of old tunes for from a public domain opera (John Gay and Johann Pepusch's *Polly* from 1777) were copied by the defendant. This was held to be infringement, because even though the relevant notes in the defendant's arrangements were not identical to the original copyright arrangements, the harmonisation in the Columbia versions clearly imitated

[73] ibid. See also D Hudson Hick, 'Making Sense of the Copyrightability of Plots: A Case Study in the Ontology of Art' (2009) 67 *The Journal of Aesthetics and Art Criticism* 399.

[74] S Harrison, 'Battle over copyright to James Joyce's works' *BBC* (12 April 2012), available at www.bbc.co.uk/news/uk-northern-ireland-17686617.

[75] *CBS Records Australia Ltd v Gross* (1989) 15 IPR 385 at 393.

[76] *Austin v Columbia* [1917–1923] MacG CC 398.

Austin's renditions. Furthermore, in the case of *Robertson v Lewis*[77] a claim was taken regarding arrangements of traditional Scottish airs. However, the Robertson estate failed to show that the recorded Vera Lynn version was derived from the Robertson arrangement.[78] This case shows that unless it is possible to demonstrate a clear case of copying of the exact notes/accompaniment/words, in practice it may be difficult to enforce rights in an arrangement of a public domain work.[79] The same principles would apply in a case involving a dramatic adaptation of a public domain play.

Comparative Insights

The UK infringement doctrine is broadly comparable to the test applied in other common law countries such as Australia,[80] Canada,[81] India[82] and Ireland.[83] For example, in Australia, per *IceTV*, it is clear that assessing the quality, not the quantity, of the part taken is crucial to determining whether infringement has occurred.[84] As in other common law jurisdictions, in cases of non-literal infringement Australian courts acknowledge that it is difficult to determine whether enough of a plot has been taken to amount to a 'substantial part'.[85] Judges must make subjective decisions – in one case the court had to decide whether a sufficient amount of the plot and characters from the screenplay to *Jaws* had been copied in a subsequent Italian screenplay/film that also featured a shark attack.[86] As elsewhere, in Australia copyright can arise in an adaptation of a public domain work;[87] although infringement will only occur if the specific new original input is taken.

In Ireland, a copyright dispute involving a new theatrical adaptation of the public domain play *The Playboy of the Western World* (written by JM Synge) was

[77] *Robertson v Lewis* [1976] RPC 169.

[78] ibid.

[79] W Cornish, 'Conserving Culture and Copyright: a partial history' (2009) 13 *Edinburgh Law Review* 8, 18.

[80] Copyright Act 1968, ss 14(1) and 31(1)(a).

[81] Copyright Act (R.S.C., 1985, c. C-42), s 27.

[82] Copyright Act 1957.

[83] CRRA 2000, ss 37–43.

[84] *IceTV Pty Ltd v Nine Network Australia Pty Ltd* (2009) 254 ALR 386; *Autodesk Inc v Dyason (No 2)* (1993) 1976 CLR 300 and *Data Access Corporation v Powerflex Services Pty Ltd* [1999] HCA 49; (1999) 166 ALR 228, 248.

[85] *Zeccola (First Instance)* [1982] AIPC 90-019; *Telstra Corporation Ltd v Royal & Sun Alliance Insurance Australia Limited* [2003] FCA 786. See also T Fox, 'To the Goggomobil: The fictional character copyright chasm' (2015) 100 *Intellectual Property Forum: Journal of the Intellectual andIndustrial Property Society of Australia and New Zealand* 19; B Chesser, 'The Art of Musical Borrowing: A Composers Guide to the Current Copyright Regime Five Years on from Larrikin' (2015) 37 *Musicology Australia* 1 and R Macklin, 'Shadows over an Oscar' *Panorama, The Canberra Times* (25 March 2000) 12.

[86] ibid.

[87] *CBS Records Australia Ltd v Gross* (1989) 15 IPR 385 at [393]. Furthermore, in light of the Australian 'Men at Work' case (*Larrikin Music Publishing v EMI Songs Australia* [2010] FCA 29) where a large quantity is taken from a short work this leads to a greater likelihood that a substantial part has been taken.

settled out of court in 2013. Even without a judgment on point, it is clear from the settlement details that emerged that the new version, staged at the Abbey Theatre, possessed sufficient originality to be protected as a work in its own right, which meant that the use of the new adaptation without the permission of the author who adapted it was infringing.[88] This is line with UK precedents such as *Sawkins*.

In Canada, *Cinar Corp v Robinson* is the leading case on originality and substantial part in this context.[89] When assessing a TV show in a case of non-literal copying, the Supreme Court of Canada held that the correct approach was to evaluate the 'cumulative effect' of the similarity; here, the characters in dispute were considered original enough to be protected because they possessed distinct appearances and had particular personalities. In other words, the characters went beyond the mere 'generic'.

In India, there have been several major cases involving the plots of dramatic works. The most notable is the 1978 Indian Supreme Court case of *RG Anand*.[90] The Indian Supreme Court considered the UK and US tests, eventually favouring a substantial similarity test based on audience perception of both works. On the facts on the case, the court found that what was common to both works – the play (*Hum Hindustani*) and the latter film script (*New Delhi*) – was too generic to amount to infringement. Similarly, in the 2004 case of *Bradford v Sahara* a novelist claimed that the plot of an Indian TV series had been copied; but the court disagreed, holding that the claimed non-literal copying was of only the central 'rags-to-riches' theme and thus only amounted to stock plot elements.[91] This is in line with the UK case of *Baigent*.

Several copyright cases of relevance have occurred in the US, making that jurisdiction's case law of significant persuasive interest.[92] In *Feist Publications, Inc*

[88] T Healy, 'Roddy Doyle Gives Up Rights to Play in Legal Battle over Playboy Royalties' *The Independent (Ireland)* (13 January 2013), available at www.independent.ie/irish-news/courts/roddy-doyle-gives-up-rights-to-play-in-legal-battle-over-playboy-royalties-29025110.html.

[89] *Cinar Corp v Robinson* [2013] 3 SCR 1168. See also *Denis Desjardins Inc v Jeanson*, [2010] QCCA 1287 (CanLII); *CCH Canadian v Law Society of Upper Canada* [2004] SCC 13 and CJ Craig, 'Transforming "Total Concept and Feel": Dialogic Creativity and Copyright's Substantial Similarity Doctrine' (2020) *Osgoode Legal Studies Research Paper*, available at https://papers.ssrn.com/sol3/papers.cfm?abstract_id=3691280#.

[90] *RG Anand v M/s Delux Films* (1978) 4 SCC 118. A Banerjee, 'How Hollywood Can Sue Bollywood for Copyright Infringement and Save Indian Cinema,' (2010) 32 *European Intellectual Property Review* 10; M Sunder, 'Bollywood/Hollywood' (2010) 12 *Theoretical Inquiries in Law* 275; A Shah, 'Is Bollywood Unlawfully Copying Hollywood? Why? What Has Been Done About It? And How Can It Be Stopped?' (2012) 26 *Emory Int'l L. Rev.* 449.

[91] *Bradford v Sahara*, 2004 (28) PTC 474 (Cal). See also *Mansoob Haider v Yashraj Films* 2014 (59) PTC 292 (Bom); *Zee Telefilms Ltd. v Sundial Communications Private Ltd.*, 2003 (27) PTC 457 (Bom) (DB); *Twentieth Century Fox Film Corp v Sohail Maklai Entertainment Pvt. Ltd.*, 2010 (112) BomLR 4216.

[92] 17 U.S.C. § 106(1). See, eg *A & M Records, Inc v Napster, Inc* 239 F. 3d. 1004 (9th Cir. 2001); *Arnstein v Porter* 154 F. 2d. 464 (2d. Cir. 1946); *Bill Graham Archives v Dorling Kindersly Ltd* 488 F. 3d. 605 (2d. Cir. 2006); *Blanch v Koons* 467 F. 3d. 244 (2d. Cir. 2006); *Bright Tunes Music Corp v Harrisongs Music, Ltd et al* 420 F. Supp. 177 (1976); *ABKCO Music, Inc v Harrisongs Music, et al* 508 F. Supp. 798 (1981); on appeal, 722 F. 2d. 988 (1983); again after remand, 841 F. 2d. 494, and again 944 F. 2d. 971 (1991); *Campbell v Acuff-Rose* 114 S. Ct. 1164 (1994); *Eldred v Ashcroft* 1123 S. Ct. 769 (2003); *Feist Publications*

v Rural Telephone Service Co the Supreme Court of the US (SCOTUS) held that in order to establish infringement the copyright owner must show copying, without consent, of original elements of the work.[93] The test used is 'substantial similarity' which involves the court parsing between the protected original elements of the work and the unprotected generic stylistic conventions.[94] Like the UK test, US courts tend to focus on quality rather than quantity in assessing the two works, whether literal or non-literal copying is at stake.[95] Like the UK test, the use of the US test can be unpredictable due to the subjective nature of artistic appreciation.[96] The unpredictability may even be more pronounced in the US due to fact that, in contrast to the position in the UK (and most common law jurisdictions), in the US juries, not judges, are tasked with deciding whether the two works in question are 'substantially similar'.[97]

In the case of drama, the 'copying' or re-use of basic scenarios or plots has been the subject of legal analysis in the US since the *Augustin v Daly* case. It remains a tricky subject for lawyers to navigate.[98] US authors including Michael Crichton and Steven Spielberg have been involved in copyright infringement litigation concerning 'plots' and stories.[99] To aid courts in this task Chafee suggests a 'pattern test' whereby the court should analyse 'the sequence of events, and the development of the interplay of the characters'.[100] When considering whether non-literal copying has occurred in the context of a plot or characters, the most iconic

Inc v Rural Telephone Service Co Inc 499 US 340 (1991); *Fogerty v Fantasy, Inc*, 510 US 517 (1994); *Grand Upright Music, Ltd v Warner Bros. Records Inc.*, 780 F. Supp. 182 (1991); *Harper & Row, Publishers, Inc v Nation Enterprises* 105 S. Ct. 2218 (1985); 85 L. Ed. 2d. 588 (1985); *Newton v Diamond* 388 F. 3d. 1189 (9th Cir. 2003); *Perfect 10, Inc v Amazon.com, Inc* 487 F. 3d. 701 (9th Cir. 2007); *Sony Corp of America v Universal City Studios, Inc* 104 S. Ct. 774 (1984); *Southco Inc v Kanebridge Corp* 324 F. 3d. 190 (3d. Cir. 2003); *Suntrust Bank v Houghton Mifflin Co.* 268 F. 3d. Cir. 1257 (11th Cir. 2001).

[93] 499 U.S. 340 (1991) at [361].

[94] N Booth, 'Backing Down: Blurred Lines in the Standards for Analysis of Substantial Similarity in Copyright Infringement for Musical Works' (2016) 24 *J. Intell. Prop. L.* 99, 104.

[95] See, eg *Peter Letterese and Associates, Inc v World Institute of Scientology* 533 F.3d. 1287 (11th Cir. 2008). See also R Casalini, 'Harry Potter, Scientology, and the Mysterious Realm of Copyright Infringement: Analyzing When Close is Too Close and When the Use is Fair' (2010) 26 *Touro L Rev* 313; J Palmer, '"Blurred Lines" Means Changing Focus: Juries Composed of Musical Artists Should Decide Music Copyright Infringement Cases, Not Lay Juries' (2016) 18 *Vand. J. Ent. & Tech. L.* 907 and MR Carter, 'Applying the Fragmented Literal Similarity Test to Musical-Work and Sound-Recording Infringement: Correcting the Bridgeport Music, Inc. v. Dimension Films Legacy' (2013) 14 *Minn JL Sci & Tech* 669.

[96] *Feist Publications Inc v Rural Telephone Service Co* [1991] USSC 50; 499 US 340 (1991) ('*Feist*').

[97] *Arnstein v Porter* (n 92). Under the Arnstein criteria it is also necessary to show that the alleged infringer had access to the copyright work. See also *Williams v Gaye*, 895 F.3d. 1106, 1119 (9th Cir. 2018) and *Skidmore v Led Zeppelin*, 905 F.3d. 1116, 1121–22 (9th Cir. 2018). See also H Bosher, 'Michael Skidmore v Led Zeppelin: Copyright infringement in music under US law' (2020) 15 *Journal of Intellectual Property Law & Practice* 321.

[98] LP Loren and A Reese, 'Proving Infringement: Burdens of Proof in Copyright Infringement Litigation' (2019) 23 *Lewis & Clark L Rev* 621; *Salinger v Random House, Inc.*, 811 F.2d. 90, 98 (2d. Cir. 1987)).

[99] *Williams v Crichton*, 860 F. Supp. 158 (S.D.N.Y. 1994). See also *Litchfield v Spielberg* 736 F. 2d. 1352 (9th Cir. 1984); *Salinger v Random House, Inc.*, 811 F.2d. 90, 98 (2d. Cir. 1987).

[100] Z Chafee, 'Reflections on the Law of Copyright: I' (1945) 45 *Columbia Law Review* 503, 513–14.

US legal statement of the idea-expression principle makes explicit reference to dramatic works – in a dispute concerning two similar plays, *Nichols v Universal Picture Corporation*, Judge Learned Hand remarked:

> It is of course essential to any protection of literary property … that the right cannot be limited literally to the text, else a plagiarist would escape by immaterial variations. That has never been the law, but, as soon as literal appropriation ceases to be the test, the whole matter is necessarily at large … Upon any work, and especially upon a play, a great number of patterns of increasing generality will fit equally well, as more and more of the incident is left out … but there is a point in this series of abstractions where they are no longer protected, since otherwise the playwright could prevent the use of his 'ideas', to which, apart from their expression, his property is never extended. Nobody has ever been able to fix that boundary, and nobody ever can.[101]

He went on to use the specific example of Shakespeare to demonstrate his point:

> If Twelfth Night were copyrighted, it is quite possible that a second comer might so closely imitate Sir Toby Belch or Malvolio as to infringe, but it would not be enough that for one of his characters he cast a riotous knight who kept wassail to the discomfort of the household, or a vain and foppish steward who became amorous of his mistress. These would be no more than Shakespeare's 'ideas' in the play, as little capable of monopoly as Einstein's Doctrine of Relativity, or Darwin's theory of the Origin of Species.[102]

In the US theatre directors have on several occasions made claims asserting a copyright interest in stage productions, but up to now there have been no definitive judicial rulings on the issue.[103] The *Guitierrez* case in 1995 concerned a production of Frank Loesser's *The Most Happy Fella*, directed by Gerry Gutierrez, who filed a copy of his stage directions, noted in the margins of the script, with the US Copyright Office. *Mantello v Hall* (1996) involved a production of the play *Love! Valor! Compassion!* by Terrence McNally. In 1994, Joe Mantello directed the original production of *Love! Valor! Compassion!* in New York. In 1996 Mantello became aware of a subsequent production, which was reportedly very similar to his own production. Mantello claimed infringement of copyright – like Guiterrez he had filed a copy of McNally's script annotated with his stage directions.[104] The case was settled. Similarly, in *Einhorn v Mergatroyd* (2006) a director's copyright claim was raised over a copy of the playwright's script with the director's stage directions written in the margins that had been filed at the US Copyright Office.[105]

[101] *Nichols v Universal Pictures Corp.*, 45 F.2d. 119 (2nd Cir. 1930) at [121]–[122]. See also *Novak v National Broadcasting Co*, 716 F. Supp. 745 (S.D.N.Y. 1989) and *Alexander v Irving Trust Co*, 132 F. Supp. 364 (S.D.N.Y. 1955).

[102] ibid, 122.

[103] *Gutierrez v DeSantis*, No. 95-1949 (S.D.N.Y. filed 22 March 1995). *Mantello v Hall*, 947 F. Supp. 92 (S.D.N.Y. 1996); *Einhorn v Mergatroyd Productions* 426 F.Supp. 2d. 189 (S.D.N.Y. 2006).

[104] J Weidman, 'The Seventh Annual Media and Society Lecture: Protecting the American Playwright' (2007) 72 *Brook. L. Rev.* 641, 647.

[105] *Einhorn v Mergatroyd Productions* 426 F.Supp. 2d. 189 (S.D.N.Y. 2006).

Weidman cites the risk of overlapping copyrights creating problems for later interpreters, noting that if these directors could acquire copyright ownership of their staging, 'then the directors of each and every one of these productions could have acquired copyright ownership of theirs as well'.[106] The result would be that the copyrights 'would clearly operate as liens on a playwright's play, restricting – often in unknown and unpredictable ways'.[107] Weidman states:

> And if directors are able to copyright their work, the day will inevitably come – and soon – when a theater decides to cancel a production simply because they have been threatened by a director who perceives – rightly or wrongly, it doesn't matter – that the theater's production will infringe on a version which belongs to him.[108]

In a letter to the *New York Times*, director Charles Marowitz offered a counter-perspective:

> As a director who has found his staging appropriated by less resourceful colleagues, I know that without the text prompting motivation, movement and gestures, no director would be able even to begin 'staging' a play. Directorial conception, however, is altogether different from staging and adds an entirely new dimension to a dramatist's work. Reinterpretations of both modern or classic plays should be entitled to copyright protection because they are the original outgrowth of a director's imagination.[109]

On the other hand, Weidman notes:

> But who decides? Who determines when a 'director's imagination' has been sufficiently activated to give birth to a copyrightable piece of work? Who decides when it hasn't? Are objective standards even possible? And isn't any line in the sand which makes some direction copyrightable and some not an invitation to an avalanche of litigation casting a cloud over some theatrical productions and paralyzing others?[110]

Also relevant is the jurisprudence surrounding *scènes à faire*.[111] These are essentially generic scenes that by their nature must follow a certain pattern. For example, in *Cain v Universal Pictures* the dispute centred on two works, both of which featured a scene where lovers were sheltering from the rain in the loft of a church, with the scenario also sharing common details of prayer and hunger; despite these similarities, no infringement was found as it was held that these scenes had to unfold in a certain manner due to their particular type.[112] Although the question

[106] Weidman (n 104) 649.
[107] ibid, 649.
[108] ibid, 650.
[109] C Marowitz, 'Letter to the Editor, Stage Copyrights; What the Director Brings' *The New York Times* (5 February 2006).
[110] Weidman (n 104) 651.
[111] *Idema v Dreamwork, Inc.*, 162 F. Supp. 2d. 1129 (C.D. Cal. 2001); *Taylor Corp v Four Seasons Greetings, LLC* 315 F.3d. 1039 (8th Cir. 2003) and *Frye v YMCA Camp Kitaki*, 617 F.3d. 1005 (8th Cir. 2010). See also RK Walker, 'Breaking with Convention: The Conceptual Failings of Scenes a Faire' (2020) 38 *Cardozo Arts & Ent LJ* 435 and L Kurtz, 'The Scènes à Faire Doctrine' (1989) 41 *Florida Law Review* 79.
[112] *Cain v Universal Pictures Co* 47 F. Supp. 1013, 1017 (S.D. Cal. 1942).

of when a plot will be infringed is as difficult to assess based on US jurisprudence as it is in the UK, the US case law does benefit from clarity on two issues: unlike the UK the US courts have confirmed that individual literary characters can be protected;[113] and we know that very short works, such as the particular expression of a joke, can be protected.[114]

How Prevalent are Disputes in the UK Theatre Field?

Authors of plays want to protect their dramatic works; yet they are also wary of being accused of copying.[115] That the copying of even a short portion of verbatim text is highly susceptible to a successful infringement claim deepens this concern.[116] Moreover, as discussed earlier, copyright infringement disputes can involve cases where it is not the literal text that has been allegedly copied, but non-literal elements. We have seen that authors including Dan Brown and JK Rowling have been involved in copyright infringement litigation concerning 'plots', characters and stories.[117] Such cases rarely succeed at trial, but they can prove costly to resolve. Here I examine the prevalence of concern about copyright infringement within the theatre community in the UK.

Empirical Insights

The question of when copyright infringement should come into play in the context of re-interpretation, and even imitation, in theatre practice is a complex one.[118] In general, the interviewees I spoke with accepted that re-interpretation, imitation,

[113] *DC Comics v Towle*, 802 F.3d. 1012 (9th Cir. 2015); *Warner Bros. Entertainment Inc. v RDR Books* 575 F. Supp. 2d. 513 (S.D.N.Y. 2008); *Burroughs v Metro-Goldwyn-Mayer, Inc.*, 519 F. Supp. 388 (S.D.N.Y. 1981) and *Warner Bros Pictures, Inc v Columbia Broad Sys, Inc* 216 F.2d. 945 (9th Cir. 1954). See also *Apple Computer, Inc v Microsoft Corp* 35 F.3d. 1435 (9th Cir. 1994). See also SJ Coe, Note, 'The Story of a Character: Establishing the Limits of Independent Copyright Protection for Literary Characters' (2011) 86 *Chicago-Kent Law Review* 1305.

[114] *Foxworthy v Custom Tees, Inc* 879 F. Supp. 1200 (N.D. Ga 1995) and *Kaseberg v Conaco* LLC 260 F. Supp. 3d. 1229 (S.D. Cal. 2017). See also *Williams v Gaye*, 895 F.3d. 1106 (9th Cir. 2018).

[115] B Salter, 'Taming the Trojan Horse: An Australian Perspective of Dramatic Authorship' (2009) 56 *J Copyright Soc'y USA* 789; CL Fisk, 'The Writer's Share' (2017) 50 *Suffolk UL Rev* 621 and D Wright, 'Playwrights and Copyright' (2015) 38 *Colum JL & Arts* 301.

[116] *Sweeney v Macmillan Publishers Ltd* [2002] RPC 35. The court stated that a short extract, comprising a small number of lines, copied from the Rosenbach manuscript of *Ulysses* did amount to a 'substantial part'. This was largely due to the value of restoring the hitherto unpublished lines to published versions of Joyce's work.

[117] Baigent (n 66) and Paul Allen (n 70). *Williams v Crichton* 860 F. Supp. 158 (S.D.N.Y. 1994) and *Litchfield v Spielberg* 736 F. 2d. 1352 (9th Cir. 1984).

[118] See generally F Babbage, *Adaptation in Contemporary Theatre – Performing Literature* (Oxford: Hart, 2017). For discussion of the complexities of theatrical texts in this context see G Harris, 'Repetition, Quoting, Plagiarism and Iterability (Europe After the Rain-Again)' (1999) 19 *Studies in Theatre Production* 6.

and even copying, are commonplace and natural parts of the theatrical process.[119] One interviewee stated that ideas and plots, even detailed ones, are re-used 'all the time' and that she had 'never thought this to be a problem'.[120] Another interviewee – an actor – stated that it is 'simply necessary' in theatre to 're-interpret existing tropes' in a new way or context and sometimes to 'quote' from existing works.[121] Another interviewee, a writer/performance artist, stated she is 'comfortable' with the notion of copying; and indeed, said she would be 'flattered', if another artist decided to re-interpret her original material even without permission.[122] She said that what mattered to her was maintaining her performance style and having the freedom to develop new material, rather than worrying about copying.

None of the 20 interviewees had ever been accused of copyright infringement by other writers/directors/theatre participants. This suggests that the lack of UK case law is indicative of a lack of disputes more generally. However, the virtual absence of formal disputes does not tell the entire story. Two examples from my interviews indicate that disputes over alleged infringement do occur, but they are not litigated.

The first of these was explained by a writer interviewee (anon 2) who told me that he had knowledge of several incidents of 'plagiarism of plots' within theatre, though it had not happened to him personally. He was aware of examples involving writer friends of his, with one in particular standing out:[123]

> I'll give you one particular example that happened to a friend of mine. His play does well in London … it goes on tour. And then some time goes by and he's watching a TV crime drama. By the end of the episode, he's seen virtually the entire plot, characters, everything – they just changed the names – on the screen, with no credit or acknowledgement, let alone payment … Of course my friend never considered litigation as an option due to the crazy costs, the time, the wasted effort.

The above example of an infringement scenario shows that copying can occur from one medium (theatre) into another (TV). The other example I encountered during my interviews concerned a writer (anon 1) who had a personal story to tell about copying within the theatre world.[124] The writer complained that 'blatant copying' – likely amounting to copyright infringement – had taken place.[125] He had discovered the 'copying' when he had gone to see another writer's play at a major UK theatre.

[119] The empirical methodology is explained in ch 1.
[120] Anon 14.
[121] Anon 7.
[122] Anon 18.
[123] Anon 2.
[124] Anon 1. Infringement of dramatic works and performances in the digital rights realm has become more widely discussed in the context of the COVID-19 pandemic, due to the fact that many theatres have made recorded performances available for streaming online. Although digital rights did not form not part of the scope of my interviews, it is worth noting that digital rights could become more importantly the years to come. In fact, an infringement dispute over royalties occurred at the UK National theatre during December 2020: G Mazzo, 'National Theatre criticised by staff director for not paying streaming royalties' The Stage (December 4, 2020) – https://www.thestage.co.uk/news/news/national-theatre-criticised-by-staff-director-for-not-paying-streaming-royalties?utm_source=newsletter&utm_medium=email&utm_campaign=4%2E%20Newsletter.
[125] Anon 1. One other interviewee – Anon 19 – a deviser/choreographer – cited examples of what he called 'direct copying', noting television shows and advertisements which had 'closely imitated'

While sitting in the audience he had noticed striking similarities between the work he was watching and his own previously staged play. Here, to avoid breaching anonymity, I have to generalise what the similarities were, rather than giving specifics, but they appeared to be substantial: in both plays there were two very similar main characters, a youth and an elderly person; and the plot of the play centred on their relationship as it developed during a time of historical, sudden climate change.[126] Yet, although there were strong similarities in the characters and plot, no direct lines of text were copied verbatim from his work. The writer was very unhappy about this alleged infringement for a number of reasons. First, it had happened without any acknowledgement or any licence. Second, the writer's play had been performed at a fringe theatre in London, but the 'infringing' play had been staged at a much larger, well-known theatre in London. Third, in the writer's opinion, the 'infringing' play 'did not do as much justice' to the scenario and the characters as his had done. Interestingly, the writer told me the similarities between the two plays were noted by numerous reviewers at the time.[127]

Here, the key question from the copyright perspective would be: could this alleged copying amount to an act of infringement? As noted above, cases of 'verbatim' copying are much easier to prove than cases where non-literal elements are taken. In this instance, it would be difficult to prove copying of a qualitatively substantial part (reflecting the author's intellectual creation) – but not impossible given the level of similarity between the characters, storyline and setting. In the end, the playwright decided not to take any legal action. This decision was made for a number of reasons. First, the writer was aware that the question of whether it was in law a case of what he called 'copyright theft' was a complex one, which meant that there was a high degree of uncertainty involved.[128] Second, he knew that the costs of losing the potential action would be extremely high given the high costs of intellectual property trials at the High Court and the 'loser pays' costs system.[129] Third, the writer was aware that there was a possibility of setting a 'dangerous precedent' which might affect the theatre community in a negative way; since scenarios and characters are constantly re-used in the theatre world, he did not want to end up regretting the decision (he expressed the fear that he might be castigated by other writers for taking the case in the first place). Finally, there was a certain amount of acknowledgement in the theatre world that unfair 'imitation' of his work had taken place. He felt satisfaction

choreographed dance routines that he had helped to devise. In some cases, virtually entire choreographed routines were used in a new context. I do not explore this example in detail here as my focus in this book is on plays. But it is notable that in this case, like the example discussed above in the main text, the deviser decided against a court case on the basis that it would be too costly and take his time away from creative activities. For commentary on choreography see M Pavis, 'Is There Any-Body on Stage? a Legal (Mis)understanding of Performances' (2016) 19 *The Journal of World Intellectual Property* 99; R Tushnet, 'Performance Anxiety: Copyright Embodied and Disembodied' (2013) 60 *J Copyright Soc'y USA* 209 and C Waelde and P Schlesinger, 'Music and Dance: Beyond Copyright Text' (2011) 8 *SCRIPTed* 257.

[126] Anon 1.

[127] Anon 1.

[128] Anon 1.

[129] Even the relatively lower costs at the Intellectual Property Enterprise Court (IPEC) are substantial in the context of theatre. See eg L McDonagh and C Helmers, 'Patent litigation in England and Wales and the issue-based approach to costs' (2013) 32 *Civil Justice Quarterly* 369–84.

that several reviewers had noted the similarity. Within the theatre field, some 'bad-mouthing' of the alleged infringer had occurred, which for the aggrieved writer provided a level of 'community acknowledgement' of the wrong.

On this issue of social sanctions for overt, unacknowledged copying I asked the writer (anon 2) who had told me about the example of the infringement of his friend's work by the TV company whether there are informal mechanisms within the theatre world allowing writers to express concerns about such cases. He stated that theatre is 'a small community', and if cases of 'plagiarism' arise, the gossip spreads quickly; nevertheless, this did not go so far as to amount to 'blacklisting'.[130]

As noted above, the writer who had experienced a direct case of potential infringement (anon 1) took solace in the fact that the alleged 'copying' had been acknowledged by peers within the field, as well as by reviewers.[131] This indicates that, as in for example stand-up comedy, there exists a normative means of resolving such disputes.[132]

Despite the lack of case law at present, it is worth exploring how the formal defences to copyright infringement under the CDPA might work in the theatrical context and to consider whether any reforms ought to be recommended.

The Defence of Fair Dealing under the CDPA

The concept of 'fair dealing' – the legitimate use of a copyright work without licence – formed part of UK copyright law even before it was given legislative recognition in the 1911 Act.[133] Today, the most important provisions which cover fair dealing are located in sections 29 and 30 of the CDPA.[134] In the UK, fair dealing applies to the areas of research and private study,[135] criticism and review,[136] the reporting of current events,[137] as well as the two exceptions introduced in 2014, quotation[138] and parody/pastiche.[139] In order for the defence to be made out, the alleged infringer must first be able to show that the dealing falls into one of these 'purpose' categories.[140] On this, it must be emphasised

[130] Anon 2.

[131] Anon 1.

[132] Oliar and Sprigman (n 6) 1825 and 1845–50.

[133] See generally M De Zwart, 'A Historical Analysis of the Birth of Fair Dealing and Fair Use: Lessons for the Digital Age' (2007) *Intellectual Property Quarterly* 60.

[134] CDPA 1988, ss 29 and 30.

[135] CDPA 1988, s 29(1) and (1C).

[136] CDPA 1988, s 30(1).

[137] CDPA 1988, s 30(2).

[138] J Parkin, 'The copyright quotation exception: not fair use by another name' (2019) 19 *Oxford University Commonwealth Law Journal* 55.

[139] CDPA 1988, s 30A. The private copy exception was struck down in a judicial review action – British Academy of Songwriters, Composers and Authors and others, *R (On the Application Of) v Secretary of State for Business, Innovation and Skills* [2015] EWHC 2041 and [2015] EWHC 1723.

[140] See *Newspaper Licensing Agency v Marks and Spencer* [2000] 4 All ER 239, 257 (Chadwick LJ) (CA), as well as *Pro Sieben Media v Carlton Television* [1999] FSR 610, 620 and *Ashdown v Telegraph Group Ltd* [2002] Ch 149 at [64]. See also *Ashdown v Telegraph Group Ltd* [2002] Ch 149. I Fhima, 'Fairness in Copyright Law: An Anglo-American Comparison' (2017) 34 *Santa Clara High Tech. L.J.* 44, available at http://digitalcommons.law.scu.edu/chtlj/vol34/iss1/2.

that in contrast to the broad 'fair use' provision in US copyright law,[141] the fair dealing provisions under the CDPA form an exhaustive list of defences to copyright infringement. In this sense, as noted in *Pro Sieben Media v Carlton*,[142] the exceptions cannot be widened beyond their specific remit, for example 'reporting current events'. That the use might be considered fair in general practice – or be a 'fair dealing' for any other purpose than the specified legislative purposes – does not provide a defence.[143]

Until recently, the fair dealing exceptions under UK copyright law could not be construed to allow purposes that consisted of creative, dialogic or transformative dealings with a dramatic work.[144] Following the 2011 Hargreaves Review the UK government introduced the quotation and parody exceptions to clarify that such dealings are acceptable in the context of quotations and parodies. These specific purposes are in line with the EU InfoSoc Directive which takes a restrictive approach to exceptions.[145]

For present purposes, it is the new defences of quotation and parody that are of most relevance to creative reinterpretation of dramatic works. I therefore do not devote specific analysis to 'research and private study'[146] or 'reporting current events'.[147] By contrast, I argue here that the case law on 'criticism and review' may be relevant to quotation and parody; moreover, I argue there is also room for a more liberal interpretation to allow creative, transformative uses. Finally, I consider EU law in light of Brexit and the possibility that the UK may alter its copyright law from 2021 onward.

The Purposes of Criticism or Review, Quotation and Parody in the CDPA

To successfully argue this defence,[148] a potential infringer must show that the use of the work is for the purpose of criticism or review,[149] that the work had been

[141] United States Copyright Act 1976, s 107.
[142] *Pro Sieben Media v Carlton UK Television* [1997] EMLR 509.
[143] S Karapapa and L McDonagh, *Intellectual Property Law* (Oxford: Oxford University Press, 2019) 109.
[144] *Gowers Review of Intellectual Property* (London: HMSO, 2006) ('*Gowers Review*'); available at http://webarchive.nationalarchives.gov.uk/+/http://www.hm-treasury.gov.uk/d/pbr06_gowers_report_755.pdf.
[145] Directive 2001/29/EC of the European Parliament and of the Council of 22 May 2001 on the harmonisation of certain aspects of copyright and related rights in the information society, OJ L 167/10, 22.06.2001. Directive (EU) 2019/790 of the European Parliament and of the Council of 17 April 2019 on copyright and related rights in the Digital Single Market and amending Directives 96/9/EC and 2001/29/EC (Text with EEA relevance.), OJ L 130, 17.5.2019.
[146] CDPA 1988, s 29(2). To make out this defence, a potential infringer must show that the dealing was for the purpose of non-commercial research or private study. See also S Karapapa, *Defences to Copyright Infringement: Creativity, Innovation and Freedom on the Internet* (Oxford: Oxford University Press, 2020).
[147] CDPA 1988, s 30(2). This defence is an important part of achieving an appropriate balance between authors' rights and freedom of speech, something that is clearly in the public interest.
[148] CDPA 1988, s 30; CRRA 2000, s 51(1).
[149] *Beloff v Pressdram* [1973] 1 All ER 241. This is usually construed liberally, as discussed in *Newspaper Licensing Agency v Marks & Spencer* [2000] 4 All ER 239, 257. See also *Pro Sieben Media v Carlton Television* [1999] FSR 610, 620.

made available to the public previously,[150] that the dealing itself is 'fair',[151] and that sufficient acknowledgement has been given.[152] It is not possible to fit a 'transformative' or 'creative' dealing with a dramatic work within the idea of 'criticism or review'.

Nevertheless, the recently enacted section 30(1ZA) of the CDPA allows quotation more broadly – 'whether for criticism, review or otherwise' – provided that it is a 'fair' dealing, sufficient acknowledgement is given, the use is no more than is required, and the original work has already been made available to the public. Evidently, quotation is not limited to criticism and review. This potentially opens the way for claims for 'creative dealings', for example where one playwright has quoted from another in a new work.[153] This may push UK law closer to the broad 'fair use' provision under US copyright law.[154] For instance, Aplin and Bently argue that – in line with Article 10 of Berne – the quotation exception in the UK can be interpreted flexibly and liberally to ground a legal principle akin to the broad 'fair use' standard, that would not necessarily breach international legal obligations.[155] It is notable, however, that the CJEU in *Pelham* adhered to a limited view of what quotation can mean in EU law (paragraph 71):[156]

- use, by a user other than the copyright holder, of a work or, more generally, of an extract from a work
- for the purposes of illustrating an assertion, of defending an opinion or of allowing an intellectual comparison between that work and the assertions of that user
- as such, the user of a protected work wishing to rely on the quotation exception must have the intention of entering into 'dialogue' with that work.

[150] CDPA 1988, s 30(1A). See also *HRH Prince of Wales v Associated Newspapers* [2007] 3 WLR 222, Blackburne J at [176].

[151] The criticism itself does not have to be 'fair' – only the dealing, as noted in *Pro Sieben Media v Carlton Television* [1999] FSR 610, 619.

[152] CDPA 1988, s 30(1); CRRA 2000, s 51(1). *Pro Sieben Media v Carlton Television* [1999] FSR 610, 616.

[153] See generally T Aplin and L Bently, *Global Mandatory Fair Use – The Nature and Scope of the Right to Quote Copyright Works* (Cambridge: Cambridge University Press, 2020).

[154] United States Copyright Act 1976, s 107.

[155] See generally Aplin and Bently (n 153). Although many scholars argue that permitted exceptions to copyright protection must satisfy the 'three-step test' as enumerated in Article 9(2) of the Berne Convention, Aplin and Bently argue this does not necessarily override Article 10(1) of Berne. Article 9(2) states that member states may allow permitted uses of literary and artistic works 'in certain special cases, provided that such reproduction does not conflict with a normal exploitation of the work and does not unreasonably prejudice the legitimate interests of the author' and Article 10(1) says It shall be permissible to make quotations from a work which has already been lawfully made available to the public, provided that their making is compatible with fair practice, and their extent does not exceed that justified by the purpose, including quotations from newspaper articles and periodicals in the form of press summaries – see eg Berne Convention, Art 9(2); Trade-Related Aspects of Intellectual Property Rights Agreement (TRIPS), Art 13.

[156] CJEU, judgment in Case C-469/17 *Funke Medien NRW GmbH v Bundesrepublik Deutschland* EU:C:2019:623 ('*Funke Medien*'); CJEU judgment in Case C-476/17 *Pelham GmbH and Others v Ralf Hütter and Florian Schneider-Esleben* [2019] Bus LR 2159 ('*Pelham*') and CJEU judgment in Case C-516/17 *Spiegel Online GmbH v Volker Beck* [2019] Bus LR 2787 ('*Spiegel Online*'). See also German

One could argue this is a case about literary works in print/online, and thus the criteria are confined to that context. In addition, although the CJEU's approach has its drawbacks, with respect to theatre it is at least arguable that if one playwright quotes from another's writer's work they could be considered as being in 'dialogue' and thus 'quotation' could provide a defence – it depends on how dialogue is defined by the court. It is true that, with the conclusion of the Brexit process in 2021, this ruling no longer binds UK courts. Yet, a more liberal approach to quotation – allowing certain creative, dialogic dealings – would require the UK courts to be open to change, and the UK courts have thus far shown caution in interpreting fair dealing.[157] A wide-ranging interpretation of quotation in the UK does not seem to be a likely outcome.

On a more positive note, facilitating parodies under copyright law has been made easier by section 30A of the CDPA, which states that fair dealings for the purpose of 'caricature, parody or pastiche' are allowed as long as the dealing is 'fair'. The UK courts have rarely considered parody in historical case law, and they have yet to rule on the breadth of the post-2014 exception.[158] The CJEU has defined parody in Case C-201/13 *Deckmyn v Vandersteen* as having two key aspects: (i) to evoke an existing work while being noticeably different from it; and (ii) to constitute an expression of humour or mockery.[159] The CJEU emphasised that the aim of copyright exceptions is to achieve a fair balance between the interests of rights holders and users. For present purposes the CJEU definition of parody is instructive, even if not binding on the UK post-Brexit.

Due to the creative nature of the theatrical context, any transformative, but unauthorised, dealing with a dramatic work must be classed as a 'quotation' or 'parody' in order to avail of the defence.[160] Even where the dealing falls within one of these purpose categories, it remains necessary for the courts to analyse whether the use is a 'fair' one.

Assessing the Fairness of the Dealing under the CDPA

The test used by the courts to consider fairness is an objective test of degree and impression.[161] The courts typically weigh up numerous factors in deciding

Federal Constitutional Court (*Bundesverfassungsgericht*), the First Senate, Metall auf Metall, 1 BvR 1585/13, 31 May 2016, DE:BVerfG:2016:rs20160531.1bvr158513.

[157] R Burrell, 'Reining in Copyright Law: Is Fair Use the Answer?' (2001) *Intellectual Property Quarterly* 361.

[158] *Hanfstaengl v Empire Palace* [1894] 3 Ch 109; *Glyn v Weston Feature Film Company* [1915] 1 Ch 261; *Joy Music v Sunday Pictorial Newspapers (1920) Ltd* [1960] 2 QB 60; *Twentieth Century Fox Film Corp v Anglo-Amalgamated Film Distributors* [1960] 2 QB 60; *Kennard v Lewis* [1983] FSR 346 (Ch D); *Schweppes Ltd and Others v Wellingtons Ltd* [1984] FSR 210 (Ch D); *Williamson Music Ltd. v Pearson Partnership Ltd* [1987] FSR 97. See A Sims, 'Strangling Their Creation: The courts' treatment of fair dealing in copyright law since 1911' (2010) *Intellectual Property Quarterly* 192.

[159] Case C-201/13 *Deckmyn v Vandersteen* [2014] Bus LR 1368.

[160] E Rosati, 'Just a Laughing Matter? Why the Decision in Deckmyn is Broader than Parody' (2015) 52 *Common Market Law Review* 511.

[161] *Pro Sieben Media v Carlton Television* [1999] FSR 610, 620; *Hubbard v Vosper* [1972] 2 QB 84.

this question, including freedom of expression and the public interest in light of the Human Rights Act 1998 and Article 10 of the European Convention on Human Rights (ECHR).[162] The key factors include whether the work is unpublished,[163] the means by which the work was procured,[164] the amount of the work taken,[165] the particular use made of the work,[166] the intention or motive of the dealing,[167] the potential consequences of the dealing at a market level,[168] and whether the purpose could have been achieved by another method of expression.[169]

In the theatre context, the good faith of the theatrical practitioner could be assessed in relation to knowledge about the key factors, for example whether the work is yet to be published, or whether there may be consequences at the market level. A 'transformative' or 'creative' dealing undertaken for a largely commercial purpose may not satisfy the market-level test (that a fair dealing should not interfere with the market for the original).[170] In such a case the court may decide that a licence would be a more appropriate means of facilitating the use of the underlying work. However, if it is a largely non-commercial 'transformative' or 'creative' dealing which has a minimal impact on the market for the underlying work, this fact ought to weigh in favour of the court finding that it is a fair dealing.[171]

[162] *Ashdown v Telegraph Group Ltd* [2002] Ch 149, Phillips LJ at [71]. See also generally J Griffiths, 'Copyright Law after Ashdown – Time to Deal Fairly with the Public' (2002) *Intellectual Property Quarterly* 240.

[163] See CDPA 1988, s 30(1), (1A) and the case of *Hyde Park Residence v Yelland* [2000] EMLR 363, Aldous LJ at [34], stating that it would be difficult to imagine 'fair dealing' of an unpublished work. See also *HRH the Prince of Wales v Associated Newspapers* [2007] 3 WLR 222, Blackburne J at [174]. This attitude stands in contrast with the Canadian decision of *CCH Canadian v Law Society of Upper Canada* [2004] SCC 13.

[164] *Beloff v Pressdram* [1973] 1 All ER 241 – it is less likely that a work that is obtained via an illegal or illegitimate channel will be classed as a 'fair dealing'. See also *The Controller of Her Majesty's Stationery Office, Ordnance Survey v Green Amps Ltd* [2007] EWHC 2755 (Ch) at [54].

[165] *Hubbard v Vosper* [1972] 2 QB 84.

[166] *Newspaper Licensing Agency v Marks & Spencer* [2000] 4 All ER 239, 257 comments of Chadwick LJ (CA) stating that commercially advantageous dealing will not qualify as a fair dealing unless there is an overriding public interest.

[167] The test is whether 'a fair minded and honest person' would have 'dealt with the work' in the particular manner – *Hyde Park Residence v Yelland* [2000] EMLR 363, 379. See also *Newspaper Licensing Agency v Marks & Spencer* [2000] 4 All ER 239, Gibson LJ (CA) at [250]. If the motive of the infringer is 'altruistic or noble', this may help the infringer's case.

[168] *Hubbard v Vosper* [1972] 2 QB 84.

[169] *Newspaper Licensing Agency v Marks & Spencer* [1999] EMLR 369, 382–83. See also *Hyde Park Residence v Yelland* [2000] EMLR 363, 379.

[170] K Erickson, M Kretschmer and D Mendis, *Copyright and the Economic Effects of Parody: An empirical study of music videos on the YouTube platform, and an assessment of regulatory options* (UK Intellectual Property Office, 2013).

[171] Berne Convention, Art 9(2); TRIPS, Art 13; WCT, Art 10.

Comparative Insights

In terms of comparative analysis, the fair dealing provisions under copyright law in Ireland[172] and Australia[173] are defined narrowly by the courts, similar to the UK approach.[174] By contrast, the Canadian courts have at times taken an activist approach to the expansion of fair dealing, developing the concept of a 'user' right in the context of educational materials.[175] However, in Canada there is a lack of case law on legitimate 'creative' dealings relevant to theatre.[176]

German case law on '*freie Benutzung*'[177] (free use) is of relevance but must be viewed in light of the recent CJEU rulings considered above, which put the effectiveness of the provision in doubt.[178] Under traditional German doctrine, there is no infringement if the materials taken are sufficiently subsumed within the new work.[179] This idea of 'free use' thus anticipates that a certain amount of creative transformation can be taken into account by the court.[180] However, in the

[172] Copyright and Other Intellectual Property Law Provisions Act 2019 (Ireland) – the Irish Fair dealing provisions follow UK style provisions and the law was recently amended to allow parody in similar terms to the UK exception.

[173] Australian Copyright Amendment Act 2006 introduced a parody exception in s 41A of the Australian Copyright Act 1968 (as amended). See also *Sydney Ltd v Shortland* County Council (1989) 17 IPR 99; *TCN Channel Nine Pty Ltd v Network Ten Ltd* [2001] FCA 108; *Network Ten Pty Ltd v TCN Channel Nine Pty Ltd* (2004) 218 CLR 273. See also B Dharmatilake, 'Reformulating the "fair dealing" defence in copyright law to accommodate transformative musical works and maximise creativity in Australia' (2015) 2 *Int. J. Technology Policy and Law* 1 and K Pappalardo, P Aufderheide, J Stevens and N Suzor, *Imagination foregone: A qualitative study of the reuse practices of Australian creators* (Queensland University of Technology, Australia, 2017).

[174] K Pappalardo and J Messe, 'In Support of Tolerated Use: Rethinking Harms, Moral Rights and Remedies in Australian Copyright Law' (2019) 42 *UNSWLJ* 928.

[175] Canadian law now includes an idea of a 'user right' as part of fair dealing – see *CCH Canadian Ltd v Law Society of Upper Canada* [2004] 1 SCR 339. See also G D'Agostino, 'Healing Fair Dealing? A Comparative Analysis of Canadian Fair Dealing to UK Fair Dealing and US Fair Use' (2008) 53 *McGill Law Review* 309, noting that this decision effectively elevated the narrow exceptions to the level of a general principle, despite the fact that a 'user right' is not reflected in the legislation.

[176] Copyright Modernization Act 2012, SC 2012, c. 20, amending Copyright Act, RSC, 1985, c. C-42. See also *Productions Avanti Ciné-Vidéo Inc. c Favreau* [1999] 177 DLR (4th) 568.

[177] German Act on Copyright and Neighbouring Rights, 1965 (*Urheberrechtgestz*) s 24–(1) 'An independent work created by fair use of a work of another person may be disseminated or exploited without the consent of the author of the work used.' (2) 'Subsection 1 shall not apply to the use of a musical work by which a melody is discernibly taken from the work and used as the basis for a new work.' (Translation by A Klett, M Sonntag and S Wilske, *Intellectual Property Law in Germany* (Munich: Verlag CH Beck, 2008) 277).

[178] *Kraftwerk v Moses Pelham* Decision of the German Federal Supreme Court no. I ZR 112/06 (November, 2008) – translation of judgment found in N Conley and T Braegelmann, 'Metall Auf Metall: The Importance of the Kraftwerk Decision for the Sampling of Music in Germany' (2009) 56 *Journal of the Copyright Society of the USA* 1017, 1034.

[179] P Geller, 'A German Approach to Fair Use: Test Cases for TRIPS Criteria for Copyright Limitations' (2010) 57 *Journal of the Copyright Society of the USA* 553, 556 at no. 13 (hereafter referred to as Geller), referring to Eugen Ulmer, *Urheber-Und Verlagsrecht*, 3rd edn (Berlin: Springer-Verlag, 1980). See also *Bundesgerichtshof* (Gies-Adler) (I ZR 117/00) (Unreported, 20 March 2003).

[180] Geller (n 179) 556–57. However, under s 24(2), 'free use' is of restrictive application in relation to the use of 'discernable' melodies in later works.

2019 *Pelham* case the CJEU reviewed the German provision, erring on the side of caution. The CJEU held that on the question of whether to allow 'free use' in a case which involved an unlicensed sample of a Kraftwerk song, a wide interpretation of free use was not permissible under EU law, even in light of the EU Charter of Fundamental Rights.[181]

Under US law on fair use, there are four standard factors that must be taken into account: the purpose of the defendant's use, the nature of the copyright work, the substantiality of the taking and the potential harm to the market or value of the work.[182] Samuelson notes that while the broad 'fair use' provision in the US is 'often decried' due to its apparent unpredictability, when the various exceptions are divided into relevant categories of exception, stable jurisprudential patterns appear.[183] For instance, US courts typically make a distinction between commercial and non-commercial uses, with the courts looking less favourably on commercially viable uses of a work.[184] Nonetheless, Beebe argues that the designation of 'commercial' or 'non-commercial' is not necessarily determinative in US courts' assessment of fairness.[185]

Creativity is important to the idea of 'transformative' use in US law, anticipating that one creator may build upon the work of another.[186] However, there is also a line of cases which stresses the idea that a 'transformative' use is one which utilises the work in order to perform a new function.[187]

Parodies have clear protection as examples of transformative use under the fair use doctrine, as seen in *Campbell v Acuff-Rose Music Inc.*[188] A parodic work – *The Wind Done Gone*, satirising *Gone With the Wind* – was also the subject of *Suntrust Bank v Houghton Mifflin Co*, a case which was eventually settled.[189] Yet, even in the cases that focus on creativity, the courts seem more open to transformative use when the use made of the work is creative in a different sense than the original work, for example parody (*Campbell*) or collage effect (*Graham*).[190] On this point

[181] CJEU, judgments in *Funke Medien*, *Pelham* and *Spiegel Online* (n 156). See also German Federal Constitutional Court (*Bundesverfassungsgericht*), the First Senate, Metall auf Metall, 1 BvR 1585/13, 31 May 2016, DE:BVerfG:2016:rs20160531.1bvr158513.

[182] United States Copyright Act 1976, s 107, available at www.copyright.gov/title17/92chap1.html#107.

[183] P Samuelson, 'Unbundling Fair Uses' (2009) 77 *Fordham Law Review* 2537, 2539. See also recent discussion of fair use in the US Supreme Court decision in *Google LLC v. Oracle America, Inc.*, 593 US (2021) and contrast with the 2nd Circuit decision in *The Andy Warhol Foundation for the Visual Arts, Inc. v Goldsmith*, decision of March 26 2021 (2d. Cir. 2021).

[184] *American Geophysical Union v Texaco Inc.*, 60 F. 3d. 913 (2d. Cir. 1994) at [922].

[185] B Beebe, 'An Empirical Study of US Copyright Fair Use Opinions 1978–2005' (2008) 156 *University of Pennsylvania Law Review* 549, 556.

[186] See generally P Laval, 'Towards a Fair Use Standard' (1990) 103 *Harvard Law Review* 1105. See, eg *Campbell v Acuff-Rose* 114 S.Ct. 1164 (1994) and *Bill Graham Archives v Dorling Kindersly Ltd*, 488 F. 3d. 605 (2d. Cir. 2006).

[187] See, eg *Kelly v Arriba Soft* 280 F. 3d. 934 (9th Cir. 2002) and *Perfect 10, Inc v Amazon.com, Inc* 487 F. 3d. 701 (9th Cir. 2007).

[188] *Campbell v Acuff-Rose* 114 S.Ct. 1164 (1994).

[189] 268 F.3d. 1257 (11th Cir. 2001).

[190] JC Ginsburg, 'Fair Use in the United States: Transformed, Deformed, Reformed?' (2020) *Sing J Legal Stud* 265.

Arewa remarks that the courts have not done enough to clarify when creative – but non-parodic – transformative uses will be allowed:

> … even if doctrines intended to enable future uses, such as fair use, are taken into account, such property rules have thus far not facilitated a clear delineation between the scope of acceptable and unacceptable uses of existing material …[191]

If 'creativity' is supposed to lie at the root of 'transformative' use, then it would be *unfair* if creative uses of dramatic works were not acceptable in the context of theatre. A further criticism of fair use is that it is litigation-dependent, and thus empowers those with the resources to take cases to court. Goodrich, Katyal and Tushnet opine:

> When First Amendment rights are expanded to allow upcoming and lesser-known artists to use parody, the doors open for well-financed artists like Richard Prince to come along and appropriate the work of less well-financed artists. The economic disparities become even more apparent where the expanding power of fair use winds up having distributive consequences that benefit some artists and leave others disadvantaged.[192]

This statement highlights an asymmetry of power between dominant players and new entrants, focusing on the wealth disparities involved. This is a useful point, but one relevant to almost any legal scenario. For all its flaws, the US system of fair use provides the broadest defence to 'transformative' or 'follow on' creators. For this reason, it is worth considering whether the UK should embrace a broad fair use standard, post-Brexit.

Exploring the Possibility of Incorporating an Open 'Fair Use' Standard in the UK

The issue of whether limited 'fair dealing' exceptions are preferable to a broad 'fair use' provision is a hotly debated one.[193] Narrow fair dealing provisions are often criticised due to their perceived rigidity. Increased flexibility is therefore the advantage of a broadly defined fair use provision. In the US, the court has freedom to assess fair use in relation to a much wider range of dealings of works than is possible in the UK.[194] This gives the court a greater ability to adjust to circumstances.[195]

[191] OB Arewa, 'Blues Lives: Promise and Perils of Musical Copyright' (2010) 27 *Cardozo Arts & Entertainment Law Journal* 573, 616.

[192] See P Goodrich, S Katyal and R Tushnet, 'Panel I: Critical Legal Studies in Intellectual Property and Information Law Scholarship' (2012) 31 *Cardozo Arts & Entertainment Law Journal* 601, 617. See also A Gilden and T Greene, 'Fair Use for the Rich and Fabulous?' (2013) 80 *University of Chicago Law Review Dialogue* 88.

[193] Burrell (n 157) 361.

[194] See generally D Nimmer, '"Fairest of Them All" and other Fairy Tales of Fair Use' (2003) 66 *Law and Contemporary Problems* 263.

[195] P Yu, 'Fair Use and Its Global Paradigm Evolution' (2019) 1 *University of Illinois Law Review* 113.

Nevertheless, while some commentators lament the narrow 'fair dealing' approach, others say that there is little practical difference between the two standards. Nimmer argues that the four factors that are applied by the US courts in cases of fair use are actually 'malleable enough to be crafted to fit' either a restrictive or broad interpretive approach.[196]

Burrell cautions that the current narrow approach of the British courts, based on 'fair dealing', may not change even if a broad fair use provision were adopted.[197] In other words, legislative reform would need to be accompanied by a change in judicial attitudes in order for a liberal interpretation of fair use to take hold in the UK.

Bearing this in mind, it is worth considering how a reformed UK fair use provision may apply in a case involving a dramatic work. Following the US, the four factors would need to be assessed as follows. Regarding the first factor, the purpose of the use would fall within Samuelson's 'transformative' category.[198] Within this category, even if the use was not an obvious parody like *Campbell*, it might still fall into a line of cases regarding transformative artistic uses such as *Blanch v Koons*.[199] In a theatrical context, a parody or pastiche would need to comment upon a previous work. An assessment of this might involve an examination of the originality of the transformative use with regard to the new work of dramatic authorship that is created. As was the case in *Blanch*, such a transformative use may be looked upon favourably by the court, though expert evidence may have to be adduced on this point. The cultural practices of theatre could be taken into account when discussing the 'commercial' or 'non-commercial' context of the use.[200] In line with the opinion of D'Agostino, it might be useful for organisations such as The Writers' Guild or Equity to produce 'fair use guidelines' for theatre.[201]

Regarding the second factor, the nature of the work would obviously be dramatic. However, in US law 'nature' covers more that this – this factor also concerns whether the work is published or unpublished, though the fact that the work is unpublished may not necessarily prevent a fair use finding.[202] US courts are generally more willing to allow fair use of factual, rather than creative, works.[203] This would have to be taken into account in relation to fair use of a play since the work would be classed as a creative one. Despite this, Beebe notes that

[196] Nimmer (n 194) 287, citing the decisions in *Sony Corp of America v Universal City Studios, Inc* 104 S. Ct. 774 (1984); *Harper & Row, Publishers, Inc v Nation Enterprises* 105 S. Ct. 2218 (1985) and *Campbell v Acuff-Rose* 114 S.Ct. 1164 (1994).

[197] Burrell (n 157) 368. In a rare case where the English High Court applied the four US fair use factors, Arnold J's approach was a well-reasoned, but ultimately relatively conservative, one – *Sony/ATV v WPMC Ltd* [2015] EWHC 1853 (Ch).

[198] Samuelson (n 183) 2548–55.

[199] *Blanch v Koons* 467 F. 3d. 244 (2d. Cir. 2006).

[200] There have been cases where interference with a core licensing market has nullified a potential fair use – *Los Angeles News Service v Reuters Television International Ltd* 149 F.3d. 987 (9th Cir. 1998).

[201] D'Agostino (n 175) 361.

[202] *Harper & Row, Publishers, Inc. v Nation Enterprises* 105 S.Ct. 2218. (1985).

[203] *Campbell v Acuff-Rose* 114 S.Ct. 1164 (1994).

a reasonable amount of the fair use findings involve 'creative' works.[204] Regarding the third factor, the substantiality of the taking would have to be assessed in light of each case. On this, it would be considered in tandem with the fourth factor, that is, potential harm to the market. Samuelson notes that 'amount taken should only be judged excessive if it harmed the market for the work'.[205] This is in line with *Suntrust Bank v Houghton Mifflin Co*[206] where it was stated that the taking does not necessarily have to be minimal. Therefore, even in a case involving a large amount of quotation from – or a broad evocation of – a prior dramatic work, this could be held to be an acceptable 'fair use', provided that it did not harm the market for the work. Overall, it is conceivable that the US-style fair use test would be useful when applied in the context of a UK case that involves the creative processes of theatre practitioners.

Understanding what 'transformative' means is perhaps the most crucial element; theatrical practitioners often give the underlying material a 'new meaning' – including, but not limited to, quotation and parody – and as such these activities are of the kind that ought to be permitted. In this regard, the meaning of 'transformative' would have to accommodate creative and dialogic use of works.

Any worries that taking a broad interpretation of 'transformative' might prejudice the rights of the author could be allayed via the 'fairness' assessment and via application of the 'three-step test' in Article 9(2) of the Berne Convention. It states that member states may allow permitted uses of literary and artistic works 'in certain special cases, provided that such reproduction does not conflict with a normal exploitation of the work and does not unreasonably prejudice the legitimate interests of the author'.[207] Analysis of the 'three-step test' by various national courts has not been uniform.[208] However, there are persuasive arguments for taking a liberal interpretation.[209] As stated in the *Gowers Review* in 2006:

> The crucial point should be whether transformative use compromises the commercial interests of the original creator or offends the artistic integrity of the original creator.[210]

Ultimately, there is perhaps no fair dealing or fair use provision that provides a perfect fit for theatre since, as noted earlier, those involved in theatre tend to avoid litigation where possible.[211] Yet, the principle at the heart of 'fair use', that is, the

[204] Beebe (n 185) 661.

[205] Samuelson (n 183) 2552.

[206] *Suntrust Bank v Houghton Mifflin Co.* 268 F. 3d. Cir. 1257 (11th Cir. 2001) at [1273].

[207] Berne Convention, Art 9(2).

[208] J Griffiths, 'The "Three-Step Test" in European Copyright Law – Problems and Solutions' (2009) *Intellectual Property Quarterly* 428.

[209] C Geiger, J Griffiths and R Hilty, 'Towards a Balanced Interpretation of the "Three-Step Test" in Copyright Law' (2008) 30 *European Intellectual Property Review* 489. See also D Gervais 'Towards a New Core International Copyright Norm: the Reverse Three-Step Test' (2005) 9 *Marquette Intellectual Property Law Review* 1, 32 and M Senftleben, 'Fair Use in the Netherlands – A Renaissance?' (2009) 33(1) *Tijdschrift voor Auteurs, Media en Informatierecht AMI* 1, 7.

[210] *Gowers Review* (n 144) 68.

[211] Given the fact that sufficient acknowledgement is a requirement in relation to fair dealing in most cases under the current law, it is likely that it would be a requirement in relation to a case of 'transformative use'. This would likely satisfy the moral right of attribution. From the point of view

encouragement of creativity and cultural progress, is aligned with the practices of theatre.[212] Interestingly, there are recent precedents for switching from a narrow provision to a broadly articulated one.[213] Israeli law historically utilised a narrowly defined 'fair dealing' clause in line with the historical link with UK law arising from the Imperial Copyright Act of 1911. However, as Afori notes, the Israeli government came to the view that the fair use doctrine is necessary to ensure a balanced copyright law.[214] In 2007 Israel adopted a broad, open-ended standard of fair use in line with the US position.[215] Countries including Sri Lanka, South Korea, Singapore, Kenya and Uganda have also moved to a broad fair use provision in recent times.[216]

Conclusion

Infringement cases in theatre can arise in a wide range of circumstances, from the literal use of short extracts of text, or via the non-literal use of detailed plots or characters. Recent precedents on copyright in small pieces of text create the potential for over-protection of short works (headlines/titles) and short extracts. The strict enforcement by copyright owners of very small parts of literary and dramatic works could in practice have a chilling effect, or even stifle theatrical creative processes. However, this danger should not be overstated. Both the lack of case law on point and the insights from the empirical case study demonstrate that infringement disputes in UK theatre are rare. The recycling of theatrical motifs, plots and scenarios is a constant part of the creative process and appears widely tolerated. Alleged incidents of infringement do occur, but rather than resulting in litigation the interviews show that when they do transpire, they tend to be resolved behind the scenes, via social norms within the theatre community. Theatre practitioners

of fair use, the court should take into account the good faith of the practitioner who made the transformative use, even in a case where correct attribution has not been given. The CDPA accepts this in s 30(1ZA)(d) saying sufficient acknowledgement is expected 'unless this would be impossible for reasons of practicality or otherwise'. The integrity right may also need to be considered in relation to the notion of 'transformative' or 'creative' use. If the author's work is 'transformed' by the use in a manner that could be seen as 'derogatory', this might negatively affect the court's opinion regarding the 'fairness' of the use. However, it might also be possible to view this requirement cautiously. Unless the court is careful to assess whether in the specific context the use of the work could actually be seen as detrimental to the author's honour or reputation, this right might end up being a barrier to the effectiveness of the 'transformative' or 'creative' use in this context.

[212] B Reiser, 'Anything You Can Use, I Can Use Better: Examining the Contours of Fair Use as an Affirmative Defense for Theatre Artists, Creators, and Producers' (2020) 30 *Fordham Intell Prop Media & Ent LJ* 873.

[213] Yu (n 195).

[214] OF Afori, 'Legislative Comment – An open standard "fair use" doctrine: A welcome Israeli initiative' (2008) 30 *European Intellectual Property Review* 85. See also Yu (n 195) and *The Football Association Premier League v Ploni* (2009) Case 1636/08 Motion 11646/08 (District Court of Tel Aviv).

[215] Copyright Act 2007 (Israel), s 19.

[216] N Elkin-Koren and N Netanel, 'Transplanting Fair Use Across the Globe: A Case Study Testing the Credibility of U.S. Opposition' (2020) 50 *Joint PIJIP/TLS Research Paper Series* 1.

tend to avoid litigation where possible. Social sanctions causing reputational damage can be used within the theatre community where copying occurs that is overt and uncredited. But in general a wide degree of copying is tolerated in part because the community's social norms seek to 'preserve the building blocks and stock elements necessary for future creativity'.[217]

Despite the lack of case law on point, it is interesting to ponder how the fair dealing defences of parody and quotation might work in the theatrical context, should there be a court case in the near future. In this regard, the social norms of theatre – the emphasis on creative recycling of ideas and tropes – could be taken into account by a court. The current law does offer some potential to allow re-use of theatrical extracts and plots. As Bently notes:

> The 'idea-expression' dichotomy operates to permit, excuse and sanction the reuse of ideas which inevitably seep from work to work, and defences of fair use and fair dealing allow the reproduction or appropriation of the text itself.[218]

Thus, either the liberal use of the quotation or parody defences (or in the future the provision of a new broadly defined fair use exception) could prove useful at mitigating some of the potential conflicts between the creative practices of theatre and copyright.

Overall, the open-ended 'fair use' system has substantive advantages over the closed category 'fair dealing' model, particularly with regard to flexibility and adaptability to emerging cultural circumstances. Therefore, the UK adopting the broader standard is to be favoured over continued pursuit of the narrower model. Post-Brexit, the UK will likely have the freedom to move to an open, US-style fair use system, compatible with the 'three-step test', following countries such as Israel, South Korea and Sri Lanka who have made this change in recent decades.[219]

However, there are two major drawbacks that apply equally to both fair dealing and fair use. First, both models – fair dealing (parody/quotation) and fair (transformative) use – are defence-based. For this reason, both systems are reliant on the possibility of infringement actions being argued in court in order for judges to establish the boundaries of the exceptions. This limits the usefulness of the law as infringement actions taken by UK theatre practitioners rarely occur in the first place.[220]

Moreover, even if cases were to come to court, judges in the UK have traditionally been quite conservative in applying statutory exemptions to copyright.

[217] K Darling and A Perzanowski, 'Introduction' in – K Darling and A Perzanowski, *Creativity Without the Law: Challenging the Assumptions of Intellectual Property* (New York: NYU Press, 2017), 1, 8.

[218] L Bently, 'Copyright and the Death of the Author in Literature and Law' (1994) 57 *The Modern Law Review* 973, 983.

[219] L McDonagh and M Mimler, 'Intellectual Property Law and Brexit: A Retreat or a Reaffirmation of Jurisdiction?' in M Dougan (ed), *The UK after Brexit* (Cambridge: Intersentia, 2017) 159.

[220] See generally E Hudson, *Drafting Copyright Exceptions: From the Law in Books to the Law in Action* (Cambridge: Cambridge University Press, 2020).

The CJEU likewise tends to interpret the existing defences narrowly.[221] As Burrell remarks, merely bringing a new exception into the law may not necessarily change the traditional attitude of the courts.[222] With this in mind, in the event of an amendment to allow transformative uses, the provision of guidelines outlining fair use 'best practices' in the field of drama would be useful. In particular, this would help to raise awareness within the theatre network. This has already occurred in the creative industries in other jurisdictions and would be welcome in the theatrical field.[223]

In conclusion, while the above legal reforms would improve the law (a good in itself), I do not recommend that theatre participants should take more infringement cases against one another. At present theatrical creativity thrives in part because members of the community tolerate copying by each other to a wide degree – and even in overt cases they do not resort to legal action. They do not rely on the provisions of the law on infringement; rather, they resolve such disputes among themselves, via social norms (community sanctions such as 'bad-mouthing'). While such normative systems are in theory open to their own problems – bullying, abuse by those in positions of power, the lack of a system of appeal, etc – in my empirical research I did not encounter examples of such problems arising as a result of disputes over copying or infringement allegations (this is not to suggest that bullying or abuse does not occur in other theatrical contexts). In fact, on copying what struck me was an ethos of sharing – the idea that the key elements of theatre, including plot, character, structure, etc. are treated as a shared resource to be reused and recycled. For many in theatre their daily life is focused not on trying to defend their past works from being copied by other artists, but on the creation of new dramatic works and new forms of innovative theatre. For them, the law will likely always be secondary to their place in the community. Theatre itself may be a haunted stage, but theatre practitioners are certainly not haunted by the spectre of copyright infringement by their peers.[224]

[221] CJEU, judgments in *Funke Medien*, *Pelham* and *Spiegel Online* (n 156). See also German Federal Constitutional Court (*Bundesverfassungsgericht*), the First Senate, Metall auf Metall, 1 BvR 1585/13, 31 May 2016, DE:BVerfG:2016:rs20160531.1bvr158513.

[222] Burrell (n 157) 368.

[223] D'Agostino (n 175) 361. Association of Independent Video and Filmmakers (ANF) et al., *Documentary Filmmakers' Statement of Best Practices in Fair Use* (18 November 2005) at 1–2, available at https://cmsimpact.org/code/documentary-filmmakers-statement-of-best-practices-in-fair-use/ and CJ Craig, 'The Changing Face of Fair Dealing in Canadian Copyright Law' in M Geist (ed), *In the Public Interest: The Future of Canadian Copyright Law* (Toronto: Irwin Law, 2005) 437.

[224] C Sprigman, 'Conclusion: Some positive thoughts about IP's negative space' in K Darling and A Perzanowski, *Creativity Without Law: Challenging the Assumptions of Intellectual Property* (New York: NYU Press, 2017) 249. It remains to be seen whether the boom in theatre streaming during the COVID-19 pandemic will lead to infringement disputes over broadcasts or streaming of dramatic works on TV or online platforms.

5

Copyright's Role in Enforcing Credit and Control in Theatre

Introduction

The issues of credit and control are at the heart of the question of who possesses the authority to perform – to speak – on stage.[1] Building upon research published in *The Modern Law Review* in 2014 this chapter explores the way the moral rights of attribution and integrity operate in the theatrical context.[2]

On attribution I explore how credit is awarded for theatrical plays and productions. I demonstrate that it is typically the case that the agreements between writers and theatres specify that only the writer should get credit as author for the script (dramatic work).[3] Nonetheless, in theatre everybody tends to get some form of credit in the programme, from the writer to the director, and from the actors to the production staff; and when plays are published the original cast and director are usually provided in the text, providing an additional layer of attribution.[4]

It is the second moral right – integrity – that is particularly fraught in this context. We have already seen how working together – sometimes radically – is

[1] CP Rigamonti, 'The Conceptual Transformation of Moral Rights' (2007) 55 *The American Journal of Comparative Law* 67. See also D Wu (ed), *Making Plays: Interviews with Contemporary British Dramatists* (Basingstoke: Macmillan Press Ltd., 2000); JC Ginsburg, 'The Most Moral of Rights: The Right to be Recognized as the Author of One's Work' (2016) 8 *George Mason Journal of International Commercial Law* 44; MT Sundara Rajan, 'Moral rights: the future of copyright law?' (2019) 14 *Journal of Intellectual Property Law & Practice* 257; P Jaszi, 'On the Author Effect: Contemporary Copyright and Collective Creativity' in M Woodmansee and P Jaszi (eds), *The Construction Of Authorship: Textual Appropriation In Law and Literature* (Durham, NC: Duke University Press, 1994) 35; J Hughes, 'The Philosophy of Intellectual Property' (1988) 77 *Georgetown Law Journal* 287 and J Hughes, 'Actors as Authors in American Copyright Law' (2019) *Connecticut Law Review* 409, available at https://opencommons.uconn.edu/law_review/409.

[2] L McDonagh, 'Plays, Performances and Power Struggles – Examining Copyright's Integrity in the Field of Theatre' (2014) 77 *The Modern Law Review* 533, as well as K Wyver, 'Not waiting for Godot: new show tackles Beckett's ban on women' *The Guardian* (18 October 2020), available at www.theguardian.com/stage/2020/oct/18/not-waiting-for-godot-new-show-tackles-becketts-ban-on-women.

[3] This envisaged by the Writers' Guild in *The Working Playwright* (Writers' Guild of Great Britain, 2019), available at https://writersguild.org.uk/wp-content/uploads/2019/08/WGGB-Working-Playwright-Agreements-and-Contracts-1.pdf.

[4] See eg C Churchill, *Cloud 9* (London: Methuen, 1984) 10, crediting the original cast.

central to the practice of drama and the creation of plays. How does this dramatic collaboration affect perceptions of the integrity of the work – and crucially the question of who gets to control the play? Cox and Kastan remark:

> Of all literary forms, drama is least respectful of its author's intentions. Plays inevitably register multiple intentions, often conflicting intentions, as actors, annotators, revisers, collaborators, scribes, printers, and proof-readers, in addition to the playwright, all have a hand in shaping the text.[5]

In this chapter I examine the concept of the *integrity-based objection* in the theatrical context, referring to theatre studies, my empirical case study, and cases where playwrights, such as Samuel Beckett, David Williamson, Clive Norris, and Bisi Adigun have made integrity-based objections. The concepts of 'aura' and 'trajectory' are useful to this exploration.[6] Analysis of Benjamin's aura concept helps to explain why playwrights often show anxiety regarding maintaining the integrity of the dramatic work – put simply, they fear the audience will fail to perceive the intended meaning of the play. This relates to what Latour and Lowe describe as the trajectory of the dramatic work from its first performance onward.[7]

Overall, the chapter considers the legal issues central to moral rights, noting that different jurisdictions (UK, Ireland, France, Italy, and the US) take varying approaches. I conclude by suggesting that in integrity disputes, the right to freedom of expression under the ECHR ought to be taken into account as well as the author's rights.[8]

[5] J Cox and D Kastan (eds), *A New History of Early English Drama* (New York: Columbia University Press, 1997) 1. See also B Sherman and L Bently, *The Making of Modern Intellectual Property Law* (Cambridge: Cambridge University Press, 1999) and J Waldron, 'From Authors to Copiers' (1988) 68 *Chicago-Kent Law Review* 841 and R Deazley, *Rethinking Copyright: History, Theory, Language* (Cheltenham: Edward Elgar, 2006).

[6] W Benjamin, 'The Work of Art in the Age of Mechanical Reproduction' in H Arendt (ed), *Illuminations* (H Zohn tr, New York: Schocken Books, 1968) 217.

[7] B Latour and A Lowe, 'The migration of the aura, or how to explore the original through its fac similes' 1, 5–6; available at www.bruno-latour.fr/sites/default/files/108-ADAM-FACSIMILES-GB.pdf – originally published in T Bartscherer (ed), *Switching Codes: Thinking Through Digital Technology in the Humanities and the Arts* (Chicago: University of Chicago Press, 2010) 275. With regard to the life and trajectory of instruments see also B Latour, *We Have Never Been Modern* (Cambridge, MA: Harvard University Press, 1993) 17.

[8] The EU has not sought to harmonise moral rights so there are divergences between eg the UK and France on integrity. The philosophical link of 'personality' between artists and their works has its roots in Kantian and Hegelian thought – J Waldron, 'From Authors to Copiers: Individual Rights and Social Values in Intellectual Property' (1993) 68 *Chicago-Kent Law Review* 841, 842; H Breakey, 'Natural intellectual property rights and the public domain' (2010) 73 *The Modern Law Review* 208, 210; A Drassinower, *What's Wrong with Copying?* (Cambridge, MA: Harvard University Press, 2015) 147; A Chander and M Sunder, 'The Romance of the Public Domain' (2004) 92 *California Law Review*; M Borghi, 'Copyright and Truth' (2011) 12 *Theoretical Inquiries in Law* 1; JE Cohen, 'Creativity and Culture in Copyright Theory' (2007) 40 *UC Davis Law Review* 1151; I Kant, *On the Unlawfulness of Reprinting* (Berlin, 1785) in L Bently and M Kretschmer (eds), *Primary Sources on Copyright (1450–1900)* (2008), available at www.copyrighthistory.org/.

Moral Rights and Dramatic Works

Traditionally, moral rights are linked with civil law jurisdictions rather than common law jurisdictions.[9] In particular, moral rights are associated with the French concept of *droit d'auteur*.[10] Under this view, the personality of the author is central.[11] Indeed, the law in France fully acknowledges the importance of both the economic and moral rights of the author.[12] This can be contrasted with UK law which gives priority to the economic aspects of copyright.[13] In spite of this, the history of moral rights shows that economic rights exercised via contract can offer a means to make moral objections to the way an author's work may be used.[14] Statutory moral rights were only brought into UK law relatively recently, with the enactment of the CDPA in 1988; and even post-1988 it remains the case that UK law only protects moral rights in a relatively weak form when compared to the law in France.[15]

A key aspect of moral rights is that they are personal to the author and they remain with the author even where the author assigns or licenses the economic rights in the work to another party.[16] These moral rights include the right to be identified as the author of the work, which is generally known as the attribution or paternity right,[17] the right to not be falsely attributed as the author of a work,[18] and the right of integrity.[19]

As discussed in chapters three to four, the copyright owner holds the exclusive economic rights eg to license and assign the work, to copy the work, to adapt the

[9] Rigamonti (n 1). For a comparative analysis of moral rights in continental jurisdictions see A Dietz, 'The Artist's Right of Integrity Under Copyright Law – A Comparative Approach' (1994) 25 *IIC* 177; A Bertrand, 'The Moral Rights of Performers: French Law, International Law and Comparative Law' (1994) 5 *Entertainment Law Review* 114 and N Dalton, 'Will Remakes or Television Adaptation of Motion Pictures give rise to Moral Rights Claims by the Original Screenwriter and/or the Director under French Law' (2002) 13 *Entertainment Law Review* 75.

[10] E Adeney, *The Moral Rights of Authors and Performers – An International and Comparative Analysis* (Oxford: Oxford University Press, 2006) 165–70.

[11] RR Kwall, 'Inspiration and Innovation: The Intrinsic Dimension of the Artistic Soul' (2006) 81 *Notre Dame Law Review* 1945, 1986.

[12] R Clark, S Smyth and N Hall, *Intellectual Property Law in Ireland*, 4th edn (London: Bloomsbury Professional, 2016).

[13] R Bird and L Ponte, 'Protecting Moral Rights in the United States and United Kingdom: Challenges and Opportunities under the UK's New Performances Regulations' (2006) 24 *Boston University International Law Journal* 213, 213–14.

[14] Rigamonti (n 1). See also I Stamatoudi, 'Moral Rights of Authors in England' (1997) *Intellectual Property Quarterly* 478; B Ong, 'Why Moral Rights Matter: Recognising the Intrinsic Value of Integrity Rights' (2003) 26 *Columbia Journal of Law and the Arts* 297; and C Rigamonti, 'Deconstructing Moral Rights' (2006) 47 *Harvard International Law Journal* 353.

[15] W Cornish, 'Moral Rights under the 1988 Act' (1989) 11 *EIPR* 449.

[16] CDPA 1988, s 94.

[17] CDPA 1988, s 77. This right must be asserted by the author under CDPA 1988, s 78, a provision which has provoked criticism for undermining moral rights – see Adeney (n 10) 398–400. The CDPA also provides that moral rights can be waived by written consent – CDPA 1988, s 87(2). Regarding attribution, see *Sawkins v Hyperion Records Ltd* [2005] EWCA Civ 565.

[18] CDPA 1988, s 84.

[19] For analysis of the integrity right see Adeney (n 10) 405–15 and J Griffiths, 'Not Such a "Timid Thing": The UK's Integrity Right and Freedom of Expression' in J Griffiths and U Suthersanen (eds), *Copyright and Free Speech: Comparative and International Analyses* (Oxford: Oxford University Press, 2005) 211.

work, and to perform it, among other rights.[20] For the purpose of this chapter, the key economic rights are those that relate to the licensing of the dramatic work by the author-playwright to the theatre company for performance.[21] Although my focus is on moral rights, these economic rights remain highly relevant.[22] When a theatre company wishes to perform a play which is protected by copyright, the theatre company will attempt to get a licence from the author, who will usually exercise the economic right via a representative, typically an agent such as Concord Theatricals (Samuel French).[23] Depending on the circumstances, this licence may cover a single performance or an entire initial run of the play. As Rimmer notes, a negotiation may occur before this licence is granted in which the playwright, as copyright owner, may seek to restrict the making of changes to the play, such as textual edits, subtractions or additions, in advance of the envisaged performance.[24] If no agreement can be reached over this issue, the economic rights (facilitated by the licence) may be withdrawn due to a 'moral rights' objection.

It is worth recalling that in the UK the duration of copyright in the work lasts for 70 years after the life of the author.[25] As a result, classic works by luminaries such as Sophocles, Seneca, Shakespeare, Chekhov, Ibsen, Shaw, Wilde and Synge are no longer protected by copyright – they are in the 'public domain'.[26] This has two major consequences: first, performances of these public domain works no longer require a licence for use from the playwright's estate; second, the playwright's estate can no longer take legal action in order to protect the integrity of the work.[27] Nevertheless, the long term of copyright means that works which were written by playwrights who died within the last 70 years, such as Samuel Beckett, Agatha Christie and Harold Pinter, remain in copyright. In France, however,

[20] CDPA 1988, s 2(1) and ss 16–27. For a discussion of the meaning of public performance see *Bamgboye v Reed* [2004] EMLR 61.

[21] M Rimmer, 'Heretic – Copyright Law and Dramatic Works' (2002) 2 *Queensland University of Technology Law and Justice Journal* 131, 133.

[22] Berne Convention for the Protection of Literary and Artistic Works (September 9, 1886; revised 1896 (Paris), 1908 (Berlin), 1914 (Additional Protocol), 1928 (Rome), 1948 (Brussels), 1967 (Stockholm), 1971 (Paris) – as amended 1979); available at www.wipo.int/treaties/en/ip/berne/trtdocs_wo001.html.

[23] See www.concordtheatricals.co.uk. The UK Writers' Workshop offers advice to authors on finding an agent; available at www.writersworkshop.co.uk/literary-agents.html.

[24] Rimmer (n 21).

[25] CDPA 1988, s 12. Under the transitional provisions in Schedule 1 of the CDPA some very old unpublished works remain protected in the UK until 2039 – this potentially includes unpublished works by playwrights whose published works are now in the public domain. See also Directive 93/98/EEC of 29 October 1993 harmonizing the term of protection of copyright and certain related rights OJ L 290, 24.11.1993 and Directive 2006/116/EC of the European Parliament and of the Council of 12 December 2006 on the term of protection of copyright and certain related rights OJ L 372/12, 27.12.2006.

[26] For in depth discussion of the concept see J Litman, 'The Public Domain' (1990) 39 *Emory LJ* 965, 969 and J Boyle, *The Public Domain: Enclosing the Commons of the Mind* (New Haven, CT: Yale University Press, 2008).

[27] It is notable that unlike the situation in the UK, in France moral rights are actually considered to be 'perpetual'. However, the French courts have confirmed that after the author's death the moral rights of the author must be relaxed – *Hugo v Plon SA* (Cour Cass 1 ch civ) 30 January 2007, (2007) 212 RIDA 248.

moral rights are perpetual, though they are assessed less strictly in the case of a public domain work.[28]

The Attribution Right

Attribution studies is a growing field within literary and dramatic scholarship, as I examined in chapter two with respect to historical debates over the authorship of eg *The Spanish Tragedy* and the *Henry VI* cycle. In addition, in chapter three I discussed the issue of credit (attribution) in some detail in the context of joint authorship in theatre. As such, I will not repeat such discussions here, instead focusing most of this chapter on the integrity issue. With this in mind, it is worthwhile to pinpoint the specific aspects of UK legislation and case law that apply to the moral right of attribution.

Under the CDPA, attribution has two faces.[29] There is the right to be identified as the author of a work.[30] The author also has the right to object to false attribution, such as where a work is published claiming a particular author has written it when, in fact, that author has not done so.[31] The moral right of attribution is not assignable, but it must be asserted.[32] The CDPA provides that moral rights can be waived by written consent, such as in the case of ghostwriting.[33] The assertation requirement and waiver provisions potentially undermine the effectiveness of moral rights.[34]

Regarding attribution, in the UK there is scant case law on this specific right that would be relevant to the realm of theatre. A rare exception is a case involving a musical work – *Sawkins v Hyperion* – where it was held that although Dr Sawkins was thanked in the liner notes to the 'Sun King' CD, because the notes did not credit him *as an author*, Dr Sawkins' right of attribution was breached.[35]

On the point of attribution, I considered credit in joint authorship contexts in chapter 3, but it is worth reiterating that in the theatre world everybody tends to get some form of credit in the programme, from the writer and director to the actors and production staff. Often, when a new play is published, the original cast of actors will be named at the beginning of the text – all the actors I interviewed found this gesture on the part of the writer to be very favourable as a means of recognition.[36] At a more practical level several interviewees acknowledged that it would be preferable to specify at the beginning of the creative process how the credit situation will

[28] ibid.
[29] CDPA 1988, s 94.
[30] CDPA 1988, s 77. This right must be asserted by the author – CDPA 1988, s 78.
[31] CDPA 1988, s 84.
[32] CDPA 1988, s 77(1).
[33] CDPA 1988, s 87(2).
[34] Adeney (n 10) 398–400.
[35] *Sawkins v Hyperion Records Ltd* [2005] EWCA Civ 565.
[36] See, eg a number of examples of the original cast or actors being credited in S Beckett, *The Complete Dramatic Works* (New York: Faber and Faber, 2006).

be apportioned the end of the project, but this does not always happen, and greater clarity on this is something *The Working Playwright* aims to achieve.[37]

A recent example of shared credit and ownership I covered in chapter three concerns the play *Blurred Lines* first staged at the National Theatre in 2014 – the credits are 'created by Nick Payne and Carrie Cracknell, devised by the Company, poetry by Michaela Coel, text by Nick Payne' with both Payne and Cracknell sharing the copyright.[38] This provides a collaborative model of credit-sharing that is laudable and which may be emulated by other productions in future.

The Integrity Right

The CDPA protects the right of integrity,[39] which allows an author to object if the work is used in a derogatory or distorted 'treatment'.[40] In the theatrical context, the concept of integrity refers to the fact that the author of the play, as the owner of the copyright, can object to changes being made to the play by other parties.[41] It is argued here that this type of objection can be broadly described as an 'integrity-based objection' because the author-playwright's primary concern is with the integrity of the work as it is proposed to be performed.[42] Although under UK law there is a specific moral right of integrity by which such an objection can be put forward, in practice the author can make an integrity-based objection by either exercising this moral right to integrity or by asserting the economic rights (or both).[43] Regardless of which right is used to enforce the objection, it is the fact that the objection is founded upon the notion of integrity that is of primary importance to this chapter.

Moreover, the theatre world represents an interesting setting for exploring this aspect of copyright because what is protected by the law – embodied by the script of the play, known under UK copyright as the dramatic work – is a performative work, that is, a work which is intended to be performed, typically by people other than the author.[44] This is of significance because those creative participants

[37] *The Working Playwright* (n 3).

[38] Contemporary reviews commented on the profound nature of their collaboration, available at www.curtisbrown.co.uk/news/3237. The credits are shown in this official National Theatre excerpt: https://d1hsr9wh84jepr.cloudfront.net/newviews-excerpt4-blurredlines-2014-15.pdf.

[39] Adeney (n 10).

[40] CDPA 1988, s 80(1)(a). *Morrison Leahy Music Ltd v Lightbond Ltd* [1993] EMLR 144 is the leading case on this kind of musical distortion.

[41] CDPA 1988, ss 80–83. The key international treaty, setting minimum standards, and to which the UK is a party, is the Berne Convention for the Protection of Literary and Artistic Works (September 9, 1886; revised 1896 (Paris), 1908 (Berlin), 1914 (Additional Protocol), 1928 (Rome), 1948 (Brussels), 1967 (Stockholm), 1971 (Paris) – as amended 1979); available at www.wipo.int/treaties/en/ip/berne/trtdocs_wo001.html.

[42] The term 'author-playwright' is used occasionally in this chapter to emphasise that the playwright is often in law the person who can assert the author's moral rights. Following on from the discussion in chapter three, I certainly do not use this designation to cast aspersions on any other claims eg to joint authorship of the work by the director or actors.

[43] CDPA 1988, ss 16–76 and 77–89.

[44] CDPA 1988, s 3(2). See also *Brighton and Dubbeljoint v Jones* [2004] EWHC 1157 (Ch); [2004] EMLR 507.

who are involved in theatrical performance, such as directors, actors and producers, commonly seek the utmost freedom to perform the dramatic work. It almost goes without saying that this necessarily includes reimagining it, sometimes quite radically, perhaps in a way which the playwright might think is inappropriate, or which the playwright did not anticipate.[45]

As noted earlier, copyright gives the author-playwright the moral right to object to this in certain circumstances. Specifically, it allows the author to object if use is made of the work which amounts to a derogatory or distorted 'treatment'.[46] As yet, there is little case law on the integrity right in the UK, and no specific cases involving dramatic works.[47] However, it is clear from *Pasterfield v Denham*[48] and *Confetti Records v Warner Music*[49] that it is necessary under the CDPA to show that the derogatory treatment of the work would be prejudicial to the honour or reputation of the author, something which appears to be difficult to establish under the current law.[50] For this reason, the integrity right under the CDPA is sometimes viewed as 'timid'.[51] At the same time, although cautious judicial interpretation has not made the right as effective as it might be, the lack of a defence to infringement of the integrity right in the text of the CDPA could potentially make it a powerful legal tool if judicial attitudes change.[52]

The French courts, by contrast, have demonstrated a much stronger adherence to the moral right of integrity than the UK courts. The French case of *Turner v Huston*[53] (explicitly referred to by the court in the UK case of *Confetti Records*) concerned the colourisation of a black-and-white movie. The French court held that the director of the film could object to the colourisation because it violated the integrity of the work. Another significant French case is *Godot*, a case where the estate of Samuel Beckett successfully asserted the integrity right with respect to a proposed performance of *Waiting for Godot*.[54] For the purpose of this chapter, the *Godot* case is a highly relevant one and it is discussed in detail later on.

Investigating the 'Integrity-based Objection' in the Context of Theatre

As outlined in chapter three, developing theatrical performances often involves a workshop process, where the director and actors perform and re-animate the

[45] AM Adler, 'Against Moral Rights' (2009) 97 *California Law Review* 263.

[46] CDPA 1988, s 80(1)(a). The case of *Morrison Leahy Music Ltd v Lightbond Ltd* [1993] EMLR 144 is the leading case on this kind of distortion in the context of music.

[47] See *Morrison Leahy Music Ltd v Lightbond Ltd* (n 40); *Tidy v Trustee of the Natural History Museum* [1996] EIPR-D 86; 39 IPR 501; *Pasterfield v Denham* [1999] FSR 168 and *Confetti Records v Warner Music UK Limited* [2003] EMLR 35.

[48] *Pasterfield v Denham* (n 47).

[49] *Confetti Records v Warner Music Inc* (n 47).

[50] Griffiths (n 19) 221–25.

[51] ibid.

[52] ibid.

[53] *Turner Entertainment Company v Huston* (Cour Cass 1 ch civ) 28 May 1991; (CA Versailles, ch civ reunites) 19 December 1994, (1995) 164 RIDA 389.

[54] *Godot* (TGI Paris 3rd Chamber) 15 October 1992, (1993) 155 RIDA 225. See also Wyver (n 2).

dramatic work, sometimes quite radically.[55] The playwright may or may not be present during this process. Yet, the playwright, who is often not the one performing the work, has the right to object to changes being made to the dramatic work, and may choose to do so if the playwright fears the play's integrity is at stake. The idea that the playwright should have a veto power on such changes is envisaged by *The Working Playwright*.[56] As explained earlier, I refer to this as the playwright's integrity-based objection.

The playwright may fear that the director and actors will contrive to harm the play's aura – a concept I explore in detail below – if the performance is misconceived and the text misinterpreted on stage. In this sense, there is considerable overlap between the notions of integrity and aura – the integrity-based objection discussed here can be said to rest to a large degree upon the author's fear that the aura of the work could be damaged. Thus, anxiety on the part of the author as to whether or not the original intended meaning will be re-conjured in the performance could lead the author to make an integrity-based objection. As we shall see, the idea the playwright should have a veto in this respect is controversial because of the argument that in the theatrical sphere the law should protect not only the author's intended meaning, via the integrity right, but also the author's 'unintended meanings' – the aspects of the text that may be reinterpreted, and perhaps even subverted, via performance, to uncover new layers of understanding.[57]

As noted above, the way the integrity right has been interpreted in the UK means it is of itself a relatively weak right in practice.[58] Despite this, as acknowledged earlier, even without using this moral right directly there is a clear way for the playwright to ensure that any changes made to the play are within certain specifications – the parties can agree to this during negotiations over the licensing of the dramatic work (eg in a scenario where the play is an existing work owned by the playwright and a theatre company wants to stage it). During these negotiations, the playwright can specify, as a term of the licence, which uses, changes and edits are acceptable, and which are not.[59] As I discuss later on in this chapter, if the play is a brand new work in the process of being devised/revised, the practices of the workshop will inevitably require the writer, director and actors to labour together to come up with the final work as performed (and if the parties cannot agree on a way to present the work, the project will likely collapse).

[55] An example of a radical theatrical performance of a public domain work was the all-female production of *King Lear* set in a female prison which took place at Donmar Warehouse, London, in late 2012. See L Gardner, 'All female King Lear? It's about time' *The Guardian* (4 September 2012); available at www.theguardian.com/stage/theatreblog/2012/sep/04/theatre-shakespeare.

[56] This is envisaged by the Writers' Guild of Great Britain in *The Working Playwright* (n 3).

[57] McDonagh (n 2). On Ibsen's nineteenth century struggles over the integrity of his intended texts amid foreign productions see G D'Amico, 'Marketing Ibsen: A Study of the First Italian Reception, 1883–1891' (2011) 11 *Ibsen Studies* 145.

[58] See *Confetti Records v Warner Music UK Ltd* (n 47) and *Tidy v Trustees of the National History Museum* (n 47).

[59] See generally B Salter and A Hui, 'Empirical Studies of Moral Rights in Cases of Dramatic and Musical Works,' (2010), available at http://papers.ssrn.com/sol3/papers.cfm?abstract_id=1641472.

Whether the work is prior-existing or newly devised/revised, power struggles and negotiations over the eventual performance are inevitable.[60] The notion of the integrity of the work is central to these power struggles and for this reason I use it broadly here, even where the specific moral right to integrity as envisaged under UK law would not apply, or where a derogatory 'treatment' may be difficult to prove in court.[61]

Although not many theatre cases on this issue have come to court – and none have involved disputes in the UK – the cases that have arisen in other jurisdictions are highly illustrative.

Godot (France)

It is well known that since Samuel Beckett died in 1989 his estate has been, and continues to be, notoriously strict about maintaining the integrity of his works. To take one example, upon viewing a production of *Footfalls* in London during the 1990s, representatives of the Beckett estate became so infuriated by the lack of adherence to the script that the estate forced the production to close.[62] To some extent, this reflects Beckett's own belief that his stage directions should be followed to the letter.[63] Indeed, Beckett was not shy about expressing his opinion where a production deviated from his express instructions – following a performance of 'Not I' in the early 1970s in New York, Beckett reportedly told the actress in the one-woman show, Jessica Tandy, that she had ruined 'his' play.[64]

In line with this, the case *par excellence* of an integrity-based objection is the case of *Godot*.[65] Here Beckett's estate successfully took a challenge to prevent an all-female production of *Waiting for Godot*.[66] Beckett had always maintained that only male actors could perform the central roles. The French courts found that his estate could use the doctrine of moral rights to prevent the proposed production from taking place. It is worth pointing out that the courts in jurisdictions other than France have not been as sympathetic to Beckett's estate – a similar case taken in Italy 'failed to stop women waiting for Godot'.[67] *Godot*, therefore, represents a rare case where the specific moral right was invoked successfully in court by the playwright's estate.

[60] Rimmer (n 21).

[61] Griffiths (n 19).

[62] See for instance the furor created over a radical performance of *Footfalls* by Fiona Shaw, directed by Deborah Warner, discussed in F Shaw, 'Buried in Beckett' *The Guardian* (23 January 2007), available at www.guardian.co.uk/theguardian/2007/jan/23/features11.g21.

[63] See, eg his directions for *Footfalls* in S Beckett, *The Complete Dramatic Works* (London: Faber and Faber, 2006) 399.

[64] N Lezard, 'Play Samuel Beckett's Mouth? Not I' *The Guardian* (8 July 2009), available at www.theguardian.com/stage/theatreblog/2009/jul/08/samuel-beckett-not-i.

[65] *Godot* (n 54). See also Wyver (n 2).

[66] ibid.

[67] As reported in the news media – see B MacMahon, 'Beckett estate fails to stop women waiting for Godot' *The Guardian* (4 February 2006), available at www.guardian.co.uk/world/2006/feb/04/arts.italy.

Heretic (Australia)

A similar dispute between an author-playwright and a director occurred in the late 1990s in Sydney concerning the play *Heretic*. The playwright, David Williamson, accused the director, Wayne Harrison, of 'taking liberties with the script'.[68] In particular, Williamson claimed that changes to one of the characters in the play, based on the historical figure of Margaret Mead, had damaged the integrity of the character.[69] The licence agreement between Williamson and the theatre company stated that no alterations to the text could be made without the author's permission.[70] Even so, Rimmer notes that the director felt strongly that the playwright was not the only one involved the theatrical process who had a stake in maintaining the integrity of the work via its performance:

> The only way a playwright can really ensure the 'integrity' of what is written is by reading/performing the text him/herself. The minute you seek collaborators you enter the territory of interpretation, subjectivity and trust. Choose your collaborators carefully, but don't impose a tyranny of integrity and singular moral rights on those you need to transform your skeletal 'map for a performance' into a play.[71]

In this case, Williams initially considered legal action, and consulted with his lawyers about the possibility of seeking an injunction to prevent the play from being performed. However, once the disagreement became public he withdrew this threat in the face of a highly negative reaction from other members of the theatrical community.[72]

Clybourne Park (Germany)

The case examined here is the 2012 dispute over the play *Clybourne Park*. The Deutsches Theatre in Berlin planned to mount a production of the play with the black character played by a white actress in 'blackface' make-up, something which the theatre claimed is relatively normal in German theatrical practice even though it is highly taboo in the US. In his open letter Norris stated:

> Disbelievingly, I contacted my agent who put me in touch with the management of Deutsches Theatre. Yes, they confirmed, it is true, we have cast a white ensemble member in this role, and we see no logical reason why we should cast an 'Afro-German'. (If you are familiar with my play at all, the reasons are self-evident.) After much evasion, justification and rationalizing of their reasons, they finally informed me that the color of

[68] Rimmer (n 21) 131.
[69] D Williamson, 'Some like it hot … but I don't' *The Sydney Morning Herald* (9 April 1996) 13.
[70] Rimmer (n 21) 134.
[71] ibid, 137, referring to personal correspondence with Wayne Harrison undertaken during 1999.
[72] ibid, 131.

> the actress's skin would ultimately be irrelevant, since they intended to 'experiment with makeup'. At this point, I retracted the rights to the production.[73]

In the letter Norris explained the nature of his integrity-based objection in detail, acknowledging the fact that use of 'blackface' is common within the German theatrical tradition. However, ultimately this made no difference to him – what worried him was maintaining the integrity of his play:

> Whatever rationale the German theatre establishment might offer for their brazenly discriminatory practice is of no interest to me. For, as little power as we playwrights have, we always retain one small power and that is the power to say no. To say, no thank you, I'd rather not have my work performed in Germany, today, under those conditions.

It is clear that in this case concern over the integrity of the dramatic work led to the withdrawal by the playwright, Clive Norris, of the economic rights to perform it.[74] No explicit recourse was made to the specific moral right of integrity, but the need to protect the integrity of his play was clearly central to Norris' decision.

The Playboy of the Western World (Ireland)

A dispute arose in 2012–13 between The Abbey Theatre, Dublin and the playwright Bisi Adigun, the co-writer (with Roddy Doyle) of a new adaptation of JM Synge's classic play *The Playboy of the Western World* (a public domain work). In the new version the protagonist Christy Mahon was changed from a rural dweller in the west of Ireland to a Nigerian asylum seeker. The new version was staged at the Abbey Theatre in 2007. A later theatrical run of the play from 2008–09 presented an altered version of the script with more than 100 changes made without the permission of Adigun. Adigun claimed copyright infringement by The Abbey and Doyle as well as infringement of the integrity right, arguing that the work had been distorted.[75] The settlement involved The Abbey paying royalties to Adigun and acknowledging in public that the alterations to the script were unauthorised and without Adigun's permission. Furthermore, Roddy Doyle agreed to transfer all his rights over the co-authored work to Adigun as part of the settlement.[76]

[73] 'A Letter from Bruce Norris' (16 October 2012), quoted at www.playbill.com/article/pulitzer-winner-bruce-norris-retracts-rights-to-german-troupes-clybourne-park-over-blackface-casting-com-198817.

[74] M Trueman and K Connolly, 'Bruce Norris stops Berlin staging of Clybourne Park after blacking up row' *The Guardian* (18 October 2012), available at www.guardian.co.uk/stage/2012/oct/18/bruce-norris-clybourne-park-blackface-row.

[75] D Flynn, 'A Comparative Analysis of the Moral Right of Integrity in the UK, Ireland and France' (2017) 7 *King's Inns Student L Rev* 108.

[76] *Arambe Productions Limited v Abbey Theatre and Roddy Doyle* (IEHC filing, settled 2013) and the related case taken by Adigun against his solicitor – *Adigun v Mc Evoy & Ors* [2013] IEHC 342. See also T Healy, 'Roddy Doyle Gives Up Rights to Play in Legal Battle over Playboy Royalties' *The Independent* (Ireland) (13 January 2013), available at www.independent.ie/irish-news/courts/roddydoyle-gives-up-rights-to-play-in-legal-battle-over-playboy-royalties-29025110.html.

Summary of Comparative Insights

In all of these highlighted cases it is clear that the playwrights and the other creative participants (directors, actors, producers) were at odds with each other over the need to maintain the integrity of the play. Given the existence of these disputes, it is necessary to weigh up the positives and negatives of the existence of this notion of integrity under copyright. The positive case for protecting the integrity of the work tends to emphasise the inherent link between the artist and her work of art, something evident in the disputes above.[77] In this vein, moral rights can be said to protect 'the superior interests of human genius' by ensuring that the work is kept 'as it emerged from the imagination of its author'.[78] The notion of a singular, Romantic author is clearly the archetype here, rather than any idea of authorship which reflects the collaborative nature of theatre.[79] It is also sometimes argued that along with the need to protect 'the personality interests of the individual artist' moral rights also protect the public interest by 'preserving' the work for the public.[80] In other words, it is not only the artist who benefits from the moral right of integrity; it is the public as well.

Nonetheless, there is also a counter-argument, one which centres on the need to allow creative reinterpretation of the work by others.[81] Adler argues that the right of integrity 'threatens art because it fails to recognize the profound artistic importance of modifying, even destroying, works of art, and of freeing art from the control of the artist'.[82] This point is an important one – as I explore later on in this chapter, it gets to the crux of why the issue of integrity is of particular significance in the context of theatre.

[77] JH Merryman, AE Elsen and SK Urice, *Law, Ethics and the Visual Arts*, 5th edn (Alphen aan den Rijn, The Netherlands: Kluwer Law International, 2006) 423, arguing that to mistreat the work is to mistreat the artist.

[78] JH Merryman, *Thinking about the Elgin Marbles: Critical Essays on Cultural Property, Art and Law*, 2nd edn (Alphen aan den Rijn, The Netherlands: Kluwer Law International, 2009) 412, quoting from *Millet*, Tribunal de la Seine, 20 May 1911 (1911) Amm. I. 27, a case where the son of the great French artist Jean-François Millet took a case to prevent the publication of reproductions of his father's paintings, allegedly because they were so poorly produced the reproductions 'distorted' his father's works.

[79] For a perspectives of authorship which take account of non-individualist practice see CJ Craig, *Copyright, Communication and Culture: Towards a Relational Theory of Copyright Law* (Cheltenham: Edward Elgar, 2011); JE Cohen, 'Creativity and Culture in Copyright Theory' (2007) 40 *UC Davis Law Review* 1151; RJ Coombe, *The Cultural Life of Intellectual Properties: Authorship, Appropriation and the Law* (Durham NC: Duke University Press, 1998) and K Aoki, '(Intellectual) Property and Sovereignty: Notes Toward a Cultural Geography of Authorship' (1996) 48 *Stanford Law Review* 1293.

[80] Adler (n 45) 270.

[81] LA Mills, 'Moral Rights: Well-Intentioned Protection and its Unintended Consequences' (2011) 90 *Texas Law Review* 443. See also MA Hamilton, 'Appropriation Art and the Imminent Decline in Authorial Control over Copyright Works' (1994) 42 *Journal of the Copyright Society of the U.S.A.* 93 and M Rimmer, 'The Grey Album: Copyright Law and Digital Sampling' (2005) 114 *Media International Australia* 40.

[82] Adler (n 45) 265.

Analysing the 'Aura' of the Work of Drama

Adding to the insights from Barthes and Foucault in the prior chapters, here I take up Walter Benjamin's famous description of the 'aura' of the work of art – a notion which at a basic level refers to the uniqueness and authenticity of the work or 'that which withers'.[83] Benjamin states that as more and more copies, images, and reproductions of a fine art work enter the public sphere, the aura of the original, authentic work begins to dissipate. It is notable that in the context of theatrical works the precise opposite is true – the more the dramatic work gets performed, or reproduced, the more the aura surrounding the play is likely to increase in esteem.[84]

Despite this – or perhaps more accurately, because of it – the playwright may fear that the director and actors will contrive to harm the play's aura if the performance is misconceived and the text misinterpreted on stage. As noted earlier, there is considerable overlap between the notions of integrity and aura – the integrity-based objection discussed above can be said to rely to a large degree upon anxiety on the part of the author concerning the possible withering away of the aura of the work.[85]

Tension is inevitable because rather than the playwright, it is those directly involved in the acts of performance who are capable of projecting and maintaining the aura of the play. Benjamin contrasts the 'stage play' in this regard with works which can be mechanically reproduced, such as films:[86]

> The aura which, on the stage, emanates from Macbeth, cannot be separated for the spectators from that of the actor.[87]

Further insight is brought to this discussion by examining the application of Benjamin's aura by Bruno Latour and Adam Lowe in their comparative analysis of 'copies' and 'performances' in the realms of fine arts and theatre respectively.[88] All three thinkers are in agreement that the aura of the theatrical play is primarily maintained via performance. Importantly, Latour and Lowe note that with respect to classic works, such as Shakespeare's *King Lear*, the audience at a theatrical

[83] Benjamin (n 6) 220–21. This can be contrasted with the opinion of Jean Baudrillard who states that sometimes the audience cannot distinguish between the original and the copy, and at other times the audience prefers the reproduction – see J Baudrillard, 'The Precession of Simulacra' in B Wallis (ed), *Art After Modernism: Rethinking Representation* (Boston, MA: David R. Godine Inc., 1991) 253.

[84] From the perspective of copyright law, it is important to note that the notion of a reproduction used by Benjamin here does not refer to 'copies' of an object or a play which effectively amount to copyright infringement eg where another playwright has taken the play, or a substantial part of it, and put his own name, and perhaps a new title to it. Instead, it refers to performances of the play which are fully acknowledged as such, and where appropriate, licensed.

[85] Latour and Lowe (n 7) 4–6.

[86] Benjamin (n 6).

[87] ibid, 228.

[88] Latour and Lowe (n 7) 4–6.

performance is prepared for their prior understanding of the play, and its aura, to be challenged and altered by what they experience:

> No one will complain on hearing King Lear: 'But this is not the original, it is just a representation!'. Quite right. That's the whole idea of what it is to play King Lear: it is to replay it … There is nothing extraordinary in considering that 'one good representation of King Lear' is a moment, a segment, in the career of the work of art called King Lear, the absolute Platonic ideal of which no one has ever seen and no one will ever be able to circumscribe.[89]

On this it is worth recalling that for more than a century after Shakespeare's death, the Nahum Tate version of *King Lear*, with a happy ending, was the canonical version as performed on stage.[90] Dramatic works have a 'multiplicitous quality' – a profound 'openness' to being re-infused with meaning which allows us to 'imagine that there are multiple artists, even when only one artist created the original piece'.[91] Latour and Lowe observe that in works of collective authorship we tend to 'attribute to the author … the power of each of the successive reinterpretations by saying that "potentially" all of them "were already" there in the Ur-text'. Yet, this tends to downplay the potentially radical authority of the interpretive work of later performers.[92]

As Latour and Lowe point out, over the lifetime of the play this re-conjuring of the author's originality into the performance aura tends to happen in ever more radical ways.[93] As I outline below, in the context of theatre it is important that the notion of originality envisaged by copyright is able to take account of multiple interpretations of the work, along the trajectory, or career, of the play.

Evaluating the 'Trajectory' of the Work of Drama

Latour and Lowe use the notion of trajectory in the theatrical context to chart the progress of a play from its first performance onwards. By putting the work itself centre stage – rather than the author figure – it becomes possible to recognise that a copyright work is an object of property which necessarily has a life of its

[89] ibid, 6. Latour and Lowe do not accept Benjamin's key insight that the aura of works of fine art diminishes with the prevalence of copies. In their view, searching for a supposed original, authentic piece of fine art is fruitless because we know that materially all works of fine art tend to wither and fade over time. Consequently, they need to be preserved, restored, repaired – something which inevitably changes their nature, and their aura. For this reason, Latour and Lowe prefer to think of works of art as having a trajectory or career within which the only question that matters is whether the particular reproduction the viewer encounters is done well or done poorly. In their view, a poor restoration of an original will do more harm to the aura of the work than a superb reproduction. While Latour and Lowe are in disagreement with Benjamin concerning fine art reproductions, they agree with him on theatre.

[90] Kwall (n 11) 1986. See also A Chander and M Sunder, 'Copyright's Cultural Turn' (2013) 97 *Texas Law Review* 1397.

[91] Adler (n 45) 278.

[92] McDonagh (n 2). See also Wyver (n 2).

[93] Latour and Lowe (n 7) 9.

own beyond that of its creator(s). In other words, it has a trajectory. Analysis of the work's trajectory brings new insights with respect to this chapter's analysis of crucial legal issues such as originality. As shown in prior chapters, mapping of the trajectories of various copyright works – passing through many persons, companies and territories over many decades – is of central concern to this book.

I argue here that a new play has three broad stages within its potential trajectory. The first 'debut' stage follows the initial development of the dramatic work all the way through to its first performance run. As I outlined in chapter three, this developmental stage can occur in a number of different ways, including where an entire, fully-formed text is written by the playwright on his own, or conversely, where there is full or partial collaboration between playwright, director and actors during a devising/revising workshop process.[94] The harsh economic realities of theatre mean that most new plays exist solely with respect to this first stage – they disappear after their first run.

The second 'exceptional' stage, which is comparatively rare, is where a dramatic work gets picked up, due to critical or popular acclaim, for subsequent performances by companies other than the initial one. This stage may encompass a long period of time, even many decades. Moreover, not every exceptional dramatic work will be comparable – within this stage there will of course be a large deviation between dramatic works which become world famous, such as *Waiting for Godot, Cloud 9* or *Angels in America* and relatively new plays which are popular, but not as well known, such as *Clybourne Park* or *Stones in His Pockets*. What is crucial for the purpose of this chapter is that the play has crossed from the debut stage to the exceptional stage – it is now a work of some popular esteem.

The final 'classic' stage is where a dramatic work enters the public domain, at the expiration of copyright, whereby it may be performed by anyone without the need for a licence from the author or the author's estate. Where popular, such dramatic works become part of the universal theatrical canon.

It can be impossible to predict which works will bear the test of time. The director Michael Frayn has remarked: 'Whether the play will go on having any resonance I don't think you can tell. You just have to see. Some plays and books seem to go on being meaningful even when they seem to be very attached to the times they were written in; some that appear to have a classical timelessness get swept away by time.'[95]

As with the exceptional stage, there will inevitably be a distinction between different plays within the classic stage – *The Cherry Orchard* is a much more recent play than *King Lear* for example – but what is important for this chapter is that via the expiration of copyright the dramatic work moves from the exceptional stage to the classic stage.[96] Thus, copyright plays a crucial underlying role along each play's trajectory, defining when it passes into the final stage.

[94] The joint authorship issues relevant to these processes are covered in chapter three of this book.
[95] Wu (n 1) 229.
[96] This is not to say that every work for which copyright has expired will be seen in a positive light. Critical and popular tastes change constantly and there are many plays that were highly popular during eg the 19th century which are never performed today.

Dramatic works in the second stage do, of course, pass into the third stage eventually – one day *Waiting for Godot* and *Clybourne Park* will enter the public domain canon, and radical productions can be staged, with no need to seek the author's permission.[97] In other words, the classic play reaches the stage where as a work of art it grows in esteem precisely because of 'the abundance of its copies'.[98]

Latour and Lowe state that 'clearly, in the case of performance art at least, every new version runs the risk of losing the original – or of regaining it'.[99] This notion, of the need to recover 'the original', is in line with Rebecca Kwall's argument that the essence of the moral right of integrity 'is the idea of respect for the author's original meaning'.[100] As noted earlier in this chapter, what the playwright fears when making an integrity-based objection is that the original expression – the intended meaning of the work – will be lost, rather than regained in the aura of performance. This links back directly to the concept of originality which lies at the heart of copyright law.[101]

As discussed in chapter three, in light of CJEU decisions the concept of originality under UK law appears to now be largely a 'dematerialised' one – one that has been stripped of material limitations set by the boundaries of, for example, literariness or musicality.[102] If this is the case, then what the law ultimately protects is a dematerialised expression of originality defined by the author's intellectual creativity. Moreover, if the concept of the aura is concerned with how the work is perceived by the audience, and the concept of originality encompasses the author's intended meaning, then in the specific case of dramatic works the aura of the performance on stage could be said to represent the re-conjuring of this originality. As noted earlier, over the lifetime of the play, this re-conjuring of the author's originality into the performance aura tends to happen in ever more radical ways, so much so that performances can move quite drastically away from the author's original intentions – and perhaps even subvert these intentions entirely.[103]

Given that this is the case, while the views of the author-playwright are of importance it is necessary to question the extent to which in a collaborative medium such as theatre, the views of one party – the playwright – ought to override the views of the other collaborators. All works of art necessarily 'evolve over time based on how they are presented and received'.[104] After all, there are examples

[97] See case of *Hugo v Plon SA* (n 27). For analysis of different types of 'canon' see HY Kang, 'Is There (Should There Be) a Law & Humanities Canon?' (2019) 16 *Law, Culture and the Humanities* 1.

[98] Latour and Lowe (n 7) 5.

[99] ibid, 6.

[100] Kwall (n 11) 1986.

[101] B Latour and A Lowe (n 7) 6–9.

[102] Griffiths (n 19). For discussion of music cases in light of EU decisions on originality see L McDonagh, 'Is Creative use of Musical Works without a licence acceptable under Copyright?' (2012) 43 *International Review of Intellectual Property and Competition Law* 401.

[103] Latour and Lowe (n 7) 9.

[104] Adler (n 45) 271.

where other parties have directly violated the author's wishes, but ended up creating works possessing even greater value and wider acclaim.[105] This point seems particularly resonant in the context of the collaborative environment of theatre. Indeed, this very argument was made by the theatre director in the *Heretic* dispute, as detailed earlier. In line with this, Adler poses the pertinent question:

> Does the artist know what's best for his art?[106]

This question, of course, is a highly complex one, and particularly so in the theatrical context because all the creative parties – playwright, director, actors – typically consider themselves to be artists in their own right, and all are given acknowledgement of their specific artistic roles in the performance programme. In fact, in a collaborative medium such as theatre it is plausible to imagine a scenario where the enforcement of the playwright's anxieties over the integrity of the dramatic work may actually end up being counter-productive to maintaining its aura. Indeed, a fresh, radical take on the text by a creative director and set of actors might actually improve the play's standing. There may be layers of meaning within the play that can only be uncovered through such subversive performances. In other words, even if the author's original intended meaning is *subverted*, the aura of the play may still be maintained, and may actually be *enhanced*.

There are divergent views on whether the playwright should have this right. Carroll argues that a dramatist's 'rights of creative control are too strong when applied to the performing arts because they fail to take account of the mutual dependence between writers and performers to fully realize the work in performance'.[107] Fisk and Hartz even make the case for a US statutory licence to perform plays as a way of limiting playwrights' veto power over performances.[108] When *The Working Playwright* was first published in 2012, it received an angry reaction from some in the theatre community, including the playwright and director Selma Dimitrijevic, who criticised the document for advocating 'a way of working in which the writer holds the lion's share of power and control over the creation of the work'.[109] In an open letter, the playwrights David Edgar and Amanda Whittington responded by saying that *The Working Playwright*'s main benefit is to recommend that writers and theatre companies put their legal relationship to one another on a solid footing so that such disputes do not arise. Nonetheless, the existence of this public row reveals once again that tensions do exist on this point of integrity in the UK theatre field.

[105] ibid, 272, referring to the example of Clement Greenberg modifying the works of David Smith as noted by R Serra, 'Art and Censorship' (1991) 17 *Critical Inquiry* 574, 576.

[106] Adler (n 45) 271.

[107] MW Carroll, 'Copyright's Creative Hierarchy in the Performing Arts' (2012) 14 *Vand. J. Ent. & Tech. L.* 797. See also C Buccafusco, 'A Theory of Copyright Authorship' (2016) 102 *Va. L. Rev.* 1229, 1246.

[108] C Fisk and A Hartz, 'Fair Treatment of Theatre Labor: A Right to Perform Plays' *ONLABOR* (27 June 2016), available at https://www.onlabor.org/fair-treatment-for-theatre-labor-a-right-to-perform-plays/.

[109] D Edgar and A Whittington, 'Defending the Working Playwright' (31 October 2012), available at http://exeuntmagazine.com/features/defending-the-working-playwright-a-reply/.

This brings us back to the central question: could, for example, the French all-female production of *Waiting for Godot* have proved to be an insightful one? An integrity-based objection was made by the author-playwright, and the specific production was called to a halt. As a result, we'll never know what the critical and popular response might have been. We will never know, in fact, whether 'the original' of the play would have been lost, or triumphantly regained, in the aura of performance – or indeed, whether the subversion of that original meaning might have actually enhanced the play's aura.

At its worst, therefore, the integrity-based objection, if applied strictly by the author-playwright, has the potential to freeze works in time, and undermine the kind of interpretive practices common in the field of theatre.

The Link between the Play's Trajectory and the Public Domain

Even if there is frustration at present with rights restrictions, at some point in the future dramatic works which are currently held under tight control by authors, or their estates, will be freely usable.[110] In fact, it seems logical that during the first (debut) and second (exceptional) stages authors may be careful with respect to the way their dramatic works are presented. Whereas, once a play has reached the classic stage its inherent quality might be so evident that even where a performance or interpretation is very weak, and the aura fails to migrate, the audience will accept that it was merely the performance that should be considered a failure. In such a case, the esteem of the underlying dramatic work itself would not be diminished. For instance, to use the primary example highlighted by Latour and Lowe – *King Lear* – there is no doubt that each year there are many modern interpretations of the play, which vary, sometimes drastically, both in ambition and quality. Yet, the anxieties over originality and integrity seem less potent in the case of *King Lear* – a dramatic work at the classic stage of its trajectory – than in the case of a new work, for which early judgements over quality will be crucial for it to pass from the first to the second stage of its trajectory. On classic works, Latour and Lowe remark:

> … spectators have no qualm whatsoever at judging the new version under their eyes by applying the shibboleth: 'Is it well or badly (re)played?' They can differ wildly in their

[110] An example given here is the slew of theatrical productions of James Joyce's *Ulysses* that took place in early 2012 following the expiration of copyright in his works, 70 years after the death of the author – see M O'Connell, 'Has James Joyce Been Set Free?' *The New Yorker* (12 January 2012), available at www.newyorker.com/online/blogs/books/2012/01/james-joyce-public-domain.html; see also the webpage for the Dublin production of Patrick Fitzgerald's *Gibraltar* – an adaptation after James Joyce's *Ulysses* which began on 1 January 2012, available at www.thenewtheatre.com/tnt_php/scripts/page/show.php?show_id=69&gi_sn=4f01b3cfa6ca7%7C0.

> opinions, some being scandalized by what they take as some revolting novelties ('Why does Lear disappear in a submarine?') or bored by the repetition of too many clichés, but they have no difficulty in considering that this moment in the whole career of all the successive King Lears – in the plural – should be judged on its merit and not by its mimetic comparison with the first (entirely inaccessible anyway) presentation of King Lear by the Shakespeare company in such and such a year.[111]

This situation is not apparent in the case of a dramatic work in the first or second stages. Indeed, a dramatic work in the first (debut) stage seems particularly vulnerable since it goes without saying that if the first performance run is a failure then the play is unlikely to have much of a trajectory beyond that initial run. However, a dramatic work such as *Waiting for Godot* or *Clybourne Park* seems less vulnerable since the play has already passed through the first stage to the second – it is known as an exceptional work. Author-playwrights may still make integrity-based objections when the dramatic work is in this second stage, and the authors of *Waiting for Godot* and *Clybourne Park* certainly did so, but it would seem logical that for the playwright the first stage may cause the greater anxiety with respect to the maintenance of the work's originality, integrity and aura.

Dramatic works in the second stage pass into the third stage eventually – one day *Waiting for Godot* and *Clybourne Park* will enter the public domain canon, as has happened to *The Playboy of the Western World*, and at that stage innumerable radical productions can be put on, with no need to seek the author's permission.[112] Therefore, upon becoming a public domain work the classic play truly reaches the stage where as a work of art it grows in esteem precisely because of 'the abundance of its copies'.[113] Nonetheless, as shown by the 2012–2013 Irish dispute over the new version of *The Playboy*, an integrity-based objection can be made over the new adaptation.[114]

In light of the above, it is clear that copyright law is relevant to the way a dramatic work is perceived along its trajectory, something which has consequences for the perception of the originality, integrity and aura of such works. These issues are further examined below with regard to the empirical research. I evaluate how each agent's role – as well as their respective capitals and habitus – affects the resolution of the power struggles that arise within the field of theatre concerning integrity.[115]

[111] Latour and Lowe (n 7) 6.
[112] See case of *Hugo v Plon SA* (n 27).
[113] Latour and Lowe (n 7) 5.
[114] Healy (n 76).
[115] P Bourdieu, *The State Nobility: Elite Schools in the Fields of Power* (Stanford CA: Stanford University Press, 1996) 264–74. See also generally P Bourdieu, *The Logic of Practice* (Stanford CA: Stanford University Press, 1990).

How Prevalent are Integrity-based Objections in Theatre Practice?

Referring once more to Bourdieu, I argue that in theatre's social field resolving power struggles successfully is crucial to the creative processes of theatre.[116] Analysis of the empirical research demonstrates that by giving one of the agents in the field – the author-playwright – a kind of economic capital in the form of the right to withdraw permission for the performance, copyright law is deeply implicated in the way such power struggles are conceived and resolved. As noted earlier, there is interplay between the notions of originality, integrity and aura, while the duration of copyright has a significant effect on denoting the trajectory of a dramatic work.

In this vein, the interview responses on integrity issues reveal a paradox – in theatre there is a great deal of respect for the writer's wishes; but also, some frustration that these wishes can restrict the ability of performers to re-interpret the dramatic work. There is awareness that the playwright has the power to control/restrict the interpretive practices of other artists such as directors and actors.

Regarding the question of how prevalent integrity-based objections are within the theatrical realm, I received a diverse range of responses. Broadly, the issue of integrity-based objections is certainly of some concern to theatre participants, but the level of this concern can vary considerably. Among my interviewees, a small number had been forced to abandon projects in their early stages due to problems resolving a creative struggle over integrity. In spite of this, the majority of interviewees expressed a positive view about the extent of their freedom to create and perform, and some provided views sympathetic to writers who wish to have their vision appear on stage. The interviews also show that most creative participants working in theatre, regardless of their roles, tend to not dwell on their failures and creative losses. Instead they simply move on to the next available project. This means that any creative loss appears to be minimal overall. Even so, a small minority of interviewees expressed quite a deep sense of creative loss. This point is borne out by the fact very few cases come to court, but those that do occur in situations where there is a profound sense of frustration, even outrage, at the 'blocking' of performers' creative practices by writers.[117]

Looking first to the detailed responses from interviewees who described themselves as playwrights, or who possessed some experience of playwriting, it is clear that the presence or absence of trust is of great significance to resolving disputes successfully. In this context, the invocation of 'trust' signifies a relationship between the parties, or agents, which is capable of enabling the creative freedom of the performers, while at the same satisfying the playwright's wishes.

[116] Bourdieu, *The State Nobility: Elite Schools in the Fields of Power* (n 115) 264–74. See also generally Bourdieu, *The Logic of Practice* (n 115).

[117] Wyver (n 2).

One established playwright I interviewed stated that it is, for him, 'fundamentally a question of trust' – he stated that he 'must have a good relationship with a director' in order for him to allow the director a large amount of freedom to re-interpret the play.[118] Another interviewee, a highly experienced and well-known actor-playwright-director, acknowledged that the director and the set of actors require a lot of freedom to interpret or reinvent the source material in the development of a performance.[119]

Some playwrights are more comfortable than others in giving this freedom to the director and actors. One experienced playwright-artistic director I interviewed stated that he considers this a necessary part of the theatrical process.[120] Thus, he had accepted that playwrights must have a loose conception of 'the original' in mind. He expressed confidence that whatever the original meaning of the play was, it would be re-gained, or re-conjured, in the act of performance – ie the aura would not dissipate – even if what was happening on stage was actually a radical interpretation of the text.

The interview data indicate that where power struggles take place concerning the creative direction of the envisaged performance, where there is a relationship of mutual trust between the parties such struggles tend to be resolved harmoniously – to the overall benefit of the project. Moreover, each party necessarily makes use of cultural and social capitals, as well as habitus, in order to maintain this level of trust. The level of experience each party has will often be highly influential here. An inexperienced playwright may possess economic capital – the economic rights to perform the work – but may still lack cultural, social and symbolic capitals. This may mean that the playwright is unable to exert any leverage over the director within the workshop and production processes.

One early-career playwright I interviewed expressed doubts as to how effective making an integrity-based objection would be in practice. He stated that for a young playwright making such an objection might be counterproductive – it might lead the theatre company to refuse to perform the work at all. This would be particularly galling for a young writer because, as he remarked, 'you really need your work to be performed'.[121] With respect to giving creative freedom to the director and actors, the young playwright also expressed a sense of openness to the input of other agents. Nonetheless, he said 'I have some red lines' – aspects of the dramatic work that he would not want to be changed in any circumstances:[122]

> As a creative person I like the idea of someone else going to town and coming up with something different to what I had written, as long as they don't cut out dialogue, and they use the pauses in the right places and so on …

[118] Anon 1 – usage of these numbered 'anon' signifiers refer back to ch 1's list of interviewees – they are used for anonymity purposes in line with my data protection responsibilities.

[119] Anon 15.

[120] Anon 17.

[121] Anon 4.

[122] Anon 4.

Another playwright, also at a relatively early stage of his career, acknowledged that the theatrical process is a kind of power struggle; but he expressed the opinion that playwrights are not the ones with the most power. He remarked that 'playwrights live in fear of directors' because they know that once the workshop process has begun the director 'takes control'.[123] In other words, the accepted position of the director within the field – as the one in charge of the stage production – means that directors are often better placed to make use of their cultural, social and symbolic capitals than writers are.

One of the cultural capitals possessed by directors in this sense relates to the ability to bring the dramatic work to life. The same interviewee playwright noted that 'you don't know what you've written' until the workshop process begins and someone else 'makes it come alive'. Indeed, 'making it come alive' is something he, as a playwright, cannot do. He said that it is necessary for a playwright to become comfortable with this process because without it the theatrical medium 'simply wouldn't work'. He remarked:[124]

> As a writer it always feels like once you've handed over the text, you've lost control.

When pressed for detail, the playwright went on to use an interesting analogy as explanation: he stated that as a playwright he feels 'like the petrol in a car' because 'without him nothing moves'; but despite this he is ultimately not the person who decides which direction the car should go in.[125] He acknowledged that the different roles the various agents play during the workshop process often leads to power struggles between the parties. Like many interviewees, the playwright stated that communication and trust are highly important to this dynamic. He noted that some directors are very good at sitting down with playwrights and 'massaging the changes', whilst others are not so accommodating.[126] In other words, for him a good director should make use of cultural and social capitals, as well as habitus, in order to maintain positive relationships between the various agents and resolve any conflicts that occur.

The same playwright said that he had never, thus far in his career, been angered by a performance of one of his dramatic works.

However, he went on to recall what happened when a friend of his – a fellow playwright – went to see the first performance of his (then recent) play. Upon seeing it performed his friend became furious and stormed out, shouting at the director. In this case, his friend felt particularly angry that 'something he'd liked in the play's text had been edited out by the director without his knowledge'.[127] Here, communication between the director and playwright had clearly been difficult, and eventually, the director had asserted creative control over the project to the detriment of the writer. In this example, it could be said that the director was able

[123] Anon 3.
[124] Anon 3.
[125] ibid.
[126] ibid.
[127] Anon 3.

to make use of his capitals and habitus to resolve the power struggle in line with his own creative vision – but he did so in a disharmonious way. Future collaboration between these specific agents seems unlikely.

Regarding the making of performance objections, an experienced playwright I interviewed argued that 'if I have given specific instructions in the text of the play, then these should be followed'.[128] As an example, he noted that 'If I have written in the text that there is no music throughout this' then this direction should clearly be followed. However, he further remarked:[129]

> If I haven't written anything then I think it is much more difficult for the writer to argue.

The same playwright also emphasised that the writer may take a different view depending on the theatrical tradition where the production is taking place. He stated that in the German-speaking world (Germany, Austria, and Switzerland) the playwright occupies 'a different position within the cultural firmament'. Within the Germanic tradition, for instance, he noted that the director and dramaturge are institutionally mandated to take the written text of the dramatic work as a stimulus in order 'to create a performance text'. He opined:[130]

> There is no sanctity of the written text like there is the UK.

The interviewee gave an example of a German production of a play by a playwright acquaintance of his whereby the German director had 'lopped off the last three pages' of the text. He observed:[131]

> If you lop off the last three pages, how can that be anything possibly like what the author intended the meaning to be?

Yet, he noted that the playwright in that case did not make an integrity-based objection because of the new possibilities that particular production opened for him within continental Europe. From the point of view of the playwright, it was worthwhile – certainly economically, and potentially creatively as well – to allow the German production to go ahead. In this respect, the interviewee acknowledged that the terms 'to protect' and 'to enable' come into conflict, whereby playwrights have a choice: 'do I protect my work or do I enable my work?'[132] In this case of the German production with the altered ending, he noted that there was a clear incentive to not be overly 'precious' about the text – to 'enable' it rather than to 'protect' it. The interviewee went on to say that with respect to the German-speaking theatrical tradition, the writer has to 'make a trade as an artist'.[133] As a playwright he said that he must accept that there is a different theatre culture in Germany, one which is less respectful of the text.

[128] Anon 2.
[129] Anon 2.
[130] Anon 2.
[131] Anon 2.
[132] Anon 2.
[133] ibid.

Thus, in different theatrical traditions the power struggle dynamic may take different forms. Indeed, the interviewee's use of Germany as an example of a country featuring a different theatrical tradition is an interesting one in light of the *Clybourne Park* example highlighted above. In that case, a power struggle arose between the theatre company and the playwright, Clive Norris, who was unwilling to make the kind of 'trade-off' noted by the interviewee here. As a result, Norris made use of his economic capital by withdrawing the rights to perform the dramatic work.

Regarding the other agents active within the field of theatre, such as directors and actors, there was a palpable sense of frustration concerning integrity-based objections among some interviewees. One actor, at the early stage of her career, remarked with some exasperation that it is 'a shame that writers can block creativity'.[134] She noted that unless actors are very well-known they typically possess little leverage when power struggles occur, noting that the role of the actor is such that in comparison with directors and playwrights actors tend to lack the cultural capital required to exert influence over re-shaping the play, and they may also lack economic and social capitals if they are in their early career.

One highly experienced director, currently working at a small regional theatre company, stated that it is quite common for conflict to occur between the playwright and the other 'creatives' during the workshop process. He commented:[135]

> We deal with this all the time.

The same director went on to say that while some playwrights can be very resistant to the making of changes, other playwrights can be entirely relaxed about the process. Again, the issue of trust came up – he observed that the outcome of the power struggle is very much determined by the director's relationship with the writer and the 'terms of agreement' discussed beforehand. In particular, he stated that it is very important for him as a director to discover early on whether the playwright will be protective over the work, and consequently, whether he (as director) will need to 'fight' the writer to get 'his' edits. However, he also noted that while he is aware such tensions are commonly felt, in his career thus far the power struggle dynamic had always led to an outcome which both parties respected – he had always felt able to do what he wanted to, creatively, with respect to the play.[136]

One well-known and highly experienced artistic-director, working at a large theatre, stated that it is very important to have a discussion with the playwright, or the representatives of the playwright, at the earliest stage possible about the processes of production of the play.[137] Meanwhile, the idea, put forward by one playwright above, that the director has the greatest sway within the power struggles

[134] Anon 7.
[135] Anon 10.
[136] Anon 10.
[137] Anon 9.

that occur, was rejected by an experienced actor I interviewed. In this respect, she recalled a specific case where she had witnessed a playwright objecting to, and eventually preventing, an actor's change of dialogue. She commented:[138]

> Most of the time, writers get their way.

This actor did, however, acknowledge that from the playwright's perspective maintaining the integrity of the dramatic work is 'obviously very important'. She also made a distinction between dealing with a playwright and dealing with an estate – she said that in her work she is generally more accommodating to requests made by playwrights themselves, rather than their estates. Similarly, one experienced director I interviewed, at the time working at a mid-size theatre in London, acknowledged that integrity-based objections commonly occur, and that such objections tend to restrict his own creativity as a director. Despite this, he said that over the course of his career he had always complied with such requests due to his respect for the position of the playwright within theatre.[139] Thus, the role of the playwright in some circumstances brings with it a certain amount of symbolic capital.

With respect to the idea that theatre may suffer a creative loss if the power struggle cannot be resolved, one producer stated that she knew of many examples where theatre companies had given up on mounting a production due to an inability to resolve such disputes. In particular, she observed that if estates demand the right to veto certain creative decisions – regarding how the performance would be mounted, how characters would be portrayed, and which time period the play would be set in – this can cause licensing negotiations to break down. When asked how often such projects are abandoned, she simply remarked:[140]

> It happens all the time.

Be that as it may, the view that the existence of power struggles between the various agents often leads to the abandonment of projects was not shared by every participant. One established actor-producer-deviser I interviewed stated that during his career he had never been prevented from doing anything except for one minor incident involving the use of a piece of music in a key scene.[141] It is also the case that some interviewees had never experienced such tensions at all. One director I interviewed, who had worked at a small theatre for many years, stated categorically that he had never been blocked by a playwright from making changes to a dramatic work.[142] At the same time, he added that since his company rarely puts on established works it is perhaps less likely to come up than in a situation involving the re-working of an existing play. The actor-deviser I interviewed made a

[138] Anon 7.
[139] Anon 11.
[140] Anon 6.
[141] Anon 16.
[142] Anon 11.

very similar point based on his own experience.[143] Meanwhile, the playwright-performance artist, who was at an early stage of her career, said that she had never encountered any issues; but she also emphasised that she almost always performs her own work, in a solo capacity.[144] Similarly, the playwright-artistic director I interviewed said that over the course of his career he had undertaken multiple adaptations of plays, some of which were in the public domain, and some of which were in copyright, and that he had never experienced any power struggles concerning the work's integrity – though he admitted all of these adaptations were intended to be quite faithful to the source material. He also stated that he had dealt once with a playwright's estate and no conflict had arisen.[145]

Regarding the notion of integrity itself, one experienced director told me that he sees his role as a positive one. He gave one recent example where stated that he had made a lot of changes to a play 'without taking away from the integrity' and 'with the aim of sharpening' the work and 'adding to its integrity'.[146] In this case, the playwright was included within the sharpening process – the director ran ideas by the writer as the play was being re-shaped. This seems to demonstrate that while a director's suggestions can potentially detract from the integrity of the work, they can also greatly add to it. Indeed, following Latour and Lowe, to say that 'the original' of the play could be merely 'regained', rather than lost, as a result of this process doesn't go far enough; the original may perhaps even be brought into sharper view due to the efforts of the director or actors.

The director Michael Blakemore alluded to this possibility, in an interview in the late 1990s:

> I don't believe that a play means something absolutely concrete for all time; it's something which alters its character according to the times in which it's presented. There is a certain sort of flexibility to interpretation, and indeed the author himself may not be *entirely* aware of possibilities within his play, and in twenty years' time a director will get the text and do something with it that the author didn't envisage. But I think if you're doing a new play you have to assume that the man who wrote it knew what he was trying to do ....[147]

Ultimately, my interview data show that playwrights do tend to fear that 'the original' of the play will be lost – and the aura of the dramatic work consequently diminished – if the performance is misconceived in some way. With regard to the directors, actors and producers, it is clear that there is some frustration within the theatre world concerning rights restrictions, especially where author-playwrights, or their estates, hold a tight grip on the kinds of interpretations that are permitted. In line with this, the interviewees' views on the famous example of Samuel Beckett and his estate are revealing.

[143] Anon 13.
[144] Anon 18.
[145] Anon 17.
[146] Anon 10.
[147] Wu (n 1) 250.

What to do about Beckett? Views from the Field

Regarding the specific, and somewhat notorious, example of Beckett and his estate, one experienced playwright I interviewed stated:[148]

> If you're Beckett, and you have an estate that's worthy of the name, and you have an idea around that estate to, and I will use the word 'protect' here, protect the authenticity and the integrity of the work, then you may say 'I don't want an all-female cast of my work in an all-male play' or 'I don't want you to change those three words to fit your rationale or context of the play – I want it played as it is written and I have the power to say that is what I want you to do'.

For this interviewee, the clarity of the playwright's stated wishes was clearly seen as important. Likewise, the experienced actor-dramaturge I interviewed asserted that if, as in the case of Beckett, the playwright's wishes are very specified, then those wishes should be followed, notwithstanding the fact that this might be frustrating to other parties from a creative point of view.[149] Similarly, while the artistic-director acknowledged that 'you can try and argue forcibly, and creatively, how brilliant it would be to do the all women production' of *Waiting for Godot*, ultimately, he accepted that the playwright should have the right to decide to allow this or not. Furthermore, he generally didn't have a problem with this:[150]

> I think writers should be allowed to say I don't want my play contrary to the way I have indicated clearly, and therefore I don't want you to do it – that seems to be entirely the writer's prerogative, or any copyright owner's prerogative. I mean that is the point of copyright.

On this issue, the actor-playwright-director put the crucial question in these terms:[151]

> Will Beckett's work live on better if it is kept the same, or will it live on better if it is liberalised and women can play it, or will that mean that the productions will get so warped and changed that people will go off Beckett?

While acknowledging that there was no clear answer to the question, the same actor-playwright-director remarked that in his performing career he does not mind 'serving Beckett' in this formal way. He stated that it is clear with Beckett that in order to 'play his game' you must play it 'strictly by the rules'. He also said that it was Beckett's right to 'demand' this of performers, and as an actor he felt this demand forced him to be 'loyal' to the words and to the stage directions. He further commented that he tends to find it difficult to grasp the meaning of Beckett's plays, which made it particularly hard to edit them. While he found individual lines

[148] Anon 2.
[149] Anon 14.
[150] Anon 9.
[151] Anon 15.

comprehensible, he stated that as whole works they remain somewhat elusive, and this makes it particularly difficult to 'tinker' with them.[152]

A notable contrast to Beckett is provided by the play *Crave* written by the playwright Sarah Kane (who died in 1999). It is well-known within the theatre community as a work open to radical interpretation because Kane 'left almost no stage directions to denote gender, time or place' and as a result, the play 'becomes fertile ground for invention' receiving its most recent radical reinterpretation during 2020.[153]

Examining the Play's Trajectory – What Makes *King Lear* Different from *Waiting for Godot*?

With regard to the three stages of a play's trajectory put forward in this chapter, one experienced playwright I interviewed acknowledged that there is a 'journey' from the beginning of the playwright's first sentence to the eventual public performance. The same playwright also gave a cogent explanation for why the initial workshop process is so crucial to the play's future life:[154]

> … on the whole, drama publishing in this country is a sub-set – publishing follows production …'

The same playwright said that since the vast majority of new plays have no life beyond their initial run, spending time agonising over how the play might be perceived with regard to subsequent performances, along with the copyright consequences that would occur upon reaching that level of success, is largely not worthwhile. Even so, he acknowledged that the revival of a play does, on occasion, unexpectedly happen, noting that some very popular plays had their first performances put on by a small fringe theatre. With regard to the possible trajectory of such a new play he remarked:[155]

> How do you plan in all conscience for something that has that kind of life when actually its first manifestation is so tiny?

Another playwright I interviewed stated that the first production of a play ought to be in accordance with the strict intentions of the writer – but subsequent productions ought to be given more flexibility with respect to radical interpretations of the text.[156] The playwright accepted that his anxiety concerning the work tended

[152] ibid.

[153] A Akbar, 'Crave review – Kane's bleak poetry is as potent as ever in taut production' *The Guardian* (Nov 3 2020), available at www.theguardian.com/stage/2020/nov/03/crave-review-sarah-kane-chichester-festival-theatre.

[154] Anon 2.

[155] ibid.

[156] Anon 3.

to be at its highest level during the debut stage of a play's trajectory. Thereafter his need to control the work would lessen.

There is a clear rationale behind such early anxieties. The playwright Howard Brenton has observed that bad early reviews can destroy a play's reputation forever; in fact, this is what happened with his play *Ugly Rumours* – after positive preview responses from audiences, the first critics panned the play, and it never recovered.[157]

The director Michael Blakemore has commented on trajectory in relation to his work with the playwright Michael Frayn, noting that once a play has been established as an exceptional piece, later productions can be given a lot of freedom to re-interpret the text:

> However, the first production of a new play is very important because it can either destroy it, or it can establish a way of doing it which then becomes *the* way to do it – and is copied all over the world. In any event, a good first production represents a backstop position. I think that one of the reasons why Michael wrote it without any stage directors was to give whoever attempts it a free hand. Certainly there have been different sorts of productions of *Noises Off* all over the place, one of which dispensed entirely with the third Act … he [the director] felt he couldn't top the second Act, so he said, 'We'll just end it here.' I think this was a production in the Balkans, not surprisingly.[158]

Stafford-Clark has admitted that it can be difficult for newly written, innovative 'of the moment' plays to have a successful afterlife:

> I think all plays are product of their time, and you have to go back to look at that time. *Cloud 9* was a difficult play … because it was a pre-AIDS play, and it's about sexual politics. So when it was revived last year at the Old Vic that was the first time that play could be revived, because it was so specific to its time. I did a play at the RSC called *A Jovial Crew* which was written in 1639/1640 by Richard Brome – and was, records tell us, the last play to be performed before the theatres were shut. Now the text seems pretty baffling, and of course it's not as coherent as the Elizabethan plays. It's about a benign landlord who becomes totally autocratic and insists on benevolence to people, and when you go back and study the period you can see it as a coded message, as a way of criticising Charles I. Once you see that, and you read about what went on during the period, then certain elements of the play become clear. So any barrier to understanding is caused by the time that's passed.[159]

Another playwright I interviewed remarked that if one of his plays was subjected to a 'shocking production' this would leave the play marooned at the first stage of its trajectory. He further noted that it would probably also have the effect of harming his reputation as a playwright – an especially acute fear at the early stages of his career.[160]

[157] Wu (n 1) 50.
[158] Wu (n 1) 250.
[159] Wu (n 1) 71.
[160] Anon 4.

With regard to the distinction between dramatic works in the second and third stages, one producer I interviewed acknowledged that public domain works, such as the plays of Shakespeare, are sometimes a more popular choice for companies because there is no possibility of interference from the playwright or the estate (as well as no need to pay for the rights).[161] Similarly, another producer I interviewed stated that her mid-size company is wary of attempting to do radical versions of dramatic works that are still in copyright, due to problems they had experienced in the past in trying to get the rights to such works.[162] Another interviewee, an actor, echoed this point, stating that because works eventually fall into the public domain this 'gave hope', since public domain works can be reinterpreted radically.[163]

In light of the above comments, the notion put forward in this chapter that a new dramatic work has three broad potential stages within its trajectory appears to be an accurate one. In addition, it does indeed appear that some author-playwrights feel most anxious about the interpretation of the play during its debut stage, and they become more relaxed once it passes into the exceptional stage (though some writers, like Beckett, do not seem to share this sense of relaxation). Finally, there is acknowledgement within the theatre world that there is a distinction between works that are in copyright and works that are in the public domain; indeed, classic public domain works are sometime favoured for radical reinterpretation because they can be performed without a licence, and thus without the possibility of an integrity-based objection being put forward.

Conclusion

From the above analysis it is clear that power struggles between the playwright and the other agents, especially the director and actors, occur frequently in the field of theatre. Furthermore, copyright law is deeply implicated in the way these power struggles are conceived and resolved. Ownership of the economic and moral rights to the dramatic work provides economic capital to the playwright, which can be used to make integrity-based objections during such power struggles. Even so, it is clear that other agents, such as directors and producers, also possess economic, cultural, social and symbolic capitals within this field, and they draw upon these to try to resolve the conflicts in line with their own creative visions.

The existence of such power struggles is not, in many instances, a negative thing. Indeed, as explored in chapter three, the eventual play/performance as staged is to some extent constitutive of these struggles. However, where a power struggle cannot be resolved harmoniously this can lead to a creative loss since

[161] Anon 5.
[162] Anon 6.
[163] Anon 7.

the project may be abandoned. Nonetheless, it appears that the majority of agents in the field of theatre tend to not spend time dwelling on these creative losses; instead, they move on as soon as possible to new projects. Thus, any creative loss is probably of minimal overall effect. At the same time, a small minority of interviewees expressed a deep sense of creative frustration. This point is borne out by the fact very few cases on point come to court globally – none at all so far in the UK – but those that do occur feature parties nursing a deep sense of frustration, even outrage, at the 'blocking' of performers' creative practices by writers.[164]

From the point of view of copyright law, the above analysis provides much food for thought. There is clear interplay between the concepts of originality, integrity and aura. Copyright protects originality on the basis of the author's intellectual creativity. It seems important in the theatrical context that this notion of originality is interpreted broadly. Originality here must encompass not only the author's intended meaning, protected via the integrity right, but also the author's 'unintended meanings' – the aspects of the text that other parties may choose to reinterpret, and perhaps even subvert, via performance, in order to uncover new creative layers within the text. Such interpretations may, of course, move away from the author's intended meaning; yet, they may still enhance the aura of the play. This should be taken into account when courts are forced to determine whether a particular performance truly threatens the play's integrity. Such concerns were insufficiently considered by the French courts in *Godot*, but they were taken into account by the Italian courts in a subsequent case concerning the same play, where the all-woman performance of *Waiting for Godot* was allowed to go ahead.[165]

In addition, it is clear that the duration of copyright has a significant effect on denoting the trajectory of a dramatic work, whereby a new play may pass through three stages – debut, exceptional and classic. The playwright will tend to be most concerned over the dramatic work's integrity and aura during the debut phase, but may retain some concerns throughout the exceptional phase. Once copyright expires, and the work reaches the classic 'public domain' stage, the issue of the author's intended meaning – protected by the integrity right – fades away. In fact, upon reaching the classic stage the aura of the work appears to stabilise at a relatively consistent level – the play tends to remain in high esteem regardless of how well or how poorly it is reinterpreted on stage. Not for the first time it is worth questioning whether the long period of copyright – life plus 70 years – is really justifiable given that it keeps works such as *Waiting for Godot* under the cloak of integrity for far longer than is necessary for the work's aura to stabilise.[166]

[164] Wyver (n 2). See also *The Working Playwright* (n 3).
[165] MacMahon (n 67).
[166] I Hargreaves, *Digital opportunity. A review of Intellectual Property and Growth* (Intellectual Property Office, 18 May 2011) 93; available at www.ipo.gov.uk/ipreview-finalreport.pdf.

6

How Should Law Respond to the Challenges of the Theatrical Context? How Should Theatre Respond to Law?

Introduction

The relationship between theatre and copyright law is complex, unwieldy, and yet, sometimes invisible.[1] The practices of theatre are profoundly social and normative, but they are also bounded by legal constructs, even if those constructs only become apparent when disputes occur.

I have shown that these constructs – dramatic work, authorship, joint authorship, infringement and the moral rights of attribution and integrity – do not have a stable, inherent meaning; they are infused with normative content only through the performance of law (which includes practices that are often more improvisational than we lawyers like to admit).[2] The activities that copyright lawyers and judges perform shape these boundaries of copyright law, which in turn regulates the way works of theatre are perceived as objects of property. At times, the attitude of legal practitioners to the dramatic work brings to mind Alain Pottage's

[1] D Miller, *Copyright and the Value of Performance, 1770–1911* (Cambridge: Cambridge University Press, 2018); S Katyal, 'Performance, Property, and the Slashing of Gender in Fan Fiction' (2006) 14 *American University Journal of Gender, Social Policy, and Law* 461; CJ Craig, 'Reconstructing the Author-Self: Some Feminist Lessons for Copyright Law' (2006) 15 *American University Journal of Gender, Social Policy, and Law* 207; JE Cohen, *Configuring the Networked Self: Law, Code, and the Play of Everyday Practice* (New Haven, CT: Yale University Press, 2012); MA Lemley, 'Faith-Based Intellectual Property' (2015) 62 *UCLA Law Review* 1328; P Jaszi, 'Is There Such a Thing as Postmodern Copyright' (2009) 12 *Tulane Journal of Technology & Intellectual Property* 105; S Stern, 'Copyright, Originality, and the Public Domain in Eighteenth-Century England' in R McGinnis (ed), *Originality and Intellectual Property in the French and English Enlightenment* (New York: Routledge, 2008) 85; P Jaszi, 'On the Author Effect: Contemporary Copyright and Collective Creativity' in M Woodmansee and P Jaszi (eds), *The Construction Of Authorship: Textual Appropriation In Law and Literature*, (Durham, NC: Duke University Press, 1994) 29; D Oliar and C Sprigman, 'There's No Free Laugh (Anymore): The Emergence of Intellectual Property Norms and the Transformation of Stand-Up Comedy' (2008) 94 *Virginia Law Review* 1787.

[2] A Read, *Theatre & Law* (Basingstoke: Palgrave Macmillan, 2016) 3. See also S Ramshaw, 'Jamming the Law: Improvisational Theatre and the 'Spontaneity' of Judgment' (2010) 14 *Law Text Culture* 133.

comment (per Bruno Latour) that law 'produces objectivity by knowing as little as possible about the object'.[3]

Yet, since at least the Elizabethan age law has been forced to utilise its legal processes and methods of reasoning in order to resolve questions concerning rights and ownership of plays. The practitioners of theatre and the publishers of plays have insisted that lawyers and legal institutions intervene in disputes. The narrative of this book has featured an array of characters, including the lawyers who have translated, written and performed plays; the playwrights who have used the theatrical forum of law (the trial in particular) in illuminative ways; and the writers, directors and actors who have fought legal battles over the ownership and control of plays.[4] I have mapped the trajectories of dramatic works, exploring how they pass through many persons, companies and territories over weeks, years, decades and centuries. This has shed light on the multifaceted continuum of authorial collaboration in theatre – and on the play as a contested object of property.

The History of Authorship of Plays and the Shifting Property Boundaries of Ownership – The Text as Commodity

I have demonstrated that in theatre the boundaries of authorship, ownership and legal protection shifted continually during the period 1558–1911. The period marked the rise of two separate property objects and sources of value – the print-text commodity (including partial reproduction of text) and the performance commodity. These two would eventually be subsumed into the legal concept of the copyright work.[5] Yet, in the Elizabethan and Jacobean eras writers lacked ownership of either of these commodities, with the Stationers possessing legally enforceable printing monopolies, and theatre companies holding a type of informal ownership of plays as performance texts.

Polyvocal creativity was essential to theatre in the period 1558–1625.[6] Masten argues that the Jacobean text *The Knight of the Burning Pestle* (ascribed to Beaumont) 'defies even the ideally liberal constraint Foucault imagines' as fiction 'passing through something like a necessary or constraining figure'.[7] A similar

[3] A Pottage, 'Introduction: Fabricating persons and things' in A Pottage and M Mundy (eds), *Law, Anthropology, and the Constitution of the Social – Making Persons and Things* (Cambridge: Cambridge University Press, 2004) 1, 23, referring to the Latour's assessment of the legal process in chapter 3 of the same volume).

[4] C Field, 'Copyright – My Story: A One-Woman Play' (2009) 17 *J Intell Prop L* 35.

[5] N Goodman, *Languages of Art* (Indianapolis: Hackett Publishing Co Inc, 1976) 99–123. See also Miller (n 1).

[6] R Barthes, 'The Death of the Author' 5/6 *Aspen: The Magazine in a Box* (R Howard tr, 1967), available at www.ubu.com/aspen/aspen5and6/index.html and M Foucault, 'What Is an Author?' in JM Marsh, JD Caputo and M Westphal (eds), *Modernity and its Discontents* (New York: Fordham University Press, 1992) 299, 305 (original essay dating from 1969 and seen by many as a response to Barthes).

[7] J Masten, 'Beaumont and/or Fletcher: Collaboration and the Interpretation of Renaissance Drama' (1992) 52 *English Literary History* 337, 352.

argument could be made about *The Spanish Tragedy*.[8] By contrast, an unstable text such as *The Taming of The Shrew* could be viewed as passing through the constraining figure of Shakespeare while still accepting the input of others in the Lord Chamberlain's Men.[9] Yet, it is Ben Jonson, more than Shakespeare, who stands out as a self-conscious 'possessive' author in theatre at this time, aware of the value of what he contributed as a writer (to the print and performance commodities), and thus cognisant of the need to assert his voice as author-figure in print and on stage.[10] Nonetheless, the Elizabethan/Jacobean periods demonstrate that it is possible for a collaborative product – the play – to be created successfully in an environment that does not prize, or reward, individual authorship through property rights.[11]

Post-Restoration, someone akin to that author-figure emerged gradually in widespread theatrical practice and, eventually, in legal personhood (author) and property objecthood (copyright in the book). By the time of the Statute of Anne 1710, the dramatist had grown in esteem and authorial attribution of plays in print and in stage playbills had become the norm. Over the eighteenth century statutory copyright enabled writers to become increasingly assertive of their rights in the legal sphere at the Courts of Chancery and Kings' Bench. Even though an author-figure began to emerge in theatrical practice and in law well before the 'Romantic' era, in the 1800s the Romantic conception of authorship helped solidify ideas of authorial ownership of texts.[12]

We can trace individualist notions of authorship and ownership as the law evolved from the Statute of Anne through subsequent case law over performance rights. This culminated in reform legislation in 1833 and 1842, whereby the law moved from the mere protection of playbooks (from unauthorised printing and reprinting), to preventing unlicensed performances of play-texts.[13] These threads were joined together by the 1911 Copyright Act, which for the first time in UK law protected not 'books' or 'dramatic pieces' as separate entities, but 'works' of drama. The commodification of the theatrical play – its transformation via law into an apparently stable object of property – provides an example of how 'legal procedures invent the tradition which they purport only to continue'.[14]

Along with collaboration, a notable recurring theme throughout the history of English theatre is the significance of informal norms. In the Elizabethan era,

[8] E Smith, 'Author v. Character in Early Modern Dramatic Authorship: The Example of Thomas Kyd and The Spanish Tragedy' (1999) 11 *Medieval and Renaissance Drama in England* 129.

[9] JJ Marino, *Owning William Shakespeare: The King's Men and Their Intellectual Property* (Philadelphia: University of Pennsylvania Press, 2011) 48.

[10] J Loewenstein, *Ben Jonson and Possessive Authorship* (Cambridge: Cambridge University Press, 2002).

[11] H Hirschfeld, 'Early Modern Collaboration and Theories of Authorship' (2001) 116 *Theories and Methodologies* 609, 619–20. See also E Ostrom, *Governing the Commons* (New York: New York University Press, 1990).

[12] J Loewenstein, 'The Script in the Marketplace' (1985) 12 *Representations* 101, 102.

[13] Miller (n 1).

[14] A Pottage, 'Introduction: Fabricating persons and things' in A Pottage and M Mundy (eds), *Law, Anthropology, and the Constitution of the Social – Making Persons and Things* (Cambridge: Cambridge University Press, 2004), 1, 6.

normative cooperation ensured different companies did not compete to perform each other's plays.[15] In the period 1770–1800 the London patent theatres cooperated to ensure plays such as *The School for Scandal* were performed at only one venue.[16] In contemporary theatre the norms of theatre practice remain of great importance – but the content of these norms is being continuously challenged by new forms of theatrical practice, such as devised theatre, as well as by legal discourse.

Copyright Law, Authorship and Joint Authorship of Plays in the Contemporary Theatre Field

For Barthes, once published the text cannot be controlled by the author, and can only be understood through mediation between reader and other texts; Foucault imagines texts circulating without the need of an author.[17] Yet, Masten argues that even Foucauldians must admit that it is, ironically enough, a form of 'pure romanticism' to imagine a culture devoid of all such mechanisms.[18] Some version of the author-figure appears to be an inevitability, even in the practices of devised theatre.[19] Yet, the theatrical text is not just a text – it is a copyright work, a multifaceted commodity, potentially underpinning value in print, performance and adaptation. Can we as copyright lawyers define the author and the work in a way that complements Barthes' and Foucault's critical literary approach while also providing a just solution to authorship disputes? How much attention should judges pay to aesthetic matters or social norms of practice? This is a precarious position for courts to be in given that 'we do not, even now, have a standard approach to the concept of the dramatic author'.[20] We as copyright lawyers sometimes fail to provide adequate answers.[21] The theatre world itself sometimes struggles to do so.[22]

[15] B Lauriat, 'Literary and Dramatic Disputes in Shakespeare's Time' (2018) 9 *Journal of International Dispute Settlement* 45.

[16] O Gerland, 'The Haymarket Theatre and Literary Property: Constructing the Common Law Playright, 1770–1833' (2015) 69 *Theatre Notebook* 74.

[17] R Barthes, 'The Death of the Author' 5/6 *Aspen: The Magazine in a Box* (R Howard tr, 1967) available at www.ubu.com/aspen/aspen5and6/index.html and M Foucault, 'What Is an Author?' in JM Marsh, JD Caputo and M Westphal (eds), *Modernity and its Discontents* (New York: Fordham University Press, 1992) 299, 305 (original essay dating from 1969 and seen by many as a response to Barthes). L Bently, 'Copyright and the Death of the Author in Literature and Law' (1994) 57 *The Modern Law Review* 973, 980.

[18] Masten (n 7) 351.

[19] A Field, 'All Theatre is Devised and Text-based' *The Guardian* (April 21 2009), available at www.guardian.co.uk/stage/theatreblog/2009/apr/21/theatre-devised-text-based.

[20] T Stern, 'Review of Authorship and Appropriation: Writing for the Stage in England, 1660–1710' (2003) *The Scriblerian* 73, 74.

[21] *Brighton and Dubbeljoint v Jones* [2004] EWHC 1157 (Ch); [2004] EMLR 507.

[22] CL Fisk, 'Will Work for Screen Credit: Labour and the Law in Hollywood' in P McDonald, E Carman, E Hoyt and P Drake (eds), *Hollywood and the Law* (London: Palgrave, 2015) 235, 240.

Despite the collaborative practices of devising/revising, *The Working Playwright* prioritizes the writer as author-figure in law, and thus as the owner, in the first instance, of the dramatic work as an object of property.[23] Yet, the empirical interview responses show that even if the role for the writer as author-figure is respected, this does not mean that the original, collaborative contributions of other parties such as director and actor should go unrecognised. Sharing credit (attribution) and ownership/royalty sharing via contract can help align the collective practices of authorship with ownership of the collaborative product.

When collaboration proceeds smoothly, certain parties (actors, directors, producers) may not need the property rights typified by authorial copyright;[24] but when disputes occur, such rights can offer leverage to one party who might otherwise be left without credit or ownership.[25]

Traditionally, when judges have been faced with assessing claims of copyright law, such as in *Brighton v Jones*,[26] they have focused more on maintaining legal coherence and continuity of ownership rather than on contextual analysis of fluid creative practices.[27] Courts can be unwilling to disrupt individualist authorship/ownership because copyright transactions are easier to complete when there are fewer owners.[28] Copyright law can thus refuse to recognise important contributions to the play during the workshop where these are classed as mere 'ideas'. In recent times copyright scholars have argued for the law to be more open to the actual creative practices of authorship.[29] The contextual approach taken in the *Kogan v Martin* case is a step in this direction and it is to be commended.[30] Fairness demands that when deciding questions of authorship and ownership, the courts must be open to contextual evidence, weighing up the claims in light of the complexities of the creative field within which the work emerged.[31] But the law cannot be expected to provide a solution in every dispute; many will never make it to court. Inclusive approaches by theatre practitioners do occur and these should

[23] B Latour and A Lowe, 'The migration of the aura, or how to explore the original through its fac similes' 1, 5–6; available at www.bruno-latour.fr/sites/default/files/108-ADAM-FACSIMILES-GB.pdf – originally published in T Bartscherer (ed), *Switching Codes: Thinking Through Digital Technology in the Humanities and the Arts* (Chicago: University of Chicago Press, 2010) 275.

[24] M Brown, 'Writers claim being excluded after creating Idris Elba play' *The Guardian* (2 July 2019), available at www.theguardian.com/culture/2019/jul/02/writers-claim-being-excluded-after-creating-idris-elbas-play.

[25] D Simone, 'Kogan v Martin: A New Framework for Joint Authorship in Copyright Law' (2020) 83 *The Modern Law Review* 877.

[26] *Brighton and Dubbeljoint v Jones* [2004] EWHC 1157 (Ch); [2004] EMLR 507.

[27] Bently (n 16).

[28] K Pistor, *The Code of Capital: How the Law Creates Wealth and Inequality* (Princeton, NJ: Princeton University Press, 2019).

[29] L Bently and L Biron, 'Discontinuities between legal conceptions of authorship and social practices: What, if anything, is to be done?' in M van Eechoud (ed), *The Work of Authorship* (Amsterdam: Amsterdam University Press, 2018) 237, 270–76.

[30] *Kogan v Martin* [2019] EWCA Civ 1645; Simone (n 24).

[31] See generally J Silbey, *The Eureka Myth: Creators, Innovators, and Everyday Intellectual Property* (Redwood City, CA: Stanford University Press, 2014) and M Iljadica, *Copyright Beyond Law: Regulating Creativity in the Graffiti Subculture* (Oxford: Hart, 2016). See also S Larsson, *Metaphors and Norms: Understanding Copyright Law in a Digital Society* (Lund: Lund University Studies in Sociology of Law, 2011).

be encouraged. Examples include two of my interviewees who agreed to share credit and ownership via contract with their respective creative collaborators,[32] and the equitable sharing of copyright in the 2014 play *Blurred Lines* between the writer Nick Payne and the director Carrie Cracknell.[33] Such practices are likely to be of great importance if theatre is to recognise the value of all those who contribute substantially to the final work.

Copyright Infringement – A Rare Occurrence in the Contemporary Theatre Field?

On infringement, while it is true that recent precedents on copyright in short pieces of text create the potential for over-protection of short works (headlines/titles) and short extracts, in reality there is little case law and few public disputes. There is little evidence to indicate a chilling effect, or stifling of the theatrical creative process. The recycling of theatrical motifs, plots and scenarios is a constant part of the creative process and appears widely tolerated in the system of norms perpetuated by theatrical practitioners. Alleged incidents of infringement do happen, but rather than resulting in litigation the interviews show that when they do occur, they tend to be resolved behind the scenes, via social norms within the theatre community. Theatre practitioners tend to avoid litigation where possible.

Despite the lack of case law on point, it is interesting to ponder how the fair dealing defences of parody and quotation might work in the theatrical context, should there be a court case in the near future. The current law does offer some potential to allow re-use of theatrical extracts and plots.[34] In the future, if cases do arise either the liberal use of the quotation or parody defences (or in the future the provision of a new broadly defined fair use exception) could prove useful at mitigating some of the potential conflicts between the creative practices of theatre and copyright. Overall, the open-ended 'fair use' system has substantive advantages over the closed category 'fair dealing' model, particularly with regard to flexibility and adaptability to emerging cultural circumstances. Therefore, the UK moving to the broader standard is to be favoured over continued pursuit of the narrower model. Post-Brexit, the UK will likely have the freedom to move to an open, US-style fair use system, compatible with the 'three-step test', following countries such as Israel and South Korea who have made this change in recent decades.[35] Yet, even if cases were to come to court, judges in the UK have traditionally been quite conservative in applying statutory exemptions

[32] Anon 1 and 15.

[33] See https://www.curtisbrown.co.uk/client/nick-payne/work/blurred-lines.

[34] Bently (n 16) 983.

[35] L McDonagh and M Mimler, 'Intellectual Property Law and Brexit: A Retreat or a Reaffirmation of Jurisdiction?' in M Dougan (ed), *The UK after Brexit* (Cambridge, UK: Intersentia, 2017) 159–79.

to copyright. The CJEU also tends to interpret the existing defences narrowly.[36] As Burrell remarks, merely bringing a new exception into the law may not necessarily change the traditional attitude of the courts.[37]

Copyright and Moral Rights in the Theatre Field – The Issue of Integrity Looms Large

On the issue of moral rights, and integrity in particular, it is clear that power struggles between the author-playwright and the other agents, especially the director and actors, occur frequently in the field of theatre. Ownership of the economic and moral rights to the dramatic work provides economic capital to the author-playwright, which can be used to make integrity-based objections during such power struggles. Nevertheless, it is clear that other agents, such as directors and producers, also possess economic, cultural, social and symbolic capitals within this field, and they draw upon these to try to resolve the conflicts in line with their own creative vision.

The existence of such power struggles is not, in many instances, a negative thing. Indeed, in many cases the eventual performance as staged is to some extent constitutive of these struggles. However, where a power struggle cannot be resolved harmoniously this can lead to a creative loss since the project may be abandoned. From my interviews it appears that agents in the field of theatre tend to not spend time dwelling on these creative losses; instead, they move on as soon as possible to new projects. Thus, any creative loss is probably of minimal overall effect. Even so, a small minority of interviewees expressed a deep sense of creative frustration. This point is borne out by the fact very few cases on point come to court globally – none at all so far in the UK – but those that do occur feature parties nursing frustration, even outrage, at the 'blocking' of performers' creative practices by writers.

If copyright protects originality on the basis of the author's intellectual creativity, then it seems important in the theatrical context that originality is interpreted broadly so that it encompasses not only the author's intended meaning, protected via the integrity right, but also the author's 'unintended meanings' – the aspects of the text that other parties may choose to reinterpret, and perhaps even subvert, via performance, in order to uncover new creative layers within the text. Such interpretations may move away from the author's intended meaning, yet still

[36] CJEU, judgment in C-469/17 *Funke Medien NRW GmbH v Bundesrepublik Deutschland* EU:C:2019:623 ('*Funke Medien*'); CJEU judgment in Case C-476/17 *Pelham GmbH and Others v Ralf Hütter and Florian Schneider-Esleben* [2019] Bus LR 2159 ('*Pelham*'); and CJEU judgment Case C-516/17 *Spiegel Online GmbH v Volker Beck* [2019] Bus LR 2787 ('*Spiegel Online*'). See also German Federal Constitutional Court (*Bundesverfassungsgericht*), the First Senate, Metall auf Metall, 1 BvR 1585/13, 31 May 2016, DE:BVerfG:2016:rs20160531.1bvr158513.

[37] R Burrell, 'Reining in Copyright Law: Is Fair Use the Answer?' (2001) *Intellectual Property Quarterly* 361, 368.

enhance the aura of the play. This should be taken into account when courts are forced to determine whether a particular performance truly threatens the play's integrity. Such concerns were insufficiently considered by the French courts in *Godot*, but were taken into account by the Italian courts in a subsequent case concerning the same play, where the all-woman staging of *Waiting for Godot* was allowed to go ahead.[38]

In addition, it is clear that the duration of copyright has a significant effect on denoting the trajectory of a dramatic work, whereby a new play may pass through three stages – debut, exceptional and classic. The author-playwright will tend to be most concerned over the dramatic work's integrity and aura during the debut phase, but may retain some concerns throughout the exceptional phase. Once copyright expires, and the work reaches the classic stage, the issue of the author's intended meaning – protected by the integrity right – fades away. In fact, upon reaching the classic stage the aura of the work appears to stabilise at a relatively consistent level – the play tends to remain in high esteem regardless of how well or how poorly it is reinterpreted on stage. It is debatable whether the long period of copyright – life plus 70 years – is justifiable given that it keeps works such as *Waiting for Godot* under the cloak of integrity for far longer than is necessary for the work's aura to stabilise.[39]Although it does not appear to be on the UK government's agenda, post-Brexit, the government can, and should, consider reverting to the Berne minimum duration – life of the author, plus 50 years.

Conclusion

In this book and over the course of this chapter I have alluded to several recommendations on legal issues. The most substantial recommendation I make in this conclusion concerns the key matter of joint authorship of plays, where I am encouraged by the approach taken by the Court of Appeal in the 2019 case of *Kogan v Martin*. As in *Kogan*, the courts must be open to contextual evidence from the theatre field when cases come to court. But it must be acknowledged that the costs of litigation – both in monetary terms and in terms of time wasted – remain such that most theatre participants tend to avoid litigation. The recent dispute over the play *Tree* is an example of this – it went unresolved by law and played out instead in the media and within the theatre community.[40] As such, although the courts should maintain conceptual openness when it comes to joint authorship, we as lawyers cannot expect this alone to suffice.

[38] B MacMahon, 'Beckett estate fails to stop women waiting for Godot' *The Guardian* (4 February 2006), available at www.guardian.co.uk/world/2006/feb/04/arts.italy.

[39] I Hargreaves, *Digital opportunity. A review of Intellectual Property and Growth* (Intellectual Property Office, May 2011) 93, available at www.ipo.gov.uk/ipreview-finalreport.pdf.

[40] Brown (n 23).

Yet, even if a large rise in case filings does not look likely, the recent judicial refinement of copyright's authorship and ownership concepts may still have a provocative impact within the theatre network.[41] For instance, it may be the case that a precedent like *Kogan v Martin* encourages more joint authorship disputes, even if these are resolved informally; by contrast, the earlier precedent of *Brighton v Jones* may well have discouraged the pursuit of such claims, even within the theatre community.[42]

Similarly, the social norms of the theatre field must be taken as relevant to resolving disputes over infringement or the right to integrity. The role of lawyers and courts should be to weigh up infringement or integrity claims by each party in a fair and rational manner, taking into account that copyright, as property, is not an absolute right; rather it must be balanced against other rights, such as the right to freedom of (creative) expression under Article 10 of the European Convention on Human Rights.

One aspect of law's response to theatrical practices that can be improved is making the law more accessible, to aid in anticipating problems and disputes that may arise, particularly over the vexed issues of joint authorship/ownership and the integrity right. On the theatre side *The Working Playwright* is in many ways a positive step – it makes public draft contracts with major and mid-size theatres in the UK. More remains to be done. The provision by lawyers of clear, readable guidelines outlining the key principles of joint authorship, infringement and fair dealing/use 'best practices' in the area of theatre would be helpful, though this would not bring copyright law and theatre into perfect harmony.[43] From a range of empirical studies it has become clear that copyright only works to encourage certain types of creation. This is true in cultural fields as diverse as Irish traditional music, French cuisine, stand-up comedy and Wikipedia.[44] IP's incentive function is insufficient to explain why theatre practitioners create. Property is relevant but it would be absurd to say that it is the central motivation. The social practices of theatre are a reminder that there are types of 'ownership' that do not necessarily imply property in the legal sense. Ownership can also mean the resource is shared.[45]

Finally, with this book I have aimed to shed light on the key aspects of the relationship between copyright law and theatre. I hope that theatre practitioners

[41] Iljadica (n 30).

[42] See https://www.curtisbrown.co.uk/client/nick-payne/work/blurred-lines.

[43] G D'Agostino, 'Healing Fair Dealing? A Comparative Analysis of Canadian Fair Dealing to UK Fair Dealing and US Fair Use' (2008) 53 *McGill Law Review* 309, 361. Association of Independent Video and Filmmakers (ANF) et al, *Documentary Filmmakers' Statement of Best Practices in Fair Use* (18 November 2005) at 1–2, available at https://cmsimpact.org/code/documentary-filmmakers-statement-of-best-practices-in-fair-use/. For a UK site aiming to assist copyright users see www.copyrightuser.org/.

[44] L McDonagh, *Does the Law of Copyright in the UK and Ireland Conflict with the Creative Practices of Irish Traditional Musicians? A Study of the Impact of Law on a Traditional Music Network* (PhD Thesis, School of Law, Queen Mary University of London, 2011).

[45] K Darling and A Perzanowski, 'Introduction' in K Darling and A Perzanowski (eds), *Creativity without the Law* (New York: NYU Press, 2017) 1, 13.

and scholars engage with this book; I hope that it provokes a response. In times of great uncertainty, it is inspiring that theatre practitioners continue to reinvent the medium and challenge the norms of authorship and ownership. Yet, even as the law becomes more open to the creative context of theatrical collaboration, theatre must not succumb entirely to legal constructs and property boundaries. Theatre is often a centre of resistance to prevailing political and cultural currents – whereas law (especially in cases of intellectual property) can sometimes, perhaps often, be the tool of the powerful. I hope theatre practitioners continue to find ways to challenge legal constructs that they disagree with, in their commentaries, their texts, their performances, or ideally in ways we lawyers cannot yet imagine.

ANNEX I – INTERVIEW QUESTIONS

In designing the interview questions, I was careful to use language that would be comprehensible to the non-lawyer. Where necessary I elaborated on the issues during the interviews in order to make sure the participant understood what I was saying. The questions were framed in order to be 'jumping-off points' for the conversation – they were intended to stimulate a response from the participant and potentially to prompt follow-up questions depending on the initial response. As a result, although the interviews followed this basic template, the follow-on questions varied slightly for each participant.

The participants were asked questions in four sections. First, questions 1–3 (Part A) were asked in relation to copyright authorship, ownership (including questions of revenue-sharing) and attribution. Second, question 4 (Part B) was asked with respect to copyright infringement. Third, question 5 (Part C), the key one for the purpose of this Annex, was asked in relation to the issue of the 'integrity' of the work. The final question 6 (Part D) was a short question about whether the participants thought copyright was important to them in their working lives – it was designed to give the participants a final chance to engage with the issues and to mention any other opinions they had on the subject.

Part A

Q.1 Copyright tends to regard the individual playwright as the author of the play – in your experience does this represent an accurate description of the way plays are actually created?

Q.2 If there is significant input from directors or actors in the creation of a new play eg via the workshop process, do you think this ought to be recognised eg in the crediting of joint authorship of the play?

Q.3 With regard to question 2, if the completed play does feature significant input from directors or actors, and it goes on to generate licensing revenue, do you think this should be shared among the various parties who contributed eg on a proportionate basis?

Part B

Q.4 Under the legal doctrine of copyright infringement, if a substantial part of a copyright work eg a portion of dialogue, a detailed plot, is taken from the author's work without authorisation/licence and used in another work, this is a breach of the author's right. If you discovered that another playwright/theatre director had, without acknowledgement, taken elements of a play you created and used them in a new work, what would your response be, if any?

Part C

Q.5 Authors have a right under copyright law, known as the integrity right, to object to a treatment of their work which could be seen as derogatory or harmful to their reputation. For instance, Samuel Beckett famously took a court case in France to prevent a production of *Waiting for Godot* with female actors. In your opinion, to what extent should playwrights be able to control the way their plays are performed eg should a playwright be able to object to a director editing the play or changing its context?

Part D

Q.6 Does copyright play an important part in your working life in theatre?

INDEX

A

Actors *see* **Performers**

Agreement on Trade-Related Aspects of Intellectual Property Rights (TRIPS) 70

Anne, Statute of 1710 *see* **Statute of Anne 1710**

Anonymity
- changing nature 26
- reconceptualisation of anonymity during seventeenth century 38–9

Artistic works
- Berne Convention 1886 61
- EU copyright law 76
- fair use 145
- Imperial Copyright Act 1911 62

Attribution
- *see also* **Right to be identified**
- commonplace shared credit and ownership 153–4
- importance of contracts 110–11
  - credit and royalty-sharing 110–11
  - effect of failing to agree credit and rights issues 108–9
- key issue 149
- key moral right 153
- overview 16–18
- scant case law 153
- Thomas Kyd – *The Spanish Tragedy* 33–5

Aura
- impact of integrity-based objections 174
- integrity-based objections 156
- interplay between originality, integrity and aura 179
- re-conjuring of the author's originality 161–2

Australia
- fair dealing defence 141
- integrity-based objections 158
- joint authorship 88
- originality 80

Authorship
- *see also* **Joint authorship; Ownership**
- absence of standard approach 114
- authorship and joint authorship in contemporary theatre 183–5
- authorship and joint authorship under 1833 and 1842 Acts 56–8
- Ben Jonson as first self-conscious author 37–8
- censorship of theatre texts sixteenth and seventeenth centuries 39–40
- centrality to moral rights 151
- comparative insights
  - overview 4
- contemporary copyright law
  - CDPA 1988 82
  - duration of copyright 83
  - overview 14–15
- deconstruction of the 'cult of the author' 7
- emergence of post-Restoration practices 182
- empirical methodology 9
- focus on individualist notions of authorship 115–16
- importance of contracts 111–12
- key concepts 1–2
- lawyers as writers and performers of plays 25
- polyvocal authorship during Elizabethan and Jacobean eras 29–31
- recognition of authors as owners – Statue of Queen Anne 1710 44–7
- reconceptualisation of anonymity during 1600s 38–9
- relevance of literary theory and theatre studies 22–3
- shifting boundaries 1558–1911 63
- shifting boundaries during 1558–1911 181
- shifting boundaries of historical perception 20
- as a social practice 91–4
- statutory reforms 1833 and 1842 53–5
- theoretical perspectives 4–6
- underlying philosophy of copyright law 65–6

B
Barthes, R. 4–8, 22, 32, 65, 114, 161, 183
Beckett, S. 18, 39, 65, 67, 71, 81, 83, 92, 99, 150, 157, 174–6, 178
Benjamin, W. 18, 150, 161–2
Berne Convention 1886
origins of international copyright 61–2
uncertain nature of the dramatic work 70
Blocking
integrity-based objections 168
major problem for early publishers 41–2
moral rights 186
sense of creative loss or frustration 179
Blurred Lines 97, 110, 116, 130, 153, 185
Brecht, B. 92, 99–100, 106, 115

C
Canada
fair dealing defence 141
infringement 129
joint authorship 89
originality 78–9
Censorship
changes to theatre culture post Statute of Anne 1710 47–9
theatre texts sixteenth and seventeenth centuries 39–40
Churchill, C. 15, 67, 93, 101, 110
Clybourne Park
different power struggle dynamic 172
integrity-based objections 158–9, 163–4
'trajectory' of dramatic work 167
Collaboration
see also **Polyvocal authorship**
authorship as a social practice 91–4
as authorship during Elizabethan and Jacobean eras 29–31
crucial aspect of creative practice 7
importance of legal-feminist thought 8
legal problems of shared ownership 113–14
musical works 72
relevance of literary theory and theatre studies 23
role of actors 103–4
role of director 102–3
role of writer 100–1
social practice involving power struggles between the various agents 104–5
struggle for visibility and legal recognition 114–15
'trajectory' of dramatic work 165–6
workshops as 'collective processes' 96
Commodification of art
claims for exclusive rights to perform plays. 49
impact of legal procedures 63, 182
shifting boundaries of historical perception 20
Stationer's Company 41
text as a commodity 181–3
Comparative insights
fair dealing defence
Australia 141
Canada 141
Germany 141–2
Ireland 141
United States 142–3
infringement
Canada 129
common law countries 128
India 129
Ireland 128–9
United States 129–33
integrity-based objections
Australia 158
France 157
Germany 158–9
Ireland 159
various approaches to need to maintain integrity 160
joint authorship
Australia 88
Canada 89
common law countries 88
India 88–9
UK 90–1
United States 89–90
originality
Australia 80
Canada 78–9
United States 77–8
overview 4
US Copyright Act 1856 58–60
Complicité 93
Contracts
importance
authorship-sharing 111–12
credit and royalty-sharing 110–11
effect of failing to agree credit and rights issues 108–9
fairness 109–10
ownership 112–13
TV/film-writing distinguished 112
legal problems of shared ownership 113–14

ownership of copyright 82
role in theatre practice 2–3
Control
acting companies 28
CDPA 1988 123
Dramatic Literary property Act 1833 54
empirical methodology 9, 11
key Chancery rulings 51
key issue 149
rationale for book 2
role of directors 13, 102
Stationer's Company 14, 24, 26–7, 45
'trajectory' of dramatic work 166
TV/film-writing 112
Copying
meaning of 'substantial part' 123–4
plagiarism 1709–1911
common practice in sixteenth and seventeenth centuries 118–19
presumption of originality from 1710 119–20
'scenario' claims 120
prevalence of theatre disputes 135
social sanctions 135
theoretical perspectives 4
Copyright Act 1956 122
Copyright, Designs and Patents Act 1988
control of 'restricted acts' 123
fair dealing defence
assessing fairness 139–40
criticism and review 137–9
parody/pastiche 139
scope of statutory provisions 136–7
meaning of 'substantial part' 123–5
Copyright law *see* **also EU copyright law**
authorship
CDPA 1988 82
duration of copyright 83
authorship and joint authorship in contemporary theatre 183–5
authorship and joint authorship under 1833 and 1842 Acts 56–8
authorship as a social practice 91–4
boundaries of 'dramatic piece' 1833–1911 58–60
changes to copyright protection 1710–1832 50–3
Copyright, Designs and Patents Act 1988
control of 'restricted acts' 123
meaning of 'substantial part' 123–5
creation of dramatic works during workshop process 97–100
development of the 'abstract notion of the copyright work' 64–5
EU copyright law
broad, 'dematerialized' requirement of originality 75–7, 164
headlines and titles as original works 74
expense of litigation 115–16
focus on individualist notions of authorship 115
infringement*see* **Infringement**
international copyright
Berne Convention 1886 61–2
Imperial Copyright Act 1911 62–3
interplay with theatre 1–2
joint authorship
CDPA 1988 83
dramatic works 83–7
musical works 87–8
jurisdictional limitations 3–4
key questions 2
original works under CDPA 1988
headlines and titles 81
literary works 73–4
musical works 72–3
short plays 81, 81–2
uncertain nature of the dramatic work 69–72
resolution of rights and ownership of plays 180–1
role of actors 103–4
role of director 102–3
role of writer 100–1
Statute of Queen Anne 1710
boundaries of copyright protection 49–50
recognition of authors as owners 44–7
statutory reforms 1833 and 1842 53–5
theatre play-texts as original dramatic works 94–7
underlying philosophy 65–6
workshopped plays as joint authorship 105–8
Credit *see* **Attribution**
Criticism and review
fair dealing defence 136
requirements for successful defence 137–9

D

Directors
ability to make play 'come alive' 170–1
control 13
integrity-based objections 172–3

notion of integrity 174
role 102–3
'Dramatic pieces'
boundaries of 'dramatic piece' 1833–1911 58–60
problem of dramatisations post-1833 55–6
statutory reforms 1833 and 1842 53–5
Dramatic works
see also **Literary works**; **Musical works**
authorship and joint authorship under 1833 and 1842 Acts 56–8
authorship as a social practice 91
Berne Convention 1886 61
boundaries of 'dramatic piece' 1833–1911 58–60
changes to copyright protection 1710–1832 50–3
changes to theatre culture post Statute of Anne 1710 47–9
changing status of theatre and playwrights post-restoration 42–4
comparative insights – USCA 1856 58–60
creation during workshop process 97–100
during Elizabethan and Jacobean eras
Ben Johnson as first self-conscious author 37–8
'blocking' registrations 41–2
case study – Thomas Kyd – *The Spanish Tragedy* 33–5
censorship of theatre texts sixteenth and seventeenth centuries 39–40
overview 25
ownership of plays 26–9
'piracy' of printed texts 40–1
publication of Shakespeare's *First Folio* 35–6
reconceptualisation of anonymity during seventeenth century 38–9
theatrical collaboration as authorship 29–31
unsettled state of theatre texts 31–3
history as print-text and performance commodity
expansion of printing during Elizabethan age 25
overview 13–14
relevance of literary theory and theatre studies 22–3
role of Inns of Court 23–5
shifting boundaries of perception 20
significance of theatre to daily life 20
'the play's the thing' 19
Imperial Copyright Act 1911 62
integrity-based objections
centrality to power struggles 157
impact on play's aura 156
weak right in practic 156
workshop process 155–6
interplay with copyright law 1–2
joint authorship 83–7
jurisdictional limitations 3
originality
headlines and titles 81
short plays 81–2
originality under CDPA 1988 69–72
problem of dramatisations post-1833 55–6
role of actors 103–4
role of director 102–3
role of writer 100–1
social practice involving power struggles between the various agents 104–5
statutory reforms 1833 and 1842 53–5
theatre play-texts as original dramatic works 94–7
theoretical perspectives 4–5
workshopped plays as joint authorship 105–8
Duration of copyright
Berne Convention 1886 62
impact on 'trajectory' of dramatic work 179
Imperial Copyright Act 1911 62
major consequences of works being in public domain 152
UK law 83

E
Economic rights
see also **Moral rights**
ability of playwright to exert leverage 169
authorship and ownership 82–3
means to make moral objections 151–2
withdrawal of integrity rights 154, 159
Elizabethan and Jacobean eras
Ben Jonson as first self-conscious author 37–8
'blocking' registrations 41–2
censorship of theatre texts sixteenth and seventeenth centuries 39–40
changing status of theatre and playwrights 42–4
overview 25
ownership of plays 26–9
'piracy' of printed texts 40–1

publication of Shakespeare's *First Folio* 35–6
reconceptualisation of anonymity during seventeenth century 38–9
text as a commodity 181–3
theatrical collaboration as authorship 29–31
Thomas Kyd – *The Spanish Tragedy* 33–5
unsettled state of theatre texts 31–3

Empirical insights
Bourdieu's work as intellectual framework 12–13
methodology of the qualitative empirical research 9–11
prevalence of theatre disputes 133–6

EU copyright law
broad, 'dematerialized' requirement of originality 75–7, 164
fair dealing defence 142
headlines and titles as original works 74
meaning of 'substantial part' 124
narrow approach to infringement 148

F

Fair dealing defence
assessing fairness 139–40
comparative insights
Australia 141
Canada 141
Germany) 141–2
Ireland 141
United States 142–3
criticism and review 137–9
'fair use' compared 143–6
parody/pastiche 139
scope of statutory provisions 136–7

Fairness
fair dealing defence
assessing fairness 139–40
'fair use' compared 143–6
scope of statutory provisions 136–7
importance of contracts 109–10

Feminist perspectives 8, 82, 92, 180

First Folio 1623 26, 32, 35–6

Fixation
EU law 75
literary works 73
originality under CDPA 1988 69, 71
revisions of a play 94
US copyright law 77

Forced Entertainment 94

Foucault, M. 5–9, 22, 30, 38–9, 64–6, 114, 161, 181, 183

Freedom of expression (Art 10) 140, 150, 188

G

Germany
fair dealing defence 141–2
integrity-based objections 158–9

Gorbudoc 25

'Great man theory' 8, 23

H

Headlines and titles
EU copyright law 74
over-protection of short works 146
UK copyright law 81

Heretic 158, 165

History of dramatic works
see also **Contemporary copyright**
authorship and joint authorship under 1833 and 1842 Acts 56–8
boundaries of 'dramatic piece' 1833–1911 58–60
changes to copyright protection 1710–1832 50–3
changes to theatre culture post Statute of Anne 1710 47–9
changing status of theatre and playwrights post-restoration 42–4
comparative insights – USCA 1856 58–60
copyright protection under Statute of Queen Anne 1710 49–50
Elizabethan and Jacobean eras
Ben Johnson as first self-conscious author 35–6
'blocking' registrations 41–2
case study – Thomas Kyd – *The Spanish Tragedy* 33–5
censorship of theatre texts sixteenth and seventeenth centuries 39–40
changing status of theatre and playwrights 42–4
overview 26
ownership of plays 26–9
'piracy' of printed texts 40–1
publication of Shakespeare's *First Folio* 35–6
reconceptualisation of anonymity during seventeenth century 38–9
theatrical collaboration as authorship 29–31
unsettled state of theatre texts 31–3

emergence of post-Restoration practices 182–3
expansion of printing during Elizabethan age 25
infringement
Copyright Act 1956 122
Imperial Copyright Act 1911 121–2
international copyright
Berne Convention 1886 61–2
Imperial Copyright Act 1911 62–3
overview 13–14
plagiarism 1709–1911
common practice in sixteenth and seventeenth centuries 118–19
presumption of originality from 1710 119–20
'scenario' claims 120
recognition of authors as owners 44–7
relevance of literary theory and theatre studies 22–3
role of Inns of Court 23–5
shifting boundaries during 1558–1911 181
shifting boundaries of perception 20
significance of theatre to daily life 20
statutory reforms 1833 and 1842 53–5
'the play's the thing' 19
Human rights 140, 150, 188

I
Idea/expression dichotomy 125–7, 147
Imperial Copyright Act 1911 121–2
India
infringement 129
joint authorship 88–9
Informal norms *see* **Social norms**
Infringement
comparative insights
Canada 129
common law countries 128
India 129
Ireland 128–9
overview 4
United States 129–33
Copyright Act 1956 122
Copyright, Designs and Patents Act 1988
control of 'restricted acts' 123
fair dealing defence 136–43
meaning of 'substantial part' 123–5
fair dealing defence
effectiveness in theatre 147
'fair use' compared 143–6
Imperial Copyright Act 1911 121–2
key concepts 1–2
narrow approach of EU law 148
need for reform 188
new adaptations of public domain works 127–8
over-protection of short works 146
overview 15–16, 117–18
plagiarism 1709–1911
common practice in sixteenth and seventeenth centuries 118–19
presumption of originality from 1710 119–20
'scenario' claims 120
prevalence of theatre disputes
empirical insights 133–6
overview 133
rareness in contemporary theatre 185–6
resolution via social norms 146–7
theatre as a 'haunted stage' 117
Inns of Court
Elizabethan boom in litigation 23–4
importance of translations in English legal rhetoric 24
writers and performers of plays 25
Integrity-based objections
comparative insights
Australia 158
France 157
Germany 158–9
Ireland 159
various approaches to need to maintain integrity 160
dramatic works
centrality to power struggles 157
impact on play's aura 156
weak right in practic 156
workshop process 155–6
overview 150
part of integrity right 155
potential to freeze works in time 166
prevalence in practice
director's ability to make play 'come alive' 170–1
directors and actors 172–3
diverse range of responses 168–9
early-career playwrights 169–70
impact on originality and aura 174
importance of theatrical tradition 171–2
notion of integrity 174

power struggles between the various agents 173–4
resolution of struggles through trust 169
theatrical paradox 168
Waiting for Godot 175–6

Integrity right
France 155
frequent power struggles between various agents 186–7
impact on creative participants 154–5
interplay between originality, integrity and aura 179
moral right 151
need for reform 188
overview 16–18
right to object 155
underlying concept 154

International copyright
Berne Convention 1886 61–2
Imperial Copyright Act 1911 62–3

Ireland
fair dealing defence 141
infringement 128–9
integrity-based objections 159

J

Jacobean era *see* **Elizabethan and Jacobean eras**

Joint authorship
see also **Collaboration**; **Polyvocal authorship**
authorship and joint authorship in contemporary theatre 183–5
authorship and joint authorship under 1833 and 1842 Acts 56–8
comparative insights
Australia 88
Canada 89
common law countries 88
India 88–9
overview 4
UK 90–1
United States 89–90
contemporary copyright law
CDPA 1988 83
dramatic works 83–7
musical works 87–8
overview 14–15
creation of dramatic works during workshop process 97–100
key concepts 1–2
musical works 73
need for reform 187–8
role of director 102
theatre play-texts as original dramatic works 95
workshops 105–8

Joint stock company 93

Jonson, B. 14, 25, 26, 33–8, 43, 47, 64, 182

L

Literary works
see also **Dramatic works**; **Musical works**; **Printing and printed matter**; **Texts**
authorship as a social practice 91
Berne Convention 1886 61
boundaries of copyright protection 49–50
concept of literary property 45–7
as dramatic work 3
fair use 145
Imperial Copyright Act 1911 62
meaning of 'substantial part' 124
originality under CDPA 1988 72–3
piracy and blocking 41–2
problem of dramatisations post-1833 55–6

M

Masten, J. 7–9, 14–16, 22, 29–40, 64–5, 73, 92, 181, 183

Moral rights
see also **Economic rights**
attribution
commonplace shared credit and ownership 153–4
key moral right 153
scant case law 153
centrality of author 151
comparative insights
overview 4
frequent power struggles between various agents 186–7
impact of power struggles 178–9
integrity right
France 155
impact on creative participants 154–5
right to object 155
underlying concept 154
interplay between originality, integrity and aura 179
key concepts 1–2
key issues 149–50
overview 16–18

Musical works
see also **Dramatic works; Literary works**
joint authorship 87–8
jurisdictional limitations 3
originality under CDPA 1988 72–3
test of substantial reproduction 125–6

O
Originality
Berne Convention 1886 61–2
under CDPA 1988
literary works 73–4
musical works 72–3
uncertain nature of the dramatic work 69–72
comparative insights
Australia 80
Canada 78–9
United States 77–8
dramatic works
headlines and titles 81
short plays 81–2
EU's broad, 'dematerialized' requirement of originality 75–7
impact of integrity-based objections 174
interplay between originality, integrity and aura 179
meaning of 'substantial part' 124
presumption of originality from 1710 119–20
re-conjuring of the author's originality 161–2
theatre play-texts as original dramatic works 94–7
theoretical perspectives 4
'trajectory' of dramatic work 164
Ownership
see also **Authorship**
acting companies 28
authorship and joint authorship under 1833 and 1842 Acts 57
Ben Jonson as first self-conscious author 37–8
contractual terms 82
development of the 'abstract notion of the copyright work' 64–5
emergence of post-Restoration practices 182
empirical methodology 9
importance of contracts 112–13
legal problems of shared ownership 113–14
plays during Elizabethan and Jacobean eras 26–9
recognition of authors as owners – Statue of Queen Anne 1710 44–7
shifting boundaries during 1558–1911 181
statutory reforms 1833 and 1842 53–5
theoretical perspectives 4
underlying philosophy of copyright law 65–6

P
Parody/pastiche
fair dealing defence 136
requirements for successful defence 139
Patents
changes post-1710 47–8, 52–3
informal norms 1770–1800 65
statutory reforms 1833 and 1842 54–5
theatre monopolies issued by Charles II 42–3
Paternity rights *see* **Attribution**
Performers
integrity-based objections 172–3
lawyers as writers and performers of plays 25
role 103
Piracy
Berne Convention 1886 61
major problem for early publishers 40–1
ownership of plays during Elizabethan and Jacobean eras 27
Plagiarism *see* **Copying**
Playwrights *see* **Authorship**
Polyvocal authorship
see also **Collaboration**
blossoming of english 'renaissance' theatre 43
challenge to modern assumptions 63
collaboration during Elizabethan and Jacobean Eras 29–31
combination of authorial and textual instability 33
importance 1558–1625 181–2
'plural and collaborative' works 34
role of censorship 39–40
Shakespeare as serial collaborator 35–6
Printing and printed matter
see also **Texts**
changes to copyright protection 1710–1832 50–3
during Elizabethan and Jacobean eras
'blocking' registrations 41–2
'piracy' of printed texts 40–1

increasing legal print rights post-1710 48–9
recognition of authors as owners – Statue of Queen Anne 1710 44–7
statutory reforms 1833 and 1842 53–5
Public domain works
link with 'trajectory' of dramatic work 166–7
major effects 152
musical works 72
'trajectory' of dramatic work 178

R
Research
Bourdieu's work as intellectual framework 12–13
fair dealing defence 136
methodology of the qualitative empirical research 9–11
Review *see* **Criticism and review**
Right to be identified
see also **Attribution**
CDPA 1988 153
history of dramatic works 43
moral right 151

S
Shakespeare, W. 6, 14, 24–40, 43, 47, 52, 57, 64, 83, 92, 127, 131, 152, 161–2, 167, 178, 182
Social norms
building blocks of future creativity 147
community sanctions such as 'bad-mouthing' 148
normative cooperation in Elizabethan period 66
ownership by acting company 14, 28
recurring theme 182
regulation of theatrical disputes 3, 112, 118, 146, 185
relevance to judicial consideration of disputes 183
risk of reputational harm 107
Speech
originality 78
protection of verbatim copies 56
theoretical perspectives 4
Stationers' Company
control of printing 26–7
expansion of printing during Elizabethan age 25
shifting boundaries of historical perception 20
Statute of Anne 1710
see also **Ownership**
boundaries of copyright protection 49–50
recognition of authors as owners 44–7
shifting boundaries of historical perception 20
'Substantial part'
comparative insights 135
Copyright Act 1956 122
Copyright, Designs and Patents Act 1988 123–9
Imperial Copyright Act 1911 62–3, 121–2
interview question 191

T
Texts
see also **Literary works**; **Printing and printed matter**
boundaries of 'dramatic piece' 1833–1911 58–60
censorship of theatre texts sixteenth and seventeenth centuries 39–40
as a commodity 181–3
creation of dramatic works during workshop process 99
history as print-text and performance commodity
Ben Johnson as first self-conscious author 37–8
case study – Thomas Kyd – *The Spanish Tragedy* 33–5
expansion of printing during Elizabethan age 25
overview 13–14
relevance of literary theory and theatre studies 22–3
role of Inns of Court 23–5
shifting boundaries of perception 20
significance of theatre to daily life 20
'the play's the thing' 19
original literary works under CDPA 1988 73–4
'piracy' of printed texts 40–1
plays during Elizabethan and Jacobean eras 26–9
recognition of authors as owners – Statue of Queen Anne 1710 44–7
role of actors 103–4
role of director 102–3
role of writer 100–1

theatre play-texts as original dramatic works 94–7
theoretical perspectives 5
unsettled state during Elizabethan and Jacobean eras 31–3
The Knight of the Burning Pestle 32, 64, 181
***The Playboy of the Western World* (Ireland)** 128, 167
The School for Scandal 48, 52, 65, 183
The Spanish Tragedy 26, 33–5, 153, 182
The Taming of The Shrew 32, 64, 182
The Working Playwright
attempt to create legal certainty 109
attribution rights 153
importance of contracts 108
need for reform 188
playwright's consent as 'default' copyright owner 110, 156
prioritisation of writer's ownership 112, 184
questions of fairness 109
reaction from theatre community 165
Theoretical perspectives
Barthes and Foucault 5–6
'great man theory' 8
relevance of literary theory and theatre studies 22–3
Seneca 4
'Trajectory' of dramatic work
dramatist's 'rights of creative control 166
effect of collaboration 165–6
first and subsequent productions distinguished 176–7
impact of duration of copyright 179
link with public domain 166–7
need to recover 'the original' 164
'of the moment' plays 177
property which necessarily has a life of its own 162–3
public domain works 178
three broad stages 163–4
TRIPS *see* **Agreement on Trade-Related Aspects of Intellectual Property Rights (TRIPS)**

U
United States
fair dealing defence 142–3
infringement 129–33
joint authorship 89–90
originality 77–8

W
Waiting for Godot 127, 157, 164, 167, 175–6
Works *see* **Dramatic works**
Workshops
creation of dramatic works during workshop process 97–100
integrity-based objections 155–6
joint authorship 105–8
social practice involving power struggles between the various agents 104–5
theatre play-texts as original dramatic works 96–7

www.ingramcontent.com/pod-product-compliance
Ingram Content Group UK Ltd.
Pitfield, Milton Keynes, MK11 3LW, UK
UKHW020811290926
15470UKWH00003B/1084